Henri Nissen:
Noah's Ark Uncovered
- an Expedition into the Ancient Past
Translated from Danish by Tracy Jay Skondin
Copyright 2004 by the author and Scandinavia Publishing
House, Copenhagen.
Cover design by Ben Alex

Print: DNT, Poland
ISBN 87 7247 813 6

Update: www.udfordringen.com/noah.htm

Layout:
The illustration on top of each page is a section of the 3,700-year-old Atrahasis tablet (right) found in Sippar southwest of Baghdad. The tablet tells of a man who survived a great deluge onboard a ship. The tablet can be found in The British Museum, London.

At the bottom of each page is a section of a relief stone plate from the 9th century B.C. with an inscription in Hittite hieroglyphics about the activities of King Uhilina and his son. The original stone plate (left) has three lines of hieroglyphics on top of each other. The pages of the book contain only one line each and are read right to left. The stone plate can be seen in the Archeological Museum of Istanbul. It was found in Hama in the northern part of Syria.
The background of the page numbers is Ron Wyatt's model of the Ark

Contents:

Foto: Sevkut Kurtius / Ilhan Durupinar 1959

PART 1:

The Boat in the Mountains

*When I first saw this object in 1983, my first reaction was that this was
just a landslide area where the object was formed naturally and by chance.
But then I saw the object from a helicopter and could see that it lay at the
beginning of the bottleneck. It looked just like when you fly over the
Atlantic and see the gargantuan boats floating down there.
According to aerodynamic and physical laws it made sense
that the "Ark" lay precisely where it did in the middle of a mudslide.
Then I understood that the formation had not emerged around the great stone
which we are quick to conclude.
It is independent of the stone. It is its own entity.*

(Dr. Salih Bayraktutan, Professor of Geology)

Chapter 1

Is this the Ark?

"There's the Ark!" said Elin Berglund and pointed toward the top of the rugged, gray-brown rock of a mountain.

"Where?" asked the rest of us, full of expectation and impatience after having traveled the past two days.

"It's there, next to that green area..."

After a while, some caught a glimpse of a symmetrical outline. I couldn't see it though and stood spying with my binoculars for a long time.

We found ourselves less than five kilometers from the site that many claim to be the actual ruins of Noah's Ark!

It wasn't on Mt. Ararat where so many Ark-hunters had otherwise searched for hundreds of years. It lay on the other side of the Aras valley, amidst a mountain range not known to most people from the western world. It lay about 12 miles southeast of the foot of Mt. Ararat - on the Iranian border.

Elin Berglund (No. 2 from the left) and the Danish Ark-hunters with a look of expectancy and hope towards the "Ark" up the mountain while Dr. Salih Bayraktutan (right) returns to "the boat-shaped object" that he has researched over the past 20 years.

A Mysterious Object Appears

Until April/May of 1948, there was nothing to see of the Ark in these Kurdish mountains. Only mud and grass covered the slope where the broadshaped object suddenly appeared out of the mud one day. For one reason or another, the slope was named "Mashur" which means resurrection.

In 1948 there were a number of earthquakes in that area of Turkey, and from one day to the next a shape of something was seen sticking up out of

The Danish expedition at the signpost indicating Nuhun Gemisi, Noah's Great Boat, just before the first trip into the mountains on the left. Journalist Joachim Frøsig from the Danish television station TV2 is on the right.

Geologist Dr. Salih Bayrak-tutan was one of our guides. Here he is together with TV-journalist Joachim Frøsig.

the mud that was not there before. From a distance, it was possible to see that the shape was an outline of what looked like a gigantic boat...

The local Kurdish people in the nearest village, Uzengili, tell that right away they associated the shape with Nuhun Gemisi – Noah's boat. Maybe it was because the outlined objcct was large and had the form of a boat, or maybe because an old woman had had a dream not long before in which she herself – by her account - was given a message that Noah's Ark would appear and that a local man by the name of Hassan was to guard it.

Reshit, the young shepherd boy who saw the strange shape first, soon told about it in the town Dogubayazit - Turkey's eastern-most city. A well-off local farmer took the news with him on a trip to Istanbul, 1,300 km west. Before the news got out to the western world, an American journalist in Istanbul had a mix-up with his geography. Until that time, interest in finding Noah's Ark had been concentrated on Mt. Ararat, and therefore, he assumed that this was once again a Mt. Ararat story. That is why he placed Reshit's find "2/3 of the way up the mountain of Ararat".

Ark hunters tried to get this new, sparse information to fit together with that which they had already collected. For many years they were convinced that this Reshit, whom they never found again, had seen the Ark on Mt. Ararat. In the meanwhile the boat-shaped object was allowed to lie untouched for 11 years...

Captain Ilhan Durupinar

One day in the summer of 1959, a Turkish captain and cartographer by the name of Ilhan Durupinar flew over the area and photographed the boat-shaped object from the air. The picture was printed, among other places, in what at that time was called LIFE magazine.

This started a great new interest in finding Noah's ark - on Mt. Ararat. It was plain to see that the boat-shaped object did not lie on this mountain, but very few had this insight. Whatever the case, it was over in the mountains - somewhere.

At the same time, an American team had come down to research the object, but they had no great success. Disappointed to find nothing but earth, they went home; again, the find was forgotten for more than a decade.

In the middle of the 70's, a very special American became interested in the object. But the leading Ark-hunters didn't take this man seriously. The Ark was supposedly located on Mt. Ararat, or so they thought without a doubt. But this special American had uncovered more and more for each year, and one day the Turkish authorities recognized his find and declared it a protected national park.

The Turkish military had constructed a gravel road so that when conditions were acceptable – that is, clear of snow - it was possible to drive almost all the way up the steep mountain road. It was relatively easy for us to find the place.

"It's time to go," shouted Elin.

We quickly got into the little bus we had rented and drove up the snowy gravel road.

When we got around the last hairpin turn at an elevation of well over 6,500 ft., the "Ark" suddenly appeared on the hillside to our left.

"It's practically in a valley! Didn't the Ark land on a mountain?" I commented to Elin who had been here before and was the guide for our trip.

"Yes, but the Ark hasn't always lain here. It sailed down here from the mountain there." She laughed and pointed up toward a steep crest of 8,800 ft. I later found out that the crest was given a Turkish name that, when translated, means "the anchor place of heroes".

There it was – the boat-shaped object – like a mighty ship on its way down the valley from its first haven, the twin mountains of Yiðityataði which can be seen in the background.

When Mt. Ararat Exploded

Dr. Salih Bayraktutan, the geologist we hired to travel with us, explained that mud from multiple enormous mudslides had washed down through the valley together with huge amounts of water from punctured pre-historic lakes. His theory was that the boat-shaped object had earlier lain up by the crest and had slid down together with the mud mass to its present position. This had happened many, many years ago, maybe multiple thousands of years.

It is possible that the mudslide happened at the same time that a big part of Mt. Ararat almost exploded under an enormous volcanic eruption[1], which blew 1/6 of the mountain away.

It is not known exactly when this happened, but it must have been an eruption of the same magnitude as Mount St. Helens, which exploded on a

"Jetzt gehen!" said the Turkish chauffeur (left).

Sunday morning, the 18th of May, 1980 in Washington State. St. Helens' explosion spread ash all the way to Japan...

The earthquake on Mt. Ararat left an enormous gap in the mountain - the so-called Ahora Ravine. Strangely enough, this same Ahora Ravine is where many Ark-hunters have searched and continue to search for the Ark in vain. Up until now, no one has found conclusive evidence of the Ark on Mt. Ararat, but the hunt has continued year after year.

Now we were here, looking at the only sign of a pre-historic ship lying here in the mountains. And it didn't lie on Mt. Ararat, but rather some 12 miles southeast, on an unknown and over-looked mountain...

Like a Mirage...

The Turkish chauffeur stopped and ordered us to get out in German, "Jetzt gehen!" He had been a guest worker in Germany. We got out to admire the fabled "ship", which at this point only looked like a peculiar heightening in the landscape. I think that we all felt the wind of history, as if we were set 5,000 years back in time to the days of Noah...

We quickly captured the area on film and in pictures, even though we would soon have the opportunity to get some better ones. We kept ourselves in subconscious reverence at a distance of 1500 ft. It was as if we didn't dare risk the chance that it could be a mirage that would disappear before we got up to it.

Could this really be the Ark...?

From our studies beforehand, we knew that we wouldn't find a well-kept wooden Ark untouched through at least 4,500 years[2] of harsh climate. We knew that it would be more of a type of imprint in the earth. The wood would either have decayed or been petrified after all of these years. But just to find the smallest sign that the Ark actually existed was an extreme sensation. And here we stood, looking at a formation that was 518 feet long - the same length the Ark had according to the Bible.

Could it be that Noah's good ship had again reared its head after all these years where the Ark only existed in stories and myths?

Salih and Hassan

While we stood atop a hill with a view of the "Ark", Dr. Salih Bayraktutan, the Turkish scientist, held a geologic lecture that we shall come back to later. Salih is a geologist and professor at Atatürk University in Erzurum. He has patiently worked with the find for almost 20 years without being able to finish his research both due to a shortage of supplies and partners that deserted him.

I tried to translate the distrait professor for the group, but his sentences were longer than the Ark itself, and in the end I let him explain without any disruptive interruptions. He was finished before he noticed that I wasn't translating anymore.

Salih was not lacking in self-irony, and he got along well with Danish television TV2's photographer, Magnus Platz, whose cunning and dark Danish humor is not for beginners.

Magnus and TV2's journalist, Joachim Frøsig, got a hold of Hassan, an old Kurd from the near-by village, Uzengili, in the meantime.

In the TV-feature they recorded Hassan claimed that back in 1948, when the object first appeared, a neighbor-woman was given a message in a dream that the Ark would be found and that he, Hassan, should guard it. Hassan does this today and willingly brews up Turkish tea for pilgrimaging foreigners that have traveled from distant lands to see his good ship: Nuhun Gemisi.

Hassan remembers when "the Ark" emerged from the mud.

The Wyatt Mystery...

The TV team stood on the edge of the hilltop and let Hassan, via a Kurdish translator, tell how one day many years ago he had seen a mystical stranger lay down and sleep on top of the boat-shaped object.

Hassan, with unbelief and caution, got closer. Turks say that Kurds always sleep with a knife on them, but this guy seemed to be unarmed. Hassan crept close to the sleeping stranger and put a gun in his face. The stranger, as in a surprise attack, tried to gather his thoughts and explained that he had been wandering about in the mountains trying to find the place that the Turkish pilot had revealed from the air. Exhausted, he laid himself down to sleep on the "Ark". This is what had happened up until the two met each other, and immediately after, they became life-long friends.

Hassan's friend was now dead. His name was Ron Wyatt from Nashville, Tennessee.

Wyatt was a mystery that I had to explain. Before we started our journey, I read many articles about this man. There were a lot of critical articles that claimed that he was a deceitful fortune hunter. Some tried to embarrass him by suggesting that he should rather have written series about Indiana Jones. Actually, Kurdish terrorists abducted him. People around him were killed; he was accused of espionage and had been imprisoned in Saudi Arabia. Comparing him with Indiana Jones was really not that far off the mark.

As usual, the source of the criticism was a group of American creationists who were convinced that the Ark lie on Mt. Ararat instead of here.

It was difficult for us outsiders to understand this discord. And it didn't make it easier finding the truth.

I asked Elin, who had known Wyatt personally and been together with him on an expedition to Egypt shortly before his death in 1999, what her impression of the man was. She had only good things to say about him.

TV-photographer Magnus Platz shot four hours of video from the first Danish expedition in May 2001. It was cut down to 9 minutes and 30 seconds before it was shown on national television.

But I took her assurance with a grain of salt.

Now it was not about getting off course, but rather finding the truth about Noah's Ark - no matter what I thought about Wyatt.

The Flood...?

Geologist Salih Bayraktutan had now finished his lecture on how the formation could not have possibly been naturally formed and why it stayed standing with its sharp edges despite the violent erosion of the landscape and the sedimentary movement underground.

Finally, we were headed toward the formation. We were finally on our way to "the Ark". We were about to walk on "something" that may have carried Noah and his family, together with a lot of animals, through the Flood over 4,500 years ago.

The Flood...? Yes, but wasn't that just a story...?

Now it was time to dive into it. We knew the American scientists had recently found new evidence of "the Flood" in the Black Sea - only 185 miles northwest of our Ark find. There had also been geological signs in other parts of the world of a catastrophic flood centuries ago.[4] The signs have been interpreted differently - all after the geologist's personal convictions.

There were both Christians and non-Christians on the team. Some believed completely and unshakingly in the Bible. Some doubted. A few had a different religion. But whatever we believed, we knew that both the Flood and the Ark were two of mankind's greatest riddles, which were not only described in the Bible but also in other ancient historic sources.

Noah and the Ark are a part of world culture. Almost all children have heard the story. It is not only found written in Christianity and Judaism but also in Islam's holy book, the Qur'an. Among Native Americans and the Chinese, this story is known. Throughout the whole earth, stories about a great and mighty flood - and eight forefathers, which many cultures have made into gods - can be found.

Were they only myths, or was there a historical happening behind them? - a part of the world's very first pre-historic story?

The further I dove into this pre-history with the ancient sources, the more exciting it got. We will come back to all of this later, and you will be amazed - just as I have been time and time again.

Could It Lie on Mt. Ararat?

While we traveled over toward the boat-shaped object, we had the mighty Mt. Ararat on our left-hand side. It stood as a constant challenge for our interest of the new find.

In the years after our first expedition to the Durupinar find, I have followed the investigation of the Ark on Mt. Ararat through books and articles. The last 50 years of research has been mostly concentrated on climbing on Mt. Ararat. There have been innumerous books written about the fantastic stories that circulate and about people that think they have seen the actual Ark on

Footnotes

[2] According to the Bible's chronology, there should have been ca. 6,000 years from the creation of Adam until now. The Flood came in the year 1656, according to this calculation - that is 2344 B.C. (ca. 4,348 years ago - in 2004). This is in agreement with the Hebrew, Egyptian, and Babylonian astronomical chronologies (according to Davidson and Aldersmith).

Author and journalist Rene Norbergen estimated ca. 3398 B.C. after having studied the *Greek* Septuagint version of the Old Testament. This version was made for the Egyptian king, Ptolemy II Philadelphus' (287-47 B.C.) large library in Alexandria. The transcriptions of this are older than the later Hebrew Massorah transcriptions.

[3] The biblical telling of a worldwide flood because of the evil of mankind can be found in Genesis, chapters 6-8 in the Old Testament of the Bible.

[4] See the map with markings of where stories of the Flood are later in this book.

the great mountain.

Therefore, it came as a shock when I heard about the Durupinar find, which wasn't on the infamous mountain at all.

If Durupinar contains the ruins of the Ark, many of these stories and accounts must not be true. This was not a nice thought. Now I had an even larger study in front of me when we returned home. In the coming chapters, we will go through the results of the research I have done.

We will also meet the oldest "survivor" of the first modern expeditions in 1960 on Mt. Ararat, the artist Elfred Lee, whom I have interviewed. He has personally known many of the people that claim to have seen Noah's Ark on Mt. Ararat. He has painted their stories. And he has also been on Mt. Ararat himself and looked for the Ark. He still believes that he knows where it is. And he is waiting for a sign from God – and then he will go out again. But until then, he is trying to keep his Ark-fever under control – that is, if the sign comes.

Some of what he can tell and that which I have found out will most likely shock many of those interested in the Ark.

But let's not dawdle.

Whether you are convinced one way or the other, the story of Noah's Ark will never again be just an innocent fairy tale after you've read this book. I can promise you that much.

We walked around "the Ark" for hours investigating it… In front ship builder Niels Lind.

We traveled to the easternmost and poorest part of Turkey...
Our route on the 2001-expedition included Abraham's town Harran and Sanli Urfa
(once Ur) in Southern Turkey and an outing to a possible Tower of Babel
under the dammed-up Euphrates River.
More on that in chapter 12.

Chapter 2

Could it be True?

We crawled up onto the "Ark" into its sternpost where a piece had fallen off so we could get up easier. In some places the sides were 20 feet high and steep. In other places they had collapsed a bit. In the middle of the "ship", a large limestone rock had drilled its way up, but the formation still stood proudly in the field making a sharp contrast to its surroundings with its high, steep edges.

It had become even more prominent after the last earthquake in 1978, the geologist told us. Inside the earth had sunk some, especially near the sides, while the mid-parts bowed upwards. When you wanted to get to the "bow" you had to go straight up. For hours, we examined the boat-shaped object both from above and just outside of it.

Who Do We Have?

We were definitely not the first people that had come to find Noah's Ark. But we may have been the first that kept all possibilities open with no pre-conceived notions. We didn't have a holy mission to complete. For us, it was not about proving the existence of God by finding the Ark, as it seems many of the earlier Ark-hunters were set on. Some of us already believed in God and didn't need that type of evidence. Others probably didn't be-lieve in God. We didn't ask each other about that.

Love of Adventure

Personally, I was driven by the love of adventure, or rather "investigative reporting". That sounds better.

For many years I have followed the accounts given by those looking for the Ark very closely. And I made up my mind many years ago that I would personally like to go to the Mt. Ararat area and see what it was all about, if the opportunity should arise.

One day, I ran across a video about the so-called "boat-formed object" or the Durupinar-find. I had also seen aerial photos of the object earlier, but in the popular accounts the photos of this find were often put together with stories about the searching on Mt. Ararat.

It was partly amateur-quality and way too drawn out. It was almost two hours long. I have to admit, I fell asleep when I saw it the first time one late evening, and my son John was offended when he woke me.

But I was aware of the fact that this amateur archeologist, Ron Wyatt, had gotten a hold of something that was worth taking a closer look at. I would later come to watch the movie many times and dig deep into the written material about "the boat-formed object". I also studied everything I could get my hands on about explorations on Mt. Ararat.

The Press Gets Interested

In Norway, Elin Berglund had already been interested in the Ark and other extra-ordinary archeological discoveries. Together with her, I started planning a trip to Mt. Ararat.

At first, I wanted to get down there to dig up a story for my newspaper. But then we got the idea to use "the hunt for Noah's Ark" as a way to get new subscribers. We promised a trip to the site as a prize for one of the new subscribers. The winner was Gunhild Gervin from Gentofte, Denmark. But by the time we drew her name, many had written in telling of their interest in the trip, and one day a journalist from Ritzaus Bureau called and asked about the trip. For a while things were quiet, so I assumed that he had sent a notice that I had probably overlooked. Then one morning around Easter of 2001, my children told me about a huge article written about our trip. It turned out that the article had been printed in most of the daily papers throughout the entire country.

I started getting new enquiries from people that wanted to join the journey, and this continued until we found ourselves in the Ararat area close to the Iranian border - nine Danes, a Norwegian and a Swede.

We were also accompanied by Danish television, TV2, which had sent a journalist and a photographer along with us in order to tell the story, which they did on the popular news program, "Dags Dato" on the 20th of May, 2001. The journalist told us that we had to give them free access to tell the story their way. We guessed their intention was to humiliate us as "naïve people" who believed we could find Noah's Ark. But on the contrary, they produced a very fine, sober feature that created even greater interest.

Traces of Rust…?

We were quite lucky in that Ark-hunter Bill Fry was on the formation the same day we were and could tell us about his observations. He had worked closely together with Ron Wyatt.

On this trip in May of 2001, he accompanied an American free-lance photographer, Barbara Patt, who sat where an iron nail had been found. The traces of rust were still visible…

In June of 1991 Ron had already found one round iron nail that resembled it. All together, the remains of four such iron nails have supposedly been found.

Barbara showed us the clear traces of rust from the nail that were found in the eastern side of the "ship" – on the port side – in something that now looked like a large rock cropping out of the railing. It was not a stone, but rather a porous material.

"It's all part of the boat," claimed Barbara.

Signs of Craftsmanship in the Stones

Bill and Barbara were there to plan a conference to be held in Ankara about the Ark in 2003. Out by the formation, Barbara found a large rock sticking out of the eastern side about 20 feet up. It looked like it had

Ron Wyatt's original 2-hour video about the possible discovery of the Ark is still available at www.wyattmuseum.com.

engravings on it. To avoid local treasure hunters stealing the stone, it was covered again after having some pictures taken.

Later in September of the same year, Bill Fry came back to examine the stone more closely, and he informed the Turkish authorities of his find. The engravings looked like long lines carved into the stone. There is no explanation for them, but Bill Fry is convinced that the stone belongs together with the "ship". Again in June of 2002, he was in Turkey and tried unsuccessfully to move the 770 pound rock into the building that has been established about 500 yards from the boat-shaped object where the rock could be kept safely. Instead, a local politician promised that it would be taken care of.

Video clip: The remains of a rivet on the eastern side of the boat-shaped object.

Below: Rivet found by Wyatt in 1991.

I realized that Bill and Barbara had another specific assignment – one which they wouldn't talk about. Later I met them again and was told by Barbara what they were looking for: an enlarged cranium that had been found in the vicinity but had since been stolen. Many things in this area had been removed or destroyed by vandals or treasure hunters. The thief now wanted an absurdly high price of $30,000 when he realized how extraordinary the cranium was. If an enlarged cranium had been found here, then what was the explanation? There is a very exciting theory about this, which I will present later in the book.

Petrified Wood…?

I went along the west side of the Ark's 10-20 foot high flanks and looked at the light stripes that, according to some of the earlier explorations, showed there had previously been rib timbers underneath underneath. The lighter stripes lay at intervals of about one meter, and it was difficult to find a natural explanation. I tried to get it on video, and while I went around filming together with Oli Tindalid from the Faeroe Islands, a funny little stone caught my eye. It had grooves as if it were a fossil. I picked it up and we looked at it a bit before I stuffed it in my pocket to show Salih later.
Not much later Gunhild Gervin found a similar stone or fossil in the vicinity. She also showed it to Salih later. He looked at the stones a bit, and then he said with a laugh:

"This is petrified wood!"

"That is what I wanted to hear," I answered, and we laughed at the situation while Salih looked at the stone yet again. He was very convinced that both my and Gunhild's stones were petrified wood. When Gunhild later had our find examined by the Geological Museum in Denmark, they could not confirm that there was talk of a fossilized piece of wood. There were "barred lime crystals" which had probably "grown in cracks as a result of water with lime content flowing over".

Bill Fry and Zafer Onay had the stone removed.

I later had my "stone" examined by a geologist that told me it was a petrifaction of a plant, because the grooves had a finger-form.

We didn't weigh these small finds too heavily.

Gunhild had also brought back a few small dark samples from the area around the "rivet" in order to have established whether it was all, as Barbara said, "part of the boat". The samples were hard as stone and had mainly a greenish color which she thought might be remains of metal.

To this the Geological Musem answered that to a large extent this rock consisted of silicate minerals. And that the greenish color was probably due to the mineral epidote which shows that the rock has been buried deeply below the earth's crust. As a consequence of this the original minerals have undergone a transformation (metamorphosis). The original rock has probably been a mud stone. As silicates are the chief ingredient of most rocks, it was actually a quite ordinary piece of rock. The funny thing was, however, that this crumbling rock had, in fact, been "deeply buried under the earth's crust" until 1949 when it turned up rather unexpectedly as part of the upper sharp contour of the boat-shaped object.

Pitch from the Ark?

While we were talking, Niels Lind came over with a piece of hard "earth" that he had broken off of the "ship". On the one side it had a black, somewhat greasy coating.

"It smells, and the odor suspiciously reminds me of pitch," noted Niels, who is a trained engineer and knows a lot about the building of wooden ships. He and Elin Berglund had crawled up to a hole in the eastern side, the port side.

The rest of us started examining the tar-like substance at the top of the huge hole. The hole was so big that both Oli Tindalid and I could sit inside of it. Skeptically and analytically Niels Hansen from Århus, Denmark thought at first it may be blackening from a bonfire, but after he had looked at the earth, he realized that the black didn't come from below, but rather from within and was also found behind the earth that he removed.

"Strange. So it can't be from a fire," he noted.

We knew that Noah, according to the Bible, was told to coat the sides of the Ark with pitch. In Genesis, chapter 6, verse 14 Noah is told by God, "Make for yourself an ark of gopher wood; you shall make the ark with rooms, and shall cover it inside and out with pitch." (NRSV)

It was almost too good to be true. It would be amazing if we found remains of pitch on the sides of this "Ark" because *the* Ark had been coated in it. It was a little difficult to believe. On the other hand, at that point in time we couldn't find another reasonable explanation as to why there was tar-like material on the inside of this particular formation.

Gertrud's stone looked like petrified wood, but it wasn't.

A Disastrous Indifference

How had that hole gotten there anyway?

Maybe it was this hole that was broken open during the first American expedition in 1960. They visited this site after Captain Durupinar from the Turkish Air Force had detected and photographed the formation from the air in 1959.

One of the members of the American expedition was Dr. Arthur Brandenberger, who was a professor at Ohio State University in Columbus, Ohio. He had earlier revealed missiles on Cuba with the help of stereoplanigraph photogrammetry – a technique where with the help of multiple photos differentiation in levels can be seen. When he was given the opportunity to study the Turkish photograph, he remarked, "I have no doubt at all that this object is a ship. In my entire career I have never seen an object like this on stereo photo".[1]

"The Ark" seen from the east. On the side of it white shades from top to bottom are clearly seen in a repeated pattern.
These shades were believed to be remnants of "rib timbers" by Wyatt and others. Notice the size in comparison to the two people on top.

Despite Dr. Brandenberger's conviction, which he later clung to, the expedition unfortunately only performed a very surface-level investigation. It seems as if they couldn't or *wouldn't* believe that it could actually be the Ark. They were most likely prejudiced by the strong focus at the time on the great Mt. Ararat as the landing place of the Ark.

In those years many Ark-interested people believed that the Frenchman, *Fernand Navarra* had found wood from the Ark on Mt. Ararat a few years before that. Later, the wood was found to be much younger, but it was kept a secret by the SEARCH Foundation, which we will come back to at a later point.[2] After two days, the expedition didn't see anything but dirt and some stones that looked like planks but with no annual rings, so they established that this was just a mound of dirt that had been made by natural phenomenon. This is a theory that Salih Bayraktutan rejects today, but the expedition in 1960 did not include a geologist.

Yet this hasty two-day survey from 1960 is used again and again as evidence to discredit the Durupinar find.

When the Turkish authorities officially recognized the Durupinar find as "Nuhun Gemisi" (Noah's boat), some of the bitter Ararat Ark-hunters tore the road sign down. Some of the people that through the years have made a name based on the interest of finding the Ark on Mt. Ararat began to attack Wyatt rather than considering the new site. This was a sad chapter in the hunt for the Ark.

Video clip of former surveyor Hans Lind, who was in charge of our metal detector scanning.

Tidl. landmåler Hans Andersen Lind
Deltager på ekspeditionen

Scannings and Small Finds

We had read that measurement of metal under the surface has been recorded by scanning, so we played with a metal detector and one day tried to search the boat-shaped object with it.

The search was performed with surveyor Hans Linds' expert skills. Every time the detector gave a positive signal, we laid a stone. After a while, we could see that the metal signals came in straight lines at intervals of about one meter. This supported the scanning that Wyatt, Fasold, Bayraktutan, and Baumgardner had taken earlier.

Afterwards, we tested the ground about 20 yards from the formation. There were signals of metal in the earth here, too. But these signals did not come in straight lines like the others.

We didn't really dare read anything into the results of the scanning, just as we didn't dare read anything into our other findings. There were a number of us that found mussel shells, which have no place at an altitude of 6,500 feet so far from the sea.

Not a Natural Formation

In the evening at the hotel we discussed together with Dr. Salih Bayraktutan, and he answered the questions about how the boat-shaped

Footnotes

[1] Quoted from "The Ark Conspiracy", by Jonathan Gray p. 14.

[2] Carbon-14 testing of the age of the tree by two American laboratories showed that the tree was only c. 1500 years old.

object could have be formed:

"How can we know that this formation hasn't just occurred naturally as the critics claim?" I asked. "They say that it could be made of mud or lava that stopped in the shape of a tail after an obstacle. There are a lot of instances where this happens, such as in deltas."

"Yes, but this formation cannot have occurred naturally by these hydrodynamic laws," explained Salih.

There is no obstacle. Actually, there is a limestone in the boat-shaped object, but it isn't located completely in the front at the bow, as it should if the formation were made because of this. It is located in the middle of the formation. And it isn't stationary, but it moves together with the formation.

The Ark-formation also begins with a point, which it wouldn't do if it were created by soil erosion."

"What about lava flow?"

"Yes, it is possible to imagine that the formation's symmetrical figure was created by a flow of lava that crossed itself two times. There are multiple examples of this over on the Ararat Mountains. But here there is no sign of lava flow," concluded Salih.

Investigating a hole in the eastern side of the formation. It smells like tar…

What Do We Have?

What we have is a formation up in the mountains that has the shape of a boat. It has the same length as Noah's Ark, according to the Bible. To be specific, 300 cubits which is about 158 meters or 518 feet.

It was apparently down in the mud before and appeared in 1948 for the first time. Over time, it has become more and more distinct. In the beginning it was only about 3 feet higher than its surroundings, but now it is 10-20 feet higher. (The following year we measured one of the sides to be 30 feet higher. Erosion took place very quickly.)

Even though the formation was obviously made of earth like its surroundings, it stood out and stayed in its position as a whole, even though the mud around it continued to slide down the valley from year to year. Something within the formation held it together.

According to the geologist, the formation had occurred naturally. But on the aerial photographs he himself had, you could see the mud stream run from the top of the mountain and down to the place where it now lay so that you got the impression that it had come "sailing" down.

"When I saw the photo, I was convinced that we had something really special here," said Salih seriously. For the past twenty years he had been working on getting this object excavated by means of a large-scale dig, drilling, dirt samples, and more. But again and again, he ran into the

Greenlander Grethe had a catch of oysters and snail shells in a curious place – up here, far from the sea…

problem of not having enough money for the work that needed to be done.
In Turkey, there were many other projects that were rightfully prioritized
for the development of their country.

Before we left, he asked us to find partners and help from Europe for a
scientific project. We promised to do what we could, and all of us were
intent on telling the world about the fantastic discoveries in Eastern Turkey.

The TV crew had already gone home, and on the May 20, 2001, the Ark
was featured on TV2's most popular news program, Dags Dato, which
created a lot of attention - at least in Denmark.

Chapter 3

Was There Actually a Flood?

When we got home from Turkey, I contacted the leader of the department of geology at one of the universities here in Denmark. I hoped to spark an interest in working together with Dr. Salih Bayraktutan and the Turkish university on a co-operative excavation of the exciting find.

I knew how well-equipped this department is with the latest technology, and if a co-operation with Atatürk University, which had the brain- and man-power, but insufficient equipment, were to happen then together they could make great progress.

I got a somewhat friendly reply, but the head of the department didn't try to hide the fact that the old account of Noah required a flood, which he had already ruled out. Therefore, there was no possibility of a co-operation. At this point I had not prepared myself that "the Flood" was practically a taboo among geologists' circles. In fact, the theory of a great flood apparently troubles the entire theoretical system upon which geologists build their knowledge and science. If Noah, his ark, and the Flood did in fact exist, then the entire house of cards was in danger of collapsing. I understood that ancient Noah could be a threat to certain modern geologists...

Faith and Science

The explanation for these negative vibrations is simply that in the past centuries two theories about the world's evolution have arisen and since then won almost total acceptance in the scientific community. They have in fact become so integrated in modern practice and theory that it has almost forgotten that these are *only working theories*. Right now they are dogma.

The first theory is Charles Darwin's well-known theory of evolution. As most of us know, this theory states, in a nutshell, that living things have developed from lower stages through a process over an unfathomable number of years. This theory is now taught in public schools everywhere. On half-scientific TV programs assumptions of this theory are tossed out without any further explanation with phrases like, "when our ancestors crawled down from the trees" and "so-and-so many millions of years ago when our ancestors were fish or unicell animals". They don't even take the time to state that despite everything, this is *only a theory* - one that is questionable and needs to be tried.

The second theory is the so-called theory of uniformity that Charles Lyell developed - also covering the previous centuries, which is very obvious. Since its introduction there have been new discoveries that speak against it, but it has been canonized as dogma and discourages independent research. Simply put, the theory says that all changes in the universe have taken place at the same pace, which can be seen today. That is to say, the pace is incredibly slow, and therefore it is supposed this happened over many

Charles Darwin's theory of evolution was first looked at with humor, but today it has become dogmatized in a way that makes it difficult to consider other possibilities.

millions of years. An example: it is popularly assumed that the geological layers have been created by millions of years of dust and other materials laying on top of each other. But anyone that has lived in other parts of the world then Lyell's safe and comfortable England knows that the pace at which the landscape erodes will surpass the tremendously slow pace at which it is supposed the layers are formed or created. Such illogical relationships exist in the theory of uniformity, which, unfortunately, is quietly accepted. Why? We often get the impression that „science" really has a good grip of all the millions of years being tossed off. But far from it!

Datings on Shaky Ground

The theory saying that it is possible to date fossils from the geological layer in which they are found is problematic because some fossils are found in several layers. They are called polystraight fossils.

E.g. you find trees and plants having their roots down in the Carboniferous layer (which means that they should be 360-286 mill. years old), whereas their trunk stands in the Permian layer (and therefore should be 286-245 mill. years old) and their top is in the Triassic layer (i.e. between 245-208 mill. years old). It goes without saying that this can't be true. And yet this system of dating is used uncritically when you are so lucky to find a fossil in one layer. It doesn't seem quite serious.

Sometimes animals and plants are also found in the „wrong layers" – according to the theory of evolution. In fact, animals and plants supposed to have become extinct millions of years ago, have been found in layers together with works of art from ancient Greece. But then they are just called „out of place" – and scientists continue using the theory confirming the preconceived opinions. Does that seem reliable?

In the book „Forbidden Archaeology"[1] Michael A. Cremo and Richard L. Thompson are among other things telling about the Nampa goddess, a small earthenware figurine found in 1889 about 100 meters down between two sedimentary layers (Pliocene and Pleistocene) so that it should actually be dated 2 mill. years back even though it is, in all probability, only some thousand years old. Quite down in the coal seams (at least 286-360 mill. years ago) several man-made objects were found in 1926 in Bear Creek, Montana, together with two human teeth. In 1912 an iron pot was found in the coal seams near the town of Thomas, Oklahoma. An iron bell has also been found in a lump of coal in West Virginia.[2] A whole human skeleton was found low down in a coal field in Italy in 1958 – even though this layer should correspond to an age about 300 mill. years ago.

In 1891 a woman in Illinois dropped her coal scoop on the floor so that the coal broke. It turned up that a gold chain was enclosed in some of the coal – supposed to have been made about these 300 mill. years ago ...[3]

In Freiburg in Germany you find a fossil of a human skull that has been found in the coal seams...[4] Also a spoon has been found enclosed in coal – and three wooden spears were found in a coal mine in Schöningen near Hannover in Germany. They are of fir and Institut für Denkmalpflege dates

Footnotes

[1] Michael A. Cremo and Richard L. Thompson: Forbidden Archeology: The Hidden History of the Human Race Publisher: BBT Science 1996, ISBN #: 0-89213-294-9

[2] Ch. E. Seller and Bryan Russell: Ancient Secrets of the Bible. Dell Publish., New York 1994. Pg. 243-247.

[3] George Mulfinger: The Flood and the Fossils, Bob Jones University Press, Greenville. Pg.5

[4] Otto Stutzer: Geology of Coal, University of Chicago Press, 1940. Pg. 271.

[5] „Archaeology" May–June 1997. Pg. 25

them to between 380,000 – 400,000 years – not because they can measure it, but because they think that man at that time had reached that far.[5] But according to the theory of the geological layers upon which this understanding of evolution is building, these spears were actually lying in layers which were 300 mill. years old ... oops!

At the same place thousands of legs of animals have been found, with marks of cuts and stings – indicating that they have been killed by men. But unfortunately, they were lying in the devon-, the coal- or the tertiary-layers – and therefore they should be 408-66 mill. years old which does not at all fit in with the model of evolution saying that man was made only a few hundred thousand years ago.

All this system of dating is ridiculous.

Today we also know from the ecological research that nature has to be constantly in circulation and balance. So that the idea that a fish may have changed into a foreleg is not as simple as Darwin thought.

The problem with these two outdated theories is that they have become so one-sided that they hinder an open-minded research, if it does not fit into the theories already in place.

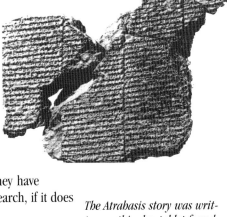

The Atrahasis story was written on this clay tablet found in Sippar (today Abu Habba in Iraq). It is believed to be from the 17th century B.C. and can be seen at the British Museum.

Room for a Creator?

You can't help but notice that these theories arose in a context in which there were religious undertones. There was a focus on getting rid of religion. But instead Darwin's and Lyell's theories became the next religious dogmas that you had to believe in - and still couldn't ask questions.

Ever since that time, atheist school teachers have tried to knock child-like faith out of their tiny pupils by claiming that the Bible was wrong about the Flood. Yes, even theology (the study of God) has been affected because certain theologians have tried to conform to that which was obviously fact.

In previous centuries Lyell and his followers categorically precluded the possibility of a flood or any other form of colossal world catastrophe. Until then, the Flood was accepted within the scientific community. It was thought that geologic layers were created by a worldwide flood that occurred some 4,500 - 5.500 years ago.

The Original Model of Explanation

The fact is that the geological layers in particular can also be interpreted as the best proof of a global flood.

For over 75 pct. of the earth and 95 pct. of the sea bed are covered by an enormous layer of sediments. This layer consists of minerals and organic material and it may have arisen *either* due to a very slow process of crumbling (Lyell's theory) *or* due to – a gigantic flood...!

The sedimentary layers are a huge burial place for all sorts of animals, fish, birds, reptiles, insects, plants and human beings. 99-100 percent of all the species that have lived on earth are according to the palaeontologists buried here. And they are lying in fairly good order with the smallest animals at the bottom and the bigger and faster on top. The huge heavy dinosaurs are lying somewhat lower. The way they would be lying if they had been caught in a catastrophe.

Nowadays animals and plants rot and decompose rapidly when they die. Why they shouldn't have done so previously is difficult to know – unless they were buried due to a catastrophe.

In the 1700's and 1800's big mass graves were found with widely different animals intertwined in a mess. Animals that didn't normally go together. Some still with grass in their mouth. Everything seems to show that they had died in a catastrophe.

Experiments with having different materials slopping around in a reservoir also show that they gradually settle down in layers – like the geological layers. It is actually very simple as long as you make room for the Flood.

But science is still injuriously affected by the fact that in the 18th and 19th centuries all the religious ideas were disposed of – and the Flood was thrown out. Later, archeologists and anthropologists realized that the Bible is not the only source that tells about a great flood. Almost all of the ancient civilized nations have accounts of it.

Discovery of the Sumerian Tablets

In 1872 – a few decades after Lyell had established that there had never been a flood – a century old telling of it from a non-biblical source was found.

By 1849 an English attorney and employee of the embassy, Henry Austin Layard, had already dug up ca. 10,000 clay tablets out of the ancient city of Nineveh (Mosul) in Iraq. These came from an extensive library that the last great Assyrian king, Assurbanipal (668-626 B.C.) had collected shortly before Nineveh was destroyed in 612 B.C. (which, by the way, was prophesied by both Nahum[6] and Zephaniah[7] in the Old Testament).

The tablets came to the British Museum in London, but it took decades to decipher the thousands of stones with inscriptions telling about law, trade, religious laws and things like food rations for political prisoners.

Then in 1872 the English assyriologist George Smith discovered an account of a hero named Gilgamesh. When he got to the 9th and 10th tablets he read that Gilgamesh in his sorrow and searching for the meaning of life visited a wise old man named Utnapishtim (which means "he who found life") – a person that surprisingly resembled Noah!

The poem has since been translated into many languages.[8] And it is considered one of the highpoints of world literature. The ancient clay tablets' contents told of the lineage of kings both before and after the Flood – and in the tablets there were up to 10 kings before the Flood (just as in the Bible's ten patriarchs), and Gilgamesh was the 5th king after the Flood. He was king in the city-state Uruk, in southern Iraq – one of the oldest cities in the world. The archeologists also found an ancient Sumerian account of the Flood in which Noah is named *Ziusudra*, a Sumerian name

Footnotes

[6] The Book of Nahum is about Nineveh. In 722 B.C. the Assyrians destroyed Samaria with atrocities as never before had been seen. But 80 years later Nahum prophesied that Nineveh, the capital of the Assyrian Kingdom, would be destroyed. In 612 B.C. this happened when The Babylonians and the Medes captured the city. The city, which was considered invincible, was penetrated by the Tigris River which made it possible for the enemy to come right in (see Nahum chapter 1:8 and 2:6).

[7] Zephaniah imparted his message in the latter part of the 7th century B.C. – most likely before 621 B.C. Zephaniah 2:13-15 says, "And he will stretch out his hand against the north, and destroy Assyria; and he will make Nineveh a desolation, a dry waste like the desert. Herds shall lie down in it, every wild animal; the desert owl and the screech owl shall lodge on its capitals; the owl shall hoot at the window, the raven croak on the threshold; for its cedar work will be laid bare. Is this the exultant city that lived secure, that said to itself, 'I am, and there is no one else'? What a desolation it has become, a lair for wild animals! Everyone who passes by it hisses and shakes the fist."
Today, scientists are the only ones who know of the beauty and majesty hiding under the fields of Mosul where the sheep graze.

[8] Translations are very different. An English translation can be found at: ancienttexts.org/library/mesopotamian/gilgamesh/index.html

for *Utnapishtim* (which also means, "he who found life"). Ziusudra was the king of Shuruppak before the Flood. According to the tablets, it was an ancient city that lay on the shores of the Euphrates. Ziusudra also built a ship and survived the Flood.

An earlier Babylonian account from approximately 1700 B.C. is about *Atrahasis* (which means the "extra wise") and is thought to come from the Sumerian period (some 1,000 years before) because it gives an account of the kings of *Samaria* before the Flood where Atrahasis was the last king in Shuruppak. Atrahasis is also saved from the Flood by building a boat. So there is no doubt that this account, too, is about the same Noah.

To sum it up, all of these ancient tablets support the Bible's account.

Which Account Comes First?

The biblical account of Noah was probably written down by Moses during the journey to Canaan with the freed Egyptian slaves. Or perhaps in the 40 years he lived as a refugee in Midjan. At least he had plenty of time.

According to the normal biblical chronology the Exodus of the Jews happened between 1446 and 1406 B.C. And with the chronology we suggest (see later) it might in stead have been around 1.585 B.C.

But we mustn't forget that the Jews could also have had older written sources. For example, in the book of Joshua and again in 2 Samuel in the Old Testament there is a reference to the Book of Jasher.[9] And Moses, as an Egyptian prince, surely had access to the most ancient sources in the royal libraries in Egypt. Whatever the case, accounts were probably handed down from the days of Abraham (around 2.230 B.C.) by word of mouth.

The important thing to note, however, is not *which* account is chronometrically the first, but rather that there are *multiple* accounts. And all of them confirm that there was a flood and a man who saved his family by building a boat. And the Sumerian accounts tell that this man and his family were the source of mankind as we know it.

Mesopotamia – the Birthplace of the World

It is not so unusual that these ancient accounts of the Flood were found precisely here in Mesopotamia. The area between the Euphrates and the Tigris is the home of the first civilizations known to man.

According to the Bible, this was also the area where most people went after the Flood. Many of the cities in this region are mentioned, for example "The beginning of his (Nimrod's) kingdom was Babel, Erech, and Accad, all of them in the land of Shinar. From that land he went into Assyria, and built Nineveh, Rehoboth-ir, Calah, and Resen between Nineveh and Calah; that is the great city."[10]

The oldest lager culture found here is the Sumerian, but there are traces of earlier peoples (before the Flood perhaps). Sumer is probably the same country known as *Shinar* in the Bible. Shinar was the great plain where those that wandered here from the landing place of the Ark built the Tower of Babel, according to the Bible. Most of what scientists know about

[11] **Agatha Christie** was married to the archeologist, Max Mallowan and wrote multiple novels connected to the excavations they experienced together. Among those works are Murder on the Orient Express and Murder in Mesopotamia whose excavation leaders are very similar to Woolley. The most autobiographical of these was They Came to Baghdad, which she wrote in Nimrod in 1951

Footnotes
[9] **The Book of Jashar,** however, may possibly have been rediscovered in the form of scrolls, as we will later see.

[10] Genesis 10:10-12.

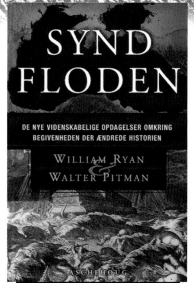

SYND
FLODEN

DE NYE VIDENSKABELIGE OPDAGELSER OMKRING
BEGIVENHEDEN DER ÆNDREDE HISTORIEN

WILLIAM RYAN
&
WALTER PITMAN

ASCHEHOUG

[13] **Noah's flood - The new scientific discoveries about the event that changed history** by William Ryan & Walter Pitman. Simon & Schuste, New York.

Mesopotamia comes from the excavations performed in the 18th and 19th centuries, not least of all being the tablets in Nineveh and thousands of other tablets found in Aleppo in Syria.

Woolley's Dig in Ur

Another great source of knowledge came in 1922 when the English archeologist *Sir Leonard Woolley* excavated the ancient city of Ur in southern Iraq. The city dates back to c. 2100 B.C., and many believe it to be the birthplace of Abraham. The British were deeply involved in the Mesopotamian excavations, and even the detective novelist Agatha Christie was present at a number of the digs in Ur, Nineveh, and Nimrod from 1930 until 1958.[11]

Relevant to Ark research was that *under* the potsheards in the ancient city of Ur, Leonard Woolley discovered another layer that was multiple meters deep. There was nothing found in that layer, but again there was another layer under that one where interesting finds appeared. The deep layer of clay was from a great flood that covered at least the entire southern part of Mesopotamia. This can be constituted because other similar flood layers have been found in that area. It is only natural to wonder if this layer wasn't from *the* Flood.

The Flood in the Black Sea?

One of the most interesting findings in connection with the question if there has actually been a great flood came just a few years ago. In connection with these findings, the distinguished Danish geologist, Minik Rosing, wrote the following: "There is good reason to believe that the biblical flood, which we started considering a fantasy-filled myth, was actually a historical event. An event which looses none of its ability to fascinate by our beginning to understand the complex correlation between climate, geology, and cultural history from which it has been born." [12]

He is only one of many geologists and archeologists that have been forced to adjust their perception of the world after new discoveries have been made in the Black Sea within the past few years by geophysicists William Ryan and Walter Pitman.[13]

Their discoveries show that around 7,200 years ago water gushed into the Black Sea with a force equal to 200 times that of Niagara Falls. On the bottom of the Black Sea they found a sand bar that couldn't keep up with the water flow. Both salt-water and fresh-water muscles have been found in the same place. This is a sign that the sea changed from being a fresh-water reservoir to a salt-water sea. Even a house has been found on the bottom of the sea… Scientists' theory is that the flood is a result of the water from the Mediterranean breaking through the Straight of Bosporus. For each hour that passed, the Black Sea was supplied with one cubic kilometer of water!

With this size figure, one can't help but think about the biblical flood connected with Noah's Ark - No more the less when one finds out that it's

[12] **Minik Rosing** in an article from the otherwise characteristically atheistic newspaper, Politiken, under the scientific topic: "Wit and Sense" (8/12/01)

dated around 7,200 years ago – not the usual millions of years ago as geologists often juggle. According to the numbers in the Bible, the Flood should have happened around 4,500-5.500 years ago. This is not exactly the same time, but the difference could be that Ryan and Pitman established the age based on the muscle shells that were found, shells which could be older than the event itself. Both events, looking at the big picture, belong to the first civilizations of antiquity, to pre-history.

Local or Worldwide?

Now, it's not normal for scientists to recognize biblical accounts in detail. There is no talk of a worldwide flood, but rather the flooding of an immense valley measuring over 1,600 miles from north to south and east to west. Here, where the Black Sea is now located, they believe lay the known "world" of that time. They also think that the flood was a result of melting during the Ice Age in Northern Europe and has been put in the Bible (and other ancient sources) as a punishment sent from God. It is a very exciting theory that is built upon the conventional theories of an ice age. But these theories have been scrutinized as not holding water because Antarctica and Greenland were evidently ice-free 3-4,000 years ago. (More in ch. 4.) Whatever the case, Ryan and Pitman have found evidence of a great flood.

Ryan and Pitman have explored the bottom of the Black Sea together with scientists from Bulgaria and Turkey. With the help of ultrasound waves and samples taken of the soil, they have established that the Black Sea was once a fresh water lake that lay hundreds of meters under today's sea level.

They image that at that time the Straight of Bosperus was closed off and that the area where the Black Sea is located today was once a very fertile valley – a paradise, one is tempted to call it – with a glorious fresh water lake at its center. Just behind that narrow isthmus that divided the Mediterranean from the Black Sea, the elevation dropped a sudden 150 meters, while the lake itself sank to a depth of 2,000 meters or 6,500 feet.

One could imagine that the valley was engulfed by a power so terrible that the entitety of the first civilization was wiped out completely with the exception of very few – possibly Noah and his family? – who drifted eastward with the strength of the wind landing around Ararat.

Evidence of a Flood Catastrophe?

Scientists have found an embankment of water-worn pebbles at a depth of 500 feet close to the Black Sea. This suggests that the coast had once been there. In deeper waters, sandbars have been found which can normally only be found at 10 feet or less.

If the water had risen slowly, the beach, along with the sandbar, would have followed. The fact that evidence of a beach has been found at such a depth suggests that the water had to suddenly rise more than 300 feet.

The Black Sea is a mighty inland sea situated between Europe and Asia. It is 721 miles long and up to 380 miles wide. The Black Sea is about 7,200 ft. deep. Through the Bosporus Strait, the Marmara Sea, and the Dardanelles there is a route leading to the Mediterranean. The Black Sea was once a fresh water lake. Today it is salty and large parts of it are dead because of a lack of oxygen.

There had to have been a water cataclysm of some kind.

From 500 feet below the surface and up to the present-day coastline there are also layers that are otherwise only found on the side of dry valleys. A thin layer of mud now covers it.

On the beach at 500 feet below, clams and muscle shells have been found. These shells are from fresh water muscles. On the contrary, the shells that have been retrieved further up the sea bottom are all of salt-water muscles.

Dating with the carbon-14 method (which, as well known, should be taken with a grain of salt) shows that the youngest fresh water muscles and the oldest salt-water muscles are of the same age. Based on their ages, the "Flood" is thought to be dated around 7,200 years ago.

A House on the Bottom of the Black Sea

On the bottom of the Black Sea – though only 311 ft. deep (95 m.) – a house has been found. Robert Ballard was the first to catch a glimpse of it miles away from land when leading an archeological exploration of the depths of the Black Sea in 2000.

The house is about 40 x 13 feet and built out of twigs and clay. A nearby dung heap – still under water – contained pieces of wood, branches, and polished stones. A man-made container and some tools were found around the house. Ballard estimates the location to be from 5500 B.C. Such an old domicile under water is almost unheard of. Wood is usually destroyed very quickly under water because of bacteria and worms, but not in the Black Sea because the oxygen level is so low that these things cannot survive, marine biologist W.B. Ryan from Columbia University told the press.

The Flood – More Than a Local Event?

One could easily believe that the flood from the Bible and other ancient sources was actually just a local, but massive flood: the Black Sea Flood. There have been attempts to explain the Flood in the same way by citing an enormous flood that occurred in southern Iraq about 5,000 years ago, of which clear signs can be found in the layers of the earth in the ancient cities of Ur and Nineveh. But there is still new evidence appearing of a great flood: Geologists Jim Teller from the University of Manitoba in Canada, Nick Lancaster from the Institute of Desert Research in Reno, Nevada, and Ashok Singhi from the Laboratory for Physical Research in India have come with indications that there was at one time a mighty flood in the Arabian Desert. And they think that the Gulf, which is only around 330 feet deep, was previously dry. They presented their findings for the American Geological Society's annual meeting in Reno in 2000.

These geologists believe their flood to be the product of shed glacial water from the ending of the Ice Age. Naturally, one is tempted to say, due to the fact that these scientists have to interpret their evidence based on the theories that already exist. But for people that are convinced that there once was a flood, the Flood, this is again evidence that a worldwide catastrophe did occur.

Chapter 4

Stories Everywhere

The author Clauss Westermann has gathered 302 flood narratives from the around the world. Others estimate that there are around 6,000 different accounts of the Flood in existence. The historian Aaron Smith counted no less than 80,000 stories in 72 languages that tell of the Flood and about 70,000 of these include a boat.[1]

No matter how many accounts there are, the fact is that stories of the Flood can be found throughout the world in old legends and myths. And most of these include the narrative of people being saved in a boat. It would be very strange if all of these stories came out of pure imagination, independent of each other. The stories don't have a Christian influence either, because many of these primitive peoples didn't have Christian influence until a few hundred years ago. Their accounts are much older. In many cases it has been established that they are 2-3,000 years old.

These accounts are, of course, full of local differentiations, but the essence is the same. They all point to the idea that there really was at one time in the history of mankind a great flood.

In the Sumerian account of the Flood, Noah is called Ziusudra (Xisuthros in Greek). In India there is a Noaic account in which Noah is known as Menu.

The old Sumerian picto-graphic sign for the earth is a boat-shaped figure with eight lines…
A remnant from the story of the beginning of the new world after Noah and the Ark with its eight survivors. In various ancient cultures you also find a world-egg that looks strikingly like the boat shaped-object.

eight

vessel

mouth

The Chinese sign for a big ship has these three signs: vessel, eight, and mouth. The vessel with the eight mouths.
Japanese signs also have remnants of the eight.

The Flood According to the Greeks

The Greeks, too, have an account of the Flood in their mythology.

Mesopotamia was conquered by the Greeks around 330 B.C. It is not sure if they took the Mesopotamian stories and altered them to fit their own mythology or if they had their own story of the Flood, but we do know that the Greek adapted a large portion of Mesopotamian religion into their own, for example astrology.

The ancient Greek myth of *Deucalion* tells us how this hero brought the population on earth back to normal "after the waters sank".

Deucalion was the son of Prometheus (which means the preconceived, or "the extra wise"). According to the myth when Zeus punished mankind by sending a flood Deucalion and his wife Pyrrha, who sailed in a box for nine days, were left as the only survivors. After the ninth day the box landed on a mountain, Parnassus. The couple then became the generator of the new human family, and their son, Hellen, became the father of the Greeks (the Hellenes).

(The Greek Noah-mountain Parnassus is a mountain chain in mid-Greece with the highest peak reaching 8,061 ft. In ancient Greece it was considered the residence of Apollo and the Muses. The oracular city, of Delphi and Castalia can also be found on Parnassus.)

Footnotes
[1] According to Werner Keller, *The Bible as History*, Bantam Books, New York, 1980. Sold 10 million copies since 1955.

Footnotes

[2] According to Rene Norbergen in "The Ark File".

[3] An English translation can be found at www.icr.org/pubs/imp/imp-214.htm

In the Greek account, as in many other older myths, the gods and half-gods play a role in the world of man. Due to that fact, the "enlightened" Western World has considered myths nothing but pure imagination. There is, however, the possibility that real events have been dressed in mythological clothing, changed through the years. Ancestor worship can be found in all ancient cultures and still is practiced in African cultures, for example. It doesn't take too many years for an ancestor to become a half-god. And not much more for him to be given supernatural powers. Thus, a myth is born. This is how it happened with Noah in some of the ancient cultures' stories of the Flood where he is considered a god. The eight that left the Ark have become ancestor "gods" in many of the ancient religions.

E.g. the Egypts' eight ancestor spirits, the AKiHaWas, reminding remarkably of Sumer's Asakus and the Greeks' Akhiyawa.

To Understand the Ancient Sources

In the biblical account it is maintained that Noah was a normal man that made mistakes like the rest of us. (He got drunk and threw off his clothes; he cursed one of his sons, etc.)

The mistakes of prophets, kings, and other great leaders are told candidly. Therefore, from a journalistic point of view, it is easier to believe the objective, critical story telling in the Bible than that of the glorified hero and god stories found in other religions and cultures. The Bible is also by far the most well-documented of the ancient writings. Thousands of original copies can be found in many different languages, while most other sources can only be found in limited numbers. Whether seen with religious or worldly eyes, it is in a class of its own. However, the other sources contain accounts of real events, too.

For many years we have had a tendency to assume that the stories from ancient cultures are fallible or fairy tales full of superstition. And we often act as pompous gentlemen based on the value of truth that exists in this era.

For example, every time the supernatural comes into play our scientists give a rational explanation. If a prophet sees something that is to come and it happens hundreds of years later, it is assumed that the prophet must have lived after the fact. The supernatural is shut out because it has no place in modern Western acknowledgement.

If ancient myths are degraded and thrown out in this manner, one misses the possibility of real events being hidden in layers of religion and language.

In this book, we will try to regard the ancient sources with great respect in order to find the answers to the mysteries of pre-historic time.

The Chinese Account of the Flood

In China legend asserts that the Chinese are the descendents of Nu-Wah, an ancestor of old whose name bares a striking resemblance to Noah. He survived the Flood together with his three sons and his three daughters-in-

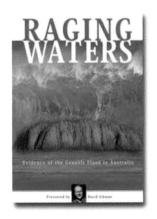

"Raging Waters" is a documentary from Keziah Films indicating that in historic time a flood transported the gigantic and out-of-place Ayers Rock to the remote desert of Middle Australia. Did Noah's Flood also reach Australia?

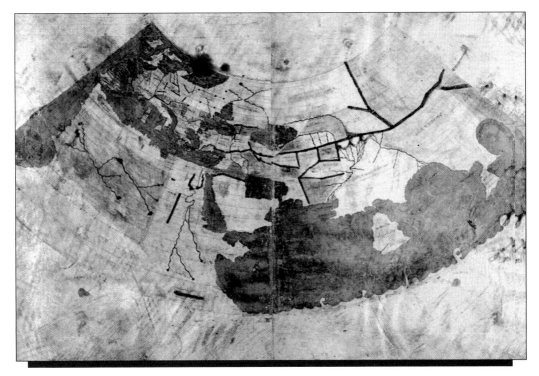

The world map Ptolomaios's "Geography" was designed around 150 A.D. It is the first known map that shows the world as a sphere, but the size of the world's circumference was known long before. This copy is from 1290 and kept in Rome. (Codex Vaticanus Urbinas). Obviously people had a rather precise idea of the shape of the world.

law – the exact same way that Noah did. The Chinese character that is used today for the word "ship" comes from a very old character that consisted of a boat and eight mouths.[2]

Among the Miao, or Miautso peoples, these ancient stories especially resemble the first accounts from the Bible. They include the story of Creation, the Flood with Noah and the Ark, and the Tower of Babel. It is quite possible that these narratives have been so well preserved from generation to generation because they are written in a type of rhyme in which accidental changes are not likely.[3]

The Miao people once governed over most of inner China but were driven into the mountains by the Chinese. A missionary, Ernest Truax, spent most of his life among the Miao people up in the mountains. He collected their old accounts and translated them into English.

According to the Miao traditions, it rained for 40 days (the same as the Bible's account) and then 55 days of haze and drizzle caused the waters to rise up over the mountains, and there was no place to go for shelter. The people were overcome with terror. But the patriarch NuWah was righteous. He built a great boat. His entire household came aboard and survived, together with both males and females of all the animals as well as birds by twos. When the time came, God commanded the waters to retreat, and NuWah released a dove (also as in the Bible). The waters receded into lakes and seas. The land was again inhabitable. Fattened animals were offered to the Mighty One, and God gave them his good favor.

The Native American Accounts of the Flood

Among the many tribes there are very different stories:

"In the tribal tales of the Cherokee Indians of the southeastern United States, the coming of a flood was told by a dog to his master. 'You must build a boat,' the dog said, 'and put in it all that you would save; for a great rain is coming that will flood the land.'"[4]

"The Tlingit tribe of northwestern Alaska told of a great flood which, driven by wind, covered all dwelling places. The Tlingits saved themselves by tying several boats together to make a great raft. They floated on this, huddling together for warmth under a tenet until Anodjium, a magician, ordered the sea to be calm and the flood to recede." [5]

From his book, *Chinigchinich*, Friar Geronimo Boscana wrote, "The Acagchememe Indians, near San Juan Capistrano in Southern California, were not entirely destitute of a knowledge of the universal Deluge, but how, or from whence, they received the same, I could never understand. Some of their songs refer to it; and they have a tradition that, a time very remote, the sea began to swell and roll in upon the plains, and fill the valleys, until it had covered the mountains; and thus nearly all the human race and animals were destroyed, except a few, who had resorted to a very high mountain which the waters did not reach."[6]

Aboriginals Have an Account of the Flood

The Australian aborigines also had their own story of the Flood long before Christian influence came. George Rosendale, who is himself a part of the Australian aboriginal race, tells[7] that his first time in Sunday school when he heard about the Tower of Babel, he protested wildly: "You whites have misunderstood. The story with the languages didn't happened somewhere in the Middle East, but rather up here by Cooktown. My grandma told me our story, and it is just like that there." The grandmother had heard the story herself as a little girl:

"Our story is that when people broke the laws of the ancestor spirit, He got mad. (The ancestor spirit is the one that created everything and gave life.) He sent a great cyclone that rained and rained until the whole area was flooded except for the top of a hill. The few that made it up there survived, the rest drowned or were eaten by crocodiles when they tried to swim to a safe place.

Also the Maori of New Zealand have a story of the Flood from pre-colonization.

Footnotes

[4] L. Patricia Kite: *Noah's Ark*.

[5] L. Patricia Kite: *Noah's Ark*.

[6] Boscana, Father Geronimo: Chinigchinich, Fine Arts Press, Santa Ana 1933. Ref. CA31291

[7] Reproduced in Creation Magazine, see Answers In Genesis.com

World map showing where flood stories occur. From Jonathan Gray's book The Ark Conspiracy.

Stories of the Flood in All Cultures

John D. Morris and Tim F. LaHaye gathered in their book, *The Ark on Ararat*[8] a list of some of the many accounts of the Flood. This became the following impressive list of over 212 accounts:

MIDDLE EAST AND AFRICA
1. Africa (central)
2. Babylon
3. Bapedi Tribe (S. Africa)
4. Chaldea
5. Egypt (Pharaonic)
6. Egypt (Priestly)
7. Hottentots
8. Jumala Tribe
9. Lower Congo
10. Masai Tribe
11. Otshi Tribe (Kabinda)
12. Persia (Ahriman)
13. Persia (Bundehesch)
14. Persia (Testrya)
15. Persia (Yima)
16. Persia (Zala-Cupha)
17. Syria

PACIFIC ISLANDS
18. Alamblack Tribe (New Guinea)
19. Alfors of Ceram
20. Ami
21. Andaman Islands
22. Australia
23. Bunva
24. Dutch New Guinea (Mombrano River)
25. East Indian Island
26. Engano
27. Falwol Tribe (New Guinea)
28. Fiji
29. Fiji (Rokora)
30. Flores Island
31. Formosa Tribesman
32. Hawaii (Mauna-Kea) Tribesmen
33. Hawaii (Nu-U)
34. Kabidi Tribe (New Guinea)
35. Kurnai Tribe (Australia)
36. Leeward Islands
37. Maori (New Zealand)
38. Melanesia
39. Micronesia
40. Nais
41. New Britain
42. Otheite Island
43. Ot-Danoms
44. Polynesia
45. Queensland
46. Rotti Tribe
47. Samoa
48. Samo-Kubo Tribe (New Guinea)
49. Sea Dyaks (Borneo)
50. Sea Dyaks (Trout)
51. Sea Dyaks (Sarawak)
52. Sumatra
53. Tahiti
54. Toradjas
55. Valman Tribe (New Guinea)

FAR EAST
56. Anals (Assam)
57. Bahnara (China)
58. Bengal Kolhs
59. Benua-Jakun (Malaysia)
60. Bhagavata-Purana
61. China (Fo-hi)
62. China (Joa)
63. China (Tao-tse)
64. China (Upper Burma)
65. India (Rama)
66. Kamars (C. India)
67. Kamchadales (India)
68. Karens (Burma)
69. Lolos (S. China)
70. Mahabharata
71. Matsya-Purana
72. Menangkabans (Sumatra)
73. Satapatha Brahmana
74. Singphos (Burma)
75. Sudan
76. Tartary Mongols

EUROPE & ASIA
77. Celts
78. Druids
79. Finland

80. Iceland
81. Kelts
82. Lapland
83. Lithuania
84. Norway
85. Rumania
86. Russia
87. Siberia
88. Transylvania
89. Wales

HELLENIC
90. Apamea (Cibotos)
91. Apollodorus
92. Aristotle
93. Athenian
94. Cos (Meropes)
95. Crete
96. Diodorus
97. Hellenucus
98. Lucian
99. Megaros
100. Ogyges (Boeotia)
101. Ovid
102. Perirrhoos
103. Pindar
104. Plato
105. Plutarch
106. Rhodes
107. Samothrace
108. Sithnide Nymphs
109. Stephanus
110. Thessalonica

NORTH AMERICA
111. Acagchemens
112. Aleutian Island Indians
113. Algonquins (Manabozho)
114. Appalachian Indians
115. Arapahos
116. Arctic Eskimos
117. Athapascans
118. Blackfoot Indians
119. Caddoques
120. Central Eskimos
121. Cherokee
122. Chippewa
123. Cree
124. Delaware Algonquins
125. Dogribs
126. Eleuts
127. Eskimos (Alaska)
128. Eskimos (Norton Sound)

129. Esquimax
130. Flatheads
131. Greenland
132. Great Lakes Indians
133. Haidas
134. Hareskins
135. Huron Indians
136. Innuit Eskimos
137. Iroquois
138. Kathlamets
139. Knistineaux
140. Kolosh
141. Koloshes
142. Lake Tahoe Indians
143. Lenni Lanape Indians
144. Luisenos
145. Mandans
146. Mantagnais Algonquins
147. Menominees
148. Montagnais
149. Natchez Indians
150. New California Indians
151. Nez Pierces
152. Ojibway
153. Pacullies
154. Papagos
155. Pimas
156. Potawatomi Indians
157. Rio Erevato Indians
158. Salteaux Algonquins
159. Sarcees
160. Smith River Indians
161. Spokanas
162. Thlinkuts
163. Thlinkuts (Yehl)
164. Thompsan Indians
165. Tinneh Indians
166. Twangs
167. Virginia Indians
168. Yakimas

CENTRAL AMERICA
169. Achagnas
170. Antilles
171. Aztecs
172. Aztecs (Coxcoxli)
173. Canaris
174. Cholulans
175. Cholulas
176. Coras (Lowland)
177. Coras (Highland)
178. Cuban Indians
179. Huichals

180. Mexico (Coxcox)
181. Mexico (Mexitli)
182. Michoacans
183. Muratos
184. Nicaraguan Indians
185. Panamanian Indians
186. Rio-Crevato Indians
187. St. Domingo Indians
188. Tlascalans
189. Toltecs

SOUTH AMERICA
190. Abederys
191. Ackwois
192. Araucaians
193. Arawaks
194. Brazilian Mountain Indians
195. Brazilian Sea Coast Indians
196. Caingangs
197. Carayas
198. Chiriguanos
199. Colombian Indians
200. Incas
201. Kataushys
202. Macusis
203. Maypures
204. Orinoco Indians
205. Pamarys
206. Peru (Bomara)
207. Peru (Guancas)
208. Peruvian Indians
209. Rio de Janeiro Indians
210. Tamanacs
211. Terra-Firma Indians
212. Tierra del Fuego Indians

[8] Morris, John D. & Tim F. LaHaye, *The Ark on Ararat* (New York: Thomas Nelson Inc., 1976), pp. 233-237.

A Common Mystical Past

Even though some people lived completely geographically isolated from the Bible's Middle Eastern world – such as the Indians of South America and the Australian Aborigines – they still have their stories of the Flood. Since these stories are placed far back in the history of these cultures, it is obvious that it is not something the whites brought with them.

The most likely explanation is of course that they originally wandered from the same region and have taken the story with them. The Norwegian explorer Thor Heyrdahl crossed the oceans in a boat made of rush on multiple expeditions from 1947-70 and thus proved that it would have been possible for our "primitive" forefathers – long before Columbus – to cross the Atlantic, Indian, and Pacific Oceans. Since then, many have crossed the Atlantic and the Pacific in even very small boats.

Right now new information is being discovered that suggests that the people of the world had connection over the seas by using ocean currents as a means of transport as far back as 3-4,000 years ago. For centuries before our time, people in Mesopotamia were emptying some of America's mines of alluvial natural copper, tin and silver.[9] They already knew about advanced ball-trigonometry, which calculates distances based on the earth being round. The Sumerians were the first to seperate the circle into 360 degrees. But unfortunately, a lot of this knowledge disappeared under the Roman militant depredation centuries before Christ, and was not truly found again until the 17th century by the Europeans.

Footnotes
[9] James Bailey: Sailing to Paradise.

Statistics over Flood stories all over the World

88%	are about a family that is saved; 12% maintain some part of this
70%	tell of a boat that saved the survivors; 30% tell of other types of rescue
95%	only tell of the Flood; 5% also tell of other causes
66%	blame the catastrophe on mankind's evilness
67%	include animals being saved
73%	include animals in some way
73%	include a worldwide Flood
53%	say that the survivors were rescued from a mountain
35%	include the bird being sent out (like in the Bible)
7%	mention the rainbow
13%	mention an offering afterwards
66%	tell that those saved were forewarned
82%	happen locally (often with a local mountain)
9%	specifically mention that 8 people were saved
37%	have coincidental reasons for the catastrophe

Local Color; The Same Event
Even though the many accounts have local coloring, there is still agreement with the biblical account.

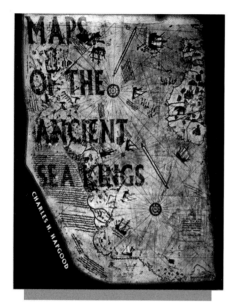

Old Maps Suggest a Different World

Ancient maps show that the knowledge of degree measuring was already in use.[10] The Greek legends even include Antarctica. But in more modern times this knowledge was rejected. On his two journeys in 1768-1775, James Cook established that the Greek accounts of a large continent around Antarctica were false. He could only see ice. But under that ice is the fifth largest continent in the world – that's what was shown by seismologic research performed in 1958. The amazing thing is that the areas of land were drawn on Oronteus Finaeus' map of the world in 1531 – which was presumably based on ancient maps. Phillippe Buaches' map of 1754 also shows Antarctica without ice and with a great fjord running through the middle of the continent between the seas of Ross, Weddel, and Bellinghausen. Buaches could only have had this knowledge from ancient maps. Modern measuring of the underground proved that these maps were accurate. How could the old cartographer know what lay beneath a layer of 2-mile thick ice? The explanation is simply that Antarctica must have been free of ice 4-6,000 years ago. W. D. Urry and Dr. Jack Hough, atomic physicists at the University of Illinois, realized this after Hough had taken some sediment tests at a depth of 2,990-3,292 meters (9,809-10,800 ft.) below the ice during the Byrd-expedition in 1949.

This information disputes the teaching that the evolution of the earth has happened at a constant rate. If Antarctica and Greenland were free of ice 4-6,000 years ago – at the time of Noah – then the world at that time looked very different than it should according to conventional theories. The climate would have been much milder but quickly changed. (The hairy mammoths of Siberia that were quickly frozen would also support this theory.) The question is: what made the poles freeze? And is it coincidental that they apparently froze directly after the point in time where the Bible says the Flood happened?

The Tower of Babel – A Common Origin?

A number of things suggest that in antiquity, which we only know from traditions and myths, a lively bit of traffic happened on the world's oceans. And the "original" inhabitants of the Americas, Australia, and the Pacific Islands could have arrived from a common starting point – namely the Middle East.[11]

Did they? If we look at the story in the Bible (and the myths of some other peoples) everyone was spread out from Mesopotamia because they began speaking different languages. God had – according to Genesis chapter 11 – confused the languages in order to stop the building of the Tower of Babel, a pyramid-shaped building of which ruins are thought to be found in Birs Nimrod about 12 miles from the ancient city of Babylon, 65 miles

Footnotes

[10] Charles H. Hapgood: Maps of Ancient Sea Kings, Evidence of Advanced Civilisation in the Ice Age. Adventures Unlimited Press. Kempton, Illinois 1996.

[11] The Norwegian author Aril Edvardsen has gathered huge amounts of information about this in his major work: Solgudens autostrada (The Highway of the Sun God).

from Baghdad, Iraq. The tower here was at least 180 feet high and consisted of 7 stories. But this is not the only ziggurat (a pyramid-shaped temple tower) that can be found in the area. The largest is found in Babylon itself. It was over 300 x 300 feet at the base and nearly 300 feet high. (According to some ancient sources, only 1/3 of the mighty tower is left behind.[12])

The Ararat Mountains – A Common Origin?

But if we don't just accept the Biblical account as truth, is there other evidence suggesting that the people of the world all originate from one region of the world? Yes, the so-called Indo-European languages can all be traced back to a so-called Proto-Indo-European language that arose from this region. The Indo-European languages include many Asian languages such as Bengali, Iranian, Kurdish, Afghan, Nepali, and Romany (the languages of the gypsies of northern India) in addition to most of the European language families (the Romance, Germanic, and Slavic language families).[13]

Old maps seem to indicate that only a few thousand years ago the world looked different - and that the theories about the development of the earth don't quite fit. Here e.g is a map by Philippe Buaches from 1754 showing an ice-free Antarctia and with a large fiord between the Ross Sea, the Weddel Sea and the Bellinghausen Sea. Later measurements through the ice have shown that it is true, but Buaches couldn't have known that in 1754 where Antarctia like today was covered by ice - unless his information built on ancient maps, but if so Antarctia would have been ice-free in historical times.

The theory that all languages had a common source was formed by Sir William Jones in 1786 in Calcutta. Jones found a clear connection between the verb-roots and the grammatical forms in the ancient Indian language of Sanskrit and Persian, Greek, Latin, Celtic, and German.

The linguist *Thomas Gamkredlidze* from the State University in Tiblisi, Georgia revised the "language tree" in 1985 and discovered that the trunk – the original proto-Indo-European language – sprang out of Armenia! The theory met skepticism from the West but in 1995 was confirmed with the help of the computer-mathematics of three researchers at the University of Pennsylvania,[14] who clearly did *not* believe in the theory.

There are also other languages than the Indo-European: Sino-Tibetan, Hamito-Semitic, Nilo-Saharan, Khoisan, and Niger-Kordofanian, Uralic-Altaic languages, Austro-Asiatic languages, the Dravidian family, and the Malayo-Polynesian. Languages which do not belong to any of these families include native American languages, Korean and Japanese, the languages of New Guinea, and the Athabascan

Footnotes

[12] The Book of Jasher 9:38 states: "And as to the tower which the sons of men built, the earth opened its mouth and swallowed up one third part thereof, and a fire also descended from heaven and burned another third, and the other third is left to this day, and it is of that part which was aloft, and its circumference is three days' walk."

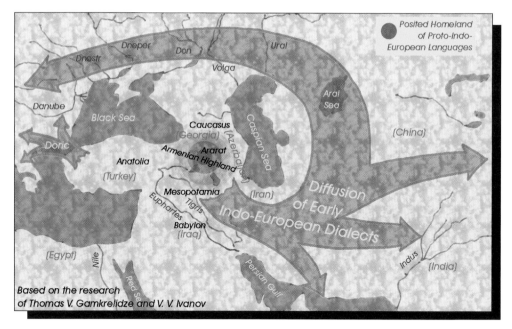

The linguists Thomas V. Gamkrelidze and V.V. Ivanov have researched the development of the Indo-European languages and have concluded that the original Proto-Indo-European language had its starting point right here in the Armenian highlands – also known as Ararat and Urartu – where the Ark was stranded. Other researchers have previously assumed that Europe was the starting point. From the highlands the development of the languages spread to the southeast via Mesopotamia.

Footnotes

[13] There are also the following independent language chains: Finno-Ugric, Turkish, Mongolian, Tungusic.

[14] Donald Ringe, Ann Taylor, and Tandy Warrow.

[15] Described in "The Nexus – Spoken Language. The Link Between the Mayan and the Semitic During Pre-Columbian Times," Isac Press. Institute for The Study Of American Cultures, Columbus, Georgia, 1993.

and Algonquian languages of subarctic Canada. According to the Bible all theses languages came from one.

A few years ago one of my contacts in Ark research, David Allen Deal, USA, discovered a clear connection in both word and written types between the language that the Maya Indians spoke and wrote in South America and the Semitic language in the Middle East.[15] And if this connection between the two languages that supposedly belong each to their own distinct family of languages does exist, then there may be absolutely no need for a division of language families but rather talk of very different languages that have the same language family as a starting point.

Chapter 5

Meteor Showers

The Sunday Telegraph in London printed a notable story the 4th November 2001: [1]

The article relates that Dr. Sharad Master, a geologist at the University of Witwatersrand, Johannesburg, South Africa has on satellite photographs located an enormous crater measuring over 2 miles in diameter in southern Iraq. He discovered this by accident when reading an article about Saddam Hussein's canals and saw a picture showing different formations - one of which was very circular. Studies of older satellite photos from the 80's show that the depression previ-

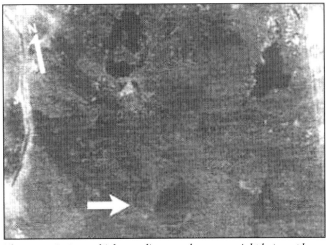

The crater in Iraq which was discovered on an aerial photograph was caused by a meteor shower c. 2,000 B.C. or earlier. Around 2,345 B.C. a sudden decline occurred in the cultures of the world. According to the traditional understanding of the chronology of the Bible, the Flood took place in 2,349 B.C. (See the chapter about new chronology later in the book.)

ously held a small lake. But Saddam drained it in his campaign against the Marsh Arab Area, causing an elevated ring-shape typical of craters to become visible in the dried-out lake.

Some scientists have suggested that this crater was formed when a meteor destructively hit the earth about 4,000 years ago. The power of this meteor's crash was equivalent to the power of hundreds of atom bombs put together. The crater is in the Al 'Amarah region, about 10 miles northwest of where the Tigris and Euphrates flow together into a delta.

The strike may have caused destructive fires and floods. Is this when the Flood started, or was it in connection with this event that the Tower of Babel came crashing down further north where fire and brimstone rained from the heavens causing the people to spread in every direction?

Here Fall the First Civilizations

The Sunday Telegraph states that this could possibly explain why many earlier cultures seemed to disappear around 2,300 B.C. This is true of the Akkad culture of central Iraq (Babylonia) with its mysterious ruler, Sargon (was this the Bible's Nimrod?); it is also true of the sudden end of the 5th dynasty of the ancient Egyptian kingdom after the building of the great pyramids and the hundreds of contemporary inhabitants of present-day Israel. Until now, archeologists have explained the fall of these early civilizations with reasons such as war or climatic changes, while astronomers have suggested a meteor being the possible cause.

Whatever the case, the crater is relatively new. The sediments in this region are very young, geologically speaking, so whatever caused this crater-

Footnotes

[1] „Meteor clue to end of Middle East civilisations" by Robert Matthews, Science Correspondent, Daily Telegraph, London. The story was followed up by more information in the Telegraph on 8th November.

like structure must have happened within the last 6,000 years, says Dr. Master, who has described his findings in the November 2001 issue of "Meteoritics & Planetary Science". His discoveries have also been cited in other journals. Dr. Master is part of a scientific group, *Impact Cratering Research Group*, which researches craters caused by meteors from outer space. Dr. Benny Peiser, who teaches on impact craters at John Moores University, Liverpool, England calls the crater one of the most meaningful discoveries from this period which confirms his own and others' research in this area. He also mentions that a crater found in Argentina dates back to this same period, which suggests that the earth was hit by a shower of massive meteors at that time.

The discovery of this crater also casts new light on the legend of Gilgamesh, which talks about "the Seven Judges of Hell" who lifted their torches setting fire to the countryside and bringing about a storm that turned day into night and created a mighty flood. [2] (See the Gilgamesh chapter.)

This epic poem normally dates backt to around 3,000 B.C.

Another source from the period in question is called "Akkad's curse" which speaks of flaming potsherds raining from the heavens.

Such Large Meteors Would Release a Flood

Shortly before the time of Christ, the Jewish astronomer, Rabi bar Nachmani, wrote in the so-called "Babylonian Talmud", that the Flood in the days of Noah was caused by two "stars" falling from the sky. "When the Holy One . . . wanted to bring a flood upon the world, He took two stars from *Khima* and brought a flood upon the world ." [3]

Was he really referring to two great meteors that were known of in the Middle East, one of which being the meteor in question falling in Iraq?

Bill Napier, an astronomer at Armagh Observatory believes there was a meteor shower. He told Science Tuesday[4] that a comet named Encke, which was discovered in 1786, is the remnant of a larger comet that broke into thousands of pieces about 5,000 years ago spreading throughout the universe and possibly hitting the earth in the early Bronze Age where a cloud of meteor debris could have darkened the sun. Napier connects these happenings with a cooling of the climate, which is measured in tree rings over the period 2,354-2,345 B.C.

According to Benny Peiser from Liverpool John Moores University a dozen or so large impact craters have been found, and due to the earth comprising of more sea than land, we can only expect that there are twice as many enormous meteors in the ocean. This would have caused great tidal waves, Tsunamis, of greater consequence than meteors hitting the land.

Do the Years Fit?

Once again, we see that the Biblical accounts and other "myths" such as Gilgamesh are not carefully crafted stories as often claimed, but can very well refer to factual events. If we were to add up the genealogies from the Flood to the time of Christ, as Irish Archbishop and astronomer, James

Footnotes

[2] ",...and the seven judges of hell ... raised their torches, lighting the land with their livid flame. A stupor of despair went up to heaven when the god of the storm turned daylight into darkness, when he smashed the land like a cup." - *An account of the Deluge from the Epic of Gilgamesh, circa 2200 B.C.*

[3] Tractate Brakhot (Seder Zerafim) chapter IX, Fol. 59a, transl. by Maurice Simon, ed. by I. Epstein (London, 1948).

[4] www.science.com, November 13, 2001.

[5] Articles: ",Time, Life, and History in the Light of 15,000 Radiocarbon Dates", Whitelaw, 1970, *Creation Res. Soc. Quart.* 7, 56-71, 83. and ",The biblical record of Creation, Flood and History in light of 30,000 radiocarbon dates", Proceedings, 15th Anniversary Convention of Bible Science Association, pp. 197-202, 1979.

[6] ",The Cause of the Deluge Demonstrated, being an Appendix to the 2nd edition of the *New Theory of the Earth*" (London, 1708).

[7] Rabbi Joshua: ",There is a star which appears every 70 years and misleads the captains of boats." A possible reference to Halley 's comet. (W. M. Feldman, *Rabbinical Mathematics and Astronomy* (New York, 1931), pp. 11, 216.

Ussher did in1650; the equation dates the Flood to 2,349 B.C.

Of course, these accounts should be taken with a grain of salt, because some generations may have been left out, and my personal opinion is that the Flood dates further back, that is around 3,500 B.C. When this does not agree with Ussher's calculation, it is due to a fault in the Hebrew (so-called Masoretic) translation and of an omission of "evil years", which we shall look into later.

If the meteor showers have to fit with Gilgamesh the meteor showers must be before 3.000 B.C. - provided that the dating of Gilgamesh is correct.

Some scientists set the Flood around 4,950 years ago based on Carbon-14 dating.[5] These show a large rise in the findings of dead humans and animals about 5,000 years ago. Actually, there are over double the amount of such examples at this time than from earlier periods, and oppositely, there is only 1/8 of that amount in the five years following. This could suggest that the population was drastically minimized.

If this was caused by the Flood, then it happened about 5,000 years ago. And the meteor landing in Southern Iraq may have been connected with the nearby Tower of Babel. This could reasonably have happened around 600 years later - and if the people spread out after that point, then it would also lead to a temporary decline in the Babylonian as well as other contemporary civilizations.

Whether the meteor in Iraq was connected with the Flood or the Tower, it is sure that a meteor strike of such caliber didn't come quietly! And it will be exciting to follow the story as scientists finally set a date as to when the meteor struck. This can be done by measuring radioactivity in any melted rocks or glass that would have been caused by the heat of such a collision. But those things have yet to be found.

Barringer Meteor Crater in Arizona is 3,900 ft.wide and 650 ft. deep. It is estimated to be 50,000 years old, but as is common knowledge, dating over a few thousand years is based upon theories that have not been proven. The diameter of the crater in Iraq is more than double this size – i.e. approx. 10,000 ft.!

Velikovsky Said It...

500 years ago Russian-American scientist, Immanuel Velikovsky, postulated a theory that the earth was hit by a number of catastrophes following a meteor and the influence of other planets whose orbit had come too close to the earth. His theories were very popular during the decades just after World War II, but he was considered a heretic in the scientific community, which held on to Lyell's dogma that the earth has evolved at an immensely slow tempo (the theory of uniformity) without major changes (catastrophes).

Today, observations from space have confirmed some of Velikovsky's theories, and the discovery in Iraq might be just one more example.

In his books, Velikovsky dishes up hundreds of examples from nature that demonstrate the fact that at least one violent and worldwide catastrophe took place in the beginning of historical time.

We will come back to Velikovsky.

Is the Comet Theory as Old as the Flood Itself?

Even before Velikovsky, astronomers and others throughout history have had similar thoughts. The best known is Englishman, William Whiston, who in 1696 published the book *New Theory of the earth*. In an appendix[6] to the book, he referred to Halley's comet, which had appeared in the sky just a few years previous in 1682 and had caused a lot of interest in astronomy. (Edmund Halley got the honor for his theory that the comet returned every 70 years, but the same observation had already been made in the 2nd century by a Jewish astronomer.[7])

Whiston believed that the comet returned at an interval of 575 ½ years and had been here in 2,346 B.C. where it caused a massive flood. Whiston also found ancient sources that spoke of a year that only lasted 360 days around 700 B.C.

Before Whiston, David Herlicius in 1619 had published writing about a comet that had shown itself in 1618. He cited Cicero that misfortune always followed comets and believed, as did his predecessors Abraham Rockenbach (16th cent.), Seth Calvisius (1556-1615), Henricus Ecstormius, Christopher Helvicus (1581-1617), and David Herlicius (1557-1636), that a comet had caused the Flood in the year 2,292 B.C.

Abraham Rockenbach tells, as the most natural fact, that in the year 1656 after the creation of the world, three days before the death of Methuselah, "a comet appeared in the constellation Pisces, was seen by the entire world as it traversed the twelve signs of the zodiac in the space of a month; on the sixteenth of April it again disappeared. After this the Deluge immediately followed..."[8] However, he doesn't quote any direct sources. He could have gotten his information from Rabbi Isaac ben Solomon (Rashi), the great Jewish expert of astronomical phenomena who lived in the South of France in the Middle Ages - the 11th century to be precise. His commentary on the Bible and the Talmud is still considered the authority among rabbis.

Footnotes

[8] In the year of the creation of the world 1656, after Noah had attained the age of 600 years, three days before the death of Methuselah, a comet appeared in the constellation Pisces, was seen by the entire world as it traversed the twelve signs of the zodiac in the space of a month; on the sixteenth of April it again disappeared. After this the Deluge immediately followed, in which all creatures which live on earth and creep on the ground were drowned, with the exception of Noah and the rest of the creatures that had gone with him into the ark. About these things is written in Genesis, chapter 7, Quote according to Velikovsky in „In The Beginning".

[9] „...who made the Bear and Orion, the Pleiades and the chambers of the south" (Job 9:9)

[10] „Can you bind the chains of the Pleiades, or loose the cords of Orion?" (Job 38:31)

[11] „The one who made the Pleiades and Orion, and turns deep darkness into the morning, and darkens the day into night, who calls for the waters of the sea, and pours them out on the surface of the earth, the Lord is his name" (Amos 5:8)

Khima?

Rabbi Rashi had commented on the stars written of in what is most likely the oldest book in the Bible - Job in both 9:9[9] (chapter 9, verse 9) and 38:31[10] as well as in the book of Amos 5:8[11]. The stars are called Aish, Kesil, and Khima in Hebrew – in English they are translated as Arcturus, Orion, and Pleiades.

He called *Khima*, translated as Pleiades (the seven sisters), "a star with a tale" - a comet. In the Jewish explanation, the Talmud, *Khima* is connected with the Flood.

Velikovsky demonstrates that translators for different ages have chosen different stars, and by comparing it with other quotes from the Talmud, he finds that this Khima must be Saturn. Therefore, Job 38:31 should actually read: "Canst thou bind the bonds of Saturn and loosen the reins of Mars?" And that makes sense because the "bonds" of Saturn can still be seen today with a telescope. There are, of course, rings around the planet. And Mars' "reins" are the two small moons in its orbit. They were already known of in Homer's time.

So what the Jewish rabbi in the 2nd century before Christ is saying is probably: "Two stars erupted from the planet Saturn and caused the Deluge." And historically Saturn was connected with water and catastrophes. The Chaldean astronomer, Berosus, tells in his account of the Flood that Saturn (Kronos in Greek) warns King Xisuthros (Noah) that a universal flood would begin on the 15th day in the month of Dasios.

Two Stars from Saturn...

Saturn was the most important star to the great civilizations of the past. Actually, Saturn was worshipped in the Chaldean, Greek and Egyptian religions. In the Chaldean, Saturn was called the star of the god Tammuz, while the Greeks revered it as their greatest god, Kronos, later removed from the throne by Zeus (Jupiter). Likewise, in Egypt, Saturn was the strongest of the gods named Osiris who

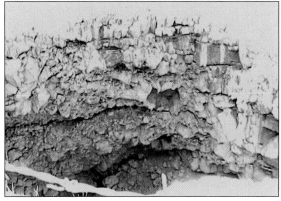

A few miles from the boat-shaped object, just before you cross the Turkish-Iranian border, there is a crater of a more recent date from the last century. It measures c. 80 ft. in diameter and on the inside you can see how the meteor has forced its way down through earth and stone. (Video clip from 2004.)

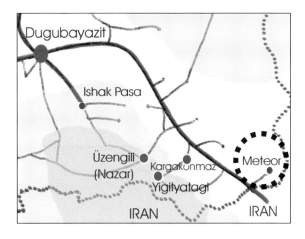

was the brother and husband of Isis (Jupiter). In India, Saturn was connected with Brahma and Siva with Jupiter. The same religious ideas ran throughout all of these early civilizations, and according to the Bible, the reason is that all people originally spread from Babel in Iraq to the various corners of the earth. Whether you believe in the Tower of Babel or not, the evidence points to a common start. The story of the Tower of Babel can also be found in the most unexpected places and cultures long before the influence of missionaries or other biblically knowledgeable people was possible. Just like Noah's Ark, this is apparently a common heritage from the beginning of mankind.

But let us conclude this chapter: we have both historical sources and modern observations suggesting that two "stars" (meteors) fell to the earth just 4-5,000 years ago bringing about a monstrous flood.

Is this what happened? One or several meteors hitting the Earth knocked a hole in the Earth's crust thus catalyzing the greatest catastrophe the Earth has ever seen?

Chapter 6

Velikovsky's Theories

Russian-American scientist Immanuel Velikovsky (b. 1895 in Vitebsk, Russia, d. 1979 in New York, New York) reported in his books[1] innumerable examples of archeological findings and geologically notable facts suggesting that the earth has experienced mighty catastrophes in our modern age.

Genius Albert Einstein found the manuscript of Velikovsky's book *Worlds in Collision* very interesting, but despite his interest, it was difficult for Velikovsky to find a publisher willing to print the book, because its contents posed serious questions to established science. MacMillan, the publishing house that accepted the book, was pressured by the scientific community to release it under a subsidiary publisher called Doubleday, which ended up causing the book to become the year's best seller.

Encouraged by the success, the publisher printed the first part of *Ages in Chaos*, which gave Velikovsky's reconstruction of the historical happenings from c. 1450-840 B.C., in 1952. The continuation, which was to cover successive years up to 33 B.C., grew into two large books: *Ramses II and His Time* and *Peoples of the Sea*.

After these books came *earth in Upheaval* in 1955, which is the most relevant for us in connection with the Flood due to page after page of geological and paleontological evidence suggesting the existence of the Flood. The book questioned the accepted theories of geology suggesting that everything we see has changed over millions of years of uniform evolution - with no dramatic disasters such as the Flood. Velikovsky was convinced that multiple cataclysms took place, also in our recent past.

After his book *Oedipus and Akhnathon* was released in 1960, Velikovsky started a manuscript that was never published. It was written about what he saw as the "common memory lapse" our culture suffers from due to our trying - seen from a Freudian point of view - to suppress the knowledge of the past.

An Exciting Heretic

An independent thinker is required to challenge established science on many levels, and Velikovsky was so independent he was unwanted at universities for a number of years. But after some of his theories seemed to be confirmed by the first vessels sent towards Venus, Mars, and Jupiter, he was asked to give visiting lectures for large groups at so many universities that he could not honor all of the invitations. In 1972 the Canadian Broadcasting Corporation, CBC, aired a one-hour special about Velikovsky and his research, and the BBC (British Broadcasting Corporation) followed their lead in 1973. Again, he found acceptance. He encouraged and mentored younger scientists following up on his theories until his death in 1979.

Who Was He?

Already as a child in Russia, **Immanuel Velikovsky** spoke multiple languages and was exceptionally gifted in Russian and mathematics as seen by his grades at Medvednikov College in Moscow where he was given a gold medal in 1913. He then traveled to Europe as well as the Middle East. For a period he studied medicine in Montpelier, France, and studied pre-med at the University of Edinburgh in Scotland. Just before World War I he made it back to Russia where he finished his medicinal studies in 1921 at the University of Moscow.

Thereafter he journeyed to Berlin where he edited the journal Scripta Universitatis, which employed Albert Einstein as the editor of the mathematics and physics section. He married violinist Elisheva Kramer and lived in what was then Palestine for 15 years where he practiced medicine and researched the newest findings of the time, Freud's psychoanalysis, and wrote articles for Freud's journal *Imago*. In 1930 he published a thesis that introduced pathological encephalograms (x-rays of the brain) to detect epilepsy, now routine practice in the diagnosis of this sickness.

In 1939, just a few weeks before the start of World War II, Velikovsky took his family and traveled to New York. While the world was at war he researched Freud's Oedipus theories and later published a book *Oedipus and Akhnathon*, in which he argues that Akhnathon was the legendary Oedipus.

It was here in April of 1940 that he worked with his first ingenious idea about disasters. He was first taken by the references in Jewish history. There was also an Egyptian story of the plagues in the almost unknown Ipuwer-papyrus housed in Leiden, The Netherlands. In this document an Egyptian wise man, Ipuwer, grouches about an event that caused the so-called Middle Kingdom to fall.

Velikovsky was convinced that Ipuwer was referring to the same situation as the Bible. Based on this, he synchronized Egyptian and Israeli history in his book, *Ages in Chaos*.

After ten years of research in the US, *Worlds in Collision* as well as the other books supporting the theories of catastrophes based on astronomical happenings was published.

Creationists - scientists that believe in some type of Creation - have proven a lack of logic in the ruling Theory of Evolution both before and after Velikovsky. One can easily wonder why their arguments have been ignored, but the explanation is simple; they were thought to be based on religious motives. What is refreshing about Velikovsky is that he cannot be suspected of being on a religious mission. He was an atheist, a Freudian, and believed in a form of evolution - not over millions of years, but an adaptation over a short period or time, which has partially been confirmed.[2]

But Velikovsky considered the ancient myths and stories - especially those from the Bible - as trustworthy and took them as a sign that some type of catastrophe really did happen even in our recent past. He claims that the last astronomic calamity took place c. 15-1700 B.C., and his theory was an attempt to give a non-religious explanation of phenomena such as the crossing of the Red Sea and Joshua's "long day" where "the sun stood still" and "waited almost an entire day"[3]. For example, he points out that before "the long day" there was a destructive rain, which Velikovsky understood to a meteor shower. "As they fled before Israel, while they were going down the slope of Beth-horon, the Lord threw down huge stones from heaven on them as far as Azekah, and they died; there were more who died because of the hailstones than the Israelites killed with the sword." (Joshua 10:11)

When God Is Not *Allowed* to Exist...

From the 50's to the 70's when Velikovsky's works were first released, there was little understanding within the scientific world of other dimensions of reality than the purely material. Therefore all things had to be explained based on the rules of positivistic science for time, space, and location - that is, things exist only if we can prove them with what we already know.

Today, when there is a better understanding of supernatural phenomena, it is almost funny to think that rather than accepting the existence of a supernatural power (God), people would rather accept Velikovsky's almost isolated astronomic explanations of Biblical happenings. For example, Velikovsky claims that the ten plagues in Egypt and the division of The Red Sea happened due to Jupiter releasing Venus as a massive supercomet that nicked earth about 1500 B.C. The 10 plagues spoken of in Exodus supposedly took place either directly or indirectly due to this encounter: dust from the comet that colored the water of the Nile blood red; the vermin that ravaged Egypt came from the comet; flies and possibly scarabs fell out of the comet, while the heat the comet brought caused the native frogs to develop with haste; and the earthquakes caused by the comet demolished the lodgings of the Egyptians, but not those of the Hebrews.

"The only thing that doesn't seem to fall from the comet is cholesterol levels to harden Pharaoh's heart," Dr. Carl Sagan sarcastically observes in a review.

"All of this apparently falls from the comet's coma, because at the exact moment Moses extends his staff over the Red Sea, it parts – either due to tidal changes caused by the gravitational force of the comet, or due to electrical or magnetic interplay between the comet and the Red Sea which is not discussed any closer. When the Hebrews reach safety on the other bank, the comet had obviously distanced itself so much that the parted Red Sea comes gushing back to drown Pharaoh's army," writes Sagan.[4]

What Sagan disregards is that in the same way what statistically is even more unlikely is arguable – a big bang leading to an immeasurably complex and magnificent swarm of species with complicated cell structures and DNA profiles that exist on our planet while all other planets seem to be lifeless. No explosion has ever caused life, but still it is considered excepted and correct to believe The Big Bang Theory.

When the supernatural and God are not *allowed* to exist and facts prove that something supernatural has occurred, the explanations brought forth with toil based on a limited understanding are quite unsatisfying.

But Still, He Was Right...

Even though Velikovsky's theories were at times speculative and doubtful, he did manage to have the focus set on two important areas:

1)   We can't just write off old "myths" based on our present, limited understanding, but we need to research these myths for their historical content with a greater respect for what they are claimed to be.

2)   He called attention to the mass of evidence suggesting that worldwide catastrophes have taken place throughout our history, as ancient myths agree with and tell us.

It would take too long to dive into all of these impressive facts suggesting disasters, but in the end of *earth in Upheaval*[5] he summarizes them. They give an impression of how extensive the evidence is: [6]

Evidence Everywhere

"Wherever we investigate the geological and paleontological records of this earth we find signs of catastrophes and upheavals, old and recent. Mountains sprang from plains, and other mountains were leveled; strata of the terrestrial crust were folded and pressed together and overturned and moved and put on top of other formations; igneous rock melted and flooded enormous areas of land with miles-thick sheets; the ocean bed flowed with molten rock; ashes showered down and built layers many yards thick on the ground and on the bottom of the oceans in their vast expanse; shores of ancient lakes were tilted and are no longer horizontal; seacoasts show subsidence or emergence, in some places over one thousand feet," writes Velikovsky.

Remains From the Flood?

Velikovsky continues and describes the "graveyard" of geological layers after a mighty disaster. It is difficult not to think of the Flood and it's major consequences/changes:

Footnotes

[1] Dr. **Immanuel Velikovsky** wrote *Worlds in Collision*, *Earth in Upheaval*, *Ages in Chaos*, *Peoples of the Sea*, *Ramses II and His Times*, *Mankind in Amnesia*, *Stargazers*, and *Gravediggers*. He wrote other works as well, and many of his books can be found on the Internet. Specifically note www.varchive.org/itb/index.htm

[2] For example, certain birds have been known to change feather color under varying environmental circumstances. And this is not over a period of millions of years, but rather only a few hundred.

[3] Joshua 10:13-14: "And the sun stood still, and the moon stopped, until the nation took vengeance on their enemies. Is this not written in the Book of Jashar? The sun stopped in midheaven, and did not hurry to set for about a whole day. There has been no day like it before or since, when the Lord heeded a human voice; for the Lord fought for Israel."

[4] An analysis of *Cosmic Collisions* by Dr. Carl Sagan, Cornell University. Translated from a quote in Danish on www.skeptica.dk

[5] *Earth in Upheaval* copyright 1955 Doubleday and Company, Inc. and Immanuel Velikovsky.

[6] Velikovsky's work is written in a stream-of-consciousness style. He uses almost nothing but commas to give the reader a chance to breathe. Therefore, some of the sentences have been changed so they are more readable.

"Rocks of the earth are filled with remains of life ex-tinguished in a state of agony; sedimentary rocks are one vast graveyard, and the granite and basalt, too, have embedded in them numberless living organisms; and shells have closed valves as they do in a living state, so unexpectedly came the entombment; and vast forests were burned and washed away and covered with the waters of the seas and with sand and turned to coal; and animals were swept to the far north and thrown into heaps and were soaked by bituminous outpourings; and broken bones and torn ligaments and the skins of animals of living species and extinct were smashed together with splintered forests into huge piles; and whales were cast out of the oceans onto mountains.

"Rocks from dis-integrating mountain ridges were carried over vast stretches of land, from Norway to the Carpathians, and into the Harz Mountains, and into Scotland, and from Mount Blanc to the Juras, and from Labrador to the Poconos; and the Rocky Mountains moved many leagues from their place, and the Alps traveled a hundred miles northward, and the Himalayas and the Andes climbed ever higher; and the mountain lakes emptied themselves over barriers, and continents were torn by rifts, and the sea bottom by canyons; and land disappeared under the sea, and the sea pushed new islands from its bottom, and sea beds were turned into high mountains bearing sea shells, and shoals of fish were poisoned and boiled in the seas, and numberless rivers lost their channels, were dammed by lava and turned upstream, and the climate suddenly changed; tillable land and meadows turned into vast deserts.

"Reindeer from Lapland and polar fox and arctic bears from the snowy tundras and rhinoceroses and hippopotami from the African jungles, and lions from the desert and ostriches, and seals, were thrown into piles and covered with gravel, clay, and tuff, and the fissures of multitudes of rocks are filled with broken bones; regions where the palm grew were moved into the Arctic, and oceans steamed, and the evaporated seas condensed under clouds of dust and built mountainous covers of ice over great stretches of continents, and the ice melted on heated ground and cast icebergs into the oceans in enormous fleets; and all volcanoes erupted.

"All human dwellings were shattered and burned, and animals tame and fierce and human beings with them ran for refuge to mountain caves, and mountains swallowed and entombed those that reached the refuge, and many species and genera and families of the animal kingdom were annihilated down to the very last one; and the earth and the sea and the sky again united their elements in one great work of destruction."

It Happened in the Recent Past

"Following the trail of geology, we were led by the merciless logic of facts and figures to the conclusion that the earth was more than once a stage on which acts of a great drama took place, and no place on earth was free of its effects," Velikovsky concludes.

"In the face of the evidence we were also compelled to concede that the most recent paroxysms of nature happened in historical times, only a few thousand years ago, when in some parts of the world civilization was already entering the Iron Age, but in other parts still lingering in the Neolithic or even, in the Paleolithic, or rude Stone Age.

"The laminations of lakes, the salt content of those without outflow, the retreat of waterfalls, the elevation of mountains, pollen analysis, and archaeological finds, as well as the recent drop of the ocean level, all show how close to our time the more recent paroxysms of nature must have occurred."

Changes in the Earth's Axis

"The evidence is also overwhelming that the great global catastrophes were either accompanied or caused by shifting of the terrestrial axis or by a disturbance in the diurnal and annual motions of the earth. The shifting of the axis could not have been brought about by internal causes, as the proponents of the Ice Age theory in the nineteenth century assumed it was; it must have occurred, and repeatedly, under the impact of external forces. The state of lavas with reversed magnetization, hundreds of times more intensive than the inverted terrestrial magnetic field could impart, reveals the nature of the forces that were in action.

"Thus from the geological evidence we came to the con-clusion to which we had also arrived traveling the road of the historical and literary traditions of the peoples of the world – that the earth repeatedly went through cataclysmic events on a global scale, that the cause of these events was an extraterrestrial agent, and that some of these cosmic catastrophes took place only a few thousand years ago, in historical times.

"Many world-wide phenomena, for each of which the cause is vainly sought, are explained by a single cause: The sudden changes of climate, transgression of the sea, vast volcanic and seismic activities, formation of ice cover, pluvial crises, emergence of mountains and their dislocation, rising and subsidence of coasts, tilting of lakes, sedimentation, fossilization, the provenience of tropical animals and plants in polar regions, conglomerates of fossils of animals of various latitudes and habitats, the extinction of species and genera, the appearance of new species, the reversal of the earth's magnetic field, and a score of other world-wide phenomena."

Velikovsky sees all of these signs as the result of astronomic phenomena which have effected the earth. That is arguable. Those that believe in God would say it was God that did it. Besides that, the two explanations don't rule each other out. If it was God that stood behind things, He could have used astronomical mechanisms.

All of the evidence Velikovsky mentions should speak clearly to anyone and everyone that a Flood really existed.

The Spanish artist José Pérez Montero has like many others tried to visualize the scene when the animals and the birds gathered around the Ark. Did they have an intuitive feeling that a great catastrophe was approaching like when animals flee from a forest fire long before people discover it? Or had Noah's family captured the many different species over the years?

Chapter 7

What Does the Bible Say About Noah?

After we had visited Mt. Ararat, stood on "the Ark", and walked through the Valley of the Eight, it was a completely new experience to read the story of Noah and his family from the book of Genesis. It wasn't difficult to imagine old Noah and Naamah (as she is called in some sources) taking evening walks in their vineyard or sitting on a boulder looking out over the lush valley where the animals were grazing and the grandchildren ran around playing.

I have gone back to the *Bible's* account of Noah innumerable times in many different languages in many translations, studying the original Hebrew text word by word in order to uncover any new information.

We shall now look at the text that Moses wrote around 3,650-3,550 years ago. He might have had a source from which he took the information. He refers to The Book of Jasher two times in the Old Testament as *Sephir Ha Yasher,* or The Book of the Upright. *(See note[1])* In some translations of the Bible there is a reference to The Book of Jasher and in others "The Book of the Upright". This book obviously disappeared later, but it has possibly been found again - more on this later. One could imagine that this book was an even older source from which Moses took some of his information.

Moses may also have had a great knowledge from the Egyptian libraries which he had access to as an Egyptian prince. Whether this is the case or not, the Jews passed down their stories through oral and written tradition.

C. 1800 B.C. Moses wrote down or collected material about creation which can be found in the book of Genesis. (See the chronology chapter.) Ill. José Pérez Montero.

Semitic Storytelling

The Semitic storytelling style found in Genesis actually resembles the journalistic method where the story is often told in two or three circles. The first circle (the title, sub-title, and captions if there are any pictures) is a short summary. The second circle (the introduction) goes back to the beginning and gives a little more information. The third circle (the article itself) goes deeper into detail. If the reader doesn't take this writing style into account, he or she will misunderstand the text so that he or she believes the same thing happened 2 or 3 times. There are 3 circles in the story of Creation. The first circle is in Genesis chapter 1, verse 1. The second circle is from chapter 1, verse 2 until chapter 2, verse 3. The final circle is found in chapter 2, verses 4-25.

Footnotes

[1] Found in the Book of Joshua chapters 10 and 13 and in 2nd Samuel chapter 1, verse 17.

[2] The text is from the New American Standard Version. The notes though are made by Bible translator Iver Larsen, who has worked for Wycliffe and others on different Bible translations for more than 25 years. The notes of the author are marked with the letters HN: in front of them.

Footnotes:

[3] **6:2** It is unclear what this text means. "The sons of God" can mean angels, rulers, or men descended from Seth – those that worshipped god according to 4:26. "The daughters of God" could then be everyday women or the women that were descendents of Cain living apart from God. The chosen translation builds on the fact that the word "gods" (*elohim*) can refer to judges or societal leaders other places in the OT. Lamech from Cain's line was the first to marry multiple wives cf. 4:23.

HN: The **"sons and daughters"** of God are later spoken of in Isaiah 43:6-7, " *Bring my sons from afar and my daughters from the ends of the earth. Everyone who is called by My name, and whom I have created for My glory, whom I have formed, even whom I have made.*" This is clearly a reference to humans. Though some believe this to be a confirmation of supernatural beings, like fallen angels, many Bible translators agree that "the sons and daughters of God" is just a phrase for the first generations of mankind.

[4] **6:3** or possibly "spirits", or "the breath of life".

[5] **6:3** or "continue in". What this word and verse mean is unsure. The 120 years can either be the normal lifespan of humans from then onwards or the period of time they were given to repent of their evil lifestyles.

HN: In the Book of Jashar it is clear that 120 years to repent is meant. Jashar 5:11 says, "And the Lord granted them a period of one hundred and twenty years, saying, If they will return, then will God repent of the evil, so as not to destroy the earth."

When Did They Go Into the Ark?

This recurring story telling style can also be found when Noah was told to go into the Ark. If one does not understand this, it seems as if Noah goes in and out of the Ark.

"And God said to Noah, "…Make yourself an ark… and you shall come into the ark, you, your sons, your wife, and your sons' wives with you. And of every living thing, of all flesh, you shall bring two of every kind into the ark… also take with you every kind of food that is eaten…" (6:13-21).

"Noah did this; he did all that God commanded him." (6:22).

At this point, from a chronological point of view, one would expect that Noah had already built the Ark and was already inside of it with all of the animals. But this is actually only a description of Noah's personal character, which is repeated a few times to make the point.

But then in chapter 7, verses 1-4 we find the following, "Then the Lord said to Noah, "Go into the ark, you and all your household… take with you seven pairs of all clean animals… for in seven days I will send rain…"

7:5 "And Noah did all that the Lord had commanded him."

Again, thinking chronologically, Noah had obviously gone out with his family again since he is told to go back and get more animals. There are still 7 days until the rain comes.

7:7-10 "And Noah with his sons and his wife and his sons' wives went into the ark… (and animals) went into the ark with Noah, as God had commanded Noah. And after seven days [*from when?*] the waters of the flood come on the earth." Did they sit in the Ark and wait for 7 days? But now the flow of water is really coming (7:11-12).

7:13-14 "On the very same day Noah with his sons, Shem and Ham and Japheth, and Noah's wife and the three wives of his sons entered the ark, the and every… creature." So they had obviously gone out again, because now it is the actual day where the water comes, and they go into the Ark one more time.

All joking aside, Noah only went into the Ark *one* time. But this is how the recurring story telling style works.

Here is what Moses tells about Noah and the Flood in Genesis chapters 6-9 with a translator's notes and my comments marked with **HN:** (note [2])

Chapter 6
The Wickedness Spreads

[1] When people began to multiply on the face of the ground, and daughters were born to them, [2] the sons of God *(See note[3])* saw that they were fair; and they took wives for themselves of all that they chose.

[3] Then the Lord said, "My spirit *(See note [4])* shall not abide *(See note [5])* in mortals forever, for they are flesh; their days shall be one hundred twenty years."

[4] The Nephilim *(See note[6])* were on the earth in those days - and also afterward - when the sons of God went in to the daughters of humans, who bore children to them. These were the heroes that were of old, warriors of renown. [5]The Lord saw that the wickedness of humankind was great in the earth, and that every incli-

nation of the thoughts of their hearts was only evil continually.

⁶ And the Lord was sorry that he had made humankind on the earth, and it grieved him to his heart. ⁷ So the Lord said, "I will blot out from the earth the human beings I have created - people together with animals and creeping things and birds of the air, for I am sorry that I have made them."

⁸ But Noah found favor in the sight of the Lord. ⁹ These are the descendants of Noah. Noah was a righteous man, blameless in his generation; Noah walked with God. ¹⁰ And Noah had three sons, Shem, Ham, and Japheth.

¹¹ Now the earth was corrupt in God's sight, and the earth was filled with violence. ¹² And God saw that the earth was corrupt; for all flesh had corrupted its ways upon the earth.

¹³ And God said to Noah *(See note ⁷)*, "I have determined to make an end of all flesh, for the earth is filled with violence because of them; now I am going to destroy them along with the earth. ¹⁴ Make yourself an ark of cypress wood; make rooms in the ark, and cover it inside and out with pitch. ¹⁵ This is how you are to make it: the length of the ark three hundred cubits *(See note ⁸ and ⁹)*, its width fifty cubits, and its height thirty cubits. ¹⁶ Make a roof for the ark, and finish it to a cubit above; *(See note ¹⁰)* and put the door of the ark in its side; make it with lower, second, and third decks. ¹⁷ For my part, I am going to bring a flood of waters on the earth, to destroy from under heaven all flesh in which is the breath of life; everything that is on the earth shall die. ¹⁸ But I will establish my covenant with you; and you shall come into the ark, you, your sons, your wife, and your sons' wives with you. ¹⁹ And of every living thing, of all flesh, you shall bring two of every kind into the ark, to keep them alive with you; they shall be male and female. ²⁰ Of the birds according to their kinds, and of the animals according to their kinds, of every creeping thing of the ground according to its kind, two of every kind shall come in to you, to keep them alive. ²¹ Also take with you every kind of food that is eaten, and store it up; and it shall serve as food for you and for them."

²² Noah did this; he did all that God commanded him.

Chapter 7
The Consequence of the Wickedness

¹ Then the Lord said to Noah, "Go into the ark, you and all your household, for I have seen that you alone are righteous before me in this generation. ² Take with you seven pairs of all clean animals, the male and its mate; and a pair of the animals that are not clean, the male and its mate; ³ and seven pairs of the birds of the air also, male and female, to keep their kind alive on the face of all the earth. ⁴ For in seven days I will send rain on the earth for forty days and forty nights; and every living thing that I have made I will blot out from the face of the ground."

⁵ And Noah did all that the Lord had commanded him *(See note ¹¹)*. ⁶ Noah was six hundred years old when the flood of waters came on the earth. ⁷ And Noah with his sons and his wife and his sons' wives went into the ark to escape the waters of the flood. ⁸ Of clean animals, and of animals that are not clean, and of birds, and of everything that creeps on the ground, ⁹ two and two, male and female, went into the ark with Noah, as God had commanded Noah. ¹⁰ And after seven days the waters of the flood came on the earth.

⁶ **HN**: **What type of giants are these?** Some believe this to be a specific race, possibly from Cain. Others suggest something above man or half gods. But this is all speculation that doesn't fit with the rest of the Bible. But what we do see here is very important: Moses tells us that at that time before the Flood and also afterwards in some instances, people were larger! We can also see over-sized men later in the Bible, like Goliath. In the area we think to have found the Ark, oversized human bones have been found. They can be found at Wyatt's Museum in the States, among other places.

⁷ **HN**: **When was it?** People are first given 120 years to repent, and many years may possibly have passed afterwards. But the evil and violence got worse. Afterwards Noah is told to build the Ark. Another possibility is that the text is based on the circular principle spoken of in the introduction. If this is the case, Noah may have gotten the whole message (via a voice, a dream, a vision, or an angel?) at the beginning of these 120 years. He is told to build the big Ark and has plenty of time in which to do it. The building of the Ark throughout these years is a warning to the people to turn from their evil ways.

⁸ **6:15** The cubit used here is either the Babylonian, 50.3 cm or 19,6", the Egyptian, 52.5 cm or 20,5" or the ancient "royal" Hebrew cubit, the breadth of seven hands, or 51.8 cm or 20,2". Later a shorter Hebrew cubit became the norm. It is 6 handbreadths or 44.5 cm or 17,36".

⁹ **6:16** Unclear meaning. Most likely it is a cubit's length between the highest side of the Ark and the roof so that light and air could come

through a row of windows or openings, cf. 8:6.)

HN: Why is the cubit that is used in later years shorter? The answer could be that a cubit is an elbow – the length from one's armpit to fingertip. Naturally, Noah used his own or the (then) contemporary cubit. If today's cubit gives an average height of 6 ft., then Noah was around 7'3".

HN: A window or an elevated roof? The extra cubit could also be an elevation in the roof in the middle. That is how it is translated is some languages. And as we will later see, it would be ideal if the ship's roof were raised 1/50 in the middle so that water could run off. This is the solution our ship experts expect. Later in the text (8:6) Noah opens a hatch. This could be one of the necessary "windows" for ventilation.

[11] **HN: How did the animals get into the Ark?** If Noah had as much as 120 years from the first warning to the entry into the Ark, then there was enough time to capture some of the various animal pairs. In the Book of Jashar a 5-year building period is mentioned. There is a supernatural influence and the animals come by themselves, gathering around the Ark. Those that bow before him, Noah takes into the Ark.

HN: How could all of the animals be in the Ark? Logisticians have worked with this question and have considered how much room they would take, food they would eat, etc. John Woodmorappe's book *Noah's Ark: A Feasibility Study* is the most thorough of these studies. In his book he looks consequently at all the problems there could be. On top of this, he used the small Ark

[11] In the six hundredth year *(See note [12])* of Noah's life, in the second month, on the seventeenth day of the month, on that day all the fountains of the great deep burst forth, and the windows of the heavens were opened. [12] The rain fell on the earth forty days and forty nights.

[13] On the very same day Noah with his sons, Shem and Ham and Japheth, and Noah's wife and the three wives of his sons entered the ark, [14] they and every wild animal of every kind, and all domestic animals of every kind, and every creeping thing that creeps on the earth, and every bird of every kind - every bird, every winged creature. [15] They went into the ark with Noah, two and two of all flesh in which there was the breath of life. [16] And those that entered, male and female of all flesh, went in as God had commanded him; and the Lord shut him in.

[17] The flood continued forty days on the earth; and the waters increased, and bore up the ark, and it rose high above the earth. [18] The waters swelled and increased greatly on the earth; and the ark floated on the face of the waters. [19] The waters swelled so mightily on the earth that all the high mountains under the whole heaven were covered; [20] the waters swelled above the mountains, covering them fifteen cubits deep.

[21] And all flesh died that moved on the earth, birds, domestic animals, wild animals, all swarming creatures that swarm on the earth, and all human beings; [22] everything on dry land in whose nostrils was the breath of life died. [23] He blotted out every living thing that was on the face of the ground, human beings and animals and creeping things and birds of the air; they were blotted out from the earth. Only Noah was left, and those that were with him in the ark. [24] And the waters swelled on the earth for one hundred fifty days.

Chapter 8
A New Beginning

[1] But God remembered Noah and all the wild animals and all the domestic animals that were with him in the ark. And God made a wind blow over the earth, and the waters subsided; [2] the fountains of the deep and the windows of the heavens were closed, the rain from the heavens was restrained, [3] and the waters gradually receded from the earth. At the end of one hundred fifty days the waters had abated; [4] and in the seventh month, on the seventeenth day of the month, the ark came to rest on the mountains of Ararat *(See note [13])*. [5] The waters continued to abate until the tenth month; in the tenth month, on the first day of the month, the tops of the mountains appeared.

[6] At the end of forty days Noah opened the window of the ark that he had made [7] and sent out the raven; and it went to and fro until the waters were dried up from the earth. [8] Then he sent out the dove from him, to see if the waters had subsided from the face of the ground; [9] but the dove found no place to set its foot, and it returned to him to the ark, for the waters were still on the face of the whole earth. So he put out his hand and took it and brought it into the ark with him. [10] He waited another seven days, and again he sent out the dove from the ark; [11] and the dove came back to him in the evening, and there in its beak was a freshly plucked olive leaf; so Noah knew that the waters had subsided from the earth.

[12] Then he waited another seven days, and sent out the dove; and it did not

NOAH

JAPHETH
Indo-Europeans
Gen. 10:6-20
Europe - Western Asia

- **Gomer**
  Northern tribes
  Cimmerians
  - **Ashkenaz**
    Allemani tribe
    Germany
  - **Togarmah**
    Harran - Carchemish
    Armenia (Turkey)
  - **Riphath**
    Northern Europe
- **Tubal**
  Tbilisi
  Georgia
- **Javan**
  Costland tribes
  Ionian
  Greeks
  - **Elishah**
    Hellenic
  - **Tarshish**
    Spain
  - **Rodanim**
    Rhodos
  - **Kittim**
    Cyprus
- **Tiras**
  Thracians
  Thor-people
- **Magog**
  Scythians
  Tartars
- **Madai**
  Medes
  Caspian Sea
  Iran
- **Meschek**
  Cappadocians
  Muscovites
  Russia

HAM
Egyptians - Africans
Gen. 10:6-20
Lybia - Canaan - Ethiopia

- **Cush**
  Cushites
  - **Seba**
    Ethiopians
  - **Sabteca**
    Ethiopians
  - **Havilah**
    Gold Country
    Armenia?
  - **Sabtah**
    Ethiopians
  - **Raamah**
    Ethiopians
  - **Nimrod**
    Mesopotamia
- **Mizhraim**
  Egypt
  - **Ludim**
    Egyptians
  - **Naphluhim**
    Egyptians
  - **Anamim**
    Egyptians
  - **Pathrusim**
    Patrusians
    Philistines
  - **Lehabim**
    Egyptians
  - **Casluhim**
    Lower Egypt
    Philistines
- **Put**
  Africans
  Lybia
- **Canaan**
  Jebushites
  Amorites
  Canaanites
- **Sidon**
  Phoenician

SHEM
Shemites
Gen. 10:21-32
Middle East - Southern Asia

- **Elam**
  Elamites
  Persians
- **Aram**
  Assyrians
  Syrians
- **Asshur**
  Assyrians
  Iraqians
- **Arpachshad**
  - **Shelah**
    - **Eber**
      Hebrews
      - **Peleg**
      - **Joktan**
- **Lud**
  Lydians
  Asia Minor

Many peoples can be traced directly back to Noah's descendants by means of sources like Josephus and Homer.
This is an attempt to trace some of the nations from the first generations. There are, of course, several theories since most of the original ethnic groups have since then split up or mixed with others.
Ill. HN

measurements of 450 x 75 x 75 feet (the equivalent of 569 railroad cars), and still there was enough room for 2,000-16,000 animals, he constitutes. His calculations are based on genus (a tact higher than species) and not species. Besides that, he includes dinosaurs and mammoths in that he assumes they still lived in Noah's day.

[12] **HN: Long life**: Everyone apparently lived for hundreds of years before the Flood. The Sumerian tablets also tell of long life for the kings before the Flood. In an ancient Chinese narrative, one of the characters wonders about and regrets that people don't live as long as they did in the past. One explanation for their longevity could be that they didn't age so quickly because the Earth may have been protected from cosmic radiation, which causes people to age. One theory suggests that a layer of ice or steam covered the globe like a bubble and that the bubble burst or the ice melted and rain came falling down creating the Flood. Afterwards the rainbow was seen for the first time, and light from cosmic radiation cut through sharply. We will look at this theory later.

[13] **HN: Which Ararat?** Due to non-meticulous translations, Europeans and later the USA, have translated "the Ararat Mountains" as Mt. Ararat. As previously mentioned, this was a calamitous misunderstanding. The Hebrew text is clear: „in the Mountains of Ararat": הָרֵי אֲרָרָ֑ט - in the plural.

[14] **7:20** Ritually clean for offerings and food.

[15] **HN: The first rainbow**: This suggests that there was a major change in the Earth's climate and supports theories that Earth was in

return to him any more.

[13] In the six hundred first year, in the first month, on the first day of the month, the waters were dried up from the earth; and Noah removed the covering of the ark, and looked, and saw that the face of the ground was drying. [14] In the second month, on the twenty-seventh day of the month, the earth was dry.

[15] Then God said to Noah, [16] "Go out of the ark, you and your wife, and your sons and your sons' wives with you. [17] Bring out with you every living thing that is with you of all flesh - birds and animals and every creeping thing that creeps on the earth - so that they may abound on the earth, and be fruitful and multiply on the earth." [18] So Noah went out with his sons and his wife and his sons' wives. [19] And every animal, every creeping thing, and every bird, everything that moves on the earth, went out of the ark by families.

[20] Then Noah built an altar to the Lord, and took of every clean *(See note [14])* animal and of every clean bird, and offered burnt offerings on the altar. [21] And when the Lord smelled the pleasing odor, the Lord said in his heart, "I will never again curse the ground because of humankind, for the inclination of the human heart is evil from youth; nor will I ever again destroy every living creature as I have done. [22] As long as the earth endures, seedtime and harvest, cold and heat, summer and winter, day and night, shall not cease."

Chapter 9
God's Covenant with Noah

[1] God blessed Noah and his sons, and said to them, "Be fruitful and multiply, and fill the earth. [2] The fear and dread of you shall rest on every animal of the earth, and on every bird of the air, on everything that creeps on the ground, and on all the fish of the sea; into your hand they are delivered. [3] Every moving thing that lives shall be food for you; and just as I gave you the green plants, I give you everything. [4] Only, you shall not eat flesh with its life, that is, its blood. [5] For your own lifeblood I will surely require a reckoning: from every animal I will require it and from human beings, each one for the blood of another, I will require a reckoning for human life. [6] Whoever sheds the blood of a human, by a human shall that person's blood be shed; for in his own image God made humankind. [7] And you, be fruitful and multiply, abound on the earth and multiply in it."

[8] Then God said to Noah and to his sons with him, [9] "As for me, I am establishing my covenant with you and your descendants after you, [10] and with every living creature that is with you, the birds, the domestic animals, and every animal of the earth with you, as many as came out of the ark. [11] I establish my covenant with you, that never again shall all flesh be cut off by the waters of a flood, and never again shall there be a flood to destroy the earth."

[12] God said, "This is the sign of the covenant that I make between me and you and every living creature that is with you, for all future generations: [13] I have set my bow *(See note [15])* in the clouds, and it shall be a sign of the covenant between me and the earth. [14] When I bring clouds over the earth and the bow is seen in the clouds, [15] I will remember my covenant that is between me and you and every living creature of all flesh; and the waters shall never again become a flood to destroy all flesh. [16] When the bow is in the clouds, I will see it and remember the

everlasting covenant between God and every living creature of all flesh that is on the earth." ¹⁷ God said to Noah, "This is the sign of the covenant that I have established between me and all flesh that is on the earth."

Noah's Three Sons

¹⁸ The sons of Noah who went out of the ark were Shem, Ham, and Japheth. Ham was the father of Canaan. ¹⁹ These three were the sons of Noah; and from these the whole earth was peopled. ²⁰ Noah, a man of the soil, was the first to plant a vineyard. ²¹ He drank some of the wine and became drunk, and he lay uncovered in his tent. ²² And Ham, the father of Canaan, saw the nakedness of his father, and told his two brothers outside. ²³ Then Shem and Japheth took a garment, laid it on both their shoulders, and walked backward and covered the nakedness of their father; their faces were turned away, and they did not see their father's nakedness.

²⁴ When Noah awoke from his wine and knew what his youngest son had done to him, ²⁵ he said, "Cursed be Canaan; *(See note ¹⁶)* lowest of slaves shall he be to his brothers." ²⁶ He also said, "Blessed by the Lord my God be Shem; and let Canaan be his slave. ²⁷ May God make space for Japheth, and let him live in the tents of Shem; and let Canaan be his slave." *(See note ¹⁷)* ²⁸ After the flood Noah lived three hundred fifty years. ²⁹ All the days of Noah were nine hundred fifty years; and he died.

Why This Intense Reaction?

Noah's reaction towards Ham is so intense that there *must* be more to it than what is mentioned here. A Jewish legend tells that Ham castrated his father while drunk so that his inherirance, one third of the world, would not be split up into smaller bits.

But who says that Noah's reaction was fair? It was, after all, not God who spoke and Noah was an ordinary human being who could get angry like the rest of us. He had made a fool of himself and maybe only in anger and in an attempt to pass on his guilt he hurled his curses of the impudent son ... Like angry fathers have done at all times. And regretted.

Whether the curse was fair or not, it looks as if it has turned out to be true as for the Africans who have been victims to slavery more than anyone else - slaves first to the Arabs (Shem) and later to the white people (Japheth).

But Ham's descendants are not *only* Africans, but many more peoples - e.g. the original Egyptians before the country was arabized. Maybe Dravidians and Aboriginals are also of Ham's stock. One of the sons, Cana'an, lent his name to the land of Cana'an - present day Israel and other countries where Abraham went. After the division it lawfully belonged to Shem and the Semites who according to the Ethiopian *Book of Jubilees*¹⁷, chapt. 8, were given most of Asia while Ham had all Africa and Japheth the North, i.e. Europe.

a „bubble" or ring of mist that protected it from cosmic radiation.

¹⁶ **9:25** Another name for Ham. After that follows a detailed description of the territories as to rivers, oceans, mountains etc. But as mentioned, *The Book of Jubilees* is not necessarily authentic or as old as what it purports to be. Like other commentaries it may be from the period after the return of the Jews from Babylon, written a few centuries BC.

¹ **HN: The Book of Jubilees** - one of the earliest Jewish so-called Midrashim, i.e. a free rabbi commentary to the Pentateuch, adding extra details of maybe doubtful character. This commentary is claimed to have been written at the time of Moses. It seeks to draw up a chronological table starting with the creation of Adam in year 1. About the division of the Earth in the days of Peleg (approx. 100 years after the Flood) it says in chapt. 8: „And it came to pass in the beginning of the thirty-third jubilee (1569 a.m.) that they divided the Earth into three parts, for Shem and Ham and Japheth, according to the inheritance of each..."

After that follows a detailed description of the territories as to rivers, oceans, mountains etc. But as mentioned, *The Book of Jubilees* is not necessarily authentic or as old as what it purports to be. Like other commentaries it may be from the period after the return of the Jews from Babylon, written a few centuries BC.

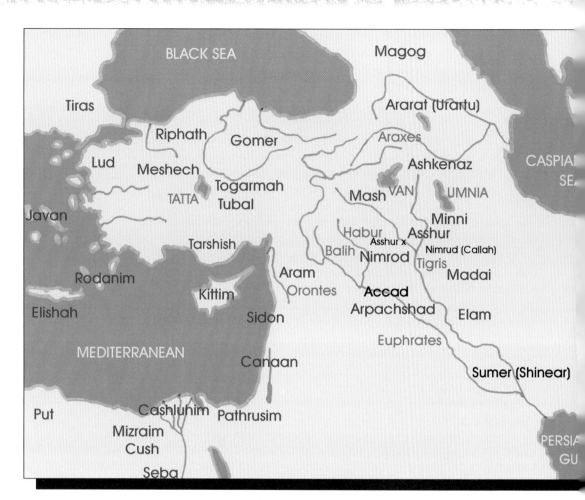

Noah's grandchildren. *On this map of the Middle East you can see where the people named after Noah's grandchildren and great-grandchildren supposedly settled (marked in reddish brown).*

Migration, war, and conquest scattered most tribes all over the world where they split into even more tribes and in some cases united again. In some cases historical sources and archaeological finds confirm where they originally lived while there is a bit more uncertainty in others. For example, we know with certainty that Javan are the Greeks whereas it is unclear whether Tarshish is the present Tarsus in Turkey or whether it was Spain. On the Internet you can find many new theories about the history of the various tribes.

Whether you recognize that the peoples in the world descend from Noah or not, it gives food for thought to see how many connections there are between the names of the people groups and Noah's descendants.

Chapter 8

The Ship Expert:
A Sensible Construction

What did Noah's Ark look like? How good was it at sailing?

An expert on ships will tell us some surprising things about this in the following chapter. The dimensions of the Ark are not only well-proportioned, but in certain areas it actually fulfills and surpasses the standards established by the international Load Lines Convention drawn up by the United Nations' International Maritime Organization (IMO), which is also used today for ship building internationally. The 4,500-year-old proportions of height and width are equivalent to what will most likely become the European Union's newest rules for the transportation of animals…

What Did the Ark Look Like?

From the Middle Ages to the present day, many have believed that the Ark was a quadrangular box. Maybe this is because it has for the most part been theologians that have devoted themselves to the study of the Ark. Maybe the artists that painted the Ark in the Middle Ages didn't know much about sailing… Whatever the case, some very baroque pictures of the Ark exist, pictures that one can almost only be amused by – a bit like the very locally-inspired northern European paintings of Maria and Joseph and a camel out in a cabin in a snow-covered forest of pine trees!

But there are also serious Ark-enthusiasts that argue that the Ark was a quadrangular box based on studies of the Hebrew word for ark (תֵבַת). This is not the same word that is normally used for a boat in Hebrew. This view is especially found among the group of Ark-enthusiast that believe the Ark is located on Mt. Ararat. This is natural enough because the so-called eye-witnesses play a great role here and they have described what they saw to artist Elfred Lee as a rectangular Ark, which looks like a great big box in Lee's beautiful paintings.

Oppositely, Ark-hunters that believe the imprint of the Ark is found in the boat-shaped object are by default forced to believe that it was, of course, shaped like a boat. The discovery of the boat-shaped object was what seriously questioned the earlier belief of the Ark being shaped like a box.

Let's Ask an Expert

But what does a ship expert say about the shape and dimensions of the Ark? With many years of consulting experience for a number of Danish ferry companies, Hans Otto Kristensen has taken part in constructing a great deal of the ferries that are sailing in Danish waters.

Simply put – he is an expert.

Graduate Engineer **Hans Otto Holmgaard Kristensen** has worked in almost every area of maritime construction. He started at the Danish Maritime Institute and Dwinger Marine Consultants before working for the shipping company Scandlines. He presently works for the Union of Danish Shipping Companies (Danmarks Rederi-forening) where he works with safety and the environment among other things. Part of this includes his position in the United Nations' International Maritime Organization (IMO).

Through his active participation in international rule setting, Hans Otto Kristensen has been a major factor in Denmark's marked influence on the development of rules and regulations, especially among fast ferries and leakage control.

In the area of environment, Hans Otto Kristensen has within the last year developed a comprehensive computer generated model whose purpose is to regulate the energy consumption and emissions of ships. This model is in use by the Union of Danish Shipping Companies and is also a part of the Danish Ministry of Transportaion's so-called TEMA 2000 model which can calculate energy consumption and emissions on all types of transportation vehicles.

Could a Box Actually Sail?

"A square box wouldn't manage as well in waves as a sailing apparatus with pointed or rounded ends, because these would break the waves, thus failing to lift the ship as much out of the water. If a ship were lifted out of the water, it would not splash down into the water quite as hard as a box would. In technical language, it would be said that the slamming (splash) would be larger for the box. The rounded ends would give calmer movements and create a more secure ship because capsizing caused by the waves would be reduced, explains Hans Otto Kristensen.

Are the Proportions Reasonable?

In Genesis chapter 6, verses 14-17, there aren't a lot of building instructions given:

Make for yourself an ark of gopher wood; you shall make the ark with rooms, and shall cover it inside and out with pitch. This is how you shall make it: the length of the ark three hundred cubits, its breadth fifty cubits, and its height thirty cubits. You shall make a window for the ark, and finish it to a cubit from the top; and set the door of the ark in the side of it; you shall make it with lower, second, and third decks.

"What does this information tell us?"

"Compared to the often very thick documents from which ships are constructed today, the description of Noah's Ark can be called an extremely short outline specification, in technical language," says Hans Otto Kristensen. "Its brevity doesn't make it of any less value in that the description withholds some facts that from a historical perspective are very exciting. Noah's Ark was most likely the first large ship built in the history of the world."

Divided Into Rooms

"The first thing we shall call attention to is that the Ark was to be furnished with rooms. What's interesting with this is that by far the majority of ships that have been built *afterwards* have been built without rooms."

One only has to think of the Nordic Viking ships where the hull of the ship constitutes a long open room where the crew's quarters and the cargo room were one and the same. Of course, one could rightly say that Noah's Ark was to be built with rooms so that there was enough room for the many animals onboard. This is obvious, and because this account is more like supervisory blueprints, I will allow myself to interpret the description of dividing the boat into rooms as a preparation or pre-cursory measure for the entire ship being filled with water, if water were to seep through a single hole. Such an anti-leakage provision is called securing the ship's aptitude to float. Until modern times, that is the 17th century, such division into rooms has only been seen in Chinese ships known as "junks". It wasn't until the 1800s that others started to subdivide the hull for practical reasons such as separating the engine room from the crew's quarters and the cargo. Another reason that room divisions became more popular was, as mentioned above, so that the entire hull was not filled with water if there was a leak due to a collision or grounding, says the ship expert. Mapping out the ship into watertight zones has today become a very mathematical science which Hans Otto Kristensen has devoted himself to for many years.

The Dimensions

"The most interesting aspect of the Ark's plans though, is the choice of principal dimensions", say Hans Otto Kristensen. "They are interesting because, on the one hand you get a feeling of the ship's size, and on the other hand, but just as interesting, because you can compare these principal dimensions' mutual relationship with the corresponding relationships that are used in modern ship building today".

One cubit was about 18 inches long or ½ meter, which gives Noah's Ark the following approximate measurements:

Length = L = 150 m (492 ft.)
Width = W = 25 m (82 ft.)
Height = H = 15 m (49 ft.)

These measurements give us a feeling of the Ark's size, which, by the way, is the same size as some of the world's largest animal transport ships that can carry about 40,000 living sheep.

In addition, it is very interesting to see that the relationship between the height and the length (H/L) of the ship and that of the length and width (L/W) of the ship are equivalent to the normal construction practice used today for modern containerships which is shown in the figure below.

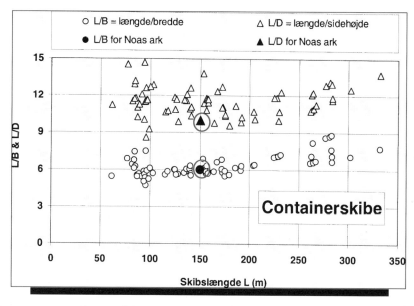

The illustration shows the length-width proportions used for modern container ships (shown with a round circle). The length-width proportions of Noah's Ark are marked with a circle filled out in black. Likewise you can see the height-length proportions according to which the different container ships are built (marked with a triangle). The height-length of Noah's Ark is marked with a triangle filled out in black. In both cases the Ark is placed in the middle, i.e. a construction very close to what is considered ideal today.

Roofing Lives Up to
International Requirements

"Another interesting thing about Noah's Ark, which for a person without knowledge of ship construction can seem meaningless, is the fact that the Ark's roof ridge was raised one cubit, that is 1/50 of the ship's width."

The roof ridge of this boat is the deck, and the deck's camber (rising) causes any water that may come onto the deck to easily flow overboard again.

When seen through the eyes of a ship builder, this little detail called a roof ridge is very notable, because the same construction is used today when building ships.

Even more interesting is the fact that the measurements used here, 1/50 of the width of the ship, is the exact same standard that has been established by the United Nations' Maritime Organization, IMO, and used internationally when building ships.

The Stability of Animal Transport
– Keeping EU Standards

"One last comment on the Ark's principal dimensions is that these dimensions would give the ship such stability that it would be able to fulfill the requirements for stability that the European Union (EU) is drawing up for animal transport ships."

Today, many of the different types of ships are too high so that animals in transport, when faced with bad weather, can be put in circumstances that surpass what an animal can bear.

The new requirements that the EU is working on (which Hans Otto Kristensen has also taken part in) will assure that animals under transport do not experience great accelerations. The Ark's principal dimensions have been chosen so well that they would fulfill all of the EU's coming requirements for stability.

Hans Otto Kristensen would like to stress that his short explanation should not be understood as scientific evidence of the existence of Noah's Ark in that such evidence cannot be given. The sole purpose is to show that from a technical point of view, there is nothing in the account from the Bible about the Ark that defies the knowledge and experience we have today about shipbuilding.

"From a technical point of view, one can't help but notice that the Bible's account amazingly agrees with modern shipbuilding principles in that the description contains details that were not made into standards in shipbuilding until many years after the building of the Ark. Some of them have not even come so far yet but most likely will within the coming years, apropos the coming rules of the European Union on the stability in transporting animals.

Chapter 9

From Where Did the Water Come?

Standing there for the first time on the earth formation - which many of us now believe to be the remains or the imprint of a huge ship – the gears started turning in the old knocker. The dear old Sunday school story of Noah's Ark with all of the animals and rainbows went from being just a colorful, marvelous fairytale to a historical possibility.

Imagine if there really was a boat lying here in the mound below us... Could any other boat than Noah's Ark have landed at 6,500 ft.?

The moment you realize that it is feasible, your brain starts finding answers to all of the apparently unanswerable questions connected with the Ark: Were there also animals in the Ark as the Bible tells us? Were all the animals represented or only certain species? How did Noah manage to get all of the animals into the Ark? Did he catch them over several years, or did they come by themselves, their instincts forewarning them of imminent disaster? How could there be enough room for all of the animals, and what did they eat? How could a "primitive" man like Noah build such a large boat? How could the water get high enough to cover the mountains?, etc., etc.

It was questions like these that used to convince people that this account was just a fairytale or a myth – that is, an edifying story without, necessarily, any historical facts. But if we were standing on the boat itself, then more serious consideration would be necessary...

A Feasibility Study

As a matter of fact, many intelligent people have been investigating these issues methodically. For example, John Woodmorappe[1], a reputable geologist has described all imaginable "impossibilities" in his book *Noah's Ark: A Feasibility Study*, published in 1999.[2] The results from his and others studies can also be found on several websites[3].

It is very interesting reading, and we might want to explain many of these calculations, but when you wander off into details, you easily lose track of things. And it is not the purpose of this book to "prove" that every detail of the biblical account of Noah is correct or possible. We want to stick to the big picture and leave it to others to deal with the details.

For me, the big picture seems to indicate that some thousand years ago a very extensive water catastrophe actually happened on the earth. Whether it was 4-5,000 years ago or more is not the most important thing. And whether the catastrophe only included parts of the earth or whether it was global is also up for discussion. But obviously there are signs all over the earth indicating that this catastrophe really happened, and if these really are the remains of Noah's Ark we've found at a height of some 6,500 ft., then we are dealing with more than a local flooding around the Euphrates

Footnotes

[1] John Woodmorappe is a noted Creation Scientist who has published extensively in creation journals. His book "Studies in Flood Geology" is a collection of papers that describe different aspects of the global flood. In particular, the paper "A Diluviological Treatise on the Stratigraphic Separation of Fossils" (Dec 1983) describes his TAB model (Tectonically-Associated Biological Provinces) for how the flood has produced the fossil record as it is found today.

The Woodmorappe website (www.rae.org/johnw.htm) contains a study guide to his book "Noah's Ark: A Feasibility Study", and a rebuttal against published objections to points made in the book.

[2] John Woodmorappe: "Noah's Ark: A Feasibility Study", 1999, Institute For Creation Research: 1-(619) 628-7640.

[3] For example, there is a power point presentation on http://emporium.turnpike.net/C/cs/ark/

or the Black Sea. Irrespective of details, however, the big question to be considered more closely is: Where did the water come from?

From Both Above – and Below

In popular versions it just started to rain and rain, but Moses is more specific in his account.

We are told that "...in the second month, on the seventeenth day of the month, on the same day all the fountains of the great deep burst open, and the floodgates of the sky were opened. The rain fell upon the earth for forty days and forty nights." (Genesis 7:11-12)

As we are told, it did not only rain – water also came from "fountains of the great deep". As a matter of fact, these fountains, or springs are mentioned before "floodgates of the sky" indicating, possibly, that they at least are of no less importance. The Hebrew word for fountain is *Mayan*. It means fountain, well, and spring. It could also be referring to the seas as the expression "the great deep" is used elsewhere in the Hebrew text about the seas.[4] So it is quite plausible that huge amounts of water were put into motion, thus creating floods. We see this today with tidal waves in the Bay of Bengal, for example, which are able to send waves up to 20 feet tall hundreds of miles into Bangladesh. We just have to multiply that by 10 or 100 to imagine the results of a giant meteor crashing into the ocean.

The abyss or "the great deep" may also be referring to subterraneous sources. [5]

When the text says that these fountains were "breaking through" or "breaking up", some people believe this to be referring to the theory that large water reservoirs once existed *below* the surface of the earth. (In the story of Creation we are told that the waters gathered in one place).

As a matter of fact there is evidence of such hidden reservoirs below the surface. It is interesting to note that due to underground pressure up to 70 percent or more of that which comes out of a volcano during an eruption is water, often in the form of steam.

40 Days of Rain

Most of the professional researchers investigating whether the world was actually deluged or not believe that if this was the case, the water must have come from below and that the rain was caused by the bad weather following the dramatic upheaval.

In Genesis 7:11-12 Moses writes, "and the floodgates of the sky were opened. The rain fell upon the earth for forty days and forty nights." If the earth had been struck by a catastrophe, maybe caused by a meteoric impact or movements of other planets, this could easily lead to storms and rainfall for 40 days. But normally rain comes from vapor rising from the earth - condensation. Therefore some scientists believe that the rain mentioned was some kind of extraordinary rain. And as a matter of fact there is a rather interesting detail in Moses' Creation account that certainly stirs the imagination.

Footnotes

[4] As in Genesis 1:2; Job 38:30, 41:32; Psalms 42:7, 104:6; Isaiah 51:10, 63:13; Ezekiel 26:19; Jonah 2:3.

[5] Ezekiel 31:4, 15.

The Firmament Above

We are told in Genesis 1:6-8 that on the second day of creation God said, "Let there be an expanse in the midst of the waters, and let it separate the waters from the waters. God made the expanse, and separated the waters which were below the expanse from the waters which were above the expanse; and it was so. God called the expanse sky."

The account continues telling how the waters below the firmament, or the expanse, gathered in one place making the dry land appear.

The word "firmament" is the same as the Hebrew word *raqiya* meaning expanse. Later we are told that the birds fly in this expanse implying that the expanse is the atmosphere.

The question is whether the waters *above* this firmament was simply a poetic way of telling us the sky is as blue as the sea or maybe a bit more technical indicating the fact that the atmosphere contains water - or was there really a blanket of vapor and mist?

Just as Saturn still has gaseous rings around it, as seen in the above illustration, the earth may have been surrounded by rings before the Flood-catastrophe, thus shielding her population from the cosmic radiation which ages us today.

Primitive Men or Men of Genius?

Modern theologians seem to regard the words about "the expanse above" as primitive people's poetic description of the blue sky. But much seems to indicate that pre-historic people were not primitive at all and that they had greater knowledge in many fields than later generations - especially people living before the Flood, who allegedly grew extremely old.

Instead of considering these kinds of curious remarks in the Bible and in descriptions left behind from various cultures as primitive, we will in this book attempt to look at them as indications of facts – although they are often surrounded by fairytale stories.

An example of this could be the "underworld" in the Greek myths which is looked upon as pure superstition; it may, however, be considered a remnant of times when prehistoric people in rush boats set out on journeys around the world exploring the "underworld" – down under as the Australians say – "where the sun shines at night and the moon during the day." (This was also true of the Americas (Atlantis?) where the Sumerians and Phoenicians possibly found their copper 3-4,000 years ago.)

So let's not underestimate the civilizations of prehistory.

Warmth and Coldness Blanketing the Earth

But is it at all possible that there could have been a blanket of water vapor surrounding the earth? Yes, it is possible. As we know, Saturn has rings around it and similar rings might have been around the earth.

The fact is the globe has different layers in its atmosphere[6] being respectively very hot and very cold. Therefore, these layers – which are now dried up – could have stored both ice and vapor.

The troposphere being closest to the earth (0-10 km) gets between 10-15 degrees colder than the earth's surface temperature for each kilometer we move away from it. At a height of 45 miles (in the mesosphere) the temperature gets as low as 65 below (-54 C). But then it turns around:

Footnotes

[6] The Earth's atmosphere is split into the troposphere (<10 km), the stratosphere (10-50 km), the mesosphere (50-80 km), the thermosphere (>100 km), and the ionosphere, which is the ionized part of the upper atmosphere. It is divided into layers: D-layer (75-90 km), E-layer (95-150 km), and F-layer (>150 km).

The outermost layers of the thermosphere (beginning approx. 100 km or some 62 miles out) are drastically heated up by UV- and other rays from the sun. Around 1,000 km (621 miles) from the earth the temperature reaches as much as 1,300 degrees! That is why space rockets have to be equipped with a heat shield when moving through the thermosphere.

The higher the temperature, the more vapor can be stored in the layers.

The Water Vapor Canopy

Dr. Joseph Dillow[7] has done extensive research on the idea of such a water vapor canopy. But the ring was not necessarily vapor; it could also have consisted of ice as we find both very hot and very cold layers surrounding the earth.

The theory developed by Dillow was later modified by Dr. Larry Vardiman who believed that much of the waters engulfing the world at the time of the Flood could have been stored in small ice particles distributed in equatorial rings around the earth similar to those around Saturn.[8]

This water vapor canopy could have collapsed, falling as rain. Or volcanic eruptions associated with the breaking up of the fountains of the great deep could have thrown dust into the water vapor canopy causing the vapor to nucleate on the dust particles thus forming rain.

The canopy, however, couldn't have been too thick as this would have caused the earth's surface to be intolerably hot. And actually, researchers at Texas A&M University have demonstrated that the atmospheric pressure at sea level was once twice as much as it is presently (760 mm).[9]

Vardiman and Rush concluded that a maximum of 2 meters (6.5 ft.) of rain could be held in such a vapor canopy.[10] Although it is quite a lot of rain, it is not enough to cover the earth completely including the mountains. Therefore, most creation scientists believe that the major source of the Flood-waters did not come from above, but from the fountains and springs of the earth by the lifting up or tearing apart of the tectonic plates causing a series of volcanic eruptions. You can almost imagine the massive amounts of water from the ocean being thrown up into the air like boiling water from mighty geysers, just to fall to the ground again over a period of 40 days. Maybe we will even one day hear of an "inner ocean" in the depths of the earth, because evidence is mounting that there is still a huge amount of water stored deep in the earth in crystal lattices of minerals due to the immense pressure.[11]

The Ocean Floor Rose

A group of scientists[12] with geophysicist John Baumgardner in the lead have been working with the possibility that the earth's tectonic plates have at one point been lifted causing great amounts of seawater to be washed over the continents. The starting point for this is that the sea floor is very "young" geologically speaking. They even think that this was formed after the Flood.

The model is as so: a piece of the earth's originally hard mantle is re-

Footnotes

[7] J.C. Dillow, *The Waters Above* (Chicago, IL: Moody Press, 1981).

[8] L. Vardiman, "The Sky Has Fallen", *Proc. First ICC*, 1986, 1:113-119.

[9] Charles E. Sellier & Brian Russell: Ancient Secrets of the Bible. Dell Publishing, New York 1994. Pg. 99-101, 236-239.

[10] D.E. Rush and L. Vardiman, "Pre-flood Vapor Canopy Radiative Temperature Profiles", *Proc. Fourth ICC*, Pittsburgh, PA, 1990, 2:231-245 - L. Vardiman and K. Bousselot, "Sensitivity Studies on Vapor Canopy Temperature Profiles", *Proc. Fourth ICC*, 1998, pp. 607-618.

[11] See L. Bergeron, "Deep waters", *New Scientist*, 1997, 155(2097):22-26:"You have oceans and oceans of water stored in the transition zone. It's sopping wet."

[12] S.A. Austin, J.R. Baumgardner, D.R. Humphreys, A.A. Snelling, L. Vardiman and K.P. Wise, "Catastrophic Plate Tectonics: A Global Flood Model of Earth History" Proc. Third ICC.

[13] However, this coal could also originate from the motion in the tectonic plates of the earth – i.e. the theory that the continents used to be connected as they fit into each other.

leased under the sea. Part of the floor starts to sink into the warmer, softer parts of the mantle. Fiery heat follows, especially around the edges, which soften and sink in a wild, accelerating tempo. This causes the plates to move even more and rips a nearly 6,000-mile long crevice in the earth's mantle. Through the crack, new hot material floods out of the inner-earth to fill the void.

The glowing material creates enormous vertical geysers (maybe the same "fountains of the great deep" spoken of in Genesis 7:11 and 8:2).

The geysers spray boiling steam far into the atmosphere where it is cooled down and later falls as rain over 40 days.

The new sea floor that quickly replaced the old, hard mantle is warmer and therefore not quite solidified. Thus, the ocean bottom rises 3-6,000 feet. This sprays seawater throughout the continents and even engulfs the mountains (the Flood).

By the new movements of the tectonic plates, new mountain ranges are created throughout the earth: the Himalayas, the Andes, the Rockies, and the Ararat Mountains – right where three of the earth's tectonic plates meet.

(In current, widespread geological timelines, these mountain ranges are said to be much older. But these are not facts that can be measured, but again, the ruling theory of uniformity raises its head telling us that all things have evolved over millions of years without any catastrophes taking place. Baumgardner and many others reject this theory as out-dated and scientifically untenable.)

According to the Bible the first human beings lived in heavenly surroundings. Illustration by José Pérez Montero.

Greenhouse Climate – and Paradise?

But let's go a bit further. With a ring of water or a bubble encompassing the earth, the result would be a near-paradise, at least climatically speaking. The earth would have had a uniform greenhouse climate being pleasantly sub-tropical to temperate all around the globe, even at the poles where there is ice today, tell Vardiman and Dillow.

This would have caused the growth of lush, succulent vegetation all around the globe. This is supported by discoveries in Antarctica of coal containing vegetation that obviously belongs to a whole other climate. The climate at the poles must have been warmer at that time[13]. Scientists have coincidentally discovered that the Arctic Ellesmere Island in the North Western Territory of Canada, now covered by ice, showed clear evidence that "the climate in this area used to be swampy and temperate." ("New York Times", September 24, 1976).

Their actual purpose was to research a theory that Europe at one time might have been connected with North America. Similar discoveries have been made in other places indicating that the climate in the not too remote past might have been quite different from what it is today, possibly due to a protective vapor canopy or ice surrounding the earth.

Last century in the artic Spitzbergen, which is almost always covered in snow and ice, scientist Oswald Heer found 136 different types of fossilized plants, among these, silver fir, common spruce, cypress, elm, hazel, and waterlillies. There is even evidence that there were once palm trees with dates in this artic area.

Similar results have been found other places which may suggest that the climate was very different in our not too distant past. And this *could* be due to a protective layer of water or ice around the earth.

The wind and cloud conditions would be quite different in this climate, and as the mountains were possibly not as high as they are today (because the mountain chains are a result of the movement of the tectonic plates) this again would have an effect on the formation of rain clouds, so it is feasible that it didn't rain at all. (According to the Bible, the pre-Flood earth was only watered by a fountain that flowed into four rivers and by the mist or dew.)

If the greenhouse theory is correct – until the water catastrophe changed it – this may explain the missing annual rings in some of the wood-like stones found near the Ark-formation and in other places around the world. (Because there were no seasons.)

Dinosaurs – and People with More Brains

A result of this greenhouse theory would be that plant and animal life was much more vigorous than today – developing into dinosaurs, mammoths and sea monsters?

Because without the direct cosmic radiation of the universe making us grow old, both human beings and animals would live much longer and grow much larger.

Analyses of fossils where flies and air are captured inside amber point to that earth once had an atmosphere with an oxygen content of 30% compared to 21% today.

In such a climate, cuts would heal more quickly and people and animals would live longer. We would even have more brains...ha! We have around 200 billion brain cells when we are born, but within the first 6 weeks of our lives, we loose around half of those, probably due to lack of oxygen and the atmospheric pressure.

So this might be the reason why the Bible and old stories from almost all cultures tell about giants and gods with extremely long life spans...?

Don't you feel that we're onto something that could possibly solve many of the great riddles?

Chapter 10

The Valley of the Eight

One day we drove out to the "Valley of the Eight".

This is the part of the valley that twists around the west side of Mt. Ararat and lies about 15 miles from both the mountain and the boat-shaped object.

The name, "Valley of the Eight" or "Region of the Eight" of course refers to the eight that, according to the Bible, survived the Flood by taking refuge in the Ark. Many ancient civilizations and religions speak of eight forefather-gods. This is a study in itself, and here we will only mention its existence rather than get lost in all of its details.[1]

The special thing about this valley is the multiple anchor stones with holes in their tops that have been found here. Ron Wyatt was the first to stumble across these large stones, and year after year more appeared, most of them in this area. He supposedly found a total of 13 anchor stones together with his employees, but some of these have either been removed by collectors or destroyed by the locals, who don't understand the foreigners' interest in these rocks. We know that in a few instances the locals cut the stones in half to see if there was a treasure or something else of value hiding inside...

"The Valley of the Eight" is approx. 13 miles away from Mt. Ararat and due to the big anchor stones found here many Ark-hunters are convinced that Noah and Na'ama settled here. Feizal, the head of the village, is showing the stone that Wyatt believed to have been Noah's altar.

We have heard that some of the villagers can be aggressive, but with the presence of Salih Bayraktutan, things go as planned.

One of our goals is the little village, Arzep. Even Ron Wyatt has incorrectly called the town Kazan before. But Kazan is a few more kilometers up the mountain.

Some believe that Ron Wyatt mixed up the names of the villages on purpose to send the treasure hunters that constantly followed him to steal these memories of the past on a wild goose chase. But this trick didn't stop the robbers from emptying the graves.

Armenian Cemetery

Many of these strange stones are found in Arzep, and some call it "the Village of the Eight".

There is also an Armenian graveyard here – partially destroyed – which probably contains the remains of crusaders and pilgrims. It is located east of the village and is no longer a beautiful sight. Many headstones have already been removed and used as building materials, while other graves are more or less open where bones are up for grabs. As we walk around the cemetery, Kurdish children run around playing with the arm and leg bones...

The atmosphere is very intense. People are yelling and screaming. We are shocked to see a boy corrected by his father – by a blow to the head with a shovel.

This cemetery is worth studying deeper. It probably contains not only bodies of the Armenians who lived here until they were chased away, but possibly also crusaders who came here in search of the Ark. But today we won't stop a thousand years ago with the crusaders; we will be going back to the days of Noah!

In another area north of the village, huge headstones that look like anchors have been found. They have – or rather had in some cases – a hole in the top. Some of the stones are still intact where we can see these holes.

We also saw a house in this town where the two halves of one of these very old engraved stones were used as building material.

Mighty Anchors of Stone

The stones can be found just northwest of the village, and only a few still have their holes intact while the others have been broken where the hole was previously, or they are set up so it is buried under the earth.

Other places in the world, like on the Nile, this method of tying a boat to a large stone with a hole in it is practiced. Normally these anchor stones are no longer than a meter, usually one half.

But here in this village and throughout the hills surrounding the Region of the Eight, eleven such stones have been found, and they are not one meter long, but 2 and even 3 meters!

Ron Wyatt was the first to discover these stones in 1977. He claims to have found 13 all together. Bill Fry has since then located 11 of these

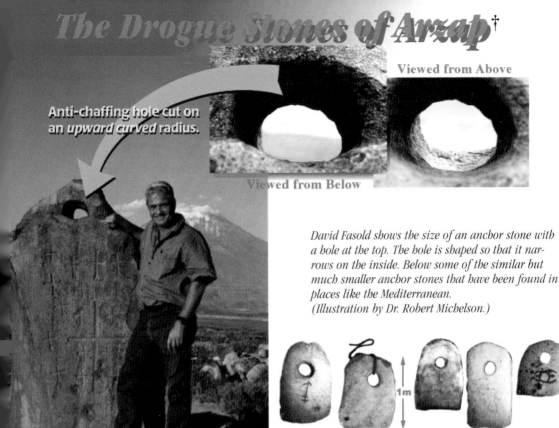

Anti-chaffing hole cut on an *upward curved* radius.

Viewed from Above

Viewed from Below

David Fasold shows the size of an anchor stone with a hole at the top. The hole is shaped so that it narrows on the inside. Below some of the similar but much smaller anchor stones that have been found in places like the Mediterranean.
(Illustration by Dr. Robert Michelson.)

1m

Anchor Stones from the Coast of Israel
(courtesy of David Fasold)

whose authenticity can be verified. (Sadly, certain local swindlers have copied these stones and placed them in remote locations in order to attract archeologists and earn money off of these false "anchor stones", so we have to be on the lookout for fakes.)

Bill Fry has not found the last two stones, which should be close to the Ark, about 15-20 miles from this site. These stones have most likely been stolen, or at best been secured by the local authorities. But gone is gone.

Dr. Salih Bayraktutan tells me later that a similar stone has been found in present-day Armenia, so there are possibly 14 or even more.

The holes in these stones are special: they slope inwards. Therefore, they are fit to tie a rope to so that the knot slides into the hole and stays put.

Stones in a Line

These stones are placed in a curved line starting in this valley and pointing toward the boat-shaped object. They could also point to Mt. Ararat with a little help.

No matter. What is really special is that there are anchor stones or just plain anchors so far up in the mountains. There seems to be no logical

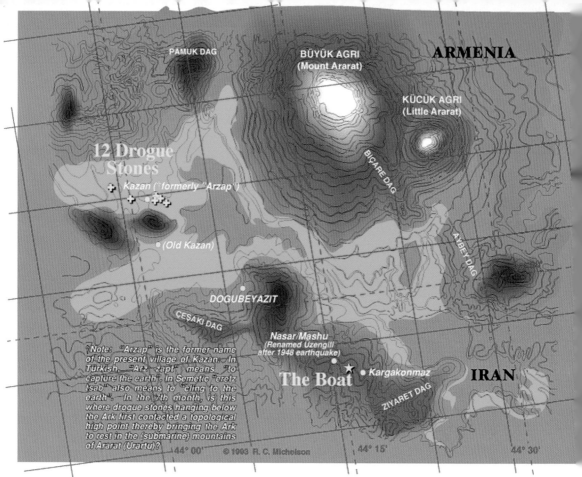

Map labels (reading within the figure):

PAMUK DAG

BÜYÜK AGRI
(Mount Ararat)

ARMENIA

KÜCÜK AGRI
(Little Ararat)

BICARE DAG

12 Drogue Stones

✠ Kazan ("formerly "Arzap")

AYBEY DAG

• (Old Kazan)

DOGUBEYAZIT

ÇEŞAKI DAG

Nasar/Mashu
(Renamed Uzengili
after 1948 earthquake)

The Boat   ★   • Kargakonmaz   IRAN

ZIYARET DAG

Note: "Arzap" is the former name
of the present village of Kazan. In
Turkish, "Arz-zapt" means "to
capture the earth". In Semetic "erelz
isab" also means to "cling to the
earth". In the 7th month, is this
where drogue stones hanging below
the Ark first contacted a topological
high point thereby bringing the Ark
to rest in the (submarine) mountains
of Ararat (Urartu)?   44° 00'   © 1993 R. C. Michelson   44° 15'   44° 30'

Robert Michelson's map of the area surrounding the find near the Turkish border leading to both Iran and Armenia. The yellow x's mark where the anchor stones have been found. Most of them near Arzep/Kazan. The huge mountain on top with the white snow cap is of course Mt. Ararat (Great Agri) – with Little Agri to the right. The Turkish name of Mt. Ararat is Agri Dagi.

The boat-shaped object is marked with a yellow star below. South of the "boat" you find the village of Kargakommaz (meaning "Restless Crow"). Further south is the mountain Ziyaret Dag (The Pilgrim's Mountain) where old graves have now been found. Northwest of the boat is the village of Uzengili which until the earthquake in 1948 was called Nazar or Mashu. See the explanation of the names in a later chapter.

explanation. The ocean and lakes are very far away.

Next, it is curious that the anchors are so exaggerated. Both things are illogical – unless a huge Ark sailed here at one point.

According to Professor Robert Michelson, Georgia Tech, the purpose of the anchor stones is "to create a drag in the water. If these devices are attached to the end of a boat, the drag produced as a wind driven boat pulls it along through the water will cause the boat's hydrodynamic pointed bow or stern to face into the wind and the oncoming wind-blown waves.

"Without such a device, a wave can hit the boat and turn it sideways to the wind and waves. The next wind impacting the side of the boat will then have a greater likelihood of rolling the boat over. Sea anchors and drogue stones effectively prevent this." [3]

The purpose of Noah's Ark was not to sail around the world but only to protect people and animals until the Flood was over. Therefore, it would have been sensible to equip it with drogue anchors that could stabilize the boat.

The name of the village, Arzap or Arzep, possibly comes from the Turkish *Arz zapt* which means "to capture the earth" or possibly further back to Semitic in *eretz tsap*, which can be translated as "to cling to the earth". [4]

At least one of the stones is on top of a hill. Maybe this was the first time the anchor stones had contact with a peak as the water began to sink. They had connected with the earth – arz zapt – Arzap.

Eight Special Crosses

Most of the stones have eight crosses on them. They look like Byzantine/Armenian crosses that curve outwards at the tips, but the vertical beam is not always longer than the horizontal.

The cross is an ancient symbol found in many cultures. For example, the ancient swastika symbol that the Nazis used comes from India. The Indians use it today, but that does not mean that they are Nazis. So it cannot be constituted for sure that these are Christian Byzantine crosses. They may date back to a pre-Christian era.

But Ron Wyatt also found anchor stones with holes that stuck out of the ground in which no crosses were engraved. This could suggest that the crosses were made after the stones were re-discovered, probably by crusaders or by the Armenians as a memory to signify the eight from the Ark.

Cult Stones?

Some critics have tried to explain these anchor stones away with the suggestion that they were merely stones used for mystical rituals by locals where the holes were used to hold candles or the like. But if this were the case, then it would be impractical that the holes narrow as they reach the center. And besides, there is no other evidence that such religious practices have existed in this area.

The Yezidi sect, which can be found in parts of southeast Turkey, is the closest we come to a fire-religion. But they have no such ritual. One offshoot of this sect worships the sun by lifting up sick children at sunrise, for example, while another group worships fire. But this is performed in dances around a bonfire.

There are neither signs of candles or fire in the holes nor signs of blackening on the stones themselves.

Rather than wild guessing about the practices of unknown religions, it makes more sense to connect these anchor stone-looking stones with that which they look like: anchor stones – likewise the eight crosses with the Ark and the eight that, according to the Bible, were in it.

Footnotes

[1] See Aril Edvardsen's "Solgudens Autostrada" Hermons Forlag (Publishing House).

[2] www.ancienttexts.org/library/mesopotamian/gilgamesh/index.html by Timothy R. Carnahan.

[3] Robert Michelson på http://avdil.gtri.gatech.edu/RCM/RCM/5RCMArkeology/6Durupinar.html

[4] In Turkish, *arzap* means to take possession of the earth or land. *Arz* meaning earth or land, and *Zapt*, means seize or take possession. (*Langenscheidt Universal Turkish*).

While in Shemetic (Hebrew in this case) *eretz* means earth, or land and *zab* means "-to cling to, as a lizard clings to a rock." (*Strong's Exhaustive Concordance of the Bible*)

Stone Reference in Gilgamesh

The Bible does not mention anchor stones, but it is possible that the use of such anchors was common practice (which finds in the Nile suggest) and thus unnecessary to mention in the short description of the Ark. When considering the Ark in the Qur'an, anchors are mentioned in Houd Sura 11: "In the name of Allah it will cast Anchor".

In the Sumerian epic poem, Gilgamesh, which we will be looking at later, strange stone things are named which could possibly be the mighty anchor stones. This happens when Gilgamesh has to sail across a body of water in order to reach Utnapishtim (Noah). In the English version, which is based on the standard Accadian version with additions from the ancient Babylonian where words are missing in the Accadian, the ferry keeper, Urshanabi, says the following to Gilgamesh:[2]

Urshanabi spoke to Gilgamesh, saying: "It is your hands, Gilgamesh, that prevent the crossing! You have smashed the stone things,' you have pulled out their retaining ropes (?). 'The stone things' have been smashed, their retaining ropes (!) pulled out!"

It sounds like a number of anchor stones have been destroyed and that the ropes that tie the stones to the boat have been pulled out.

Later we will come back to Gilgamesh, the Bible, and the Qur'an to see what they have to say about the Ark.

Mrs. Birthe Nissen and the author by one of the famous anchor stones that have been found in "The Valley of the Eight" just 13 miles from Mt. Ararat in the background and the boat-shaped object situated to the right of the mountain.

Chapter 11

Why Did They Grow So Old?

The Bible, the Mesopotamian kingly geneologies, and several other pre-historic accounts tell that pre-Flood people lived for hundreds of years. The Mesopotamian tablets mention so many thousands of years that they are most likely referring to weeks, while the biblical accounts don't exceed 1000 years. Could these be mere exaggeration?

Methuselah

It is a matter of common knowledge that Methuselah is the oldest human being to have lived. "Methuselah lived 969 years and then he died." Furthermore, he died the same year in which the Flood occurred. Actually, his name means "when he dies, it will occur." Likewise, the other people mention from the pre-Flood time had very long life spans – Noah, for example, had attained 600 years before the Flood; and, "after the flood Noah lived three hundred fifty years. All the days of Noah were nine hundred fifty years; and he died." (Genesis 9:28-29)

Not surprisingly Bible critics have called these mentions of long life spans mythical and evidence that the Bible is unreliable as we all know that people do not normally live more than 80 years or so, though we hear about very rare accounts of people who have lived for as much as 120 years. The improved conditions of life and access to new medicine may have risen the average duration of life by some decades in some countries. Despite intense research over the past century, we have not been able to significantly increase the maximum age of mankind.

Maybe the old stories have secrets hidden within. As a matter of fact, the historian Moses himself mentions that something happened just around the time of the Flood. Moses, of whom we must assume based his facts on ancient handed down traditions, says in Genesis 6:3, "Then the Lord said, 'My Spirit shall not abide in mortals forever, for they are flesh; their days shall be one hundred twenty years.'" After that the genealogical tables show the lifespan of the succeeding generations to be shortened after the Flood. Moses himself, by the way, lived to be a perfect 120 years old.

We Do Not Die from Hard Work

To people who do not believe in an almighty God, it is, of course, just as mythical that man's lifespan was suddenly shortened over only a few generations. But now new research has proved that it only takes slight changes in one's biochemistry and the amount of cosmic radiation to obtain longer lifespans, and scientists have even discovered a Methuselah gene that, when mutated, is able to prolong one's lifespan.

Instead of regarding our own lifespan as normal and that of the first human beings as extreme, we should consider why human life expectancy has dwindled. The reason is not that the human body is incapable of withstanding more than 80 years. We do not die due to hard work, but rather because we are being exposed to some kind of poisoning from the chemistry of the body itself and from cosmic radiation which means that the cells of the body are being destroyed – thus causing us to grow old and die. If we were not exposed to this poisoning and radiation, we might be able to live for 900 years like in prehistory!

Dying Via Supernova

There are several astronomical phenomena that might have affected human lifespans then and now. Cosmic radiation from the universe is, indeed, one of the main factors that limits human life expectancy. According to scientists, a star known as Vela exploded about 20-30,000 years and is the largest factor for the deadly cosmic radiation that silently bombards the earth today. [1]

A supernova is a rare celestial phenomenon: the explosion of most of the material in a star. And had it not been for this supernova Vela, long life spans *would* actually have been possible. Therefore, some people think that the Flood occurred at the same time the radiation from the supernova reached earth. This implies, however, that the Flood happened further back in prehistoric time. But even if we don't juggle around with the placement of the Flood on our timelines, supernova Vela could still have played a significant role.

As mentioned in chapter 10 "From Whence Came the Water", some Flood scientists believe that there was once a layer of vapor or ice around the earth, which dissolved in connection with the catastrophe. If there were such a layer around the earth, it would have worked as an effective protection against this cosmic radiation!

In other words: the people living in the "greenhouse" before the catastrophe were not exposed to this age-limiting cosmic radiation. After the layer of vapor disappeared their radiation exposure started, but apparently it took a few generations for the harmful effects to have a lasting influence.

In the same way other astronomical phenomena that are not yet fully known might have had an effect on their life spans. As previously mentioned the myths seem to indicate a meteor shower – maybe from an explosion on Saturn. But there are other possible explanations for our aging.

Biochemical Explanations

In their efforts to procure longer life expectancy, scientists have discovered that biochemical mechanisms may in some cases increase life expectancy by nearly 50%.[2] Experiments with fruit flies and worms have proved that. Therefore some scientists believe that in the near future it will be possible to manipulate genes or even remove those that cause us to age, in effect extending our life span as a species. Whether they are being too optimistic or not, only time will show. But with their discoveries they have

Footnotes

[1] B. Aschenbach et al., "Discovery of Explosion Fragments Outside the Vela Supernova Remnant Shock-Wave Boundary," *Nature* 373 (1995), 588. - A. G. Lyne et al., "Very Low Braking Index for the Vela Pulsar," *Nature* 381 (1996), 497-589.

[2] Simon Melov et al., "Extension of Life Span with Superoxide Dismutase/Catalase Mimetics," Science 289 (2000), 1567-69. - Judith Campisi, "Aging, Chromatic, and Food Restriction - Connecting the Dots," Science 289 (2000), 2062-63.

"incidentally" revealed a number of plausible explanations as to how human life expectancy could drop from 900 to 120 years relatively quickly.

Below you will find some of these reasons; and we can't avoid the complicated language:

Reactive Oxygen Species (ROS) Slowly Killing Us

The free radical theory of aging is one of the leading explanations for senescence.[3]

When a molecule contains an unshared electron it becomes highly reactive because the unshared electron aggressively "seeks out" another electron with which to pair. Some free radicals produced inside the cell are derived from molecular oxygen (O2) and are called *reactive oxygen species* (ROS)[4]. They play a central role in harvesting energy.

However, *reactive oxygen species* damage the cells. In their search for other unshared electrons they attack such things as molecules that make up cell membrane, proteins, and DNA. Since this damage to the cell is cumulative, the damage continues to grow – and so does the aging process.[5] But our cells are able to defend themselves against the damage that the free radicals cause. For example, the enzymes Super Oxide Dismutase (SOD) and catalase hunt the free radicals super oxide and hydrogen peroxide. Also enzymes, glutathione, peroxidase, and vitamins E and C protect against the attacks – but not enough.

A team of pharmacologists recently demonstrated that the aging effects caused by the reactive oxygen species can be largely subverted by augmenting the cell's native antioxidant defenses by using enzyme mimetics. The pharmacologists gave enzyme mimetics to worms which in turn extended the average life span of the worms by 44%.[6]

Researchers have also been able to extend the life span of fruit flies by about 40%. Instead of using enzyme mimetics, they manipulated the fruit flies' genes causing them to produce more SOD and catalase for the defense mechanism.[7]

SOD and catalase are vital to our ability to defend ourselves against aging and illnesses.

If humanity had a decrease in level of SOD and catalase in connection with the water disaster and the change of environmental conditions, then this may explain our reduced life span.

ECs Contribute to Our Aging

Researchers have also discovered that by selectively reducing food intake (calories) by 30-70%, life span can be extended by up to 40% for a wide range of creatures from yeast to mammals.[8] (Therefore, a vegetarian diet may give longer life because consumption of vegetables yields fewer calories and prevents the intake of toxins that accumulate in animal flesh.)

For years, scientists have thought that caloric restriction extended life expectancy by causing a decrease in metabolic rate which, in turn, leads to reduced production of ROS, i.e. the above-mentioned reactive oxygen spe-

Footnotes

[3] Toren Finkel and Nikki J. Holbrook, "Oxidants, Oxidative Stress and the Biology of Aging," *Nature* 408 (2000), 239-47.

[4] Sandeep Raha and Brian H. Robinson, "Mitochondria, Oxygen Free-Radicals, Disease and Ageing," *Trends in Biochemistry* 25 (2000): 502-08.

[5] Robert Arking, *The Biology of Aging*, 2nd ed. Sunderland, MA: Sinauer Associates, 1998, 398-414.

[6] Melov et al., 1567-69.

[7] Raha and Robinson, 502-08.

[8] Leonard Guarente and Cynthia Kenyon, "Genetic Pathways that Regulate Ageing in Model Organisms," *Nature* 408 (2000), 255-62.

Footnotes

[9] David A. Sinclair and Leonard Guarente, "Extrachromosomal rDNA Circles - A Cause of Aging in Yeast," *Cell* 91 (1997), 1033-42.

[10] Su-Ju Lin et al., "Requirement of NAD and *SIR2* for Life Span Extension by Calorie Restriction in *Saccharomyces cerevisiae*," *Science* 289 (2000), 2126-28.

[11] Sir2 is activated when a cell's energy status drops, which will happen under calorie-limited circumstances. When Sir2 is activated, it causes the chromosomes to condense and the genes in the chromosomes to be subdued. As a result the production of EC's dwindles resulting in an extended lifespan for the yeast. A well-worn strand of DNA will produce poisonous EC's that would in turn shorten its lifespan. But because Sir2 can subdue the genes in a chromosome, the DNA strand is not worn down as quickly. Therefore, it doesn't produce poisonous EC's and the body doesn't age as rapidly.

[12] Elizabeth Pennisi, "Old Flies May Hold Secrets of Aging," *Science* 290 (2000), 2048. - Blanka Rogina et al., "Extended Life Span Conferred by Contransporter Gene Mutations in *Drosophila*," *Science* 290 (2000), 213740.

[13] Yi-Jyun Lin et al., "Extended Life Span and Stress Resistance in Drosophila Mutant methuselah," Science 282 (1998), 943-46.

[14] Andrea G. Bodnar et al., "Extension of Life-Span by Production of Telomerase into Normal Human Cells," *Science* 279 (1998), 349-52.

cies which damage the cells. But recent studies with yeast seem to indicate that the extended life span is due to another biochemical mechanism.

This mechanism is not less complicated, but here it is in a somewhat simplified version: within chromosomes there are genes that code for rDNA. Sometimes these genes are excised from the chromosome. These excised genes form individual circular pieces of DNA (called extra chromosomal DNA circles, or ECs). These ECs are self-replicating and accumulate. They start competing with the genome for vital enzymes and other cellular materials. Therefore, ECs are toxic to cells and decrease longevity.[9]

A team of researchers from the Massachusetts Institute of Technology has now found that the enzyme Sir2 plays a significant role in reducing the accumulation of the toxic ECs in yeast, thereby extending its life span. [10]

As Sir2 is not only found in yeast but also throughout the biological realm, including humans, Sir2 is possibly one of the substances that could prevent us from aging.[11]

The Methuselah Gene

Researchers at the University of Connecticut have identified a mutation in fruit flies that disables a gene. The loss of this gene's activity means that the organism cannot extract energy from food very efficiently. This limits the energy available but, similar to caloric restriction, leads to longer life spans. Fruit fly life spans *doubled* as a result of this mutation.[12]

Oppositely, a mutation of a single gene in connection with the Flood may have led to shorter life spans. Actually, researchers have recently discovered another gene appropriately called the Methuselah gene. Again, experiments were carried out on fruit flies. Interestingly, many organisms seem to be genetically programmed to hasten mortality. When it comes to fruit flies, life expectancy is extremely short. But recently scientists have discovered a gene mutation that leads to longer life spans. The full function of this Methuselah gene has not yet been discovered, but when mutated it has been shown to extend life spans.[13]

Chromosome Disorders

Humans have 23 pairs of chromosomes; one member of each chromosome pair comes from the mother and the other from the father. Prior to cell division each chromosome duplicates, and after cell division the parent and daughter chromosomes separate from one another.

In connection with cell division and DNA replication telomerase has a function. Telomerase is en enzyme complex that maintains the so-called telomeres, the terminal ends of DNA strands in chromosomes. Without sufficient telomorase activity, telomeres become successively shorter with each round of cell division, and if the telomeres disappear, chromosomes lose stability and the cell's ability to replicate is compromised – leading to aging.

Therefore, telomerase activity is important. Researchers have been able to extend life spans by introducing telomerase into cultured human cells that lack telomerase activity.[14] This leads one to wonder if the human body didn't cease telomerase activity in connection with the Flood, thus expediting the process of ageing.

Genome Size

Scientists from Glasgow University in Great Britain[15] have recently uncovered a significant relationship between genome[16] size and longevity. The term genome refers to the entire DNA makeup of an organism. The Glasgow team surveyed 67 bird species and found that larger genomes head to longer life. Humans have a large genome – three billion base pairs (genetic letters) but only 28,000 to 120,000 genes. This means that non-coding DNA makes up roughly 97% of the human genome. We have, in other words, wider prospects than we are currently using, and one may wonder whether it was different in prehistoric times.

Researchers are on the threshold of additional breakthroughs in understanding the endocrinology and hormonal control of aging as well as deciphering Werner's syndrome (a disorder leading to premature aging). Also, as mentioned in chapter 9, increased amounts of oxygen in our atmosphere could have caused humans to lose half of their brain cells within the first six weeks after birth. So there can be many reasons as to why the first humans lived longer and were larger (and smarter) than we are today.

Footnotes

[15] Pat Monaghan and Neil B. Metcalfe, "Genome Size and Longevity," *Trends in Genetics* 16 (2000), 331-32.

[16] The word *genome* refers to an organism's full DNA nature. Genomes include genes (that decode information necessary for cells to produce proteins), RNA (building molecules), and non-coded DNA.

Before the Flood people apparently lived for hundreds of years. After the upheavals our lifespan has steadily gone downhill, but the fact that the first generations lived comparatively longer seems to indicate an accumulated influence. The survey is based on the genealogical tables according to the Greek Septuagint translation which also mentions Arpakshad's son Kenan. He is not mentioned in the later Masoretic text upon which most Bible translations are based. But Luke also mentions Kenan (Luke 3:36) which seems to indicate that Jesus and his contemporaries used the texts which formed the basis of the Septuagint in c. 300 B.C.

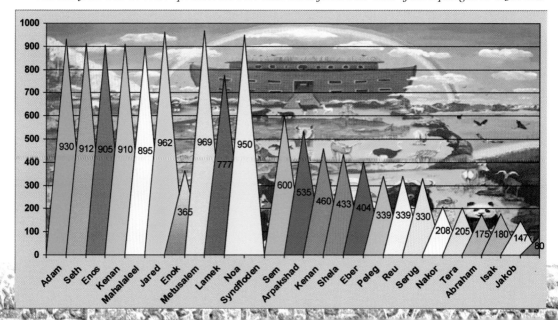

Evening picture from the Isaac Pacha Castle from where successive rulers could control the Silk Road from Europe to the mystical East.
Down in the valley in front of the castle you find Dogubayazit which is the eastern-most town in Turkey. Less than 100 years ago the town lay around the castle up in the mountains, but now it lies close to the new road running through the valley into Iran . "The Valley of the Eight" is situated between the mountains in the back-ground. Mt. Ararat is to the right and cannot be seen on the picture.

Chapter 12

The People of the Ararat Mountains

Behind the Castle of Isaac Pasha, which lies on the eastern side with a view out over the magnificent valley and the two Ararat mountains, lies an even older castle. It is almost hewn into the rocks and some of us crawl up the steep steps, into the caves.

Caves cut into the sides of rock like this can be found in various other locations in Eastern Turkey where the Hurrians lived at least 4,000 years ago. If we believe the Noahic narrative, that would place them here just after the Ark stranded in these mountains.

The Hurrians are the oldest people group archeologists have found signs of here in the mountains. But maybe a new and older culture will soon be revealed. At any rate signs of graves and dark spots after ruins have been found in the mountains around the boat-shaped object. So far these graves have not been dated, but as you will see in a later chapter it may be the legendary town of Naxuan or Mesha.

Approx. 18 miles from both Mt. Ararat and the boat-shaped object you find a cave-castle probably dating back to the time of the Hurrians – a few centuries after Noah.

Metsamor

There have also been found objcts from a very old culture in the Ararat Valley in the Armenian state on the northern side of the Arax River. This is the Metsamor-find, discovered near the nuclear power station bearing the same name,

Footnotes

[1] "The Kurds .....are descendants of two great groups of races: The Pre-Arian peoples like the Gutians, Lulluians, Khurrians, Kassites .. etc. and the Indo-European peoples of which the Medes are the most known. The former who talked a hitherto unknown group of language generally called Asiatic or Caucasian appeared from the third millennium B.C. and remained to the first millennium B.C. while the immigration of the Medes and other Indo-European peoples started from the early second millennium B.C."- According to Ancient History of Kurdistan from Islamic Group in Kurdistan/Iraq - see http://www.komall.org/httpdocs/e/e-kurdistan/e-ancientkurdhist.htm

[2] Akhenaten's World - www.geocities.com/Athens/Acropolis/7987/hurria_1.html says: "The first appearance of Hurrian personal and place names comes from Mesopotamian records of the late 3rd millenium. These reveal that the region east of the Tigris river into the Zagros Mountains was the Hurrian homeland."

[3] The Book of Jashar 30:28 and 31:65.

[4] The Khabur river is 200 miles long, rising in SE Turkey and flowing generally south through NE Syria to enter the Euphrates River near Dayr az Zawr. The Khabur valley, which has now about 4 million acres (1,6 million hectares) of farmland, is Syria's main wheat-producing area. In ancient times the Khabur was known as the Habor; along its banks in Gozan the Israelite captives from Samaria were settled in the 8th Cent. B.C. (2 Kongs 17.6; 18.11) http://www.geocities.com/Athens/Acropolis/7987/mitann_1.html.

which supplies Armenia with approx. 40 pct. of its electricity.

The old Metsamor has been a centre of both metal extraction and astronomy. People are supposed to have been living here as far back as 5,000 B.C. and up to the 17th century. As early as 2,000 years before the Babylonians, people here had set up a stellar observatory (like Stonehenge) allowing them to fix a calendar of 12 months. There are also signs indicating that the zodiac was known here before it turned up in Mesopotamia.

The old town covers an area of approx. 10 hectares whereas a neighbouring town has covered 100 hectares. Towards the end of the Iron Age, Metsamor has probably been one of the largest cities in the world - some put the number of inhabitants to 50,000. The Metsamor excavations may throw light on the first days up here in the mountains. But until then the Hurrians should be regarded as the oldest people group.

The Hurrians - "The Tall"

The name can mean the "tall" or "noble". Another translation is "people that live in caves". Hurrians can also be spelled Khurrians – which leads one to think of the Kurds, which were later found in the area. Maybe they were here all along. The Kurds in Iraq themselves claim to descend from among others the Khurrians.[1]

We don't know from where the Hurrians originate, but the first mention of them is in the end of the third millennium in Mesopotamia – over 4,000 years ago. It is evident from this ancient find that the Hurrians' homeland was the region east of the Tigris River in the Zagros Mountains.[2] These mountains are just south of Ararat. The kingdom of the Hurrians was called Hurri.

The Hurrians Go West

From the third millennium before Christ the Hurrians spread out in the Southwest in the area around Lake Van. They also lived in small groups in northern Mesopotamia around the Euphrates River.

Around 1700-1500 B.C. they invaded Mesopotamia and Eastern Anatolia in Turkey. From here a number of them continued all the way into modern day Syria and Israel.

At this time most of the countryside between the two rivers was under the Amorites in the Babylonian kingdom, which centralized power and introduced a system of law and order (the Hammurabi code of laws). But around 1600 the kingdom was plundered from Turkey in the north by the Hittites, a neighboring people that resembled the Hurrians.

The Hurrians were most likely Indo-Europeans – based on the names of their kings and such things as chariots, which are of Indo-European origin. They worshiped gods that are connected to the Aryans in Iran and India such as Mithra and Varuna. The Hurrians also worshiped some of the same gods, as the neighboring Hittites that dwelled further west in Turkey. They used some of the same names, and they had some of the same myths. The Hittites were also Indo-Europeans. The Hurrians eventually began to use the Mesopotamian mixed religion and culture, spoke Babylonian, and used the Mesopotamian system of writing when putting their own language down on clay tablets. But even though many texts written in the Hurrian language have been found, the language has not yet been decoded.

The Hurrians Are Also in the Bible

In Genesis chapter 36 the *Horrite,* Seir, and his clan are called the *Horrites (Hurrians).* The Mountains of Seir, which was the harsh mountainous country south of the Dead Sea, is named after him. Esau and his sons captured the area, and Esau let his daughters marry the sons of the Seir's chieftains.[3] The country in the southern region of present-day Israel and Jordan was later named Edom (after Esau). Esau probably lived

The Eski Beyazit Castle built into the Mountains of Ararat dates back to at least the Urartu civilization (c. 800 B.C.) and was the forerunner of the town of Dogubayazit. Before that a still older cave-castle probably existed here.

between ca. 2145-1995 B.C. (See ch. 13) And these *Horrites* may possibly be some of the same Hurrians that spread out from Ararat and the Zagros Mountains all the way to Syria and Israel.

The Kingdom of Mitanni

As time went on, the Hurrians became a major power, and around 1550-1250 B.C. King *Sudarna I* established the Hurrian kingdom of *Mitanni.* The capital was *Washukanni* on the Khabur River,[4] a large tributary of the Euphrates in northern Syria.

This kingdom existed at the same time as an almost unknown people from the East, the Cassites, invaded Babylon where they reigned from 1530-1170 B.C. They were also Indo-Europeans like the Hurrians and the Hittites, so we can see that Japheth's descendants had gained control and power over the entire area after the ruling of Ham's and later Shem's sons.

Eventually, the Hurrians ruled all of upper-Mesopotamia.

In 1475 B.C. the Egyptian king, Tuthmosis III, reclaimed Syria, but the Hurrians' king sought peace through marriage with Egyptian princesses. Later the Kingdom of Mitanni was attacked on two fronts from Hittites and Assyrians respectively and was later annexed in c. 1270 B.C. to the Assyrian Empire. Only one little Hurrian stronghold, Hayasha, survived in the Ararat Mountains. Regardless, the Hurrians were some of the first people in the Ararat Mountains after Noah.

They Wandered in the East

Most of the ancient, known history of the world comes from Mesopotamia. According to Moses, this is where people went after the Flood.

They apparently followed the rivers to lower land in the southwest because this is where Genesis, chapter 11 continues after we hear about the Ark. In most translations chapter 11 reads, "As they migrated *eastward*, they came upon a plain in the land of Shinar and settled there."(verse 2).

But it is probably a translation mistake that they went "eastward", because otherwise they would not have ended in Mesopotamia, but in Iran.

In some translations the text has been adjusted to read "as they migrated from the east" (NRSV) or "as they journeyed east" (ASV).

Today's English Version writes, "As they wandered about in the East, they came to a plain in Babylonia and settled there." The New International Version uses continued "eastward".

According to the Book of Daniel, chapter 1, verse 2, the plain of Shinar and the later Babylonia were one and the same. Shinar was the land between the Euphrates and the Tigris. It is easy to imagine that Shinar is a Semitic version of the name Sumer.[5]

Sumer is the first "country" known of in the area between the two rivers. Whatever the case, this is one of the first civilizations on earth, from around 3,000 B.C. There are also signs of even older inhabitants like the Ubaid civilization that must have come before the Flood.

Normally, Sumer is placed in the southern most part of Iraq, but maybe Sumer (or Shinar) was comprised of the entire span between the two rivers until the new centers of power, Babylon and Akkad, arose. There is actually an area called Cinar (Shinar) that is located all the way up in northern Mesopotamia - in southern Turkey - to which road signs refer even today.

If it is this Shinar that existed, then "eastward" can be read with an understanding that the Euphrates turns eastward just after the river flows down from the mountains. There is also a plain here.

The explanation of the east-west mix-up is that the Hebrew word for east basically means "in front of". This is because at that time the rising of the sun was considered the point from which one differentiated between right and left. The Hebrew text is as such, "And it was as they traveled *from "in front"*. They found a level valley in the land of Shinar. And they lived there."[6] In the Greek version LXX "*from the rising*" is stated.

Mesopotamia

The areas between the Euphrates and the Tigris are called Sumer, Akkad, Babylonia, Chaldea, and Mesopotamia. Between these two rivers, in modern day Turkey, Syria, and Iraq, over the next two thousand years bloody wars were fought for reigning power of the Middle East.

According to the Bible, all of these people groups originally came from the Mountains of Ararat. In the beginning they all spoke the same language, but in the 5th generation there was a language confusion and the people split up. This happened in connection with a great tower called the Tower of Babel, which, according to the Bible, was built on the Shinar plain. And that is where remains have been found of multiple large pyramid-like towers, so-called ziggurats, which could possibly be that same tower. It could also possibly be the temple-tower in Etemenanki, north of Baghdad which the Chaldeans later restored under King Nabopolassar and his son Nebuchadnezzar II of Babylonia.

Footnotes

[5] Aril Edvardsen has the same theory in his 4-volume series about the "Autostrada of the Sun God"

[6] "And-it-was as-they-travelled from-the-east they-found-a-level-valley in-the-land-of Shinar. And-they-lived there" (Interlinear Bible by J. P. Green.)

What Happened in the Mountains of Ararat?

The Bible doesn't clearly state who stayed in the Ararat Mountains. Instead we follow those that traveled down to Mesopotamia - some of Ham's descendants - and afterwards the Semite Abraham who lived in Ur but traveled to the present day Israel with a sidetrack to Egypt among other places. Later we will come back to one of these descendants, namely Gilgamesh who lived in Sumer.

The closest we get to answering who settled in these mountains is *the sons of Joktan*. What is written about them is that they lived in the Mountains of the East from Mesha to Sephar. (Later we will look more closely at David Deal's theory that Mesha lay in the Mountains of Ararat and that Mesha and Nazuan are the same place - close to the boat-shaped object.)

The sons of Joktan are the fifth generation after Shem, the oldest of Noah's sons. Joktan's brother is named *Peleg* because "in his days the earth was divided, and his brother's name was Joktan." (Genesis 10:25) According to the Bible, it is here that people began to wander in different directions - surely a reference to the current events of the Tower of Babel in Mesopotamia.

The World Divided in Three

If we take other less reliable sources into account such as the Book of Jasher[7], then Noah split the world between his three sons in this way:

The descendants of Shem got the Middle East and the East.

Japheth was given Europe and maybe Russia west of the Don River as well as the "distant islands".

Ham got Yemen, Egypt, and the rest of Africa.[8]

There was plenty of room in which to grow. Their descendants could have just gone in three different directions, but instead most of them obviously conglomerated in Mesopotamia and soon began to fight. Ham's son, Canaan, begins with taking the land of Canaan (Lebanon and Israel), which belonged to the sons of Shem. There are also some that travel to Egypt and plant themselves along the Nile, while others go to India and build a new civilization around the Indus River. These two civilizations start around 3,000 B.C., but that is a whole other story.[9]

The first ruler in Mesopotamia was Ham's grandson, Nimrod. For centuries his line continued to ravage the Assyrians and Babylonians (both of which were Semitic, that is of Shem's lineage) and later the Hittites and Hurrians, both Indo-Europeans (Japheth's descendants). Instead of living in each his country, they go back and forth between trying to plunder each other and gain control.

According to the Book of Jasher, Shem remained with Noah. And because some of the place names up here are close to the names of Joktan's sons, one could imagine that the Semites were the first to live up in the Mountains of Ararat.

Footnotes

[7] A Jewish text found in the Middle Ages of the same name as the book twice referred to in the Bible. It was released in Hebrew in Venice in 1625 (possibly 1613) and then translated and released in smaller editions in Krakow, Prague, Frankfurt, Constantinople (Istanbul), Amsterdam, and Calcutta. Later in English, 1839, in the USA. It is not sure that this source is authentic.

[8] Also in the "Edda" written by the Icelandic historian Snorre Sturlason (approx. 1200 A.D.) the earth is described as three continents: Africa, Europe and Asia. "Near the centre of the world was built the very reputable house and hostelry which is called Troy - that which we call "Turkland," he writes. In 1870 the archaeologist Schliemann found the ruins of Troy - in Turkey!

According to local tradition Turkey's largest lake, Lake Van, photographed here from NASA's Land Satellite in September of 1984, supposedly encompassed the Garden of Eden.

Another theory is that some of Japheth's descendants stayed in the mountains. The Armenians, who have been in the area for thousands of years, claim that they are descendants of Haig who was the son of Togarma (Genesis 10:3). He was the son of Gomer, the son of Japheth - Shem's brother. And if we look at the first known people that archeologists have connected to this area, we hear of an Indo-European people, the previously mentioned Hurrians.

Onward to Lake Van

After some time in the shadow of Mt. Ararat, we are now traveling further south. We follow curving mountainous terrain down to Turkey's largest lake, Lake Van. It is an enormous lake that like Loch Ness has its own monster as well as a unique breed of white cats, the Turkish Van cat, which is said to be fond of swimming, contrary to most other cats. They are also known for their two different colored eyes.

Lake Van is located at 1,720 m. (5,650 ft.) above sea level. It is more than 74 miles (119 km) across at its widest point and covers an area of 1,434 square miles (3,713 square km) with salt water, for there is no run-off from this high-altitude lake.

According to local folklore, the Garden of Eden can be found on the bottom of Lake Van, but no one is known to have dived there to explore the depths for hidden treasure. Something appears to be hiding it, if it is a relic from the Flood. Here is a very exciting challenge for the divers.

On the southeast bank of Lake Van lies the provincial capital, Van. Outside of Van lies an ancient castle, which is more or less hewn into a rock. This originates from the ancient Urartian kingdom that came into being around 1300 B.C. and continued until 584 where the Medes finally beat the Urartu and destroyed their capital after centuries of Assyrian attempts.

The Urartian Kingdom

The Urartu were possibly the same people as the Hurrians after their downfall. Whatever the case, there was some kind of connection between the two. The Assyrians otherwise reigned the majority of the smaller kingdoms in the area, but the Urartu pushed eastward when the Assyrians were driven back by the Aramaeans[10] (1078-977 B.C.) from Syria.

From ca. 850-584 the Urartian kingdom had its center in Tushpa just west of the city Van on Lake Van, a few hundred kilometers south of Mt. Ararat.

The Urartu were often at war with the Assyrians. *Shalmeneser III* conquered one Urartian king after another, but the Urartian King Menua (c. 800 B.C.) eventually gained control of all the highlands. The Urartu later moved their capital further east to Erebuni (all the way up around modern-day Yerevan in Armenia) and under King Sarduri II (764-735) reached all the way to the northern border of Syria. But it seems they spread themselves too thin. The next year, in 743 B.C., the infamous Assyrian ruler, *Tiglath-Pileser III*, pushed the Urartu back and won control of northern

Footnotes

[9] The first king of Egypt, Scorpion, is dated to around 3,100 B.C., but the list of kings is built on thin evidence. The Indus civilization is the earliest known civilization in South Asia. It flourished from 2600-1800 B.C., but signs of older habitations exist – possibly from before the Flood.

[10] The Aramaeans descend from Aram, one of Shem's sons. They lived in Syria, which is often called Aram.

[11] Genesis 8:4.

[12] 2 Kings 19:37b.

[13] Isaiah 37:38.

[14] Jeremiah 51:27.

Syria. Eight years later the Assyrians attacked the Urartian kingdom again and took both Urmia, on the great lake with the same name in Iran, and occupied Tushpa on Lake Van - but were unable to conquer it. In 714 the new Assyrian ruler, *Sargon II*, attacked the Urartian king, Rusa I (735-714) and beat his army.

But the Urartu regrouped and gathered their strength again, not to be conquered until 584 by the Medes to the southeast in present day Iran. They destroyed the capital, and from this point on the Urartu disappear as a people group known by that name. They were possibly later resurrected as the Chaldeans.

The Urartu civilization existed from c. 1300 to 584 B.C. and mostly had its center in Tushpa on Lake Van. Its expanse covered the Mountains of Ararat and at times the entire northern part of Iran, today's Eastern Turkey and Armenia, as well as parts of Georgia and Azerbaijan.

The Ark Stranded on the Mountains of Urartu

The Urartu are named multiple times in the Bible. The first mention is in connection with the stranding of the Ark "on the mountains of Ararat".[11] Actually it should say "on the mountains of Urartu", because there is no doubt that this is the kingdom which is being referred to. This is what the area was called during the time Moses wrote this account.

The next mention of the Urartu is in the Book of Kings where the Assyrian king, Sankerib, is told to have been struck down by his sons Adrammelek and Sareser while he was praying in his temple. "…and they escaped into the *land of Ararat*. His son Esar-haddon succeeded him."[12] The Mountains of Ararat were a good place to hide.

This happens around 681 B.C. while the Urartian king, Rusa, was building a new capital close to Lake Van.

The account is repeated in the Book of Isaiah.[13] Both times it is the same word, RRT, which is also used in the telling of the Ark. But in many translations of the Bible, the land of Ararat is translated as the land of Armenia, because this later came to cover the same area.

The Urartu Attack Against Nebuchadnezzar

The prophet Jeremiah also names the Urartu when he prophesied around 600 B.C. that the world power, Babylonia would be destroyed. He names three kingdoms that will attack it: "Raise a standard in the land, blow the trumpet among the nations; prepare the nations for war against her, summon against her the kingdoms, *Ararat, Minni, and Ashkenaz*".[14]

The attack came in 539 B.C. when the Persians gathered an alliance of Medes and other tribes in Iran and eastern Turkey in order to attack Babylonia. Among these tribes were *the Urartu, the Minni* (the kingdom of Mannai south of Lake Umnia in Iran), and the *Ashkenaz*,[15] probably a Scythian[16] race from between the Black Sea and the Caspian Sea - behind the Ararat area.

A street sign in southern Turkey showing the road to Cinar (Shinar?)

Some people connect the ruin hill in Cinar in southern Turkey to the Tower of Babel. Most people believe that the Tower was located near Baghdad.

This alliance destroyed the new Babylonian Empire, which the Chaldeans had controlled from 612-539 with rulers such as Nebuchadnezzar on the throne. The new Persian regents actually let the Jews who were forced to move to go home. So here was a prophecy that came to pass.

Who Were the Chaldeans?

From Lake Van, we drive west to Diabaktir, the copper city.

We have now come down from the mountains and are crossing a wide-spreading plain. The landscape is as flat as a pancake, only interrupted by small eminences where smaller cities once lay. While we cross the Tigris River, Elin Berglund tells me her theory about the Chaldeans who in 612 B.C. gained control of Babylon. She believes that the Chaldeans came up here from the Mountains of Ararat.

"You know the Bible tells about 'Ur in Chaldea' as the birthplace of Abraham", she says.

"Most people today believe that Abraham's birthplace is the Ur which has been found and excavated in southern Iraq. Therefore they also assume that Chaldea is located down around Babylon where Nebuchadnezzar ruled. But the Chaldeans originally came from up here where we are now", believes Elin and gives the following support:

"Nebudchadnezzar's co-ruler was named Nabonidus. He and his mother came from Haran, which was up here in Turkey. Inscriptions found c. 80-100 meters south of the find in Babel prove this. He worshiped the moon god, Sin, which was a known god in Haran.

Another inscription in Argitis near Lake Van reads: 'This is the spoil of the cities which I obtained for the people of the Khaldis in one year... To Khaldis, the giver, to the Khaldises, the supreme givers, the children of Khaldis the almighty...'[17]

"Caldian or Khaldian was a term used for the people who practiced Khaldis, a system of 79 heavenly gods with the moon god, Sin, in the center," Elin elaborates. The Greeks acclimated portions of this system of gods in the Pantheon in Rome, built with a ceiling open toward the gods.

Maybe the Chaldean rulers in Babylon came from the mountain country in the north when they in 612 B.C. invaded Mesopotamia.

This happened at approximately the same time as the Armenians' move into the mountains, which could suggest that the Chaldeans had deserted it.

Footnotes

[15] The *Ashkenaz* people were named after Japheth's grandson.

[16] According to the Jewish historian Josephus, the Scythians were the same people that the Bible calls *Magog*, normally considered to be the Russians. Josephus writes in *Antiquities*, p. 1,123 that *"Magog founded the Magogians, thus named after him, but who were by the Greeks called Scythians"*.

[17] www.fact-index.com/k/kh/khaldis.html.

[18] Genesis 11:31: And Terah took Abram his son, and Lot the son of Haran his son's son, and Sarai his daughter in law, his son Abram's wife; and they went forth with them from Ur of the Chaldees, to go into the land of Canaan; and they came unto Haran, and dwelt there.

Haran, the City of Abraham

Later on we get to Haran, which lies close to the Syrian border. This is where Abraham escaped to from Ur. The name is derived from Abraham's oldest brother, Haran. Laban, Rebekah, Rachel and Leah[18] also came from this place.

Today Haran is just a large village, but it was once the capital, done so by an Assyrian king. Haran lay strategically placed by the Balikh River, which connects to the Euphrates, and the city also lay on the road between Nineveh and Carchemish.

We hike behind the city and see the ruins of the university the Greek Alexander the Great's army destroyed when he took control of the Persian Empire. We walk around in a large, tiled courtyard surrounded by crumbling walls with a well in the middle and with hundreds of carved stones and pillars that have also been destroyed.

"I have a theory that it was Abraham that founded this school", says Elin. She refers to Abraham's visit to old Noah in the Book of Jasher to acquire wisdom from him and the stars. Whether this is the case or not, a school, the world's first university, was established here around 2,000 B.C. and had connections with Egypt. Astrology became the worshiping of idols, just like in the rest of the Assyrian and Babylonian kingdoms.

The city adapted and held on to its religious status under the later Persian world war from the 6th-4th century B.C. and after Alexander the Great captured the city for his Greek Empire.

When the Roman Empire became Christian, the heathen philosophers in Rome and Athens escaped to the east and founded a new Platonic academy in Haran where the ancient Chaldean paganism was mixed with newer Roman forms. In the 6th century Islam came to the area, and an Islamic University was founded under the caliph, Umar II. He let the professors of heathen wisdom continue, and they succeeded, just like before, in surviving the changing control. But they held their occult knowledge a secret from the Muslims. The Crusaders built a castle here that is still standing on top of one of the two centrers of the moon god in the city. On top of the other center is the Mosque.

The houses of Haran are up to 12 feet tall and built with clay. The purpose is to keep the heat out. It gets up to 131^0 F here so it's no surprise that they worshiped the moonlit nights…

Just over a mile from the castle comes a hill. On the way we pass two gates that mark the entrance to "The House of Aran", which was Sarah's family.

We have previously mentioned the Aramaeans in this chapter. They de-

Harran was Abraham's city and it later became the center of worship for the moon god Sin – also known as Nanna. Was it Noah's wife Na'ama they worshipped? At one time Haran was the capital of an Assyrian kingdom. The Greeks were here too, and the Crusaders' castle in the background tells the story of another important era with Haran at its center.

Alexander the Great is called Alexander the Cruel here. He destroyed, among other things, the famed university of Harran – maybe the first one in the world.

scended from Noah's grandson *Aram* who was a son of Shem. The original language of the Aramaeans was *Hurrian*, but later they got their own language *Aramaic*, developed under the influence of Akkadian, according to linguists. (Or maybe a Tower of Babel had an influence?) Anyway, Aramaic later became the most used business language in the Middle East and had ousted Hebrew among the Jews at the time of Christ.

Jacob's well. The people in Haran certainly know where the Jacob from the Bible met his Rachel. It was right here by the well where all of Harran's inhabitants came for water until only a few years ago.

Romantic Haran

Sarah, or *Saraj* which was her original name, was the wife of the patriarch Abraham and she is described as "very beautiful". So beautiful that Abraham had to lie twice telling that he was not her husband - afraid of being killed by two kings who were both courting Saraj.

They lived in Haran for quite a long time after Abraham and his father Tera having escaped from Ur in Chaldea. Maybe their Ur was the *Urfa* lying only about 30 miles from here. But he may also have been escaping from the Ur which was excavated in the 30'ties in the southern Iraq.

One of Abraham's brothers was *Nakor*, the other was *Haran*, but he died before they left Ur so they probably named the city after him.

Haran had a fatherless son, Lot, whom Abraham brought along when he and Sarah went to Canaan (the later Israel) after having stayed in Haran for some years. Lot settled in the fertile Sodom, but after a divine hailstorm the region was transformed into the barren Dead Sea region. But that is another story.

Sarah and Abraham get the son Isaac and he is definitely not to marry the local Canaanitic women, they agree, so they send their servant back to *Haran* to find a wife for Isaac. The servant meets the - also very beautiful - Rebecca right here at the well. She is a grandchild of Nakor, Abraham's brother, who still lives in Haran.

A generation later when Isaac and Rebecca's twins Esau and Jacob have become mortal enemies, Rebecca advises her favourite son Jacob to escape back to her brother Laban in Haran. When he reaches the country "Paddan-Aram" (Aram's plot - i.e.. the country of the Aramaeans) he meets the beautiful *Rachel* - at the well. And they fall stormily in love with each other. But father Laban cheats him so he works seven years just to marry her sister Leah - and first after that he marries Rachel (It costs another 7 years!)

So Haran has been the scene of the most romantic accounts from the Bible enveloped in the fragrance of the mystery of the East.

On top of the hill we find a *tel,* a small hill with the original city and here it is possible to dig one's way layer by layer through the long history of the city. A few digs have been made, but nothing like if there were money for it.

And that is very unfortunate as Haran could surely reveal a great deal about the first people here and in the Mountains of Ararat.

We spend the night in *Urfa*, or *Urhai* as it was called in Aramaic. *Sanliurfa*, the shining Urfa, has been its name since 1983. Inscriptions on tables found in Ebla do, in fact, mention a town by the name of Ur, lying near Haran. Therefore, there probably was a time when Urfa was called Ur, but this does not necessarily mean that it was Abraham's Ur.

In Urfa we visit among other things the cave under the Citadel of the city where Abraham, according to local tradition, is supposed to have been kept hidden by his father, general Tera. *Nimrod*, the ruler, would kill the boy. Also that is a fantastic story - but maybe not quite in accordance with the truth.

Abraham's cave, where he is said to have been kept hidden for Nimrod as a child, is found under the Citadel of Urfa in the town's large mosque which used to be a church.

So we end our going through the people in Urartu with the Armenians who are together with the Kurds the people who have lived in the Mountains of Ararat for the longest time.

The Armenians

From 612-559 B.C. the Armenians lived in the Urartu Mountains under the control of the Medes.

From 559-331 they went into an alliance with the Persians under King Kyros and his successor. King Darius I names Armenia as his 13th satrapy (province) in his writings.

No one knows where the Armenians come from, but they spoke an Indo-European language. One theory is that they came from Iran. Another suggests that they came from an area north of the Black Sea. A third says that they came from Phrygia in the west.

The Armenians occupied the area until recently, but mostly under the rule of others:

The Greeks: After having been a satrapy under the Persians, the Armenians found themselves under Greek control in 331 B.C. but were given their own kings and remained independent until 200 B.C.

The Seleucid: Armenia found itself under the Seleucid (the eastern part of the Greek kingdom) for a period but achieves its freedom when the Seleucid fall to the Romans in 189 B.C.

Armenia Independent Again: Now there is a period where there is no world power governing Armenia after the fall of the Mesopotamian Empire, and for a short while Armenia has the chance to expand.

Under Tigranes I the Great (c. 95-56 B.C.) Armenia almost becomes a world power. But the Romans under Lucullus and then Pompejus push them back reducing the size of their lands. In 66 B.C. Armenia bows down to this great power and becomes a Roman colony.

The Romans and Parthians (a people who lived in present day Iran and Afghanistan) fight for the area and vacillate between their respective vassal kings.

The Byzantine and the Persians: After Armenia's conversion to Christianity in the 4th century, the struggle continues between the later states of Byzantium and the new Persian Empire, which tries to force the Armenians to convert to Zoroastrianism.

Islam: From the 7th century the army of Islam struggled with the Byzantine over the plagued land. In the 11th century a great deal of the people escaped from the perpetual depredation and rooted themselves in Cilicia (the area between the Taurus Mountains and the Mediterranean Sea in present day southern Turkey), which was later called Little Armenia. This country allied with the Crusaders despite religious differences and had kings from the Cilician family in the 14th century.

The Osmans moved in and took over the area in the 15th century and held on to it, vacillating with Persia until 1922 where it continued as a part of the modern Turkish state.

The Russians: In the 19th century the Turkish and the Persians had to hand over parts of Armenia to Russia. The Turks and Russians fought over the area, and the Armenians sought help with the Russians against their Turkish lords. But their rebellion flopped, and they were forced into the north and the south by violent ethnic cleansing under the Sultan in the end of the 19th and the beginning of the 20th centuries.

The Kurds, which were already in the area in small numbers, also took part in the genocide with the Turks' knowledge. They took over the Armenian areas and often gave them new names.

We found this 1916 Russian 2-Kopek coin in Arzep – the Village of the Eight. Probably a remnant from World War I where part of the Armenian sector was under Russian rule for a short period.

The Soviet Union: In 1920 the northern part of Armenia became a part of the Soviet Union which created the Soviet Republic of Armenia in 1936. Today Armenia is an independent state, but the area including Mt. Ararat, became a part of Turkey after World War I.

Yet the strife continues between the Turks and the local Kurds, of which some are fighting for an independent state.

Even though the Ark landed in an area that is considered in the middle of nowhere for many Europeans and Americans, the country has been involved in international conflicts throughout history.

Chapter 13

Confused Chronology

James Ussher, Irish archbishop (1580-1656), was also a competent astronomer. In 1650 he drew up a chronology of historic events from pre-history but overlooked some of the "years of evil" not mentioned.

When trying to establish when Noah lived and when the Flood took place, it is natural to backtrack with the help of the chronologies we find in Genesis 5 and 11. But most theologians and other Bible experts would prefer to skip these accounts of long lifespans and recapitulate without considering or worrying about them. Actually, most of the numbers are based on a formula the Irish archbishop and astronomer James Ussher (1580-1656) made back in 1650. According to these chronologies, the Flood occurred 2,349 years before Christ, and there is no doubt that Ussher did a serious and qualified job with his calculations.

The problem, however, is that he assumed all generations were included. Another mistake he made was that he did not account for holes from the "years of evil" under foreign rulers that could have simply been left out, as was common practice in other Middle Eastern countries.

When considering the pre-Flood period, Ussher innocently lost over 1,656 years because he based his calculations on the *Masoretic* version of the Old Testament in which many numerical mistakes have been found when compared with the older Greek Septuagint. Quotes from the New Testament show that the Greek was closer to the scriptures Jesus referred to.

Please note that it is not our purpose to question or discuss the infallibility of the Bible[1], but rather we are looking at a rewritten Hebrew version of the Bible that arose around 100 years after the death of Christ. This translation was in part a protest against the first Christian church. In addition to the chronological mistakes, the Hebrew edition had built-in mistakes because of the new lettering system which consisted of letters that were more quadratic.

In the 800's more mistakes apparently snuck their way in with the addition of dots and dashes, which equip the Hebraic consonants with vowel sounds. However, this translation has been used by the Church in the Western world since the 4th century, because it was assumed that the Hebraic was the most correct. But actually, we should rely more on the Greek version, which the Egyptian king, Ptolemy, allowed 72 Jewish scribes to work on 250 years before Christ for the royal library in Alexandria, the so-called Septuagint or LXX.

Not 2,349 but 3,537 before Christ

But even if we use the Hebrew version that was the basis for the Old Testament, there is evidence that Ussher's dating of the Flood to ca. 2,349 B.C. was wrong. It needs to be moved back to ca. 3,537 B.C.

The following is based on Australian Barry Setterfield's detailed article, "Creation and Catastrophe Chronology", which he published in 1999.[2]

So lets follow Setterfield back in history:

Footnotes

[1] Some Christians focus on the "infallibility" of the Bible. Others are more liberal and do not consider the Bible a credible source. Still others – the author included – focus more on the *inspiration* of the Word. Since the Bible is a collection of scriptures written by men, they admit that it can contain human mistakes such as what we are considering in this chapter. But they believe that the authors and scriptures were *inspired* by God's spirit and is believable, also from a historical point of view.

2 Timothy 3:16-17 says, "All scripture is *inspired* by God and is useful for teaching, for reproof, for correction, and for training in righteousness, so that everyone who belongs to God may be proficient, equipped for every good work." Whether you agree with the one or the other, the Bible is still the best possible source for true Judaism and Christianity.

Barry Setterfield
[2] Updated on www.setterfield.org/
scriptchron.htm
Setterfield has also written an exciting work about astronomy and the varying speed of light entitled *The Atomic Constants, Light, and Time*. His conversions of atomic light years into earth years mean that the geological layers from the Flood ca. 3,536 B.C. fit into the infra-Cambrian period, which is set at 600 million years ago. Even though he is really a Creationist, he has encountered a great deal of opposition from Creationists in the US due to his unorthodox ideas. Among these smites is a report from The Institute for Creation Research in which his ideas are refuted. This report is entitled "Has the speed of light decayed?" printed in IMPACT No. 179, May 1988 by Gerald A. Aardsma.

Fixed Point: 586 B.C.

We will take the destruction of the temple in Jerusalem by King Nebuchadnezzar in **586** B.C. as a fixed point which is well documented. There is widespread agreement on this date, plus or minus 1 year.

The prophet Ezekiel, who is a captive in Babylon, reports in his book (Ez. 4, verses 1-5) that the worshiping of idols had taken place for 390 years, from the split of judges in Judah and Israel until the fall of Jerusalem. When Salomon died the kingdom was split up, in **976** B.C. [3]

Salomon reigned for 40 years, and the building of the temple started in his 4th year, or **1012** B.C.

The period from the crowning of the first king of Israel, Saul, until the temple was destroyed was $40 + 40 + 4 + 426 = 510$ years. So Saul became king in 1096. [4]

The Exclusion of the Years of Evil

Throughout history Kings have been known to periodically remove years from their annals in which foreign rulers had taken control (the exclusion principle). King Salomon apparently did the same thing when he in 1 Kings 6:1 spoke of 480 years from the exodus of the Israelites from Egypt to the beginning of the building of the temple, because Luke, in Acts, suggests that there were 573 years!

Luke tells us that there were 40 years in the desert (Acts 13:18), 450 years of judges (Acts 13:20), 40 years under Saul (Acts 13:21), 40 years under David (1 Kings 2:11), and 3 years under Salomon before the temple was started (1 Kings 6:1). Altogether, that gives 573 years, or 93 fewer than Salomon mentions in 1Kings 6:1.

Does that mean that Salomon was a bad mathematician? No, he just removed the years of evil.

If we look closely, Israel was under foreign rule for exactly 93 years: 8 years under the King of Mesopotamia (Judges 3:8); 18 years under the King of Moab (Judges 3:14); 20 years under the King of Canaan (Judges 4:2-3); 7 years under the Midianites (Judges 6:1); and 40 years under the Philistines (Judges 13:1). When added up, these numbers give 93 years – the exact same number of years removed from the lists in 1 Kings 6:1. The chronologies worked out by the first Church Fathers indirectly confirm this.[5]

Salomon was able to remove the years under foreign rule quite easily, and therefore we should be cautious of accepting biblical numbers as dogma. The exclusion principle could possibly have been used. Years of evil, or maybe an evil person that no one wants to talk about could have been removed from the slates. This does not mean that the Old Testament is not credible; it just means that we need to understand its oriental counting methods. This principal of exclusion is actually used in all of the ancient cultures. Egypt and ancient Babylon have experienced later rulers removing their predecessors from lists and monuments.

The Exodus Took Place Earlier than Assumed

We can now continue even further back in time. The temple was built in **1012** and the period from the exodus out of Egypt to the temple's building was 573 years. So the Exodus occurred in **1583** B.C. plus or minus 6 years.

About 40 years after the Exodus the Hebrews began the fight for Canaan (Israel) under the leadership of Joshua. The date was about 1545.

Typically, the Hebrews were thought to have left Egypt around 1400 or 1200, at the end of the late Bronze Age in this area. But certain facts confirm our earlier dates.

According to the Bible, Joshua conquered the fortified cities in Canaan, like Jericho for example. Archeologists have often pointed out that there were no cities to conquer around 1400 because the cities of Canaan were already destroyed at that time based on digs. An archeological journal, *Biblical Archaeology Review*,[6] claims that the cities of Jericho, Gibeon, Hebron, Hormah/Zephath, Ai, and Arad (Tell Arad and Tell Malhata) did *not* exist at the end of the Late Bronze Age. On the other hand, all of these cities, as well as Debir, Lachish, Hazor, and Bethel, existed at the end of the Middle Bronze Age.

Actually, most of the cities were surrounded by walls, as mentioned in the Bible. And they were all destroyed at the end of the Middle Bronze Age II-C. (The only exception is Ai, which may not be the true Ai.) On the other hand, Khirbet Nisya fulfills both the biblical and archeological requirements. Gibeon was also abandoned at this time. Its destruction is mentioned in Joshua 9:27.)

The archeological evidence confirms that Joshua would not have had any cities to defeat if he didn't come until 1400, but all of the cities were there – and were defeated – when Joshua invaded them, according to our corrected chronology.

+ 430 Years in Egypt

Now we are going to attempt another step back. In Exodus 12:40-41 Moses writes that the Exodus occurred on the same day Jacob and his family came to Egypt, just 430 years later. As an Egyptian prince, Moses would have known the exact date based on the royal registry.

This agrees with Genesis 15:13 where God told Abram (= Abraham) that his descendents would "be oppressed for four hundred years". This is also spoken of in Acts 7:6. So both the New and the Old Testament agree. The first Church Fathers also confirm that the Hebrews spent a full 430 years in Egypt.[7]

We know that the Hebrews were accepted at first when Joseph was in power, but after this they were used as slaves. This could have happened some 30 years later when Joseph lost power as the next pharaoh took the throne.

Based on other sources, Barry Setterfield states that the massive change took place 39 years after Joseph was named an official and 41 years before his death at 110.

Footnotes

[3] This can be cross-checked in the lists found in the 2 books of Kings.

[4] These dates can also be cross-checked in 2 Chronicles 36:21 and Jeremiah 25:11 which tell us that the Babylonian imprisonment lasted for 70 years. This would also give the Jews a year of sabbath every 7th year. They did not do this, which is why they were put into captivity for the next 70 years. So 7 x 70 years = 490 years in which they did not keep the sabbath year. In the book of Haggai 2:16, we are told that this came to an end in the 2nd year of the reign of King Darius, ca. 520 B.C. If the 490 years ended in 520, then the temple was built in 1010 B.C. – very close to the 1012 we arrived at earlier.

[5] "Theophilus to Autolycus" in *The Ante-Nicene Fathers*, Book III, Chs. 23-30, A. Roberts and J. Donaldson, eds. Eerdmans Publishing Company.

[6] *Biblical Archaeology Review* for September/October 1987, pg. 53.

[7] Others have tried to shorten the Egyptian period to 200 years because they cannot get the generations to fit, but Barry Setterfield thinks that the Hebrews often left out generations born under Egyptian slavery. The first and last are enough, but the middle joints are left out in the same way we saw before. Also, if the Hebrews were only there for 200 years, they would not have been able to create a population of 2 million. So we will continue working with all 430 years.

Back to Abraham 2305

Now we've gone back 1,585 plus 430 years - altogether **2,015** years B.C. (+/-6 yrs.). We even know that it was probably April, because the Exodus (and with that the arrival) happened during the Jewish Passover.

At the time (2015 B.C.) Jacob and his sons traveled into Egypt, Jacob was 130 years old.[8]

Since Isaac was 60 when he had Jacob, and Abraham was 100 when he had Isaac, we can go back 160 years before Jacob was born in **2145** and set Abraham's birth at **2305** B.C. (2145+160).

This is confirmed by the first Church Fathers, who most likely had their information from the Apostles, who had it from the Master himself. According to Theophilus of Antioch, Abraham was born 760 years before Moses died.[9] It is interesting that both the Qur'an and Arabic tradition set Abraham's birth at ca. 2300 B.C.

Interestingly enough, the 17,000 so-called Ebla tablets (found in 1975-76 in northern Syria) are from that exact period (2,400 – 2,250). They include writings about cities in Canaan (Israel) which were previously thought to have come from a later period: Salim, possibly Melchizedek's city,[10] Hazor, Lachish, Megiddo, Gaza, Dor, Sinai, Ashtaroth, Joppa, and Damascus. Urusalima (Jerusalem) is mentioned here for the first time in history. Professor of Archeology D. N. Freedman from the University of Michigan is convinced that the account of Abraham's meeting with Mekchizedek (found in Genesis 14) and the stories about Abraham that follow come from the Ebla Period, not a later millennium as was once believed.[11]

Inconsistent Translations

Abraham's birth being fixed at 2305 B.C. +/- 6 years is not dependent on the Old Testament (OT) translation, but the chronology before Abraham is very much affected by our using the Masoretic or the Greek Septuagint. The two translations are different, and therefore it is important to know which text is the original.

For example, we can look at the OT quotes Jesus and his disciples used. Sometimes they don't quite match the Masoretic OT, which is the basis for modern translations. They are, however, in accord with the Greek Septuagint, which is over 300 years older.[12] We can see that one of Paul's important quotes from the Pentateuch is not even found in the Masoretic version.[13]

Ezra and Nehemiah's Compilation

The prophet Ezra[14] and governor Nehemiah[15] are thought to have collected the books of the Old Testament, which were recognized shortly afterwards by the so-called Great Synagogue (ca. 440 B.C.). The source written in ancient Hebrew is called the *Vorlage*. In time this text served as the source for three different versions.

1) The first was the *Samaritan Pentateuch* (SP), the 5 first books of the

Footnotes

[8] Genesis 47:9.

[9] Theophilus of Antioch pointed out that there were 660 years from the birth of Isaac to the end of the wilderness wanderings and death of Moses. This comprised Isaac's 60 years to the birth of Jacob; then Jacob's 130 years at his entry into Egypt; then the 430-year Sojourn in Egypt; and finally the 40 years in the wilderness - a total of 660 years. As Abraham was 100 when Isaac was born, this inevitably means that Abram himself was born [660 + 100 = 760] years before Moses' death and Israel's entry into the Promised Land. This information from Theophilus indicates that both Abram's birth date of 2305 B.C. ± 5 years, and the 430-year Egyptian Sojourn is in complete accord with the teaching of the Church Fathers. (Barry Setterfield)

[10] Genesis 14:18.

[11] D. N. Freedman: *Archaeology and Biblical Religion* 1978: 'It is now my belief that the story in Genesis 14 not only corresponds in content to the Ebla Tablet, but that the Genesis account derives from the same period. ... Briefly put, the account in Genesis 14, and also in Chapters 18-19, does not belong to the second millennium B.C., still less to the first millennium B.C., but rather to the third millennium B.C.' (quoted in *Ebla Tablets - Secrets of a Forgotten City* by Dr. Clifford Wilson, p.126-127, Master Books, 1979).

Bible written by Moses, also written in Paleo-Hebraic from c. 408 B.C. Tobias the Ammonite took a copy of this when he was thrown out of Nehemiah's temple (see Neh. 13:4-9 and Ezra 4:1-4). This makes up the holy scriptures for Samaritan Israelites today.

2) The other version was the *Septuagint* (LXX), which was translated from the original c. 250 B.C. by 72 Jews trained in Alexandria. This version was necessary due to the growing number of Greek-speaking Jews who lived in Egypt under the Greek Ptolemaic Dynasty. Most authorities agree that the LXX translation of the Pentateuch and the Book of Joshua were very precise because of the revered position they held in the canonical scriptures. The Eastern part of the Christian Church still considers the Septuagint translation to be the official OT text.

3) Much later, around 100 A.D., the ancient *Hebrew* text was re-written to the so-called *Masoretic* version with the quadratic "modern" Hebrew signs, and then around 900 A.D. vowel signs were added. Unfortunately, this version is the basis for many versions of the Old Testament. In *Our Bible and the Ancient Manuscripts*,[16] Sir Frederick Kenyon wrote that this double procedure could easily be "a significant source of fallacy".

The Dead Sea Scrolls Reveal Changes

The Dead Sea Scrolls, found after World War II, withhold scriptures written over a period from approximately 300 years before Christ to the 1st century after. The texts before year 70 are the same as the Septuagint as well as the OT quotes used by Josephus, Jesus, and the apostles in the New Testament.[17] The scrolls written *after* the year 100, however, fit the Masoretic text.[18]

Professor Sigried Horn writes that he is "*sure that Mathew quotes from a Hebrew text that agreed with the source the Greek translator (of the LXX) used.*" These Hebrew and Greek texts existed and were quoted from before the destruction of Jerusalem in 70 A.D. by Titus. They were, with Professor Horn's words, "*the Hebrew Bible, which circulated while Jesus and the Apostles worked.*"

Why was the text changed? Because of the Synod in Jamnia, which took place around 100 A.D.

Horn writes that at the end of the 1st century, a compilation was standardized. Not even one single copy of a divergent text survived (accept for the Dead Sea Scrolls which had already been hidden).

Rabbi Akiba ben Joseph was the incontestable head of the Synod.

In his old age Akiba supported Bar Kokba's rebellion against the Romans with all that he owned. He was even celebrated as the Messiah.

Akiba was eventually captured and sent to Rome where he was executed in 137 A.D. at the age of 82.

The Synod in Jamnia rejected the original Hebrew versions and the LXX version which was based on the Hebrew. According to Professor Horn, it was because "*...it had become the Christians' Bible.*" Horn, Sir Frederick Kenyon, and other experts agree that the 'rivalised version' was the Masoretic

Footnotes

[12] Examples: Jesus' quote from Psalm 8:3 in Matthew 21:16 or the Apostle Paul's quote of Hosea 13:14 in 1 Corinthians 15:55, or his quote from Isaiah 64:4 in 1 Corinthians 2:9. Based on such a comparison it is obvious that quotes from the New Testament follow the LXX almost exactly. If, on the other hand, we were to compare NT quotes with the more modern OT, we would find a discrepancy in our OT version. It is quite obvious that our modern OT was translated based on the Masoretic version.

[13] In Hebrews 1:6 Paul quotes Deuteronomy 32:43. He writes, "*And again, when he brings the firstborn into the world, he sys, "Let all God's angels worship him."* If we look at the passage in Deuteronomy, we see that Paul's important quote about the Messiah's divinity is not there! It is left out of the Masoretic text but can be found in the Greek, just as Paul quotes. Actually, the Masoretic leaves out another important part of the verse, but the Greek continues: "And let all of the son's of God be strengthened in him."

[14] Ezra was a Jewish priest, the author of the Book of Ezra, and possibly 1st and 2nd Chronicles. He tells of the events toward the end of the Jewish exile in Babylon, the period from the release of the Jews in 538 B.C. by King Kyros of Persia, and Ezra's reformation in Israel in 458 B.C.

text (MT), which was the basis for most of the OT translations since the 4th century, with few exceptions.

Unfortunate Compilation Becomes Standard

Around 200 A.D. the Christian Copt, Origen of Alexandria, collected a six-fold version of the Old Testament. Since 5 out of the 6 versions were built on the Masoretic version, the compilation was full of mistakes. [19]

Sir Frederick notes, "...Origen's work was not to find the original version of the Septuagint LXX, but to bring it in harmony with the Masoretic Hebrew text which was used at that time, and for that purpose, he made changes in the text with great freedom."

Luckily, Bishop Taulus of Tella in Mesopotamia produced a Syrian translation in 617 A.D. which gave a detailed look at Origin's changes. As a result, the LXX was kept in its original version and still exists today. In most cases the differences between the texts are relatively minor, but the chronologies have some very significant differences. The chronology with a genealogical table of the 21 generations from Adam to Abraham can be found in Genesis 5 and 11. Genesis 5 delineates the patriarchs from Adam to Noah (and the Flood), while Genesis 11 covers the period from the Flood (and Shem) up to Abraham.

Septuagint's Chronology Is Correct

If you compare the Septuagint, the Samaritan Pentateuch, and Josephus' historical writings, they agree in every aspect except in the case of Lamech, where Josephus and the MT agree. The adopted chronology is accepted by the majority. All of the texts are in agreement when it comes to Noah, while the MT also agrees in relation to Jared and Methuselah. Besides this, Genesis 11 agrees completely with the LXX and the SP in its genealogy, while Josephus supports 6 out of the 11. Majority rules here as well. All of the texts agree about Abraham, and the MT also supports Shem.

Therefore the LXX is confirmed by Josephus in Genesis 5 and by the SP in Genesis 11. This proves that the LXX gives a chronological picture that is exactly the same as that which was found in the original source.

Based on this, there is a greater probability that the MT does not agree with the original source when considering Genesis 5 and 11, as quoted by Christ and the Apostles, than the LXX and Josephus.

The Church Fathers' chronologies follow the LXX in Genesis 5 and 11. These agree with the teachings of the Apostles, which must have been based on the scriptures in the original source or the LXX. Actually, the Gospel of Luke includes Kenan in its lists from the period after the Flood, just as the LXX does. This strongly supports the LXX chronology.

The differences between the LXX and the MT are of great importance. In chapter 5, the difference is 600 years. In chapter 11, the difference is more than 700 years. Because the MT went through the double process of changing the Hebrew signs and the later addition of vowels, we must suspect that the MT is the mistaken version.

Footnotes

[15] Nehemiah wrote the Book of Nehemiah (c. 430 B.C.) and was a high Jewish official under King Artaxerxes of Persia. In 445 B.C., as the Persian king's governor, he was given permission to rebuild Jerusalem. He completed his work over the following 13 years and then returned to the royal court in Persia. Nehemiah returned two years later to fight corruption and decline.

[16] *Our Bible and the Ancient Manuscripts*, page 49 (Eyre and Spottiswoode:London).

Footnotes

[17] Sigfried H. Horn, emeritus professor of archeology at Andrews University, Berrien Springs, Michigan, in "Ministry", November 1987: "The Old Testament texts in Antiquity".

[18] Frank Cross in 1953 in *The Bulletin of American Schools of Oriental Research*, No. 132, pp. 15-26.

[19] It was made up of the three Greek versions, which were built on the Masoretic version, as well as the MT in Hebrew, the MT in Greek, and finally the LXX edited by Origen.

It looks like a figure for 100 has disappeared or been systematically omitted in the copying from the Paleo-Hebraic to the MT in these important chapters.[20]

Multiple archeological discoveries confirm the credibility of the Septuagint too. When Joshua died he was buried "at Timnath-serah, which is in the hill country of Ephraim, north of Mount Gaash" (Joshua 24:30). The LXX adds an important remark: "*In that grave where they buried him they placed there the stone knives with which he circumcised the sons of Israel in Gilgal.*"

Stone graves can be found in a cliff face near Joshua's village Kef'r Ishu'a. In 1870 a large number of stone knives were found in one of the graves on the north side of the mountain.[21]

Year of the Flood: 3.537

We have already established that Abraham was born in 2305 B.C. +/- 10 years despite the text used, so we can use this as a starting point and then build up our timeline in a backwards fashion to get to the Flood.

Using the ages of the patriarchs when their specific sons were born according to the Septuagint LXX version, **the Flood** occurred 1232 years before Abraham's birth, in **3537** B.C. And the creation of Adam was then 2256 years earlier, or *5793* B.C.

This is quite in agreement with the understanding of the Ancient Church. Theofilus of Antioch (115-181 A.D.) dates Creation to *5537* B.C., Hippolit mentions *5500* B.C., and Julius Africanus (who died in 240 A.D.) sets it at *5537* B.C. The Annals of Axum establish it to be *5500* B.C., while the Talmudist (Petrus Alliacens) offers a date around *5344* B.C. Arabic documents say *6174* B.C.

Unnecessary Conflict with Archeology

It is remarkable that the Masoretic text, which is the basis for most Bible translations, cannot set the date earlier than 2657 B.C. for the Flood and 4313 B.C. for Creation.

And here is where the biblical digits come – unnecessarily – in conflict with various archeological finds.

For example, in the USA there are bristlecone pines that are up to 4,900 years old. It has been proven that they grow very slowly and are more prone to skip a ring rather than add one. So the general age is probably correct. The oldest of these trees started growing around 2900 B.C.

That means that these trees would have to have survived the Flood if we follow the shorter Masoretic chronology, while the first started growing not just after the Flood in 3537 B.C., but also after the happenings in Babel in c. 3302 B.C. and Peleg's "division of the world" in 3006 B.C.[22]

Even the ancient pines tell us that the Flood took place at an earlier time.

The new revised date for the Flood fits much better with the archeological finds[23] and our knowledge of the Egyptian and Sumerian civilizations, which we can clearly see were AFTER the great deluge.

Footnotes

[20] This also happened in the New Testament. In Acts 27:37, it says that there were 276 people on board Paul's ship when it wrecked in the storm. According to cross-checks, some manuscripts say 76. The figure for 200 has been omitted.

[21] Professor Werner Keller conveys on page 163 of *The Bible as History*

[22] Peleg (which means scattered) was called such "for in his days the earth was divided". Some believe that this refers to the separation of the continents.

[23] But there are still unsolved mysteries. A few archeological finds of humans are set to periods thousands of years before Adam and Eve were created. Here are two possibilities: the dating can be faulty, or another civilization could have existed previously starting with Adam. There are some people that consider the story of Creation in the Bible to be a "re-creation" after a previous period of chaos. (We are ignoring the dating that is not based on carbon-14 tests and are only looking at theories of the age of geological layers or other million-year-theories, which are not proven either.)

If we mix the biblical and the archeological information, the result is the following time-table (with some reservations, of course):

New time-table of pre-historic times

Adam and Eve's creation according to the Bible	c. 5,793 B.C.
Metsamor-culture in Armenia – metalwork, etc.	c. 5,000 B.C.
Signs of the first people in Mesopotamia (now Turkey-Iraq)	c. 5,000 B.C.
Noah's birth according to Gilgamesh in Shuruppak on the Euphrates	c. 4,137 B.C.
Ubaid culture in Mesopotamia (potsherds, temples, knowledge of iron)	c. 3,900 B.C.
Warka culture in Mesopotamia (proliterate period)	c. 3,600 B.C.
The Flood destroys all ancient cultures (3,537-36)	c. 3,537 B.C.
The Tower of Babel and dispersion	c. 3,302 B.C.
Noah dies – he most likely lived in the Ararat Mountains	c. 3,187 B.C.
The earth (continents?) is "separated" (in Peleg's time)	c. 3,006 B.C.
Decreased in size to 1/8 (based on 30,000 C-14 measurements)	c. 2,950-2,450
Sumerian city-states arise in southern Mesopotamia/Iraq	c. 2,900 B.C.
The first Ur Dynasty in southern Mesopotamia	c. 2,750 B.C.
Egypt's 1st dynasty and the beginning of the Egyptian Sothis calendar	c. 2,770 B.C.
Indus civilization blooms in Pakistan and western India	c. 2,500 B.C.
Cooling of the climate measured in three tree rings	c. 2354-45 B.C.
Sargon I (Nimrod?) starts the Acadian kingdom in Mesopotamia	c. 2,340 B.C.
Fall of the Acadian and Egyptian cultures, probably around	c. 2,300 B.C.
The birth of Abraham	c. 2,305 B.C.
Abraham flees from Ur to Karan (after his clash with Nimrod?)	c. 2,250 B.C.
Abraham leaves Karan (Turkey) and travels to Canaan and Egypt	c. 2,230 B.C.
3rd Ur Dynasty in Mesopotamia	c. 2,100 B.C.
Jacob enters Egypt	c. 2,015 B.C.
Moses is born, discovered by princess Meris and raised as a prince	c. 1,665 B.C.
Moses collects materials and writes of the Creation and the Flood	c. 1,600 B.C.
Exodus - Moses leads the Hebrews away from slavery in Egypt	c. 1,585 B.C.
The Hyksos People invade a weak Egypt that doesn't put up a fight	c. 15-1600 B.C.
In the end of the Bronze Age II, the cities of Canaan are destroyed	c. 1,550 B.C.
Joshua leads the Israelites into Canaan – wins cities	c. 1,545 B.C.

Chapter 14

Gilgamesh Visits Noah

Back to the days of Noah. Five generations after Noah, a man by the name of Gilgamesh lived in Iraq.

Thousands of clay tablets have been found in the ancient city of Nineveh by the Tigris River which also tell a long, fascinating story of this Gilgamesh. Gilgamesh was a king in the city Uruk in Sumer in southern Iraq. At one point he visited a sage named Utnapishtim up in the mountains. This wise man was probably old Noah.

This is why the story of Gilgamesh is an exciting piece in our search for the existence of Noah's Ark and where it landed.

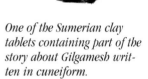

One of the Sumerian clay tablets containing part of the story about Gilgamesh written in cuneiform.

We have here a very, very old source, maybe older than the Bible that also tells us about the Flood and a man that survived it. Even more so, the hero visits this man and hears his story.

The tablets from Nineveh (as well as tablets found other places) have texts written in Sumerian, Akkadian, Babylonian, Assyrian, Hittite, and Hurrian. The account that is normally translated about Gilgamesh is the Akkadian account from c. 700 B.C. with some additions from the other versions in order to fill out some of the holes.

There is a lot of variation in how the account is given, but there is no doubt that the reference is to the same event.

Before and After the Flood

"The Flood was even more deeply rooted in the Babylonian historical consciousness than ours. They split up their past into 'before the flood' and 'after the Flood'; and everything which lay 'before the Flood' was mysterious prehistory" write the two Danish experts, Ulla and Aage Westenholz in the preface to their new 1995 translation of Gilgamesh.[1]

The Sumerian tablets tell about a line of up to 10 kings that reigned before the Flood and a line of kings that reigned afterwards. The Bible also tells about 10 kings or forefathers that were before the Flood.

King in One of the First City-States

In order to place Gilgamesh in a historical context, we are again going to look at both archeological and biblical views. Archeologists are somewhat in agreement that around 3,000 B.C. and after, a number of small city-kingdoms began to pop up in ancient Sumer. At this point there was no assembled kingdom, but some of these cities had created a cooperative union.

One of these city-states was Uruk in southern Iraq. According to the ancient tablets, the fifth king of Uruk after the Flood was Gilgamesh. Even though archeologists and prehistorians date Gilgamesh to be around 2900

Footnotes
[1] Gilgamesh – Enuma Elish. Guder og mennesker i oldtidens Babylon. By Ulla and Aage Westenholz, Carsten Niebuhr Institute at the University of Copenhagen. Spektrum Publishers, 1995.

B.C., Gilgamesh living much later cannot be ruled out. Gilgamesh is first spoken of as the king of Uruk in a source written in 1820 B.C. The Akkadian version, the source most translated, is from the 7th century B.C.

When scientists want to establish a date, they are often walking on shaky ground and have to set their dates based on assumptions of fixed points in time which can later be moved based on new findings. For example – a seal cylinder has been found which is confirmed to be from around 2120 B.C. This cylinder apparently has a scene from Gilgamesh on it. We can thus conclude that Gilgamesh lived before this time. In the story Gilgamesh takes a warning, and we know (or think) that portending was practiced between 2000 and 1850 B.C. He could have lived at this point, but because it is believed that he lived earlier, this portending is assumed to be an addition at this point.

But as mentioned above archeologists and prehistorians assume that Gilgamesh lived around 2900 B.C. According to the old Septuagint version of the Old Testament the Flood can be fixed at around 3537. Noah dies according to this cronology c. 3187. When Gilgamesh visits Noah (called Utnapishtim) while he is still a young hunter with much strength and before he becomes king in Uruk, he has probably not been more than 40 years old. But Gilgamesh's description of Noah as a man who has gained eternal life could lead to the assumption that this happens in the Noah's old age. My guess is that Gilgamesh has come to see him around 3185 and that Gilgamesh himself has lived from c. 3225 and that the city states in Sumer arose a bit earlier than normally assumed. (Some historians actually believe that the cities began to pop up already around 3300 B.C. so here is no big difference of opinion.)

Gilgamesh can very possibly have lived at the time where descendants of Noah's sons and daughters had populated Mesopotamia. He might even have been one of Kam's great-great-grandchildren.[2]

Thousands of Clay Tablets

The clay tablets that tell about Gilgamesh, among other things, were first brought to light in the 19th century through a number of digs completed further north in Nineveh on the Tigris in northern Iraq. Nineveh was the strongest city in the Middle East when the Assyrians ruled in the last century before Christ.

At that time the Assyrian King Sargon II (722-705 B.C.) established a library here in Nineveh made up of burned clay tablets. Under his successor, King Assurbanipal (669-627 B.C.), the library was expanded so that it contained at least 3,000 tablets, which are now broken into 24,000 bits and pieces. Despite the 2,500-3,500 years, the inscriptions on the tablets are relatively well kept because they have lain underground. It is an enormous jigsaw puzzle to put the pieces back together again, but luckily, archeologists are a very patient sort.

The story of Gilgamesh is written in Akkadian and other languages onto 11 clay tablets.

Footnotes

[2] In Mesopotamia there is also evidence of earlier habitations - the Ubaid culture (potsherds, temples, knowledge of iron) c. 3900 B.C. and the Warka culture (the so-called Proliterate period) c. 3600 B.C. If these datings are correct and if the time of the Flood is correct, they have consequently belonged to the culture BEFORE the flooding. Utnapishtim (Noah) actually mentions in the Gilgamesh poem that before the flooding he used to live by Euphrates in the town of Shuruppak. According to the Bible civilization before the flooding dates back to c. 5793 B.C.

[3] Some believe the "firmament in the midst of the waters" spoken of in Genesis 1:6-8 to be a layer of steam in the thermosphere which filtered cosmic radiation out causing humans to age more slowly than after the Flood. Inside of this "bubble" the Earth would be like a greenhouse where people, plants, and animals would have lived longer and grown larger. This theory may also explain the monsters of the past like the dinosaurs and mammoths, which were only found in prehistory.

Only about half of the poem is preserved, but most of the story of Noah can be found though there are many holes in the sentences.

The main characters are King Gilgamesh and his friend, Enkidu, who conquer a supernatural bull. After his friend dies, Gilgamesh, in desperation, seeks out his forefather, Utnapishtim, in order to find the meaning of life. Utnapishtim is described as immortal after having survived a great flood, which very much resembles the biblical Flood. That Noah is considered immortal is not difficult to understand. He came from the generation before the Flood – a generation which lived many more years than later generations[3] - and Noah lived through many of the following generations, those of his descendants.

What Does Gilgamesh Tell Us?

The story about Gilgamesh's meeting with Noah (Utnapishtim) starts on tablet IX and continues on tablets X and XI.

Besides being a magnificent story from a literary point of view, the story of Gilgamesh may give us some relevant information, though wrapped in rhetoric and poetic wording. Here we'll have to do with citing only a few strophes from this very extensive poem.

There are four factors that lead me to believe that we are dealing with more than a mere poem - that the poem is based upon a true story:

1. Gilgamesh can be found named on the list of kings of Uruk as the fifth king in a city that does exist and is located in southern Iraq.

2. Gilgamesh travels through geographical surroundings that could reflect the journey from Sumer to the mountains of Ararat. The entire Anatolian plateau is full of mountains he had to pass.

3. Gilgamesh is surprised by the fact that Utnapishtim is a normal person. Even though the poem is later turned into a fairy-tale like story, the original ingredients can still be found.

Our working theory, therefore, is: Gilgamesh existed, and due to his search for the meaning of life or immortality, he went on a journey to find ancient Noah (Utnapishtim). On the way he comes to the Twin Peaks (Mashu), he sails over a lake (possibly Turkey's largest lake, Lake Van), he sees some mighty anchor stones, and he speaks to Noah. When he comes back again, he tells his story which is later retold and written down by a poet as a

Noah is called Utnapishtim in the Gilgamesh story and came from Shurrupak. His father was Ubara-Tutu. This name is actually found in the list of kings from the ancient city of Shurrupak, known as Fara today, which lies northwest of Uruk. All of this evidence indicates that the Gilgamesh poem is more than just a story ....

dramatic and mythological poem based on the successive, somewhat unrealistic account.

When a person such as me has been in the area where we believe the Ark lies, it makes it very easy to imagine Gilgamesh's journey – now he's there or there, etc.

Tablet IX starts as such in lines 1-8: [4]

> *Over his friend, Enkidu, Gilgamesh cried bitterly, roaming the wilderness.*
> *"I am going to die!—am I not like Enkidu?!*
> *Deep sadness penetrates my core,*
> *I fear death, and now roam the wilderness—*
> *I will set out to the region of Utnapishtim, son of Ubartutu,*
> *and will go with utmost dispatch!*
> *When I arrived at mountain passes at nightfall,'*
> *I saw lions, and I was terrified!*

After this a fight with a pride of lions follows.

Our knowing that Utnapishtim is not just an imaginary figure is based on the naming of his father. And this Ubara-Tutu can be found on the lists of kings from Shurrupak, modern Fara, northwest of Uruk. He is the only king of Kish besides Utnapishtim that is named in the list of kings before the Great Flood.

Footnotes

[4] We will be quoting from an online translation, which can be found at the following address http://www.ancienttexts.org/library/mesopotamian/gilgamesh/
A parenthesis ( ) shows that part of the tablet is missing, while a (word) in parenthesis shows that the translator has inserted a word that is known from another version.

In line 37 Gilgamesh is by Mashu, the "Twin Peaks":

> *The mountain is called Mashu.*
> *Then he reached Mount Mashu,*
> *which daily guards the rising and setting of the Sun,*
> *above which only the dome of the heavens reaches,*
> *and whose flank reaches as far as the Netherworld below,*
> *there were Scorpion-beings watching over its gate.*
> *Trembling terror they inspire, the sight of them is death,*
> *their frightening aura sweeps over the mountains.*
> *At the rising and setting they watch over the Sun.*

These "twin peaks" lead one to think of the mountain with two crests towering above the boat-shaped object – the so-called Yigityatagi, "the cradle of the heroes", which is also called the Wall of Heaven because of its vertical slope and two peaks.

There is also a passageway on the road from Erzurum to Dogubayazit between two tall mountainsides. During the Urartu kingdom's reign many a battle was fought here when their enemies had to travel through this passageway. But none of these mountains are as extreme as the description of the Twin Peaks. It is more likely that Gilgamesh was describing Big and

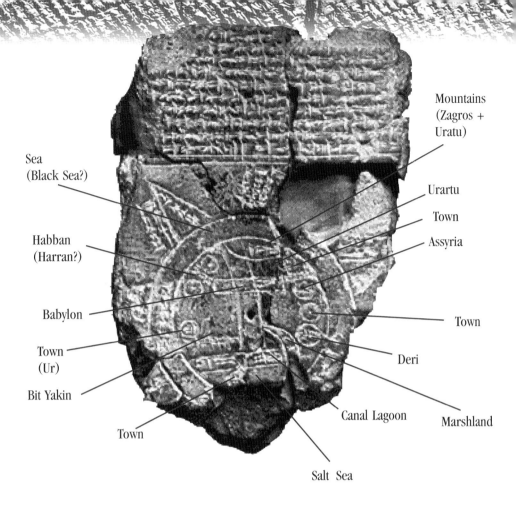

Mountains
(Zagros +
Uratu)

Sea
(Black Sea?)

Urartu

Town

Habban
(Harran?)

Assyria

Babylon

Town

Town
(Ur)

Deri

Bit Yakin

Canal Lagoon

Marshland

Town

Salt Sea

Little Ararat, which are twin peaks connected by a saddle between them.

Naturally, Gilgamesh didn't wander *through* the mountains – there were no tunnels – but rather *between* them. Instead of walking around the 12-mile wide mountain, he scaled it. And that could have taken a number of days and nights, which coincides with the poem, which tells us that he can see nothing in the dark as he journeys.

However, we cannot be sure that Big and Little Ararat actually existed at that time. As we know, they are volcanic mountains and dr. Bayraktutan believes that they have come into existence at a later time. So let us try to consider one of the two first possibilities: the steep mountain Yigityatagi.

As already mentioned some English translations use the original name of *Mashu* instead of Twin Peaks and as it appears from the chapter about the mysterious place names, the names of *Mashur* and *Masher* are found near the boat-shaped object.

Masher means Judgment Day. - "Mashur" means "risen". And it is worth noting that for some inscrutable reasons the places had these names long before the earthquake in 1948.[5]

As mentioned, Yigityatagi / Masher is not a very high mountain today with crests towering the "foundations of Heaven". But it still has two (twin)

A map of the world from the 7th century B.C. describing the Babylonians' understanding of themselves in the world with the two rivers Euphrates and Tigris and oceans surrounding the country in a circle – or the earth as a circular globe? The mountains and Urartu are marked to the north. The map, drawn on a clay tablet, is now in the British Museum.

peaks. And if you stand at the foot of the mountain, you may feel that it is towering into heaven.

If we stick to my theory that Gilgamesh is real and has returned to Sumer with his account, how would he then descibe Mashu to people living in the flat Sumer? Maybe as: "Mashu was a mountain towering straight into heaven!"

When you have seen the steep crest you will understand what he means, otherwise you will think that he is referring to an extremely high mountain. This is the way -I think - that the myth about Mashu, the Twin Peaks, arose.

The Valley of Paradise - or of the Eight

Finally Gilgamesh reaches a lush garden full of gemstones. In Sumerian mythology the Noah figure found himself in a paradisical location known as Dilmun. (A place that has later been placed to some island in the Golf which is a misunderstanding).

I believe Gilgamesh has been telling about the "Valley of the Eight" where, according to the local tradition, Noah lived and grew his grapes after the flood. The beautiful valley must have been like an oasis to Gilgamesh after a challenging trek through the mountains and in the early morning after the terrible night it may have shone like crystals to the exhausted Gilgamesh. Here he meets a tavern keeper, Siduri, whom after scaring with his jaded appearance he converses with in tablet X.

The Stone Things?

He asks for directions, and she leads him to Urshanabi, Utnapishtim's ferry keeper who has "the stone things" (line 88). Possibly a reference to the anchor stones Gilgamesh told of?

Shortly afterwards Gilgamesh gets in a fight with the ferryman and ends up breaking the stone things. From line 156:

> Urshanabi spoke to Gilgamesh, saying:
> "It is your hands, Gilgamesh, that prevent the crossing!
> You have smashed the stone things,' you have pulled out
> their retaining ropes (?).
> 'The stone things' have been smashed, their retaining ropes
> (!) pulled out!

As it appears from the chapter about "The Valley of the Eight", 13 such anchor stones have been found here, all with a hole at the top through which you tied a rope and used them for manoeuvring the ships. If these are not the anchor stones referred to by the ferryman, what else could it be? Instead Gilgamesh is now sent into the wood to debark poles. (300 for good measure ....!)

Which Sea?

The question is where did this "sea" lie? It could, of course, be the

Black Sea northwest of Ararat, but it is sort of too much off course. It is more likely to be Lake Van, south of it, which is the biggest lake in Turkey. Gilgamesh has probably reached this lake on his way from Sumer to Ararat. (It is, of course, before the Twin Peaks, but the poet may have reversed the order of events.) In the poem we hear about the "Dead Sea" - and Van Lake is actually a salt-water lake without outlet - a dead sea.

Another explanation would be that the valley between the mountains was not drained like now. Dr. Bayraktutan believes to have geological signs showing that the water has reached as high as 1500 mtrs. in the area around Dogubayazit and the Ark. Today only a river flows through the valley, but the strata of earth show signs that there used to be much more water in the area before.

Through Pathless Mountains

Gilgamesh tells of his grief and search for eternal life repeating that he went through pathless mountains - quite different from the flat Sumer he knows. From line 249:

> *Gilgamesh spoke to Utanapishtim, saying:*
> *"That is why (?) I must go on,*
> *to see Utanapishtim whom they call 'The Faraway.'"*
> *I went circling through all the mountains,*
> *I traversed treacherous mountains, and crossed all the*
> *seas— that is why (!) sweet sleep has not mellowed my face,*
> *through sleepless striving I am strained,*
> *my muscles are filled with pain.*

Afterwards Utnapishtim tells him not to worry himself for all shall die and no one knows when. From line 298:

> *You have toiled without cease, and what have you got!*
> *Through toil you wear yourself out,*
> *you fill your body with grief,*
> *your long lifetime you are bringing near*
> *(to a premature end)!*
> *Mankind, whose offshoot is snapped off like a reed in a*
> *canebreak, the fine youth and lovely girl ... death.*

Just a Man

On tablet XI the conversation continues. From line 1:

> *Gilgamesh spoke to Utanapishtim, the Faraway:*
> *"I have been looking at you,*
> *but your appearance is not strange—you are like me!*
> *You yourself are not different—you are like me!*
> *My mind was resolved to fight with you,*

Footnotes
[5] According to Fasold, Ark-Update May - June 1991.

(but instead?) my arm lies useless over you.
Tell me, how is it that you stand in the Assembly of the Gods,
and have found life!"

Utnapishtim Tells the Story of the Flood

Utanapishtim spoke to Gilgamesh, saying:

"I will reveal to you, Gilgamesh, a thing that is hidden,
a secret of the gods I will tell you!
Shuruppak, a city that you surely know,
situated on the banks of the Euphrates,
that city was very old, and there were gods inside it.
The hearts of the Great Gods moved them to inflict the Flood.
Their Father Anu uttered the oath (of secrecy),
Valiant Enlil was their Adviser,
Ninurta was their Chamberlain,
Ennugi was their Minister of Canals.
Ea, the Clever Prince(?), was under oath with them
so he repeated their talk to the reed house:
'Reed house, reed house! Wall, wall!
O man of Shuruppak, son of Ubartutu:
Tear down the house and build a boat!
Abandon wealth and seek living beings!
Spurn possessions and keep alive living beings!
Make all living beings go up into the boat.
The boat which you are to build,
its dimensions must measure equal to each other:
its length must correspond to its width.
Roof it over like the Apsu.

From this explanation one would think that the boat should be as broad as it is long - but what is said is that the sides should *correspond* to each other. And that is something quite different. The sailor and Ark hunter David Fasold read this as an instruction to build the boat according to the universal rules for boat building which he afterwards explains in full.[6]

I understood and spoke to my lord, Ea:
'My lord, thus is the command which you have uttered
I will heed and will do it.
But what shall I answer the city, the populace, and the Elders!'
Ea spoke, commanding me, his servant:
'You, well then, this is what you must say to them:
"It appears that Enlil is rejecting me
so I cannot reside in your city (?),
nor set foot on Enlil's earth.

Footnotes
[6] David Fasold: The Ark of Noah, chapter 5.

I will go down to the Apsu to live with my lord, Ea,
and upon you he will rain down abundance,
a profusion of fowl, myriad(!) fishes.
He will bring to you a harvest of wealth,
in the morning he will let loaves of bread shower down,
and in the evening a rain of wheat!"'
Just as dawn began to glow
the land assembled around me-
the carpenter carried his hatchet,
the reed worker carried his (flattening) stone,
... the men ...
The child carried the pitch,
the weak brought whatever else was needed.
On the fifth day I laid out her exterior.
It was a field in area,
its walls were each 10 times 12 cubits in height,
the sides of its top were of equal length,
10 times 12 cubits each.

The field in area mentioned as the size of the deck is one IKU - the old Babylonian area unit. Approximately equaling the deck of the boat-shaped object, according to Fasold.

I laid out its (interior) structure and drew a pic-
ture of it (?).
I provided it with six decks,
thus dividing it into seven (levels).
The inside of it I divided into nine (compart-
ments).

Here Fasold points out that these decks have a resemblance to the big pyramid in Babylon where the measurements of the different levels mysteriously enough correspond to specific geographical places on the earth like e.g. Stonehenge. So maybe there is a connection between the harmonious measurements of the Ark and the pyramids. Noah / Utnapishtim continues:

I drove plugs (to keep out) water in its middle part.
I saw to the punting poles and laid in what was neces-
sary.
Three times 3,600 (units) of raw bitumen I poured into the
bitumen kiln,
three times 3,600 (units of) pitch ...into it,
there were three times 3,600 porters of casks who carried (veg-
etable) oil,
apart from the 3,600 (units of) oil which they consumed (!)

*and two times 3,600 (units of) oil which the boatman
stored away.*

Also in this Sumerian poem is mentioned that the Ark is rubbed with
bitumen and asphalt, cf. the information in the Bible.

*I butchered oxen for the meat(!),
and day upon day I slaughtered sheep.
I gave the workmen(?) ale, beer, oil, and wine, as if it were
river water,
so they could make a party like the New Year's Festival.
... and I set my hand to the oiling(!).
The boat was finished by sunset.
The launching was very difficult.
They had to keep carrying a runway of poles front to back,
until two-thirds of it had gone into the water(?).
Whatever I had I loaded on it:
whatever silver I had I loaded on it,
whatever gold I had I loaded on it.
All the living beings that I had I loaded on it,
I had all my kith and kin go up into the boat,
all the beasts and animals of the field
and the craftsmen I had go up.*

*Shamash had set a stated time:
'In the morning I will let loaves of bread shower down,
and in the evening a rain of wheat!
Go inside the boat, seal the entry!'
That stated time had arrived.
In the morning he let loaves of bread shower down,
and in the evening a rain of wheat.
I watched the appearance of the weather—
the weather was frightful to behold!
I went into the boat and sealed the entry.
For the caulking of the boat, to Puzuramurri, the boatman,
I gave the palace together with its contents.
Just as dawn began to glow
there arose from the horizon a black cloud.
Adad rumbled inside of it,
before him went Shullat and Hanish,
heralds going over mountain and land.
Erragal pulled out the mooring poles,
forth went Ninurta and made the dikes overflow.
The Anunnaki lifted up the torches,
setting the land ablaze with their flare.
Stunned shock over Adad's deeds overtook the heavens,*

and turned to blackness all that had been light.
The... land shattered like a... pot.

The South Wind

All day long the South Wind blew ...,
blowing fast, submerging the mountain in water,
overwhelming the people like an attack.

Again a special point worth noticing. In the first line it reads: "All day long the South Wind blew" - and if Noah's boat was to drift from Shuruppak in Iraq to the Mountains of Ararat in the north, it had to blow from the south. Utnapishtim continues:

No one could see his fellow,
they could not recognize each other in the tor-
rent.
The gods were frightened by the Flood,
and retreated, ascending to the heaven of Anu.
The gods were cowering like dogs,
crouching by the outer wall.
Ishtar shrieked like a woman in childbirth,
the sweet-voiced Mistress of the Gods wailed:
'The olden days have alas turned to clay,
because I said evil things in the Assembly of the Gods!
How could I say evil things in the Assembly of the Gods,
ordering a catastrophe to destroy my people!!
No sooner have I given birth to my dear people
than they fill the sea like so many fish!'
The gods—those of the Anunnaki—were weeping with her,
the gods humbly sat weeping, sobbing with grief(?),
their lips burning, parched with thirst.
Six days and seven nights
came the wind and flood, the storm flattening the land.
When the seventh day arrived, the storm was pounding,
the flood was a war—struggling with itself like a woman
writhing (in labor).

The sea calmed, fell still,
the whirlwind (and) flood stopped up.
I looked around all day long—quiet had set in
and all the human beings had turned to clay!
The terrain was as flat as a roof.

The Boat Grounds on Nisir

I opened a vent and fresh air (daylight!)
fell upon the side of my nose.

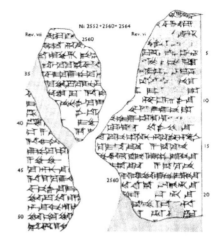

The epic poem of Gilgamesh is found on several cunei-form tablets where the cuneiform script has been pressed into the wet clay and the tablets were afterwards dried and burnt. Due to missing pieces and cracks in the tablets, people deciphering the inscriptions often have to guess at the words.

I fell to my knees and sat weeping,
tears streaming down the side of my nose.
I looked around for coastlines in the expanse of the sea,
and at twelve leagues there emerged a region (of land).
On Mt. Nimush the boat lodged firm,
Mt. Nimush held the boat, allowing no sway.
One day and a second Mt. Nimush held the boat,
allowing no sway.
A third day, a fourth, Mt. Nimush held the boat,
allowing no sway.
A fifth day, a sixth, Mt. Nimush held the boat,
allowing no sway.

Has Nisir Been Found?

Utnapishtim tells Gilgamesh that the Ark grounded on Nimush. Previously this has been read as Nisir or Mount Nisir, now it is translated to *Nimush*. But the word KUR, meaning mountain, in line 140 in tablet XI, "*a-na KUR ni-ir i-te-mid GIŠ eleppu*" doesn't mean mountain in Sumerian but rather hill or countryside or area.

Robert M. Best, who wrote a book in which he claims the story of the Ark to be nothing more than a localized flood of the Euphrates River[7], translates this line to read "in country Nisir grounded wooden boat." And he goes even further to argue that the Ark landed on a sandbank or an elevated surface! It is quite drastic when one changes a text to fit one's own ideas. The Nisir Gilgamesh talks about, however, is not necessarily a tall mountain but a hill, a little mountain, or just an area called Nisir.

This is *very* interesting, because present day Kurdish villagers in Uzengili, the closest neighbors to the boat-shaped object, say that they renamed their village from Nisir[8] to Uzengili after the object appeared in 1948. It was originally called Sar or Nasar or Nisir.[9] This means "to sacrifice" or "to show". Uzengili can be translated as "a promise".

As you see, here are several clues which we'll return to in the chapter about mysterious place names.

The Dove and the Raven

Utnaphisthim continues:

When a seventh day arrived
I sent forth a dove and released it.
The dove went off, but came back to me;
no perch was visible so it circled back to me.
I sent forth a swallow and released it.
The swallow went off, but came back to me;
no perch was visible so it circled back to me.

Footnotes

[7] Robert M. Best, Noah's Ark and the Ziusudra Epic, Sumerian Origins of the Flood Myth. Enlil Press.

[8] David Fasold's interview with a (+/-) 60 year old Kurd named Reshit from Uzengili, 1984.

[9] As found on old maps (David Fasold, The Discovery of Noah's Ark. 1990, pp. 108-114.)

[10] According to Fasold's theory these "Seven Sages" may be the seven ancestors in Kain's tribe who were exterminated together with the Flood. As is well known Cain was the first murderer - he killed his brother Abel and was exiled to the country called Nod - east of Eden.

I sent forth a raven and released it.
The raven went off, and saw the waters slither back.
It eats, it scratches, it bobs, but does not circle back to me.
Then I sent out everything in all directions and sacrificed
(a sheep).
I offered incense in front of the mountain-ziggurat.
Seven and seven cult vessels I put in place,
and (into the fire) underneath (or: into their bowls)
I poured reeds, cedar, and myrtle.
The gods smelled the savor,
the gods smelled the sweet savor,
and collected like flies over a (sheep) sacrifice.

After this a discussion breaks out among the gods where Enlil is requested never to send a flood of such magnitude again. Enlil blesses Utnapishtim and turns him into a half-god.

Utnapishtim then gives Gilgamesh a test: he is not to sleep for 7 days and 6 nights. He fails. The epic ends with Gilgamesh taking a bath and being sent home. He is given a plant that will give him eternal life, but a snake eats it on the journey home - a clear parallel to the serpent in the Garden of Eden.

At long last he comes to his hometown Uruk, which, it is noted, was established by the "Seven Sages" while he himself has reinforced the walls.[10] Uruk - or Erek as it is called in the Bible - may very well be a rebuilt town from before the flood. According to Berosus the first generations after the flood went back to the towns in Iraq that had been buried to rebuild them.

The Same Event

Despite the religious context, in Utnapishtim's account we find the same events as those in the biblical narrative of Noah.

1. The gods are/ God is angered by evil.
2. Both Utnapishtim and Noah are warned of impending disaster.
3. Both Utnapishtim and Noah are to build a boat to save life on earth.
4. The boat consists of numerous levels and is caulked with pitch.
5. The boat is lodged on a mountain.
6. Both Utnapishtim and Noah open a hatch.
7. Both Utnapishtim and Noah send out a dove and a raven.
8. Both make sacrifices to God/the gods.

Regardless of the differences, there can be no doubt that these stories are referring to the same incident.

Are Atrahasis and Ziusudra Older?

Even older accounts can be found. In Akkadian, the main character is named Atrahasis (the extra wise). Even further back, we find the Sumerian narrative of Ziusudra. The original version has been lost, but copies that were written down later still exist.

It is up for debate whether the Bible's or the Sumerian-Akkadian account is older. As far as we known, Genesis was written after the first clay tablets were used, but this is not decisive. Before both versions there were long *oral* traditions.

The story Moses tells, however, is more objective and precise. It doesn't give a picture of the supernatural in detail but only mentions God as the one behind it all. Moses, as an Egyptian prince, most likely had access to the libraries of Pharaoh and the wise men as well as Hebraic oral tradition.

What's important is not which was written down first, but rather that they *confirm* each other. Various phrases are so identical that there can be no doubt that they are talking about the same flood. When this story is found in the first Mesopotamian civilizations – and most other ancient civilizations, for that matter – it suggests that we're probably not talking about a number of local floods occurring at the same time, but a common catastrophe.

The story of the Flood is an inheritance the various people groups took with them when they spread out from the Mountains of Ararat and the plain of Sinear to all over the world. Or maybe more correctly: All over the oceans.

The Bible is not the only source that talks about this kind of populating (in connection with the Tower of Babel). In chapter 5 we saw that the linguists Thomas V. Gamkrelidze and V.V. Ivanovs had traced all the Indo-European languages back to their starting point in Armenia - i.e. back to the Mountains of Urartu. To the place where Gilgamesh probably found Utnapishtim - and the purpose of his life.

Chapter 15

Berosus Confirms

One of the most exciting of the ancient sources is the Chaldean astrologist Berosus, who lived in Babylon and later moved to Greece. Unfortunately, none of Berosus's original works exist today. Berosus's works are only known from quotations and other philosophers' and historians' books.[1] Therefore, one could fear that much has been lost through translation and citation.

When we talk about biblical texts, we have thousands of copies upon which to build our knowledge, and the Babylonian tablets are well kept at the British Museum.

Not so with Berosus. We have to depend on quotes of quotes…

Berosus's lost works were cited in the following generation by a Grecian man named Polyhistor (105-35 B.C.),[2] whose works have unfortunately been lost as well. But his citations of Berosus are quoted again by the Jew, Josephus (37-100 A.D.),[3] a Grecian, Athenaeus (200 A.D.)[4], the Coptic bishop, Clement of Alexandria (150-215 A.D.),[5] and another Grecian, Abydenus [6] (4th century A.D.).

Abydenus's manuscript has also been lost, but he is referred to by the Bishop of Caesarea, Eusebius (264-338 e. Kr.),[7] and the Byzantine monk and historian, Syncellus (9th century A.D.),[8] who also cites some of the early sources which came after Berosus.

It would not be wrong to say that the possibility for mistranslation exists. Despite this fact, Berosus is known as an important historical, though indirectly so, source of prehistory – and Noah's Ark.

The reason that such importance was put on Berosus is that until the clay tablets were found in Mesopotamia in the 19th century, Berosus was almost the only source other than the Bible that we had about life in Babylon.

Who Was He?

Berosus lived in Babylon when the Greeks conquered Persia in 330 B.C. under Alexander the Great. He was probably born around 350 B.C.

The Persians had reigned in Babylon for nearly 200 years, c. 539-330 B.C. The Persian Empire included Egypt, Palestine, and Assyria as well as other areas. And a great deal of the Empire's knowledge and common history were gathered in Babylon. For a man like Berosus who studied all of this information, it must have been like living in the Library of Congress.

Unfortunately, Alexander the Great destroyed much of the cultural treasures of this society when taking over the Empire.

When in Haran, Rebecca, Rachel, and Leah's city in southeast Turkey, we saw the ruins of the university which was destroyed by the Greeks - the university which possibly dated back to Abraham's time, considered the first in the world. Haran plays a role in occult literature.

Footnotes
[1] Berosus is quoted by the following people, among others:

[2] **Alexander Polyhistor** (c.105 - 35 f.Kr.) a Greek philosopher, geographer, and historian. Originally he was a slave in Rome, later promoted to citizen. His works have been lost, but he is quoted by Eusebius, Syncellus, Josephus, Atheneus, and Clement of Alexandria.

[3] **Flavius Josephus**, a Jewish priest and historian (37-100 A.D.). Quoted Alexander Polyhistor.

[4] **Athenaeus** (200 A.D.) Greek grammatician and author. Quoted Alexander Polyhistor.

[5] **Clement** (150 -215 A.D.) Bishop of Alexandria. Quoted Alexander Polyhistor.

[6] **Abydenus**, a disciple of Aristotle, the Greek philosopher and scientist who lived in the 4th century. His manuscript has been lost, but he is quoted by Eusebius and Syncellus.

[7] **Eusebius Pamphilius** (264 - 338 A.D.) Bishop of Caesarea. Quotes Abydenus, Apollodorus, and Alexander Polyhistor.

[8] **Syncellus** (early 9th century A.D.) Byzantine monk and scribe known as "George Syncellus". Quoted Abydenus, Apollodorus, and Alexander Polyhistor.

Berosus Moves to Kos

Berosus left Babylon when the Greeks sacked the city. He was possibly taken there as a prisoner. Back then, the most qualified or best trained citizens were taken captives and used to work in their captors' capital.

Whether voluntarily or not, Berosus ended up on the Greek island of Kos where he built an observatory for astronomy as well as a school. Due to his great knowledge he taught in Athens where a copper statue with a gold-plated tongue – a credit to his speaking abilities - has been erected in his honor.

Berosus wrote three books around 290 B.C. Unfortunately the originals have been lost, but they have been cited in so many other books, we know what they were about.

Book 1 described Babylon, the story of Creation, and "the fish man", Oannes, who taught arts and sciences.

Book 2 and 3 were written about the 10 kings[9] before the Flood, the story of the Great Flood, a list of Chaldean and Arabic kings, as well as the history of Assyria, Babylon, and Persia.

On top of these, other works describing Berosus have been found. They are often called pseudo-Berosus, because experts doubt their authenticity.[10] In these works, details that didn't exist in Berosus's work, such as one of Noah's names being Arsa and cities being named after him can be found.

The History of the Chaldeans

In his writings, Babylonica describes Berosus's world before and after the Flood based on ancient sources from the Temple of Bel in Babylon. The original inhabitants of Babylon were the Chaldeans. Their name comes from a group of celestial gods they worshiped called "Kalda".

Some scientists believe that the Chaldeans originated from eastern Turkey because evidence of Kaldese practices have been found in this area around Lake Van, not far from the Ark's supposed residence. The Chaldeans were direct descendants of Arphaxad, who was born only two years after the Flood according to Josephus (the Jewish historian who put together the history of the Jews for the Romans at the same time Jesus lived).

Arphaxad was together with Elam, Assur, Lud, and Aram, all of whom were sons of Shem as well as Noah's grandchildren.[11] These people were the namesakes of various nations, for example Assur was father to the Assyrians and Aram was father to the Armenians - whose language later became the language of trade in the Middle East. (Jesus spoke Aramaic).

The Jews also consider Arphaxad as one of their forefathers, because he was grandfather to Eber (father to the Hebrews).

Berosus's Famous Clay Tablets

It is obvious that Berosus writes his story based on written sources; clay tablets existed when the ancient Sumerian work was written. Berosus's writings of the pre-Flood period also include a number of fairy-tale like

Footnotes

[9] In Genesis 5 Moses gives us a list of the ten kings – the patriarchs – before the Flood.

[10] These were made public in 1498 by a Dominican priest named Giovanni Nanni, from Viterbo, which is north of Rome. He was also known as Annius of Viterbo. He also publicized fragments of Manetho, an Egyptian historian, who was a contemporary of Berossus. His collected works, along with his commentary, was called Antiquities. Six years after Giovanni's death, Petrus Crinitus claimed that they were false. The pope then seized all of the manuscripts and hid them in the Vatican.

[11] According to Genesis 10:22–23.

[12] According to some of the ancient writings, Nabonid was Babylon's last king and father to Belshazzar, who ruled Babylon together with him in the last part of his reign. This is the same King Belshazzar the Book of Daniel speaks of in chapter 5, explaining how in a drunken orgy he sipped from the holy vessels of gold and silver taken from the temple in Jerusalem. Afterwards he sees a hand write on the wall, "mené, mené, teqél, peres". Daniel interpreted it as such: "mene, God has numbered the days of your kingdom and brought it to an end; tekel, you have been weighed on the scales and found wanting; peres, your kingdom is divided and given to the Medes and Persians." (Dan. 5:26-28). The same evening the Persians came and Belshazzar was killed.

stories about a fish-man to whom he gives the Greek name, Oanes.

But once in a while there are interesting coincidences between this account and the one from the Bible. An example: the presence of 10 kings before the Flood is equivalent to the patriarchs of the Bible, of which Noah was number 10. Their names, of course, are different because the names at that time had meaning and therefore changed according to the language one spoke. Noah means "to be of solace". In English he could have been called *Comforter*, in French *Consolation*. Besides that, a name changed its meaning depending on the place of reference. For example, Alexander was hardly called "the Great" by his enemies, maybe more like "the Gruesome".

Berosus's Noah was named *Ziusudra* (or in Greek *Xi-suthros*) which means "he who found life". Utna-pishtim, the name used for the Noahic figure in Accadian, one of the ancient languages from Mesopotamia, has the same meaning.

The Sumerians and Babylonians called Noah *Atra-hasis*, that is "the especially wise one".

Wisdom Is Buried

Even though Berosus follows the story from the clay tablets, he also adds some things that can't be found on the tablets. Namely, the Sumerian Noah, Xisuthros, was told before the Flood to bury his tablets in Sippar, which is located outside of present-day Baghdad. Xisuthros was also raptured to heaven after the Ark was stranded, and he more or less heard a voice from heaven telling him to travel to Babylon and remain there and dig up the tablets.

One could easily accuse Berosus of claiming his own people, the Chaldeans, to be better than the Greeks based on their direct descent from the Great Forefather. But Berosus could also just be referring to the Babylonian dig in Sippar which took place under the Aramaic king, Nabonid[12] (555 B.C.) in order to find the ancient writings.[13]

Berosus also has a set date for the Flood, something that is not found in the ancient tablets, but he gives no year.

Berosus's Text [14]

"Kronos[15] revealed himself to him (Xisuthros) in a dream and said, 'mankind shall be destroyed by a great flood on the fifteenth day in the month of Daisios.'[16] He (Kronos) commanded that he should bury all of the ancient, middle, and final (that is, all) writings and lay them in the city of Si[s]parenes (=Sippar[17]), the Sun City, and he is to build a ship and go onboard with his relations and close friends. He is to bring food and drink and load it with birds and beasts. And when he had finished this, he was to set sail.

"He asked to where he should sail and he (Kronos) answered, 'to the gods to pray that it may be well for mankind.' He obeyed and built a ship five laths long and two laths wide. He did all which he was commanded and brought his wife, children and close friends with him into the ship."

Footnotes

[13] According to Komoróczy (1973) pp. 134-….

[14] Translated to English from the Danish version by Mogens Weitemeyer, *Herodots og Berossos beskrivelæse af Babylonien*, Published by Museum Tusculanums Forlag, The University of Copenhagen, 1995, ISBN 87 7289 356 7. This version is built on a collection of the safest/earliest sources. The first portion is from Synkellos's Byzantine edition from the 9th century, but in Eusebios's Armenian translations from the 4th century, the measurements of the Ark are given to be the length of 15 shots of an arrow and the width of 2.

[15] The Greek name from the Babylonian god Ea, the same as the Sumerian Enki, also known as the Lord of Eridu (Eden).

[16] Daisios is a Macedonian month. The date is equivalent with the 11th of either May or June.

[17] Ancient city near present day Baghdad.

The Birds Are Released

"When the Flood took place and stopped again, Xisuthros released a few birds. They found neither food nor place to rest and thus returned to the ship. After a few days Xisuthros released the birds again; these came back to the ship with food and had clay on them. When he released them for the third time, they did not come back to the ship. Xisuthros understood that the earth was not visible. He loosened a part of the joint of the ship and saw that the ship had landed on a mountain; he along with his wife and daughter and the captain on the ship got out, fell to the ground on their knees, and built an Altar and offered to the gods. Together with those who went out from the ship, he disappeared."

The Bible contains the same elements in Genesis, chapter 8: the release of a bird (verses 6-12), the removing of the roof of the ship (verse 13), and the sacrifice of thanksgiving at the altar (verse 20).

Xisuthros Just Disappears

After this comes Berosus's addition of the disappearance of Xisu-thros. This is not in agreement with The Epic Poem of Gilgamesh where Gilgamesh seeks out Xisuthros, who lives together with his wife and looks like a normal man.

"When Xisuthros and his companion did not come back, those that had waited in the ship disembarked in order to look for him and yelled out his name. Xisuthros was nowhere to be seen, but a voice came from the sky commanding them to be god-fearing, for he had been taken away to dwell with the gods and his wife and daughter and the captain of the ship shared in the honor.

"And he said they were to go back to Babylon, and he commanded them to take the writings from Sipparos and give them to mankind; He also said that they found themselves in the land of Armenia. When they had heard this, they made offerings to the gods and walked to Babylon."

Where Are We?

It's interesting that Berosus confirms that the Babylonians also came from Armenia, from which they wandered by foot. The people are told that "they found themselves in the land of Armenia", but at the same time we are told that they originally came from Babylon, which they now have to go *back to.*

"The ship landed in the middle of Armenia in the mountains of the Kordyai (Kurds), and some scraped asphalt off of the ship and took it with them to use as amulets."

This "*asphalt*" is the Berossian equivalent of the more precise instructions found in the Bible. There Noah is told to cover both sides of the ship in pitch to make it water-proof.

"After they came to Babylon and unburied the written pieces from Si[s]paros and while they established many cities and built temples, they rebuilt Babylon."

Footnotes

[18] Myths from Mesopotamia: Creation, the Flood, Gilgamesh, and Others (Oxford World's Classics) by Stephanie Dalley. Berossos and Manetho, Introduced and Translated: Native Traditions in Ancient Mesopotamia and Egypt, by Gerald P. Verbrugghe.

[19] Gilgamesh speaks of an IKU, which equals the measurements found in the Bible.

[20] Most of this information comes from Jonathan Gray's book, *The Ark Conspiracy*.

Babylon (or Sippar), according to Berosus, had existed before the Flood, and it is from here that the survivors originally came. Berosus does not confirm the modern criticism of the Bible either, which is found in the form of a theory that the Flood was only a local occurrence in which the Euphrates River flooded. If this were the case, the Ark would not have landed in the mountains in Armenia, over a thousand kilometers away.

Astronomical Numbers – or a Mistranslation?

Berosus' numbers are completely exaggerated. If they are true, then there were 432,000 years from Creation to the Flood – a time period in which only 10 kings reigned… There is probably a mistake in the translation, just as when Berosus or the clay tablets give other numbers.

One of the world's leading experts in clay tablets, Professor Stephanie Dalley of Oxford, England has looked at the Babylonian numbers, and she thinks that these 432,000 years should be divided by 5. This would give 86,400 weeks, which is precisely the same at the Bible's 1,656 years from Creation to the Flood.[18]

Berosus's numbers should not be taken for their worth when talking about the Ark either. Berosus writes that the Ark was 5 laths long and 2 wide. This is the equivalent of 960 x 384 meters (3,150 x 1,260 feet). An American Football field is only 360 ft. long (including end zones) and 160 ft. wide. That means that according to Berosus's measurements, there was enough room for almost 70 entire football fields on the deck of the Ark alone! This is about 80 times as big as the statistics Moses and Gilgamesh give.[19]

Was He Telling Where They Were?

David Fasold, one of the pioneers in Ark-research, had a background as an officer in the Marines and had been a treasure hunter on the bottom of the ocean. Fasold's knowledge of ancient navigation helped him to discover an incredible coincidence. The length of the Ark, when converted to degree minutes, is equal to the distance from the grave of King Darius. If one knew the length of the Ark, one could calculate its exact location!

It sounds too good to be true, so let us review the evidence and afterwards let the intelligent reader make his or her own decision as to whether this is possible or not.[20]

Fasold got the idea that the measurement of 5 x 2 laths was possibly a reference to degrees rather than the Ark's size. That instead of laths, they were to be used as a proportion. Berosus could have been alluding to the Egyptian measurement (a so-called mr) which was used in both navigation and pyramid building.

The mighty Persian Empire (c. 490 B.C.) stretched out from Libya to India. Just a few centuries later, at the time of Berosus, it was conquered by a new empire, the Greek one.

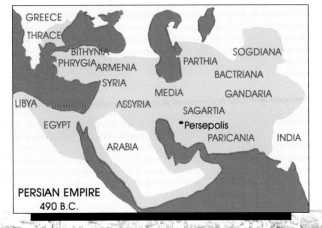

GREECE
THRACE
BITHYNIA
PHRYGIA ARMENIA
SYRIA
LIBYA
ASSYRIA
EGYPT
ARABIA
MEDIA
PARTHIA
SOGDIANA
BACTRIANA
GANDARIA
SAGARTIA
•Persepolis
PARICANIA   INDIA

PERSIAN EMPIRE
490 B.C.

The instrument makes a triangle with a right angle (90 degrees) and an acute angle of 36 degrees. The proportion being 5 x 2.

The Center of the World Was the Great Pyramid

Both the Persians and the ancient Egyptians knew how to calculate both latitude and longitude. They knew that the world was round, and they divided it into 360 degrees (something the Europeans didn't discover until the Middle Ages).

The Egyptians considered themselves, naturally, the center of the universe, and they also placed the geographic center of the world just outside of Cairo, where they constructed the Great Pyramid of Cheops. This was not only a form of self-centeredness, because if one divides the world into four equals parts with the Pyramid of Cheops at the center, each quarter withholds an equal amount of continental mass. So they could rightfully say that this was the center of the world.

The Center of the World is Moved to Persepolis

When the Persians established their world empire and conquered the Egyptians in 525 B.C., this knowledge was also obtained. But they had no intentions of letting the center of the world stay in a foreign country, so they simply moved the center of the world to Persia! To be a bit more specific, it was moved to a location just west of Persepolis.

From this point on, a great monument of King Darius[21] marked this location as the geographic center of the world. Based on the position of the sun and stars, the Persians and all of their subjects on land and sea could determine their location anywhere on the earth in relation to this common point of origin.

Today we use Greenwich in England as the center of the world, or at least as the meridian from which lines of latitude are determined. For longitude we use the Equator as a starting point.

Both the Egyptian and the Persian geographic centers lay on the same latitude, 30 degrees north. (30 degrees north of the Equator.)

The new center according to Persia was simply moved eastwards. It was located at 52 degrees 50 minutes east (of Greenwich).

The Point of Intersection?

Fasold assumed that Berosus's dimensions of 2 x 5 referred to the navigation triangle and that by using this instrument, one could find the exact location of the Ark. Fasold unfolded the map and drew an acute angle of 36 degrees based on the meridian in Persepolis, just as the people of Berosus's time would have done.

He assumed that the Ark lay north of Persepolis because the ancient sources name the Kurdish mountains or Armenia. Therefore, it must lie in the North following the sun westward. But how is one to find the point of intersection between a 36 degree angle and a 90 degree angle?

So he thought about the word "length". Maybe Berosus incorrectly trans-

Footnotes

[21] King Darius (or Dareios) is also mentioned in the Bible, in the Book of Ezra chs. 5-6 and again in the Book of Daniel, ch. 6. Daniel, a Jew forced to move, saw "the writing on the wall" for King Belshazzar. "That same night Belshazzar the Chaldean king was slain. So Darius the Mede received the kingdom at about the age of sixty-two." Dan. 5:30. Daniel became one of the three royal counsel men but was thrown in a den of lions because he would not bow down to a statue of Darius. When he survived the den, the king put his faith in the God of Israel and commanded the entire kingdom to "fear and tremble before Daniel's God".

King Darius's tomb in Persepolis was considered the Greenwich of that time.

lated "five laths wide". The length of the Ark could be the answer.

If one were to convert the 300 cubits to feet, it would equal 515 feet (provided that the Egyptian cubit was used.[22]). If these 515 feet were converted to 515 minutes on a map, they would equal 8 degrees, 35 minutes. (A degree minute is 1/60 of a degree, and we know that the Babylonians used this system. We got it from them.)

If we go 8 degrees, 35 minutes west, where do we end up? 44 degrees, 15 minutes east of Greenwich. And on which latitude do the two angles cross?

The point of intersection is 39 degrees, 26 minutes north (of the Equator).

So where is that? Grab a map and see where the two cross each other! Or even better: a digital map of the world (like Encarta World Atlas) with precise latitude and longitude measurements with the help of the mouse. Shall I say that the point of intersection is exactly there where our expedition was? Just outside of Uzengili, the village in the "mountains of Ararat".

Divine Planning or…?

But how can it be that the Ark landed exactly 515 degree minutes west of Darius's grave? (The same amount of degree minutes as its length in feet?)

The explanation is, of course, the opposite:

The landing point of the Ark was so important for the world after the Flood that when the Persians wanted to move the "center of the world" over to themselves, some geographical nerd made sure that it would be placed exactly 515 degree minutes east of the Ark.

And as if that's not enough: Both the Egyptian center, the Great Pyramid of Cheops, and the Persian center, Darius's grave, can both be found on 30 degrees north latitude. Which is 9 degree and 26 minutes south of the Ark - or 566 minutes which equaled the 566 feet of "one height and length of the Ark".

Well, I guess that's just a coincidence?

Coincidence?

Ark's length:
300 cubits = **515** feet
+
Ark's height:
30 cubits = 51 feet
=
Ark's length + height:
330 cubits = **566** feet

The Ark is **515** minutes (Or 8 degree 35 minutes) West of the old Persian prime meridian

The Ark is **566** minutes (Or 9 degree 26 minutes) North of both the ancient Persian world navel (Darius' grave) and the ancient Egyptian navel (the Cheops pyramid).

Footnotes
[22] Assuming that the Ark's 300 cubits were the same as the Egyptian 20.6 inches, making 515 feet. That is, the exact same as the boat-shaped object in Duripinar.

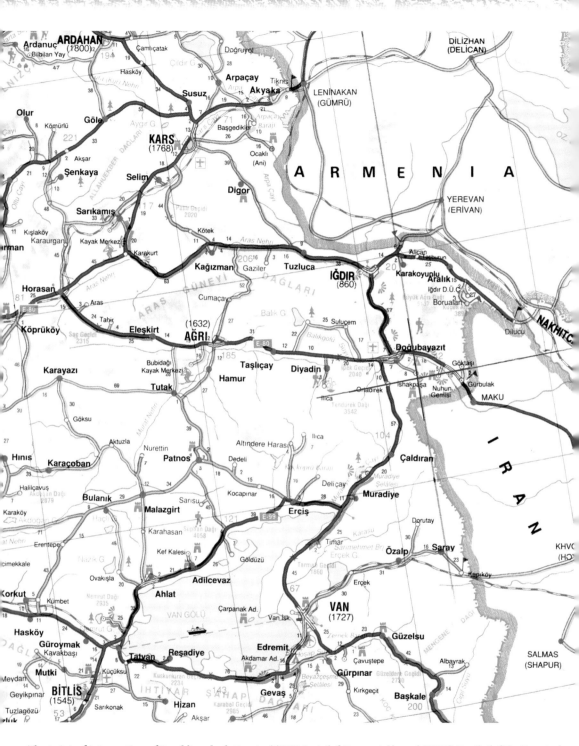

The point of intersection of Fasold's calculation is 44*15' East (of Greenwich) and 39*26' North (of the Equator). This is extremely close to Uzengili, also known as Mesha. Nazar, the village up in the Mountains of Ararat where the boat-shaped object lies is marked on this Turkish road map. Is this just a coincidence...?

Chapter 12

From Josephus to the Middle Ages

Roman bust which is said to be of Flavius Josephus, the man who at first rose against the Romans and later joined them (from Les Dossiers d'Archéologie 2001).

The name **Flavius Josephus** (37 - c.100 A.D.) often pops up in Ark research due to his book *The Antiquities of the Jews*, which names the Great Flood, the Ark, and Noah.

Josephus fought against the Romans in the Jewish Revolt that led to the destruction of Jerusalem in the year 70 A.D. He was captured and later released after which he settled in Rome. Here he wrote *The Jewish War*, describing the war between the Jews and the Romans, as well as the Jews' own story in *Jewish Antiquity*.

Josephus has been a magnificent non-Christian source from which facts about Jesus and the first Christians can be derived. Thanks to him we have confirmation from an almost enemy source that Jesus, John the Baptist, Pontius Pilate, James, and others lived. He can also confirm other details from the gospels (Matthew, Mark, Luke and John). But the reason that Josephus is such a great source for this information is that the events in question took place in his lifetime or immediately before.

Contrarily, when Josephus writes about the distant past, he has no choice but to depend on the other written authorities such as the Books of the Law (Genesis, Exodus, Leviticus, and Numbers, all written by Moses), the works of Berosus or Nic(h)olas of Damascus, or whatever tradition suggests. In superficial articles and books about the Ark, authors often write, "Josephus writes" that pitch was scraped off the Ark. But they are forgetting, or don't know, that in this instance Josephus is just quoting Berosus.

Josephus Speaks:

…in process of time they were perverted, and forsook the practices of their forefathers; and did neither pay those honors to God which were appointed them, nor had they any concern to do justice towards men … For many angels of God accompanied with women, and begat sons that proved unjust, and despisers of all that was good, on account of the confidence they had in their own strength; for the tradition is, that these men did what resembled the acts of those whom the Grecians call giants. But Noah was very uneasy at what they did; and being displeased at their conduct, persuaded them to change their dispositions and their acts for the better: but seeing they did not yield to him, but were slaves to their wicked pleasures, he was afraid they would kill him, together with his wife and children, and those they had married; so he departed out of that land.[1]

It seems that Josephus either wrote his own continuation to the reference to giants in Genesis – or he supports Jewish legend.

Now God loved this man for his righteousness: yet he not only condemned those other men for their wickedness, but determined to destroy the whole race of man-

Footnotes

[1] *Antiquities of the Jews* - Book I, Ch. 3.1. Translated by William Whiston. Irrelevant sentences have been removed and marked with ellipses (…).

kind, and to make another race that should be pure from wickedness; and cutting short their lives, and making their years not so many as they formerly lived, but one hundred and twenty only … God suggested to him the following contrivance and way of escape: - That he should make an ark of four stories high, three hundred cubits long, fifty cubits broad, and thirty cubits high … Now this ark had firm walls, and a roof, and was braced with cross beams, so that it could not be any way drowned or overborne by the violence of the water.

This calamity happened in the six hundredth year of Noah's government, … and this was two thousand six hundred and fifty-six years from Adam…[2]

Josephus follows Genesis' information very closely here, but interestingly enough he adds an extra story onto the Ark and adds 1,000 years to the biblical chronology, which seems to have 1,656 years from Creation to the Flood according to Bishop Ussher's generally accepted calculations. In Paul L. Maier's translation of Josephus there are 2,262 years from Creation to the Flood. For more see the chapter "Confused Chronology".

… the water poured down forty entire days, till it became fifteen cubits higher than the earth; … When the rain ceased, the water did but just begin to abate after one hundred and fifty days, (that is, on the seventeenth day of the seventh month,) it then ceasing to subside for a little while. After this, the ark rested on the top of a certain mountain in Armenia; which, when Noah understood, he opened it; and seeing a small piece of land about it, he continued quiet, and conceived some cheerful hopes of deliverance. But a few days afterward, when the water was decreased to a greater degree, he sent out a raven, as desirous to learn whether any other part of the earth were left dry by the water, and whether he might go out of the ark with safety; but the raven, finding all the land still overflowed, returned to Noah again.[3]

Like the Greek version of the Books of the Law in the Septuagint version of the Bible, Josephus, who originally wrote in Aramaic and was later translated to Greek, uses the name Armenia instead of the Hebrew Urartu or Ararat, which originates from a time when this kingdom existed in Armenia. There is no doubt that here Ararat and Armenia are synonyms for the same location. Josephus continues:

And after seven days he sent out a dove, to know the state of the ground; which came back to him covered with mud, and bringing an olive branch: hereby Noah learned that the earth was become clear of the flood. So after he had staid seven more days, he sent the living creatures out of the ark; and both he and his family went out, when he also sacrificed to God, and feasted with his companions. However, the Armenians call this place, *The Place of Descent;* for the ark being saved in that place, its remains are shown there by the inhabitants to this day.[4]

Stranded

The William Whiston translation of Josephus from 1737 suggested in a footnote that the Greek name of the location where the Ark "stranded" or "descended" ("apo bah tay reon" in Greek) was a derivation of the name of an Armenian city, Nachidsheuan, which was supposedly the first city after the Flood. He writes[5]:

Josephus the Historian, represented here in William Whiston's English translation.

Footnotes

[2] *Antiquities of the Jews* - Book I, Ch. 3.2-3. Translated by William Whiston.

[3] *Antiquities of the Jews* - Book I, Ch. 3.5.

[4] *Antiquities of the Jews* - Book I, Ch. 3.5.

[5] Note 18 Antiquities of the Jews.

[6] *Antiquities of the Jews* - Book I, Ch. 3.6.

[7] Matthew 14.

This (apo bah tay reon), or Place of Descent, is the proper rendering of the Armenian name of this very city. It is called in Ptolemy Naxuana, and by Moses Chorenensis, the Armenian historian, Idsheuan; but at the place itself Nachidsheuan, which signifies The first place of descent, and is a lasting monument of the preservation of Noah in the ark, upon the top of that mountain, at whose foot it was built, as the first city or town after the flood. See Antiq. B. XX. ch. 2. sect. 3; and Moses Chorenensis, who also says elsewhere, that another town was related by tradition to have been called Seron, or, The Place of Dispersion, on account of the dispersion of Xisuthrus's or Noah's sons, from thence first made. Whether any remains of this ark be still preserved, as the people of the country suppose, I cannot certainly tell. Mons. Tournefort had, not very long since, a mind to see the place himself, but met with too great dangers and difficulties to venture through them.

Today a city called Nakhichevan (or Naxcivan) exists in an enclave of Azerbaijan between Iran and Armenia about 100 kilometers southeast of Mt. Ararat. There is also a small town north of Igdir on the border with the same name. Linguists cannot agree whether the name comes from the "landing place" or not. And as we shall later see, the original Nachidsheuan or Naxuan has possibly been found much closer.

Josephus continues quoting sources:

Berosus the Chaldean … when he is describing the circumstances of the flood, he goes on thus:
"It is said there is still some part of this ship in Armenia, at the mountain of the Cordyaeans; and that some people carry off pieces of the bitumen, which they take away, and use chiefly as amulets for the averting of mischiefs."
Hieronymus the Egyptian also, who wrote the Phoenician Antiquities, and Mnaseas, and a great many more, make mention of the same. Nay, Nicolaus of Damascus, in his ninety-sixth book, hath a particular relation about them; where he speaks thus: "There is a great mountain in Armenia, over Minyas, called Baris, upon which it is reported that many who fled at the time of the Deluge were saved; and that one who was carried in an ark came on shore upon the top of it; and that the remains of the timber were a great while preserved. This might be the man about whom Moses the legislator of the Jews wrote."[6]

His Contemporaries

Nicholas of Damascus (born 30 B.C.) is associated with the Jewish king, Herod the Great, whose biography he wrote. He also wrote about the history of the world. As mentioned above, he wrote about the Ark in the first century, just shortly before Josephus' time.

It's very interesting that Nicholas writes about the timber using the past tense. It was "long preserved", but now it is obviously gone or hidden.

We also notice that the writer doesn't keep to the biblical account. Here it is not only Noah and his family that are saved, but "many fugitives" crawl up this awesome mountain even though the Bible tells that even the tops of the mountains were flooded and everyone perished.

This is worth noting because Nicholas writes in a Jewish context, whereas the Biblical account must have been simpler. But it was well known that Herod was not especially God-fearing, and the people with whom he kept company were not either.

When Nicholas refers to Noah landing on Baris (which is probably the same as Marris, the Armenian name for Mt. Ararat), it's not a fact from the Bible either, but rather it tells that Baris is obviously the highest mountain at this time. That is, the volcano had grown larger than all of the other mountains in Armenia at this point in time.

Was the Ark Hidden by a Volcanic Eruption?

We know that at some point a great volcanic eruption threw a sixth of Mount Ararat in the air leaving a gorge, Ahora Gorge, on the northeast side of the mountain. We're not talking about the 1840 earthquake that annihilated the village and monastery here. No, this was a much greater explosion that happened maybe even thousands of years ago.

Along with such an amazing act of God, ash, lava, stone, and earth are spread over a very large area. The explosion of Mt. St. Helens in Washington State in 1980 is comparable in strength.

This great explosion on Mt. Ararat could have obliterated or hidden the Ark under ash, earth, and lava while at the same time making the surrounding area uninhabitable and killing the population so that no one after this time could tell exactly where the Ark lay.

We also know that there was a mega volcano on the other side of the border in Iran and that there are regular earthquakes in the vicinity.

If these/this volcano exploded around Jesus' time or before, that would explain why no one knows, based on early sources, where the Ark lies, but insecurity has set in because the Ark has actually disappeared.

Of course, our ancestors knew that the Ark was located in Ararat – but they didn't know exactly where. Based on the information from Genesis that the Ark landed in "the Mountains of Ararat" it has been assumed, understandably, that this must have been the highest mountain in the area. It was also Mt. Ararat Western Europeans later called the mountain actually named Barris, Marris, or Agri Dagh. The West European name has strengthened the misunderstanding of "the Mountains of Ararat".

The First Christian Sources

With the onset of Christianity, a new interest for Noah's Ark was also to be found. Many from the Church wrote about the Ark:

Bishop Theophilus of Antioch in northern Syria (180 A.D.) restates the biblical facts but also adds:[8] "And of the Ark, the remains are to this day to be seen in the Arabian mountains..." Is it plausible that the Kurdish Mountains were also called the Arabian Mountains? Or does this Theophilus have his own theory?

The Church Father **Eusebius** wrote in the 3rd century that *a small part of the Ark* could still be seen in the "Gordian Mountains". Again, we are in the Kurdish Mountains, but he is probably quoting Berosus.

Footnotes
[8] Marcus Dod's translation of Ante-Nicene Fathers, II, 117.

[9] Cyprus

[10] Quoted from Jonathan Gray's *The Ark Conspiracy* p. 10.

[11] Isidore of Seville, Etymologies, in *Scriptorium Classicorum Bibliotheca Oxoniensis*, (1911), XIV,8,5, trans. Montgomery, p. 80.

The historian, **Faustus of Byzantium** (4th century), who was a Greek and wrote about Armenian history, also placed the Ark in the Gordian (Kurdish) Mountains in the Canton of Gordukh. He does this in connection with the tellings of St. James (Bishop of Nisibis, now Nusaybin c. 100 km from Cudi Dagh in Syria). Legend has it that St. James tried in vain to find the Ark but was instead awarded a piece of it by an angel. Later retellings locate the occurrence on Mt. Ararat, but James was a bishop in Syria.

Eusebius (264-340) as pictured by André Thevet in Les Vrais Portraits et Vies Hommes Illustrés, 1584.

Bishop Ephiphianus of Salamis[9] (4th century) also states that the Ark landed in the Gordian Mountains. He also asserts that the remains can still be found, and if one searches well, one can also see the altar that Noah built to thank God for his salvation. In 380 A.D. he argues the truth of Christianity and writes: "Do you seriously suppose that we are unable to prove our point, when even to this day the remains of Noah's ark are shown in the country of the Kurds?" [10]

Or course, this could also just be empty rhetoric, but this Greek bishop also states as late as 380 A.D. that the Ark "even to this day" is shown – in the land of the Kurds. Since the Kurds have never had their own country, he must be referring to the areas where the Kurds traditionally lived.

The Confusion Begins

Isidore of Seville (560-636) from southern Spain also places the Ark in the Kurdish Mountains but adds without any explanation that, "*Ararat is a mountain* in Armenia, where the historians testify that the Ark came to rest after the Flood. So even to this day wood remains of it are to be seen there." [11] Isidore, as the first West European source, introduces confusion about Mt. Ararat with his comment here. Possibly it is due to a poor translation of the Bible that doesn't include the plural "mountains". In any case, West Europeans start discussing one specific mountain, even though the Bible clearly talks about a specific area, the *mountains* of Ararat.

We know that there was no mountain in Armenia called Mount Ararat at that point. The Armenians, Kurds, and Turks all have their own names for the largest of their mountains. But in Europe, the largest mountain, from this point on, came to be called Mt. Ararat.

We only know Isidore writings from a quote in the 16th century, so a later rewriting of names is also possible.

Muslim Understanding

The Qur'an – the holy book of the Muslims written after the 7th century.

Here Noah is considered one of the prophets and it is written, "The Ark came to rest upon Al-Judi" (Houd 11:44).

According to Muslim tradition, multiple Al-Judi mountains exist. One of them is Cudi Dagh, or Jabal Judi, on the border between Syria and Iraq. Cudi is pronounced Yudi, with a soft j or y sound. This mountain has been connected with Noah's mountain. Place names all over the mountain also refer to Noah and the Ark.

Another possible location is the Judi Mountains in Saudi Arabia, which are geographically closer to Islam's two holy cities, Mecca and Medina.

The third Al-Judi Mountain is precisely the same place where the boat-shaped object has been found – on the border to Iran.

Mohammed was very interested in both Judaism and Christianity, and some experts believe that he was a member of a Jewish-Christian monoteistic sect in Saudi-Arabia before he began a new religion.

Many biblical stories can also be found in the Qur'an, but the stories have been given their own character. The account of Noah in the Qur'an, for example, is about evil people refusing to worship only one God. This was the exact same problem Mohammad had with the heathens in Saudi Arabia. He had stopped serving many gods and argued, like the other "hairs" (monotheists = Jews and Christians), that there was only one God.

That Mohammed didn't directly refer to the same Kurdish mountains as the then contemporary translations of the Bible did but rather names one specific mountain suggests that he might have had supplemental information about the Ark.

As a merchant, Mohammad might have traveled along the "Silk Road" just past the Ararat Mountains, or he could have traded with other traveling merchants that had traveled along that way and thus heard the story.

Therefore it is worth noticing that The Quran mentions one specific mountain - Al Judi. But... in Arabic, Al Judi means "the high one" and doesn't have to necessarily be one specific mountain.

Confusion About Where the Ark Is

Bishop Eutychius was the bishop in Alexandria in the ninth century, and he says, "the Ark landed on the mountains of Ararat" as it says in the Bible, but he also adds that, "it is Jabal Judi near Mosul". This city is all the way down by Nineveh, over 150 miles south of Mount Cudi Dagh, the other Al Judi. I feel obliged to point out on his behalf that he lived in Egypt.

Al Masudi constitutes in the 10th century that the Ark landed on "Jabal Judi" – and in addition adds that it is about 25-30 miles from the Tigris River. This description fits Mount Cudi in Syria.

Ibn Haukal (10th century) also calls the mountain Al-Judi but puts its location around Nesbin (today Nusaybin in Syria) where Noah supposedly built a city at the foot of the mountain.

In the 12th century, **Benjamin of Tudela** writes that a certain Omar Ben al-Khatab removed the Ark from the twin peaks and re-established it on an island in the Tigris known as Jizireh Ben Omar. He writes, too, that the aforementioned lies at the foot of Mt. Ararat, but it lies at the foot of Cudi Dagh. So the conclusion must be that he either didn't know what he was talking about or that at this time some people called Mount Cudi Mt. Ararat. Due to a lack of information, the confusion multiplies.

The Silk Road to the East

One day we were standing together with Dr. Salih Bayraktu-tan studying one of these so-called "anchor stones" on a little mountain around the Valley of the Eight.

Just below us a small road ran which reminded me of the narrow roads that run between the fields in Denmark. It twisted and turned up through the mountains until it disappeared.

It was the ancient Silk Road. By means of this road **Marco Polo** (1254-1325) and the other adventurers and travelers had journeyed by foot, horse, or camel on their way to the Far East in search of silk, spices, and other rare goods in order to bring them to the West and sell them for large sums.

The Isaac Pasha Castle

These travelers also had to pass the local kings' castles. One of these castles was the Isaac Pasha Castle, which is located with a view over the valley. It is only 400 years old, but before this castle was built, another castle existed, chiseled into the face of the mountain just behind the Isaac Pasha castle. The caves here date back to the Urartu (1300 B.C.), and probably even the Hurrians (c. 2000 B.C.), which were also called cave dwellers.

From the harem the women could overlook the beautiful landscape and imagine themselves far, far away.

The traders most likely paid a polite visit to the castle on their way. For the most part they were welcomed with great hospitality; invited into the beautifully decorated guest hall at Isaac Pasha's castle and were given food and drink while they told of news from distant lands through which they had traversed. They may also have traded with these kings, but gifts were definitely bestowed upon them.

From the dining room stretched a corridor to the master's harem where the most beautiful women, often from far-away lands, spent their lives behind these very walls. From the harem's quarters a staircase led to a small, closed-in garden where they could enjoy the rays of the sun up in these somewhat cold heights. They never came outside of the castle walls, but they could always look out over the majestic landscape and dream themselves away. They surely were not allowed to speak freely with the travelers. Women and men were kept at a distance, but through the eunuchs the women may still have heard news from the lands where they once lived before they were given away as gifts.

Ararat Could Not Be Overseen

The travelers from Europe had to come through this exact valley where the impressive Mt. Ararat with a snow dressed Ataturk top towers with its 16,945 feet. They surely thought about the biblical account of Noah's Ark. And if it didn't land on the highest mountain, then where did it land?

Many travelers told of the mammoth Mount Ararat "where Noah's Ark landed", but besides this cheap assumption, there were no serious stud-

The Dominican monk Vincent of Beauvais mentioned "the first city Noah built" by the name of Laudume, and it was supposed to lie at the foot of the mountain. (Painting from Il Capitolo del Domenicani.)

ies. Comments like, "people say it's still up there" continually arise, but there isn't any fast evidence among these thin claims.

Let's meet some of the traders that took the Silk Road past this spot. Even if they can't tell us much about the Ark besides that "people say it's still up there", they can tell us something about the setting and environment:

William of Rubruck (1255), a Franciscan monk, was sent by King Louis IX of France to the Mongolian emperor. He writes that, "near this city (Naxua) there is a mountain of which is said, here lies Noah's Ark. The one (is) larger than the other, and Araxes (River) flows at the foot of them; and there is a city they call Cemanum, which, when translated, means "eight", and they say that it is named after the eight people that came out of the Ark and who built it on the great mountain.

"Many have tried to climb it but have not been able to...".

And then he retells the story, with a bishop as the source, about the pious monk who tried in vain to climb the mountain and was finally stopped by an angel who gave him a piece of the Ark, which is now kept in the Etchmiadzin monastery in Dadjivan.

William ploddingly adds that, "the mountain doesn't seem so high to me that men shouldn't be able to climb it." But he finds an explanation in the local mythology:

"An old man gave me a good reason why not to try climbing it. The mountain is called Massis, which is (the) feminine (form) in their language. 'No one' he said, 'should climb the mountain. It is the mother of the earth'." (Now we know that the word Massis is not feminine. That type of word doesn't have a specific gender in Armenian, but the mountain could have been understood as a mother anyway.) [12]

William naming "The City of the Eight", as he calls Cemanum, makes this story about the Ark particularly interesting.

At this time the area was still inhabited by Christian Armenians, even though they had fallen under Turkish rule. They *could* have shown him The Valley of the Eight with its ancient monuments as well as the village that is now called Arzep, which we visited to see the anchor stones. But we cannot know if it is the city that he calls "The City of the Eight".

Vincent of Beauvais writes in the 13th century:

"In Armenia there is a noble city called Ani where a thousand churches and a hundred thousand families or households are to be found. The Tartars captured this city in twelve days. Near it is Mount Ararat, where Noah's Ark rests, and at the foot of that mountain is the first city Noah built, called Laudume. Closer by the city flows the river Ararthosi, which traverses the plain of Mongan where the Tartars winter, and empties into the Caspian Sea…"

That city Noah supposedly built, Laudume, could possibly be the same city William of Rubruck calls Cemanum – the City of the Eight. It could

Footnotes

[12] John Montgomery: *The Quest for Noah's Ark*, 2nd Edition, 1974.

[13] *Lonely Planet: Turkey* pp. 623-624.

[14] John Montgomery: *The Quest for Noah's Ark*, 2nd Edition, 1974.

also be the city Rubruck calls Naxua. We will come back to that later.

But the big city with the thousand churches is hard to find. Today Ani is a ghost town 45 km east of Kras. The city still has a one-kilometer long wall and many ruins. It was partially destroyed by an earthquake in 1319, and the Silk Road took another route, causing the city to lose its significance. But according to Lonely Planet's guide for Turkey, Ani should have had almost 100,000 inhabitants.[13]

Odoric of Pordenone (1286-1331), a Franciscan monk from northern Italy also visited this area and wanted to climb the mountain. He doesn't name Ararat, but Sarbiscalo, which is most likely the same mountain, and he also states that the local people believed that no one would ever be able to climb this mountain because it doesn't please "the highest one" (God).

There is also **Jordanus**, a French Dominican and missionary to India, who around 1330 describes the mountain, supposedly inhabited by great snakes and wild animals. He doesn't scale the mountain either but believes he has been to the location where Noah planted his vineyard.

The last part is very interesting because there actually is a place in The Valley of the Eight which some connect with Noah and his vineyard because of its ancient stone walls.

Marco Polo is often named in association with travels past Mount Ararat in the 14th century, but even this great adventurer does nothing more than retell local legends about the mountain.

He writes: "In the central part of Armenia stands an exceedingly large and high mountain upon which it is said that the Ark of Noah rested." And he mentions that the upper regions of the mountain never thaw. (The Travels of Marco Polo, New York, Crown Publishers, 1958).

Marco Polo the famous explorer who adorns the Italian bank notes also passed Mt. Ararat – but he didn't explore it more closely.

Sir **John Mandeville**, who from 1322-1356 traveled around the world, and Jean de Barbe or Jean de Bourgogne from Liège in France, are possibly one and the same man. He tells that people went from Erzerum (a college town today) to a mountain he called Sabissocolle. This name sounds very familiar when considering Odoric's city name, Sarbiscalo. But John Mandeville continues:

…and there beside is another mountain called Ararat, but the Jews call it Taneez, where Noah's ship rested, and still is upon that mountain; and men may see it afar in clear weather. That mountain is full seven miles high; and some men say that they have seen and touched the ship, and put their fingers in the parts where the devil went out, when Noah said "Benedicte." But they that say so speak without knowledge; for no one can go up the mountain for the great abundance of snow which is always on the mountain, both summer and winter, so that no man ever went up since the time of Noah, except a monk, who, by God's grace, brought one of the planks down, which is yet in the monastery at the foot of the mountain. And beside is the city of Dayne, which was founded by Noah, near which is the

Adam Olearius mentioned that the Ark might be petrified.

Footnotes

[15] Tim La Haye and John Morris: *The Ark on Ararat*, Thomas Nelson Publishers 1976.

[16] This location was later examined by Navarra, among others, and it was established to be nothing more than a rock projection.

[17] Research of Mount St. Helens' eruption – which was very similar to Mt. Ararat's – shows that everything was destroyed within a 45-mile radius, but the vegetation came back at an amazing pace after the catastrophe.

city of Any, in which were one thousand churches.[14]

John Mandeville is most likely referring to Vincent of Beauvais' account. But that he writes this after the earthquake of 1319 without pointing out its effect on the city makes a man question how much research he did.

The Spaniard **Gonzales de Clavijo** (1415) also describes the mountain and mentions that there is a city at its foot, a city that Noah supposedly built but has since been deserted. It may be *Laudume* or C*emanum.*

Other than this, he doesn't have anything new to tell about the Ark.

Adam Olearius (1647) describes the great Ararat Mountain and states that "the Armenians, and the Persians themselves, are of opinion, that there are still upon the said Mountain some remainders of the Ark, but that Time hath so hardened them, that they seem absolutely petrify'd." Then he mentions a wooden cross that was supposedly made of wood from the Ark...[15]

A contemporary of Olearius, the French traveler **Boulé Legouze,** drew sketches of both Big and Little Ararat in 1647, but they were unfortunately completely unrealistic views made in accordance with the style of the time. Besides placing the Ark at its peak and pointing out St. James and the small mountains, the sketches tell us nothing of interest.

A Dutch traveler, **Jans Janszoon Struys**, was told in 1694 by a friend from a convent in the vicinity of Ararat (presumably St. James') that, "the Ark is not destroyed, and that after so many centuries is still as whole as the first day it landed here". But he didn't see it.

The Englishman **Sir John Chardin** made a woodcut in 1711 of Ararat seen from Echmiadzin that is more realistic than Legouze's. It shows the Ark in an almost legendary way on the mountain's peak. You can also see that it was made before the earthquake of 1840 where the Ahora Gorge grows in breadth.

People Say…

In popular books about the Ark these travelers' and explorers' accounts are often retold, but the only thing they really tell us is that, "people say it's up there" (on Mt. Ararat). Every now and then a black dot was pointed out on the mountainside and claimed to be the Ark[16], but none of the locals had ever been up there. They didn't dare to attempt Mt. Ararat because of superstitious fears.

All knowledge of the Ark's location had evidently disappeared, presumably after the enormous volcanic eruption which had already blown away the one side of Mt. Ararat (either around the time of Christ or in the following few centuries) and left the countryside desolate.[17]

Foto: Henri Nissen 2004

PART 2
The Wrong Mountain?

"That mountain is full seven miles high;
and some men say that they have seen and touched the ship,
and put their fingers in the parts where the devil went out,
when Noah said 'Benedicte'.
But those that say such things are speaking without understanding,
for none can forge the mountain due to the masses of snow,
always covering the mountain summer and winter,
so no one has ever been there since the days of Noah
– except a monk, who, by God's grace, brought back a plank
which is now found in the monastery a the foot of the mountain."

Sir John Mandeville, 1322-1356

Chapter 17

At the Foot of Mt. Ararat

We were staying at a cold hotel outside of the largest city in the region, Dogubayazit, which has been the point of origin for many of the Ark hunts. The city lay only a few kilometers from the Iranian border. Many famous Ark-hunters had stayed here before us.

The hotel was still ice cold after the long, hard winter that the locals experience every year up here in the mountains. This area of Turkey enjoys the same temperatures as the mainland the rest of the year, but gets a dry cold of down to 50-60 degrees below zero in the winters. But Dogubayazit isn't without its advantages. It is at an elevation which is 1,600 ft. lower than Kars and Erzurum, which lie at a very windy 6,500 ft.

The summers are very warm, especially around the volcanoes in the Ararat Mountains where it is much warmer than it otherwise would be at that elevation. But even though it was May and the snow was melted and the sun was shining in the blue sky, it was still so cold here that the radiators couldn't warm up the rooms.

The Twin Mountains - Mt. Ararat

From the hotel we could see out over the mighty Mt. Ararat. With its 16,945 feet and mammoth circumference, it traveled majestically into the clouds so that seeing its snow covered top was a rare experience.

Towards the northwest it slid into a chain of mountains, but otherwise stood almost completely alone, a cone shaped volcano piercing the flat plains, which grasped up to a height of 2,500-4,500 feet. Above that only a freestanding mountain was to be found. From around 8,800 feet it started to steepen considerably. At 11,000 feet the grass stopped growing, and at 12,877 feet and 16,854 feet respectively the mountain ceased its ascent in the form of two twin peaks, which in the West are called Little Ararat and Big Ararat. Big Ararat is always an igloo above 14,000 feet.

The mountain was originally called Massis in Armenian. The two twin peaks were named Pokur Massis (Little Ararat) and Medz Massis (Big Ararat). In Turkish it is called Büyük or Agri Dagi, and on the other side of the border in Iran its Persian name was Koh-i-nuh, Noah's mountain.

The circumference of the mountain was enormous. If you tried to walk around it on the plateau, you would have to expect around 50 miles of trekking.

Not all mountains seem so impressive, but because Mt. Ararat stood alone on the landscape, one could see its glorious summits from a long distance. Therefore, it was impossible to avoid being completely fascinated by this colossal and magnificent mountain. It was like a magnet.

No wonder so many travelers believed this to be the mountain whose pinnacle hid Noah's Ark in its never-ending snow.

This was also what the locals told them time and time again – along with fantastic stories of how dangerous or even impossible it was to climb the "holy" mountain - The Mother Mountain.

How Did They End Up with Ararat?

Mount Ararat…!

This gorgeous mountain lay as a constant work against us.

Why were we not searching for Noah's missing Ark on Mt. Ararat as hundreds of other mountain climbers have done throughout time?

Isn't it this mountain that held so much mystique?

Is it not this same mountain on which multiple eyewitnesses claimed to have seen *the* Ark and others had found wooden fragments...?

Is it not this exact mountain that everyday people connected with Noah's Ark?

Yes, it is. Maybe we should look more closely at how all of this interest culminated on this specific mountain.

There are two obvious reasons:

1. Some Bible translations have mistakenly translated that the Ark landed "on Mt. Ararat" instead of "on the Mountains of Ararat" - plural.

2. Mt. Ararat is presently the highest and most impressive mountain in the area, and Ark-hunters have assumed that the Ark must have landed upon the highest mountain.

Let's look at these two reasons.

Was It in the Bible?

As mentioned, the stories of the Ark and the Flood can be found in the folklore of many folk traditions and religions, but it is the biblical account that has caused many hunters to search for the Ark on Mt. Ararat. In the original text of Genesis, chapter 8, verse 4 we see that the Ark hit ground at "RRT's" mountains. Hebrew doesn't use vowels, only consonants. Consequently, this RRT was translated differently over time.

The Hebraic Text of the Bible gives us, as mentioned, the mountains of RRT. This can be read as both aRaRaT and uRaRTu. The most reasonable assumption would be that it should be read as Urartu's mountains (the name of the kingdom), which existed from c. 1300-600 B.C.

The Septuagint is the Greek translation of the Old Testament (3rd century B.C.) It translates RRT as Ararat. Even though the place name Ararat is being used, it is not referring to a specific mountain, but rather a topographical area and its mountains.

The Targum is a distinctive designation of Aramaic translations or paraphrases of the Old Testament (c. 5th century B.C.). It tells of the Ark landing on the Quardu Mountains (the *Kurdish* Mountains).

This is *very* important. The reason that the Targum was written in Aramaic was because it was written specifically for homeward bound Jews that

Footnotes

[1] See chapter 15 about Berosus.

[2] A location close to where the boat-shaped object is now found called Ziyaret means "voluntary pilgrimage".

had forgotten their language (Hebrew) while in captivity in Babylon. Aramaic ended up partially replacing Hebrew in Israel at that time. The Targum was the written version of what had otherwise been orally passed down during the Babylonian captivity. And the Targum updated RRT to The Quardu Mountains.

From their time in Babylon (Iraq), the Jews identified RRT with the Kurdish Mountains. The Babylonians or Persians possibly knew in degree minutes where the Ark lay.[1] That is why it is very crucial that the Targum names the Kurdish Mountains. My personal theory is that not only the landing place of the Ark was known, but even the Ark itself was visible and accessible during the beginning of the Babylonian Empires - where the location was probably a holy place of pilgrimage.[2] We know for a fact that Gilgamesh pilgrimaged there.

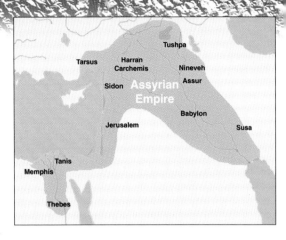

The Samaritan edition of the Law, the **Pentateuch**, which is made up of Moses's five books (from the 5th century B.C. or later) also describes the Ark's landing point as the *Kurdish* Mountains, north of Assyria.[3] (That is north of present-day Iraq.) This is also important. The Samaritans were a mixed people of Jews and foreign people. Therefore they were not considered pure Jews. (Look at the story of Jesus and the Samaritan woman.) In their version of the Books of the Law the names and places were updated. Therefore, when the Pentateuch specifically names the *Kurdish* Mountains north of Assyria, it is speaking of Eastern Turkey.

The authors of the Pentateuch perhaps knew of geographic places that other Jews didn't know about.

The first Syriac Christians also had their version of the Bible - the **Pershitta**, which was laid out 400 years after Christ. In this version of Genesis 8:4 the Ark landed on "the mountains of Quardu" - that is, the Kurdish Mountains.

All of these original translations clearly point to "the Kurdish Mountains" without naming one specific mountain. But when the Bible was translated to the European languages, the name Ararat (from the Greek text) stuck in people's heads along with the idea that there was only one specific mountain, namely Ararat.

The King James Version (1611) translated RRT in Genesis 8:4 as Ararat but translated *the same word* as "Armenia" in 2 Kings 19:37 as well as in Isaiah 37:38. This creates confusion, making it difficult to differentiate between Armenia and Ararat, a confusion for which there was no basis. Afterwards, the location of the Ark was no longer understood as a mountain range, but rather a specific mountain: Mt. Ararat.

[3] **Assyria**: an ancient kingdom located around the Tigris River with the city-state Assur. Established pre-2,000 B.C. by Semites. According to Genesis 10:22, **Assur** was one of Shem's sons. The Assyrians were his descendants. Around 1200 B.C. the Assyrians became a major power throughout the Middle East based in Assur and later Nineveh, Kalah, and Sargonsborg (Korsabad) — all along the Tigris in Mesopotamia.

The Assyrians fought against the **Mitanni** in Syria to gain the Mediterranean and rival the **Hittites** of Asia Minor (present-day Turkey). **Babylonia** and Assyria traded power back and forth from 1200-900 B.C. After 900 the Assyrians took over Armenia, Syria along with Phoenicia, Palestine, and Babylonia. **Babylon** was levelled to the ground in 689 B.C. Shortly after in 671 the Assyrians culminated their power in the conquest of Egypt.

Egypt's breakdown ensued, starting with a movement toward independence and the unification of its enemies. In 614 Assur was taken and Nineveh in 612, which was destroyed along with many Assyrians. The Assyrians were known for their **inhumane treatment** of the downtrodden and for their **administrative competence**. They erected great palaces and watering systems in their capitals.

So we can conclude that the Bible does *not* say that the Ark landed on Mt. Ararat, but rather that it grounded somewhere in the Mountains of Ararat - in the plural form - on the mountains of the Kingdom of Urartu, which later were referred to as the mountains of Armenia, or the *Kurdish* Mountains. And all four of these references are one and the same.

So Where Are These Kurdish Mountains?

Everyone knows that the Kurds live in the mountains of northern Iraq today. But they also live in the mountains in eastern Turkey and western Iran. This is the same area the ancient Urartu occupied, so when we say the Kurdish Mountains, our search includes the mountains between Iran, Turkey, and Iraq where the Kurds originally lived and still live today.

Today's Kurds believe that their Kurdistan should lie in parts of Turkey, Iran, Iraq, and Syria and be larger than France. This Kurdistan is bordered by the Taurus Mountains in the west, the Iranian Plateau in the east, the Ararat Mountains in the north, and plains in Iraq to the south. The Kurdish area mainly consists of mountains and plateaus, even though the Kurds have now come down into the valleys. But their origin is in these mountains. The Kurds are a mountain folk, and the Kurds' mountains have almost always been a play thing for feuding powers. The Kurds have never been strong enough, nor been able to see eye to eye enough, to create their own state, despite many attempts.

It wasn't until the 1200's that the name Kurdistan appeared, which, at this time, was a reference to the area in which they lived. The Kurds have been known as a people for a much longer time. The word "Kurd" can mean "the first", so maybe this tribe was the first in the mountains.

When the Jews referred to the Kurdish Mountains, not the Urartu, during their captivity in Assyria and Babylon (today's Iraq), they did so because the Urartu no longer existed around 700 B.C., and from then on the eastern part of this area was known as the Kurdish Mountains.

As previously mentioned, there is a mountain close to the boat-shaped object that is called Al-Judi or Al Cudi (pronounced almost exactly the same). Both of these words are Arabic, and it would seem there is a connection to the *Al-Judi* (the high ones) in the Qur'an (Al-Judi being the place where the Qur'an says the Ark landed.) *Al Cudi*, on the other hand, means "the Kurdish". Because of the importance of Islam for both the Turks and the Kurds, many Arabic words can be found in their respective languages.

This does not mean that the Ark *could not* have landed on Mt. Ararat, but we cannot limit the search to only one mountain.

But Mt. Ararat Was the Tallest Mountain...

Yes, today Mt. Ararat is clearly the tallest mountain in this region, and therefore the conclusion that the Ark landed on Mt. Ararat is completely understandable.

But how do we *know* that the Ark landed on the tallest mountain? It would be much more impractical, almost impossible for both animals and people to come down from such a tall and steep mountain as Ararat.

Actually, nowhere in the biblical account - or other texts for that matter- does it say that the Ark stranded on the tallest mountain. It landed somewhere in a chain of mountains.

Well, if there were other mountains that were taller than the one the Ark landed on, would Noah have noticed them?

No. Noah couldn't see anything when he sent the bird out to find dry land. The text clearly states that he didn't look out until *after* the covering roof was removed. The first thing he does is open a hatch or window, which must have been in the ceiling:

Genesis 8:6-9

> Then it came about at the end of forty days, that **Noah opened the window of the ark which he had made**; and he sent out a raven, and it flew here and there until the water was dried up from the earth. Then he sent out a dove from him, **to see** if the water was abated from the face of the land; but the dove found no resting place for the sole of her foot, so she returned to him into the ark, for the water was on the surface of all the earth. Then he put out his hand and took her, and brought her into the ark to himself.

If Noah could have seen the area around the Ark, he wouldn't have needed to send out a raven and later a dove. But he had obviously constructed the Ark such that it was not open from above but rather had an elevated roof so that water could run off without needing to have any holes where the water could also come in. ("You shall make a window for the ark, and finish it to a cubit from the top" – Genesis 6:16)

The Ark probably only had that one window. But of course, based on the few pieces information given, we can not know for certain.

A week later Noah sends the dove out one more time:

> v. 11 The dove came to him toward evening, and behold, in her beak was a freshly picked olive leaf. So Noah knew that the water was abated from the earth. 12 Then he waited yet another seven days, and sent out the dove; but she did not return to him again. (Genesis 8:11-12)

It is not until here that Noah gets the chance to see the surroundings for himself:

> v. 13 Now it came about in the six hundred and first year, in the first month, on the first of the month, the water was dried up from the earth. **Then Noah removed the covering of the ark, and**

looked, and behold, the surface of the ground was dried up.

In the second month, on the twenty-seventh day of the month, the earth was dry. (Genesis 8:13-14)

Not until Noah removed the covering of the Ark and looked out did he see that the ground was dry. Therefore one can't assume that the Ark landed on the tallest mountain or that there weren't any taller mountains around.

Mt. Ararat Is a Volcano

- But wouldn't the birds have found this mountain that was taller and landed there?

- No. Not if this mountain were a volcano that was still erupting. If it had finished erupting, it would still be barren, and there would surely not be any leaves for the dove to find. With the circumstances the earth was going through, it is not unlikely that volcanoes were still erupting.

Mt. Ararat *is* a volcano, and there is evidence that it was formed under water and had not reached it's height of over 15,000 ft. at this time. The volcano is active, and can still be heard grumbling from time to time. Only 120 years have passed since the last large volcanic eruption in Ahora Gorge. Geologist Salih Bayraktutan believes that at least the last mile of the mountain has arisen since Noah's time.

For example, it is notable that Mt. Ararat does not withhold the same fossilized sea creatures and plants as do the other non-volcanic mountains in the area. Mt. Ararat's present day form shows no signs of being immersed in water, but there is evidence that the lowest part of the mountain could have been formed under water in the form of quickly cooling lava, similar to the well-known oceanic volcanoes of Hawaii and Iceland.[4]

This seems only to confirm that the volcano came into being under catastrophic changes that could have been brought on by a mega flood.

But the Ark-hunters on Mt. Ararat have had little interest in geology and the arguments it poses. Climbing has been the only methods they have used to find the Ark. Maybe that's why they haven't found it yet?

Footnotes
[4] This theory has been pointed out by PhD. Clifford L. Burdick in Ararat the Mother of Mountains, among others.

Chapter 18

Soldiers and Adventurers

After a few centuries of rumors, someone finally decided to check if the Ark really was up on that mountain.

The Russian doctor and professor of physics, Dr. Johann Jakob Friedrich Parrot, climbed Mt. Ararat with an expedition as early as 1829.

The First Mountain Climber

When the Russian doctor and professor, **Dr. J. J. Friedrich Parrot**, scaled Ararat with a team of 5 around 1829, he discovered what the locals thought of this mountain. Superstitions had been formed which taught that anyone attempting to climb the mountain to see the Ark - which they just as superstitiously claimed was up there - would never live to tell about it. Parrot defied their disbelief, climbed to the summit, and there placed a cross. Easy as pie!

But he didn't *see* the Ark, even though it is inferred in such films as David Balsinger's "The Incredible Discovery of Noah's Ark". Parrot wrote in his book *Journey to Ararat* that he neither saw the Ark nor pieces of it.

But Parrot did start mapping out the mountain, and a large glacier on the north side has been named after him: The Parrot Glacier.

In 1835 **Carl Behrens** climbed to the top and attested that Parrot's cross was still standing.

Now begins the line of long-lived rumors that some of the Ark-hunters of Mt. Ararat emphasize so greatly.

One wandering tale tells of a shepherd from the village Bayazid (now Dogubayazit) that saw a large wooden ship.

A Turkish expedition in 1833 apparently confirmed the shepherd's story. They found "a wooden hull, sticking out of the visible glacier in the summer time." And an expedition in 1840 revealed the same discovery. This information hasn't been verified, but it was disproved by Carl Behrens when he in 1835 conquered the same mountain mentioning nothing of the sort, which was claimed to have been seen just two years previous.

The earthquake that Demolished Arghuri

In 1840 when the second expedition professedly saw the Ark once again, a violent earthquake took place in the Ahora Gorge, killing 2,000 people. Therefore, it seems unreasonable that an expedition was sent up.

The earthquake of June 20th hit in the evening and destroyed the 200 or so houses that made up the village Arghuri (Ahora) built around St. James's Monastery. Apparently, all of the victims were killed within moments of the quake, whose underground roar sent rocks from the skies raining down over the village, the monastery, and the Kurdish shepherds alike.[1]

In 1845 German-born **Dr. Herman von Abich** arrived and also mastered the mountain. The eastern tip and two glaciers have his namesake:

Footnotes

[1] Described by James Bryce in the book: Transcaucasia and Ararat.

Abich I and Abich II. Apparently, this German doctor had no interest in finding the Ark. He wanted to see if one could see the stars better if one came to a sufficient altitude as not to be blinded by the surrounding light. After von Abich came the Russian, **Colonel Khodzko**, who took on Mt. Ararat in 1850 with a team in order to systematically comb the mountain and find the Ark. He found no such thing. Neither did British major **Robert Stuart** and his team in 1856.

In a location north of the Ahora Gorge you find hundreds of volcanic stones probably dating back to the first huge eruption several thousand years ago when 1/6 of Mt. Ararat was blown away leaving the Ahora Gorge behind.
2000 men were killed by the 1840 earthquake...

The Unbelievable Story

Among the many unbelievable stories, one that stands out is from the same year - 1856.

Haji Yearam, or Jeremiah Pilgrim as he was called after being in Jerusalem, claimed that his father had been on Mt. Ararat as a guide for three Western, atheist scientists. They wanted to prove that the Ark did not exist, but when they got up the mountain, they saw it. Now they are threatening Haji's father never to tell anyone. Haji was an Adventist. His spiritual leader, Reverend Williams from Brocton, Massachusetts, claims that Haji's incredible story was confirmed by one of the three scientists, who on his deathbed in London confessed everything. This was supposedly printed in an article in 1918 in either Brocton or Boston. Haji died in 1920.

Despite strenuous searching, this article was never found. The only case that even came close was a liberal scientist from The Royal Geographic Society in London, Henry Danby Seymour, who climbed Ararat in 1845-46 and possibly again in 1856. He might have been in a debate about Noah's Ark with a Christian scientist and politician named James Bryce, who climbed the mountain 20 years later in 1876.

This story is a good example of an account which many who believe *want* to believe, because it indirectly confirms the Ark's existence and suggests that it is being held a secret by atheistic men. There are most likely pieces of truth in his story, for example that some atheist scientists ascended Mt. Ararat. But if they truly had found the Ark, they would not be so atheist any more, and it would have been impossible for all three of them to keep such an amazing secret.

The previously mentioned **James Bryce** (1838-1922) was a recognized English politician and author, who through intense study was convinced that the Bible's historical accounts were true. Bryce climbed Ararat in

Footnotes
[2] Retold by Violet M. Cummings: Noah's Ark: Fable or Fact? Spire Books 1975.

The Ahora Gorge arose from a series of amazing earthquakes. In 1840 a village and a monastery beneath the gorge were destroyed. The pictures here were taken in June 2004 where we followed the road north of the mountain into the Turkish corridor between Armenia and Iran into Nachevan. Below you can catch a glimpse of the gorge and above a close-up details where so many have searched in vain for the remains of the Ark.

1876 where he was forced to trek the last leg alone after his guides had given up at the snow line. There he found a 4-foot long piece of formed wood in the snow at over 13,000 feet.

Those of you that are quick to jump to conclusions and assume this wood must have been from the Ark forget that Parrot, Abich, and Khodzko had set wooden crosses on Ararat's summit many years before, and they are all missing.

The earthquake of 1883

May the 2nd, 1883 - the Ararat region is again shaken by a powerful earthquake. A village was buried under rock and ice. The Turkish government sent authorities to assess the damages, and along with them came the British colonel **Gascoyne** who was an attaché with the embassy.

He and the Turks were so convinced that they had seen "an enormous stern of very dark wood sticking out of a glacier," that they told world-wide media about the find that locals had known about for 6 years.

An original press release has not been found. The closest thing to it was an article printed in the British religious magazine, "Prophetic Messenger"[2]. This article tells the story in a different light. It tells how they went through a dark forest in order to get there, but such a forest does not exist anywhere in the area. The Turks disclosed that the Ark was intact. The sides were the only thing that had suffered damage. A ship isn't made up of much more than sides. The ship was build of gopher wood, and according to the Bible, the Ark *was* build of gopher wood, but how did they know that it was gopher? No one knows was gopher wood is...

Chances are this is another example of someone thinking they saw something - from a distance - after which they fly to the press and the snowball effect ends up throwing them smack dab in the middle of the Ark. But when a Russian expedition (**Markow and Kovalewsky**) in 1888 tried to find the Ark again, they were unable to substantiate the find.

A False Bishop?

In 1887 the "Nestorian archbishop of Jerusalem and Babylon", **Dr. Nourri**, led an exploration for the source of the Euphrates River. He took on Ararat and reportedly saw a hull through the eternal snow. "The only things accessible were the ship's bow and stern. The middle part was covered in ice. The Ark is made out of dark red planks of a very thick wood."

Who was he? Later he was unable to prove his fine titles, and his explanations were not convincing in that he boasted of fine details but had only seen "the Ark" from "a rifle shot's distance".

Also, the ice is not usually melted to such an extent during April when he supposedly saw the Ark...[3] Was he a religious fanatic - or a liar? Maybe both.

Wood Again

In 1888 **E. de Markoff**, a member of the Royal Russian Geographic Society, recounts that he has found wood above the timber line close to 14,000 feet. But in the wood the initials C.B. were carved. These initials matched two earlier Russian mountain climbers, so it is possible that they had carved their initials in the wooden cross Parrot planted.

Armenian Shepherds

There is also the story of an Armenian, Arthur Churchian, b. 1915, who lived his whole life in the USA. In 1975 he asserted that his father, **Jakob Churchian**, saw the Ark in c. 1890. Arthur has described the Ark in such detail that one would believe that he was the eyewitness. But when the same person tells "The Ararat Report" that he also believes that little people are living inside of the earth, and they are being kept secret by the authori-

Footnotes

[3] According to Lloyd Bailey: Noah, University of South Carolina, 1989.

[4] Violet M. Cummings mentions this in her book, Noah's Ark: Fable or Fact pp. 176-177 in connection with Al Judi.

[5] Bill Crouse argues this in The Ararat Report

[6] Noah's Ark: Fable or Fact. Spire Books 1975.

ties, he somehow loses his credibility…

Other Armenian shepherd boys can also remember stories the older boys have told about seeing the Ark, but big boys are known for trying to impress.

Another shepherd boy who showed his face 70 years later in the U.S. telling bewildering stories was one George Hagopian. We'll get back to him later.

Soldier Chronicles?

After World War II a small group of 6-7 Turkish soldiers announced they had seen Noah's Ark on their way home from Baghdad.

They were illiterate, but once they found out that Americans were interested in Noah's Ark, they got a friend who could write to send a letter to the American Embassy in Turkey in 1946 to offer their services as guides for Americans that wanted to search for the Ark.

My first thought was that these soldiers were only out to earn money.

But whatever the case, it was Mt. Ararat where they saw the Ark. It is interesting that they used the word "Ararat" when identifying the mountain on which they saw the Ark, because today Turks use "Agri Dagh" in the vernacular as well as on modern maps. In Turkey other mountains traditionally thought to have been "Noah's mountain" are also typically called Ararat[4]. The route described by these two soldiers is more reminiscent of the road to Mt. Cudi (also called Al Judi), which lies in southern Turkey. This road would also take them past the Tigris River[5] (not to confuse this Al-Judi with the Al-Judi that is near Mt. Ararat, which we will take up later.)

As far as is known, no soldiers have been requested as guides for Americans, and since then these soldiers haven't shown their faces.

The Russian Version

In August 1916 a Russian pilot, **Vladimir Roskovitsky**, says that on a reconnaissance flight he saw an ice-covered lake where the one end included a gigantic hull breaking out of the ice. One fourth of the wreck was covered in ice. One side was torn up, and the other side had a large door with two stories, but the one was missing. Roskovitsky's superiors apparently flew over the area afterwards and confirmed the existence of the wreck.

After this sighting, Tsar Nicholas II sent out an expedition. 150 soldiers worked on the mountain for a month. A scientific expedition measured the Ark and took some photos as well as samples of the woodwork. But "unfortunately" everything disappeared under the revolution.

This long-lived story of the Ark has come into Violet Cummings' book, *Noah's Ark: Fable or Fact*[6] along with many other sources.

The strange thing about this story is that is was proven to be a fake a few years ago. But still, some facts are mixed in with it.

The first time the story came out was in an American religious magazine, *New Eden Magazine,* in 1939. Author **Floyd M. Gurley** has confessed - unfortunately not until 1986 - that the details of the story were the work of

James Bryce (1838-1922), English politician and author, climbed Mt. Ararat in 1876 and found a 4-foot-long piece of processed wood (125 x 13 cm) in the snow above the 13,000 ft. mark.

imagination[7]. But he told Ark-hunter Eryl Cumming that he had received some of the information from a Russian immigrant. Cummings also says that he has knowledge of a British copy of a religious publication that Floyd M. Gurley copied almost word for word[8].

The problem is that people like Gurley who deal with Noah's Ark on a very superficial basis don't think about the consequences that follow publicizing or copying rumors, whether for interesting journalism or to promote religious interests. This type of "evidence" of Noah's Ark hurts more than it helps.

Benjamin Franklin Allen, a retired officer, constituted after the article that Gurley had uncontrollably added on to certain facts that he knew to be true, namely that two Russian soldiers had told about a pilot that had seen something that could have looked like a ship, after which infantry was sent out. They concluded that "it must be Noah's Ark".

Unfortunately, someone seeing a strange boulder or block of basalt on Mt. Ararat and claiming that "it must be Noah's Ark" has happened all too often, and we just can't trust these suppositions.

But was there more behind it?

Yes. **Alexander Koor**, a Russian colonel had actually written a similar anonymous account of the Ark that was much more detailed then Gurley's version. It was published in the Belarusian newspaper, *Rosseya*, in 1945. He claimed that he didn't know of Gurley's story which was printed five years previously. (Author and journalist Rene Noorbergen doubts this statement and believes that Koor actually used Gurley's account but just added more detail.)

Koor (who died in 1971) had been stationed in the Ararat-region during the Great War where he pointed out 20 historical sites that should be looked into more deeply. Many things were found, among these was a Sumerian inscription (from a period shortly after Noah's time) in Karada near Ararat that read, "God sowed the word's seed in the water … the water filled the earth, it came down from above...his children landed on the mountain".

In a statement[9] he explains that a Russian lieutenant named **Zabolotsky** probably saw something from his aircraft in 1916 that could resemble Noah's Ark. Koor later hears in 1921 second- and third-hand accounts of the follow-up that took place in 1916 and 1917 where some believed the Ark to be found in the "saddle" between Big and Little Ararat.

Violet Cummings has a vivid and detailed description of how the Ark supposedly looked with many rooms, etc., that it measured 500 x 50 feet, that it was covered in a dark brown wax-like material both in- and outside. The wood was well-kept except for a hole in the bow and the entryway in the side where it was a bit deteriorated and crumbled at the touch. The wood was supposedly cedar or larch wood. The Ark also supposedly lay with one side in the ice.

In the surrounding area, burned wood was found and something that could look like a stone altar, which, naturally, was meant to lead one's thoughts to Noah's sacrifice after the Flood.

Footnotes

[7] In a letter to David Fasold, forwarded to the editor of The Ararat Report, Fasold writes, "I have a letter from Floyd Gurley, with Floyd Gurley's personal letterhead on top center in blue, that he sent me from Hawaii to San Diego. When I tried to reply I was told he had died. I sent for a copy of his death certificate, and also have that. In this letter he confessed to me that the Roskovitsky story was a total fabrication for his magazine. Even the name was his friend who drove a street car in San Francisco. He said that he "hangs his head in shame" for all the problems caused by publishing the story." (David Fasold in a letter to Mathew Kneisler, February 20, 1998, published on Kneislers website.)

[8] The Explorers of Ararat, p. 376.

[9] Richard C. Bright: The Ark, A Reality?, Guilderland NY, 1989, p. 45.

[10] Violet M. Cummings: Noah's Ark: Fable or Fact pp. 57-58.

[11] The Explorers of Ararat, p. 388.

All of this information, with photographs and drawings, was supposedly sent via courier to the commander-in-chief by order of the Tsar[10].

But the tsar-regime was ended in 1917, and most of the tsar's family and many leaders were murdered under the Bolshevik Communist Revolution. Along with the royal family, this evidence also disappeared - that is, if it ever existed at all.

We cannot know whether they really found an Ark, described it in such detail, and took pictures of it, or if this is a story that speculation and rumors have built on, based on a true event that took place in 1916-17.

Despite the Revolution, it is very strange that none of the people that had been inside the Ark kept records of what happened, either by journaling or holding onto some of the many photographs or other evidence. It leaves us short of proof that this documented Russian expedition ever found a thing.

The last Russian tsar, Tsar Nicholas II, is said to have sent an expedition of 150 soldiers to Ararat to measure the Ark.

Stories about Russian Photos

There is also an instance where three Russian pilots - who where on the expedition - confirmed to a Mr. Evans along with their names and rank that the Ark was "as good as new" and that they had measured it and performed other tests. The door was gone and they took pictures and film, which were sent to the Russian government. Evans' daughter, Mrs. **Gladys Evans** gives this account. But unfortunately the document disappeared while cleaning.

A Mr. **Alvin Holdenbecker** from Minnesota tells that his aunt Eva had a father that was a medic for the Russian Ark expedition. Aunt Eva at 19 helped out in the house of the tsar-family, and her father, who was a good friend of the family, showed her the pictures.

She claims that the Bolsheviks killed as many of the expedition members they could find and that they confiscated all of the photos and rapports and that she was the only survivor because she was sent to the court of Keiser Wilhelm in Germany.

She has described the Ark in the pictures as three stories tall with an eave on the top that had openings for light and ventilation.

But her word is the only evidence we have. Or more correctly – her nephew's.

Research hasn't been able to confirm the Russian expedition either. The previous head of the KGB denied the existence of an Ark file to Armet Arslan, an Armenian Ark-hunter.

A Sunday-school teacher, Sister **Bertha Davis** of Hotville, California, showed photos of the Ark in 1935-41 that could have resembled the Russian claims. Three people say that they saw these photos: Joe Bosse, Walter Hefner, and his sister Maurine[11]. But were they real pictures or just paintings?

Two American soldiers from the 2nd World War, **Dale Nice** and **Roy Tibbetts**, gave a taped interview in New Mexico in 1977 where they tell that they both saw similar photos that an Australian soldier, **R. Taylor**, showed them. He claimed that he had taken the pictures himself.

Filmed?

The Russian expedition continues to haunt us. **Ray Lubeck**, an American machine worker on Midway Island during WWII claims that in 1942 he, along with about 30 others, saw a black and white film of approximately 50 Russian soldiers marching past "Noah's Ark" near the top of Mt. Ararat. The approximately 30-second long silent clip had an American commentator who said that the Russian soldiers were on their way to attack the Turkish soldiers. But Lubeck believes that the soldiers were from WWI based on their olive green-grayish uniforms. How in the world, though, did he see this on a black and white film?

Lubeck describes the Ark as 75 feet wide by 50 feet tall and hundreds of feet long. He says it was completely intact, lying out in the open in an area without any snow.

Lubeck didn't publicly disclose his story until after he had been to a seminar with painter Elfred Lee in the 1980's. Despite multiple attempts, no such film clip could be found in the archives in Washington, and likewise Lubeck has been unable to find any of his 30 buddies that supposedly saw that same film.

So too, this clue leaves us at ground zero...

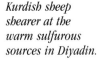

Kurdish sheep shearer at the warm sulfurous sources in Diyadin.

Chapter 19

Fernand Navarra:
- I Found the Ark

Frenchman Fernand Navarra was a big contributor to the rising interest in climbing Mount Ararat that has grown over the last half of the 20th century. The title of his book *I Found Noah's Ark*[1] got everyone to open their eyes. And his lifelike descriptions made many believe that the Ark had now been found, even though it was possibly hidden beneath a layer of ice.

Navarra pulled French military duty in 1937 in the Middle East one solitary time. In his spare time he climbed mountains together with an Armenian refugee, Alim, who once told him on Hermon Mountain about the holy mountain of his homeland – Ararat.

Another man told Alim that the Ark was still up there. The next 15 years Navarra gathered all the material he could find about the Ark, the Flood, and the countries that lie adjacent to Ararat.

In 1952 Navarra drove across Europe, into Turkey, and another thousand kilometers until he reached the border to Iran. Back in the early 50's it was much more difficult to travel than it is today.

When he reached his goal of eastern Turkey he, together with some locals and a few Turkish soldiers, climbed Ararat and made it all the way to the top of 16,854 feet.

French Fernand Navarra with the shaped piece of wood that he believed was from Noah's Ark because he found it high up on Mt. Ararat. The first examinations actually indicated that the wood was some 5,000 years old, but two carbon-14 tests showed that it was only between 1300 and 1900 years old.

A Myth is Put to Rest

After they got there they attempted to reach the west side of the mountain where a black shadow lay, one which the monks had pointed out claiming it to be the Ark hidden in the ice. No locals had ever bothered going up there to check it out. When Navarra got there he was disappointed to find the "half Ark" only to be a protrusion of rock.

At least the legend was put to rest.

But Navarra had also heard tales of the Ark in which it lay in a lake. Therefore, they tried to get to Lake Kop, found at some 13,000 ft. Navarra continues his story and tells us that his companion leaves him here unable to face the cold any longer. Navarra then continues on alone, which is very dangerous, until he reaches Parrot's glacier. And then he makes his incredible discovery at 2:00 p.m. on August 17, 1952:[2]

"It Must Be the Ark"

"I am alone on the ice where the light is clear and naked. I am so excited that I cannot feel my exhaustion. In the heavens above, an eagle is circling regularly, lifted by the wind.

I cross an arm of the glacier and ascend a glacial deposit. On the one side I can see a chunk of ice striped with crevices; on the other a steep rock face; and on the bottom between them, a dark mass.

It stands out very clearly. There are curves and straight lines embracing each other. In its entirety, it is at least one hundred and twenty meters long, and the form is very similar to the rail of a ship.

I have never been one to see things. I am a very sober-minded person and put my trust in the ability that sets the visionary apart: common sense.

What could it be? And at this height in the middle of an icy nothing? Maybe the ruins of a building? A church, a refuge, a forgotten house never rediscovered by visitors to this area? Or the remains of a crashed airplane? Even in the heroic years of flying, beams of this size were never used in planes.

There is no way around it: it is the remains of the Ark. It just cannot be anything else. In all likelihood, there lies what is left of the biblical ship's flat bottom after the rest of the construction was torn off. Does Berosus not tell us that during his time people in the Ararat area broke off pieces of the Ark to scrape off the pitch that was covering it?

The planks that they left have lain there untouched through time and protected by nature. And they are protected still today. Across from the steep rock face, enormous blocks have loosened and lie on top of the dark shapes.

The Ark is there, but you cannot reach it. Even if I had the necessary equipment to get down there, I would inevitably be crushed by these blocks. The only thing I can do today is to imprint this image into my mind with as much detail as is possible and then return to my companions. But I swear, I will return."

"It Could Only Be the Ark!"

It is typical of Navarra and many other Ark-hunters to jump to conclusions, assuming that it is the Ark they have found when they stumble upon a shadow in the ice or some wood. As Navarra has written multiple times, "because it couldn't be anything else" at an altitude of almost 16,500 ft.

But there are many other explanations for finding wood on a mountain. It could have been brought there to deceive someone. It could have been used by the monks or a hermit when building something of wood. The climate could have been much milder 1,500 years ago which would include trees growing at a higher altitude. The wood could have been catapulted to this height by the powerful volcanoes or earthquakes. Or... or...

Footnotes

[1] Fernand Navarra: J'ai trouvé l'arche de Noê.

[2] He writes the following in his book, *I Found Noah's Ark* pp. 101-102.

[3] B.J. Corbin *The Explorers of Ararat*. California, 1999.

or... We can't be satisfied with the conclusion, "it must be the Ark".

A New Climb in 1953

As promised, Navarra returned – in 1953 – but he fell ill, possibly due to the altitude, and was forced to give up. He claims that he had been a mere 300 feet from the Ark this time.

The following year an American named **John Libby** claimed to have been less than 100 feet from what he now believes to be the Ark. This helped Navarra decide to turn back for a 3rd time in 1955.

This time he takes his wife and three sons with him appearing to be a tourist family in order not to draw too much attention. Together with his oldest son Raphael, only 11, he climbs Ararat from the west. On the 2nd day around 7 in the morning they reach Kop Lake. They continue to the glacier where Navarra believes to have seen a shadow of the Ark under the ice. They are exhausted and set camp. Again Navarra unexplainably panics, and while Raphael is sleeping, he takes some cocaine he has with him...

As night presses in, the weather gets worse, and a block of lava rock falls on top of them. The next day they both fall, it starts to hail, etc. Eventually they reach a deep rift in the ice where Navarra re-discovers a wooden plank he had seen a few years previously.

"This must be the Ark," he concludes optimistically. However, it is only a glacial deposit.

Afterwards they nearly freeze to death during a 13-hour long snow storm but later dig a wooden plank out of the ice.

Despite all of their hardships, they come down alive, and later Navarra has the wood dated by an expert in Egypt who says it is c. 5,000 years old. Navarra then publishes his book, which is a huge success.

Fernand Navarra, in the foreground, resting on Parrot Glacier where he led the SEARCH expedition in 1969 with team members such as Harry "Bud" Crawford and Hugo Neuberg, seen in the background. Elfred Lee took the photo.

Doubt of Credibility

Then things start cooking.

Navarra's compadre, Alain Seker, denies being with Navarra on the expedition in 1952-53. Of course, this could be due to the fact that - according to Navarra - he left the expedition because he was freezing.

Navarra's son, Raphael, who accompanied Navarra in finding the wooden plank in 1955 has since then refused to comment on the find.

Navarra's friend and co-explorer from the first expedition in 1952, J. A. de Riquier, has also since then brought forth a serious accusation against Navarra for trying to acquire a piece of wood from an ancient construction in a village at the foot of the mountain with plans to "find" it on the mountain.

A Turkish lieutenant by the name of Sahap Ataly who says he scaled the mountain together with Navarra in 1952 made public an accusation that Navarra brought a piece of wood with him up the mountain in order to earn money from the sale of books and pictures. This was brought to light by Ataly in connection with Navarra's final expedition with SEARCH in 1969[3]. Navarra has never professed to having Sahap Atalay with him on the expedition of 1952.

And last but not least, a carbon-14 test of the wood shows that it could only be between 1300 and 1900 years old - all too young to have been from Noah's Ark. This information didn't come into the public eye until many years later. There may even be some of you that are reading this for the first time right here.

American Interest

But due to Navarra's findings, interest in the Ark – and finding it on Mt. Ararat – boomed, especially in America.

Various organizations were formed to equip expeditions to travel to Ararat in order to possibly find the Ark. The first organization that was of marked importance was SEARCH, which was led by previous Adventist minister, Robert (Bud) Crawford.

In 1969 SEARCH sent an expedition to Turkey - with Navarra as the pathfinder.

But on this expedition a painter and photographer, Elfred Lee – the oldest living, retired Ark-hunter from the SEARCH period – went along, too. He has played a central role in the latest period of Ark-hunting, and therefore, I asked him to tell about his inside information, to which he agreed.

Chapter 20:

An Interview with Elfred Lee

- Elfred Lee, you have played a key role in the search for Noah's ark. When did you get involved in the search?

- In 1968-69 right after I came back from Vietnam. I was contacted by the SEARCH Foundation, which needed somebody with my skills. There had been other groups that were looking for the Ark, but we wanted to add scientific research and credibility to the search. So I moved to Washington D.C. and lived there for many years, explains Elfred Lee.

As a missionary child born in Korea in 1940, he went through World War II as a child in a prison camp in the Philippines for three years. He personally experienced starvation and witnessed torture and was saved from execution by American paratroopers in 1945. Five years later he was once again rescued by American troops from the Communist invasion in Korea.

Because of these experiences he volunteered in Vietnam as a photographer and an illustrator for the U.S. Army and was shot down in a helicopter while taking movie footage for the Pentagon. After Vietnam he worked in Silicon Valley illustrating space shuttles among other things.

Besides being an ark hunter Elfred Lee is also a reputable artist who has painted quite a number of well-known persons as e.g. the actress Loni Anderson. Here a somewhat humorous painting of president Ronald Reagan – as a barbarian ....

- Were you employed by SEARCH?

- Well, when they had money I was given a little… I was a member of the board and one of the early pioneers. The work was based on information from the Frenchman Fernand Navarra from Bordeaux. He had written the book *I Found Noah's Ark*. He made a lot of claims, and we wanted to prove it, to verify it, and my job was to document it.

- You went on an expedition with Navarra in 1969 and 1970?

- Yes, in 1969 we had a very good expedition with Navarra and his son Coco, who spoke English. We had a scientist from the Arctic Institute of North America, and a British scientist who had worked at the South Pole. There were Ralph Lenton, Hugo Neuburg, Ross Arnold, John Bradley, and the Crawfords… These men were very strong physically and scientifically, they brought equipment. Queen Elisabeth had even honored one of them for heroic work in the Arctic. They were good with ice – we needed people who could see what was inside the ice. They brought coring augers and depth-sounding electronic equipment. I was the photographer, and I recorded the movie that has been shown on television over and over.

Wood from the Ark?

- When you went up the mountain with Navarra, he found wood again…

- Yes, more pieces of wood, and exactly in the right place where he said he had seen it earlier in 1955. Even Hugo Neubergen, the worst critic that was with us, accepted this. He and Navarra didn't get along too well. Hugo was very well educated and could speak German and Russian and more languages – and he was built like Rambo or Arnold Schwarzenegger… Navarra hated him from the very beginning and called him a boy scout and a cowboy…

- When Navarra and SEARCH had found this wood, you called a press conference in Istanbul. Why?

- I did not. It was Navarra and Ralph Crawford, the president, who wanted this. Crawford had some personal problems with money and drinking and… He had his own agenda. I honor him for the hard work he did. But I do not like the way he wanted publicity. My caution was: Please gentlemen, let us not have a press conference here in Istanbul. Let's get back to the States and have the wood dated first by scientists and others.

But I was very young, 29, and they out-ruled me. Crawford and Navarra were two of the same kind. They loved publicity. So we had our 15 minutes of fame. We had found Noah's Ark, and our photos and names went all over the world. Now when I look back, I see it was ridiculous, but I do admit I was caught up in the excitement.

- Yes of course. But then you had the wood tested…

- Yes, then the men went traveling through Europe, and I brought the wood back home. I had carried it down the mountain every day in my backpack. I went directly to the University of Pennsylvania that had the finest carbon dating lab at that time. I turned it over to them, but I did something that nobody knew about. I was testing Navarra. I had been to his home and he gave me some wood from his discovery in 1955. Even though I trusted him, I wanted someone smarter than me to verify it. So I marked two samples of wood; N for Navarra's wood and O for ours.

Nobody knew. They were all in Europe.

- What did the test reveal?

- Everything came out exactly the same. It showed that Navarra found his wood on the same spot as we did. That is very important, for some of the critics that were with him in the first place said he had planted it. They were also charismatic prima donnas who envied him and his fame.

- Do you think they criticized him because of that?

- That was part of it. We need critics. That is why I'm talking to you, provided you will publish this. I want to clear the record. I want honesty, and if I'm lying please tell me.

Elfred Lee on horseback on the SEARCH expedition in 1969 before climbing Mt. Ararat. (Photo: Elfred Lee)

- *Okay, I will.*
- The wood had been soaked in the same melting water, the test showed. It could not have been taken from a village nearby as some implied. When the men came home from Europe they also had the Forestry Department test the wood and both of them said the wood was a species of white oak.

- *But the wood was too young to be from Noah's Ark…*
- Yes, the test showed that it was between 1700 and 1900 years old.

The Facts Were Hidden
- What happened when you showed the result to Crawford?
- Crawford had been talking too much in public about Gopher wood and "5,000 years old". When I showed him the reports he immediately said, "Hide the report! Don't publicize the reports. They will use it against us. There is something wrong." So we put it in a file.

- *How did you feel about that?*
- I felt bad.

- *Later you got a letter…*
- Then Jean A. de Riquier (who was Navarra's climbing partner in 1952) wrote a letter accusing Navarra of attempting to purchase a piece of timber from an ancient structure in a nearby city. I went to the president and showed him the letter. Hugo Neuburg was in the office that day and translated it

from French. And immediately Crawford said, "Destroy that letter. It's wrong, something is wrong. Don't say anything about this letter."

I felt bad about that too. In my heart I thought: What is the truth then? I wasn't ready to give up – but I would not go on TV or publicly tell falsehoods.

My attitude was that all the report was still not in, and we needed to look at it all and make a report.

Then Rene Noorbergen came along. He was a good author and had already written a best selling book, and he and I became good friends. I saw his family and so on. He had also been through World War II as I had been.

He, of course, was very critical.

Then Navarra turned over to us his test that had been made in Bordeaux, Cairo, and Madrid. These people did not use carbon dating. But they were very good at ancient dating – especially in Cairo. They studied the cell modification from Navarra's wood. And this is why I'm so thankful I also sent in a piece of the Navarra wood and knew there was a connection. Any studies on Navarra's wood applied to ours, and vice versa. These people were very good at studying ancient material with lignite[1] formation, cell modification, the amount of fossilization, growth rings, etc. They concluded that this wood was 5,000 years old. So Crawford was happy again.

Help from National Geographic

We started to get a lot of help from the Smithsonian Institute and from National Geographic. I got to know the editor. And we were told that white oak was used a lot for ocean ships, because it is a good material for that purpose. If it was Gopher wood we don't know. Nobody knows what gopher wood is, but Don Shokey believes it is wood made in a process, a lamination of wood with layers and bitumen pitch between. And there was bitumen pitch in the wood we found.

The American SEARCH organisation persuaded Fernand Navarra (in the middle) to lead an expedition to the place where he had found wood on Mt. Ararat in 1955. In 1968 the expedition had to be cancelled due to his spraining the foot. But in 1969 these five men went to Turkey. Here Hugo Neuberg, Ralph Lenton, Navarra Harry Crawford and Elfred Lee in Dulles Airport.
(Photo: Elfred Lee)

The wood was saturated all the way through. It was very hard, like stone. It was like petrified, fossilized. Very dense and black, you could almost not see the growth rings, which also helps to prove some of the other theories of the world before the Flood with the hydrosphere[2]. All of this was coming together.

To that comes that Dr. Libby, who invented the carbon dating system, told us that there was some problem with the reliability of this theory. The wood we found had been influenced with carbon from melt water running through it for centuries. So it wasn't as obvious as it might look.

- Then the mountain was closed – Why?

- There was an uprising in Turkey at the universities at that time, and Turkey and Greece had their problems with Cyprus, and as usual there were anti-American demonstrations because we tried to be friends with both the Greeks and the Turks…

Anyway Crawford went to Greece, which wasn't very wise at that time, and he even boasted that he was working for the CIA. That of course spoiled everything. Now it came out in the news that we were illegal scientists working on Mt. Ararat. So the expedition in 1970 was called off, and the mountain (Mt. Ararat) was closed for 12 years…

So Crawford was sent back to Denver, Colorado, and he was later killed in a tragic and mysterious car accident in the middle of the desert at two o'clock in the morning. It's suspicious. He talked too much…

Jim Irwin Gets Involved

When Jim Irwin, the astronaut, got involved, he managed through his political connections to get permission. He had planted a Turkish flag on the moon – he was the one driving around in a moon-car, and he also discovered the "Genesis stone" on the moon, which showed that elements were created, not evolved. He was converted on the moon. He came back as a Christian and wanted to get involved in the search for the Ark. And that was when I got involved again.

- What did you do in the meantime?

- In the meantime I was also involved with answering questions, helping people with information and the next thing I knew, they were on TV or making film, and I was here in debt. But that's okay – it's not my project, I just happen to be involved longer than any other living person now and happen to know more about the location of Noah's Ark than anybody we know. If anybody knows more stand up. I was there at the right time, and I had the skill and education and training needed. I have a Master's degree

Fernand Navarra, Harry Bud Crawford and Hugo Neuberg climbing the Parrot Glacier in their attempt to find the Ark in 1969. (Photo: Elfred Lee)

Footnotes

[1] Lignite, variety of coal, also known as brown coal, intermediate in quality between peat and bituminous coal. Geologically, lignite is of comparatively recent origin, occurring in Cretaceous and Tertiary strata. It is usually brownish-black in color and often shows a distinct fibrous or woody structure. Lignite is inferior in calorific value to ordinary coal because of its high (30-75 per cent) water content and low (60-68 per cent) carbon content; the high (52.5-62.5 per cent) content of volatile matter causes lignite to disintegrate rapidly on exposure to air. The heat value of lignite is 7,807 kJ (7,400 BTU) per lb. (Encarta® 2002.)

[2] Lee refers to the theory that there was a hydrosphere in or above the atmosphere before the Flood.

The SEARCH team in 1969, photographed in the base camp: From the left Fernand Navarra Jr., son of the French explorer Fernand Navarra, then Harry "Bud" Crawford, who was general secretary of SEARCH, Fernand Navarra himself, Elfred Lee and in front the two scientists Hugo Neuberg and Ralph Lenton. (Photo: Elfred Lee)

and a Doctorate in archaeological illustration.

While we were waiting to get permission, we raised money – probably over a million dollars. We hired fundraising firms and there was a Korean firm that specialized in raising money from Christians. So we paid Colonel Pak $37,000 for a mailing list. Later we found out that he was using our money to raise money for Sun Myung Moon to support the Moonies.

The interview with Elfred Lee continues in the next chapters.

Chapter 21

Hagopian's Story

The year after Navarra and SEARCH had "found wood" from the Ark on Mt. Ararat and before it had been confirmed, so-called eye-witnesses showed up claiming to have seen the Ark! One had even been in it. His name was George Hagopian, who in 1970, at the age of 72, told his unbelievable story to Elfred Lee.

Hagopian's Story

As a ten-year-old, George Hagopian followed his grandfather on an 8-day trip to the top of Mt. Ararat in 1912. On this trip, claimed Hagopian, they both saw the Ark.

Even as an old man after living most of his life in the US, Hagopian could obviously remember in detail what the Ark looked like. He was helped along, however, by Elfred Lee, who painted the Ark according to Hagopian's description. Lee tells:

Elfred Lee spent hours and days with George Hagopian in order to retell his story about the Ark, which Hagopian claimed to have seen as a child in Armenia.

> - We got a letter from a lady, Mrs. Mary Board, Maryland, who knew George Hagopian. She wrote that he was an old Armenian and that he had walked on the Ark and was raised on Mt. Ararat. As a child he and his father had been on Mt. Ararat with their sheep every summer.
>
> He lived alone in his garage next to his too big house. He was broken hearted, old, sick, and lonesome, and she wanted us to get his information. Other expeditions had also received letters from her, but they had not followed up.
>
> So I went out to Maryland to talk with him. He was about 72 at that time. He had a very heavy Armenian accent, and it was very difficult to understand him at times, but because of my foreign background from Korea, I understood him. I interviewed him for hours. I made sketches from all that he explained from the mountain. At that time the border was on the other side, and he had to go into Russia – into the Republic of Armenia - to go up Mt. Ararat.

Doubtful Information

But if one goes a bit deeper into Hagopian's history, there are some things that could cause one to doubt whether his fantastic story is true.

He says that he went with his uncle to find grass after four years of drought. There were four years of drought from 1901-04, but if Hagopian was 72 in 1970, then that means he was born in 1898 which means that he was only

6 years old in the fourth year of drought. He says that he was 8-10 years old.

He also says that two years later he went up at the age of 12 and saw the Ark again. That would have been in 1906 (two years after the drought) or 1910, if his birth certificate is correct.

He claims that the uncle, grandfather, and many others in their village (which was at least 150 miles away from Mt. Ararat, on Lake Van) had seen the Ark. But if the Ark had been visible for a number of years, why is he the only one that has told about it? Especially considering the fact that people lived in the vicinity…?

Lake Van is a salt lake, but its surroundings are quite lush. So why did they go to the barren mountain 150 miles north in order to find grass? And how could they climb the mountain if they had animals to keep? It would take many days and be very difficult for such a little boy to conquer the elements that even rugged mountain men and astronaut Jim Irwin couldn't pass. And Hagopian even mentions that his legs were sore from the long walk from Lake Van. Altogether the trip took 8 days.

Even though Hagopian was only 5'4" - 5'5", he claims that he was one of the Sultan's body guards. Would a sultan be guarded by such little men? Would he lay his life in the hands of a man that was a part of an oppressed people that he later ordered into exile or be destroyed by the hundreds of thousands? Hagopian claims to have attended three of the Sultan's "murders", where Hagopian says a stand-in was hit. Why has no one else heard about these three failed assassination attempts? Did they always happen behind closed doors where Hagopian was present?

Hagopian claims that he fled when the Turks were eradicating the Armenians but was caught on the Russian border with a false passport and sent to work in Siberia for 18 months. But thousands of other Armenians fled to Russia where they were given safety and not sent to prison camps.

When he came out he only weighed 97 pounds and lived off of selling warm water and bread in Yerevan, the capital of Armenia. From this he earned enough money to travel to the US. Not too shabby.

He claims that in 1922 he was threatened by American government officials in uniform and representatives of the Turkish Embassy at the Mayflower Hotel to keep quiet about the Turkish assault on the Armenians. This is the reason he gives as to why he had not told about seeing the Ark that everyone was looking for until now as a lonely, old man. But why would the American authorities threaten him into silence?

Hagopian estimates the Ark he saw to be about 1,000 feet long and 600 feet wide, about double the length and seven times the breadth of the Biblical measurements 517 x 86.[1]

Hagopian also says that the Ark was whole and he was even inside of it. But a later "eye-witness", Ed Davis, claims that in 1945 it was split in two. Some Ark-hunting Ararat supporters think that Hagopian only saw the one half. If this was the case, then the Ark would be four times as long and 14 times as wide as the biblical specifications.

Footnotes
[1] Notice that these measurements are based on the Egyptian cubit, not the later English. If you compare them with the English, then Hagopian's measurements are even more exaggerated.

Who Can Vouch for Whom?

I asked Elfred Lee about some of these critical questions that can be formed about Hagopian's account, and therefore Lee's own material from the Ark.

- *What do you think of Hagopian's story today – thirty years after he told it to you?*

- Hagopian is one of the most valuable sources we have.

- *You still believe him?*

- Yes. I even let the hard-nosed Rene Noorbergen listen to the tapes, checked his account, and he passed a lie detector test. And everybody who knew him said he was an honest man. In fact he told us not to use his name and he didn't want money. He said, "I want you to listen to me and go back and find it."

It took me a year and a half to get all this information, and no one else on the earth has it.

- *But Hagopian claims that he was a lifeguard for the Sultan and saw stand-ins for the Sultan assassinated three times. But would a Sultan use a lifeguard from the Armenian people who were his enemies and whom he ordered destroyed…?*

- He became a lifeguard because he was a champion wrestler. He was a very strong man.

- *But small though…*

- He was in the Turkish army and kept quiet about his Christian faith,

Did Noah's Ark look like this?

In his seventies Armenian George Hagopian told that as a child he had seen the Ark on Mt. Ararat and that it looked like the one in the picture as he had "dictated" for artist and Ark-hunter Elfred Lee. Please note that in Hagopian's memory the Ark is nearly square with only slightly rounded edges, looks as if it were assembled in the middle, and includes a box with a row of windows set on top. The dimensions were bigger than those in the Bible as well…

evidently. And because he was a respected wrestler, he became a guard for the Sultan. And you can check out the whole story, and all the facts fit the time.

- But it was at the time of World War I, and the Sultan was fighting with Russia about the Armenians.
- He was a guard, and when the persecutions began, he got in trouble. Before this time the Armenians were like the Jews in Germany before the Nazis. After the war the Sultan was killed, and Ataturk took over the country and renamed the Ottoman Empire after him, called it Turkey, and then the massacres began.

- There were massacres before – the worst was in 1915.
- But Hagopian was in Turkish uniform and went to his own town and witnessed the massacre of his own family with long knives. The captain turned to him and said: You are next. The only thing saving you is your Turkish uniform. You have 24 hours to decide whether to become a Muslim or remain a Christian. So he was scheduled to die, and he fled with a Greek friend. And they ran every night and hid during the days. One day they were so hungry they stole a sheep and then hid in a tree. And the owner of the sheep, who was an Armenian, caught them and wanted to kill them. And George said, "I'm an Armenian." But the man said, "No, you are in Turkish uniform. If you are Armenian recite the 23rd Psalm. He did in perfect Armenian, and the man helped them out of the country."
But across the border he was questioned and they didn't believe him, so they said, "This is a false passport. Do you want us to send you back or send you to a prison camp in Siberia?" Hagopian said, "Send me to hell – but not to Turkey." So they said, "We will send you to Siberia, it is a lot cooler…"
He went to prison camp, but because of good behavior he was released and went to Yerevan and sold hot water for coffee and black Russian bread. He saved every penny and bought a ticket to France, and from there he got to New York.

- Did he work in France to buy the ticket?
- No, in Yerevan.

- But how could he possibly save so much money by selling hot water and bread in a poor country?
- He is Armenian…! They are good businessmen. He also had help from the church. His first objective when he came to America was to go back to Turkey with a photographer, and he actually went and got to Ishmir. But because of a war between Turks, Armenians, and Greeks, they couldn't go further. And the photographer took lots of movies from the famous Ishmir incident, where the Turks took Armenians and Greeks and threw them into the water. And there was an American gunboat there, and they

ran to the captain and asked him to save the people. But he answered that he had orders not to get involved in this local conflict.

They went back to the Mayflower Hotel in Washington and called for a press conference where they showed the film. He saw some Turks, and later people came up with official papers and said, "You must not talk about this again." They took all their movies, and the Turks threatened their lives. Then he retired to Maryland, sold carpets, kept quiet, bought an estate, and that's where I finally met him.

- And you believed him?
- Yes. I knew him well. He would not lie. There were times where he had a hard time remembering, but then I questioned him again from all directions always cross checking. I took out Ralph Crawford the president, and he didn't want me to publish it, because Hagopian disagreed with the place we had found.

But I didn't care because I thought that it would altogether bring us to the right place. And it has, because Hagopian and Ed Davis (another eyewitness) have been able to put together two conflicting ideas on where it was. Hagopian said on multiple occasions that the people in his village and the entire Armenian nation knew the secret of the location of Noah's Ark. We can't find anybody now living. He might have been the last one who had actually seen it.

- If this were true, then a lot of Armenians would know today…
- But they haven't been there. The new generation of Armenians is so secular and westernized – just like the Jews. They are very atheistic. They have been through holocaust, and they don't want to talk about their Armenian heritage.

- Couldn't it be that these old people just believe in their own imaginations?
- That's why I questioned him over and over again.

- You painted the Ark as Hagopian and Davis remembered it. But it looks like the Ark on the old medieval paintings. It doesn't look much like a boat. Wasn't it supposed to sail?
- The Ark was a bark. It's a box, like the Ark of the Covenant. (That's not a boat, but a box where the Israelites had the Ten Commandments.) It was not made to travel. It was made to float. And Hollywood took my drawings to San Diego long before I moved here, and the Navy built a scale model from my drawings. I didn't know before it came out in the movie. And they tested it – they were testing Hagopian and me. But they found out it was the most seaworthy ship they ever saw and that Noah's Ark, according to these drawings, could sustain tidal waves over 200 feet high.

- According to a ship's engineer I have talked to, a rectangular ship-

box like that would not be as able to break the waves as a ship with a pointed keel.

- Well, it was rounded a little.

Doubt from an Ararat-Supporter

Bill Crouse – who belongs to the Ararat hunters – has been trying to approach both Lee and Hagopian cautiously in the Ararat Report. He writes that Hagopian's accounts are "difficult to falsify" and that Hagopian is "no longer among us" which makes it difficult to judge. But after a few introductory maneuvers, he takes courage and writes:

> Do I have any problems with the Hagopian story? Some, but they are not enough to dismiss the story. Something that troubles me is the fact that the testimony itself is secondhand. From experience, I am skeptical of the way testimony has been elicited from alleged witnesses by Ark researchers in the past. When one wants to believe a story, as Ark researchers desperately want to do, it is often difficult to maintain the proper neutrality. Often words are put into their informants' mouths. Negative or contradictory facts are simply ignored. I am also troubled by the great length of time from Hagopian's boyhood until the time of his testimony (70 years). The years can really dim the details. But on the other hand, some elderly people have vivid memories of their early years.
>
> Another matter hard to dismiss is Hagopian's social situation. He was apparently a lonely man with no relatives and few friends. With this condition it is easy for someone needing to feel important to embellish their past! Ask any psychiatrist.[2]

Answers to Accusations

- *Dave Fasold claims in a letter[3] that you, Elfred Lee, painted on the staircase even though Hagopian didn't tell about it.*
- Dave Fasold knows nothing about me. I have met him at Mt. Ararat, and I respect him for what he was trying to do. But he got it wrong with this. I painted the ladder on the Ark according to the instructions of Hagopian. I didn't want it there. I said, "Uncle George – the Bible doesn't say that there was a ladder on the side of the Ark." And he said, "That's what I saw – so paint it." And I kept working on it, and it was very difficult, explains Elfred Lee.

- *Jonathan Gray, the Australian writer, states that you painted the Ark onto a photo used in the film "In Search of Noah's Ark".*
  Quote:
  A gentleman named Elfred Lee PAINTED IN the boat-shape onto a photo of Ararat. That's right. And what is more, a gentleman named Sellier, who prepared a picture for the film "In Search of Noah's Ark",

Footnotes

[2] From "The Ararat Report", reprinted in *The Explorers of Ararat*, July 1999.

[3] In a letter to Mathew Kneisler, February 20, 1998, published on Kneisler's website, he writes: "Despite Roskovitsky and Hagopian's story and Elfred Lee's artistic rendering of what they saw, the Bible says that Noah removed the roof covering. The question is then, who put the roof back on? While in Dogubayazit, I buttonholed Elfred Lee in the little pastry shop across the street from the Ararat Hotel (as it was named then) and asked him, "are the stairs on the bow [front] or the stern [rear end] of this eyewitness account of Hagopian's Ark on Ararat? His answer was the stairs were his idea. So much for the eye witness account of what Hagopian's Ark looked like."
http://arksearch.com

The Ark as described by George Hagopian and painted by Elfred Lee. Notice the steps on the back of the Ark that David Fasold accused Lee for having added. But it was the other way around, Lee claims. He didn't think that the steps should be there at all. Hagopian, however, insisted on their inclusion.

took a tiny stone about an inch high, shaped it into a model of the Ark and placed it against some soil in a little dry wash-out about a foot high in Utah. The film commentary stated: "This is in a canyon on Mount Ararat." They also placed it against some snow and photographed it close up in such a way you couldn't tell how big it was." – Jonathan Gray in Discoveries: Questions Answered pg. 54.

- *Well, did you paint in the Ark?*

- Jonathan Gray is making claims that are stupid. He doesn't know me. He is making claims of falsehood on falsehood. It is absolutely wrong. I would never do that. My whole goal in this is to honor God with my work in a scientific and honorable way.

I don't even know what he is talking about. But I know that somebody else did paint in an Ark on a picture, and I publicly accused them of it. There is a photo that was used in a documentary film produced by Charles Sellier and Dave Balsinger called "In Search of Noah's Ark". My movie was the first. It was called "Search for Noah's Ark". (The name SEARCH Foundation also came from me. They had a different, more religious name, and I changed it because we must be scientific and keep religion out and have other people check us. Let them have the fame and glory, and we must shut up. But we didn't – and we got in trouble.)

The other foundation was called Holy Ground Foundation. They used a photo that had been taken by Eryl Coming, if I'm not mistaken. He and Violet were all of our grandparents, and I knew them intimately. Now that he has passed away, I have had free access to their files, because I have contributed freely to all of his books.

He took a photo in the Ahora Gorge looking up – and I don't know how it got into the hands of the Holy Ground Foundation, but I know a re-touched photo when I see it. I know how to do it. But this was a bad job. When they measured it they found out that it was 200 feet high, and Noah's Ark was not at all that big. Then they went and claimed that it was Noah's Ark. They deceived a lot of people including Jim Irwin. And I said, "No, no, no! This is a retouched photo."

So, you see there are people who have illusions that they are going to find Noah's Ark and that God has anointed them. I have had to step back and ask myself: Do I want to find Noah's Ark, or do I want it found? It is not Elfred Lee's project. I'm an idiot that doesn't deserve any glory or credit. I'm just an instrument. If God can use me – fine – if not, I have other work to do. I'm busy.

- What about the model of the Ark in Utah?
- It is true that Sellier and Balsinger made a model of the Ark out of my painting and put it in the mountains of Utah. They re-enacted people's expeditions. That is how Hollywood does it. No big deal.

- But is it also clear and obvious for the people who view the film that this is not real – that is has been made up?
- Okay – I wish they had put in a disclaimer a little bit more loudly. There is a photo in one of the many books that have been published that has a photo of this scale model built for the movie. And if they don't tell that it is a scale model, I'm sorry. That's wrong.

Chapter 18

Other Eyewitnesses

Ed Davis discussing his eyewitness account with the Armenian Ahmet Arslan at a secret meeting in 1987. Photo: Elfred Lee

Next to George Hagopian, retired sergeant Ed Davis is probably the Ark hunter that has been taken most seriously.

Ed Davis claims that while he was stationed in Iran during the Second World War he saw the Ark – broken in two – on Ararat.

He explains that he had helped some locals with water and that out of their gratitude they wanted to take him up the mountain. Eight locals (from Iran?) led the way. Three of which continued all the way to the place where on the 5th day they went through the Kurds' "secret routes" to the place they had hidden from the Turks, "The Cliffs of Judgment Day".

Ed Davis describes it as a true adventurer, "I guess it's called that because it's a place you could easily die and many have. Some not of their own doing." [1]

A statement like that probably gets your alarms going even though Davis passed a lie detector test with an okay score. How does Davis *know* this?

The legendary Lawrence of Arabia is also in Ed Davis' fantastic story. He claims that he had been at a cave where Lawrence had once hidden. Since then no one has ever come across such a cave nor has anyone heard rumors of Lawrence on Ararat.

Davis and the three Kurds come to a protruding rock. The weather is gray and foggy, but suddenly the sun shines through the mist, and the Muslims pray to Allah. Afterwards they point to a specific spot and say, "That is Noah's Ark". Davis can't see it at first, but then he does. It's, "a huge, rectangular, man-made structure partly covered by a talus of ice and rock, lying on its side. At least a hundred feet are clearly visible. I can even see inside it, into the end where it's been broken off, timbers are sticking out, kind of twisted and gnarled, water's cascading out from under it."

How is it possible that Davis can hardly see the Ark one moment and the next he describes it in such vivid detail? But there's more. His companion, Abas, now points another direction where the other half of the Ark is lying a bit further down. And the Kurds say that the Ark is broken into multiple pieces.

Davis contends that he can see "at least three stories" in this end of the Ark, and Abas says there are 48 compartments in the top. Davis also believes he can see passageways inside the Ark. But they must wait until the next day to crawl down there with ropes, says Abas.

Footnotes
[1] From his eyewitness account at the Ark-a-thon meeting in Farmingdale, USA, 1986, restated in The Explorers of Ararat, 1999.

And would you believe that the next morning it snowed? So there were no further explorations, according to Davis.

Was Davis On Another Mountain?

The question is did Davis ever see the Ark other than on the painting Elfred Lee made for him in 1987 based on his descriptions. There were windows here that didn't exist in his first description from 1986, Ark-hunter Doris Bowers pointed out. Another Ark-hunter, Bill Crouse, was also skeptical. He noted 6 discrepancies in Davis's explanations,[2] which are abbreviated here:

1.   Davis has explained that he was in Harmadan, Iran, and could see Mt. Ararat. But the distance from here is over 400 miles. The curvature of the earth would make this impossible.

2.   Davis claims to have driven from Harmadan to Abas's village below the mountain in just one half of a day. This would also be impossible on such poor roads in 1943.

3.   It appears[3] that he traveled with Kurds. But Davis said that Abas was *Lourd*, which is the people group from around Harmadan. A Lourd would not be a village chief on Ararat, which is surrounded by Kurds.

4.   If the Ark were there where Davis alleges (about 13,000 feet above sea level), it would be visible in the summertime.

5.   Davis tells us that Abas and his people have previously found honey still in the jars on the Ark as well as feathers in cages, fish bones, and beans that can still be eaten.

6.   Davis also claims to have seen the Garden of Eden. Exactly 50 miles from Harmadan there is a mountain called "Kuh e Alvand" which is also traditionally the landing place of Noah's Ark[4] as well as the Garden of Eden. It is 11,700 feet high and only covered in snow part of the year. Many things suggest that if he was anywhere, it was here. Davis died in 1998.

He Knew Too Much

I asked Elfred Lee about some of these critical objections:

- *Davis claimed that he had received threats and mysterious phone calls from people accusing him of betraying Abas's family's secret and therefore "Allah's black hand" was over him. Are you sure that he was credible?*

- Yes, he had too much information and knowledge to be completely discounted. He was about ninety, and I have been to his home and met his wife. When you get to know a person's relatives, you can check out their credibility very quickly. When I first met him, I didn't believe him. I was skeptical.

- *Bill Crouse had some critical points on Ed Davis. He checked out that Davis couldn't have seen Mt. Ararat from where he was in Iran – 400 miles away.*

Footnotes

[2] In "The Ararat Report".

[3] From his account in Don Shockey's book, The Painful Mountain, Pioneer Pub. Co., 1986.

[4] In Dr. John Montgomery's book The Quest for Noah's Ark 2nd ed. Dimension Books, 1974, he presents a French map from a 1730 lexicon of the Bible (Dictionnaire historique de la Bible, Calmet) drawn by Pierre Daniel Huet. Here the "Arche de Noe" is on a mountain that – with a bit of good will – could be Kuh e Alvand or Alvand Kuh-Mountain in Iran. But Mount Ararat lies right next to it. The map is not a precise map either, but rather a fabled map of "earthly paradise" including The Garden of Eden marked to lie in southern Iraq.

Ed Davis claimed to have seen a large ship with multiple decks broken in two lying in a deep gorge on Mt. Ararat. Here we see Elfred Lee's painting according to Ed Davis's description. The two pieces of the Ark are seen lying at the top of each side of the gorge.

- Bill Crouse will find anything negative, but that's okay. He's my friend. Anyway, he didn't know Hagopian or Ed Davis. There are details that I don't know about. I know that the way he describes everything fits with Hagopian's story.

- *Davis might have known about Hagopian's story before he told his story to you...*
- Possibly, but he said he didn't know about Hagopian. And I know from first hand that Ed Davis has been there. He could not have described it and agreed with Hagopian so well without being there.

- *Where did you meet him?*
- After the 1985-expedition when we were chased out by AK47-guns and the tent and everything was burnt by the terrorists, we vent to Farmington, New Mexico, the home of Eryl Cummings. There we had an "Ark-a-thon". I had the opening devotional talk. I told about all the early expeditions that I had been involved in, and I talked about the disunity, disharmony, and dishonesty, and I said that we will never have success unless we put aside this disunity. And we all went in a circle and prayed for unity. We also

prayed for Ed Davis, who couldn't be there because he had had a stroke, I think. Then the phone rang, and it was Ed Davis on his deathbed – he was now feeling much better and wanted to come.

So somebody went and picked him up, and he came later that evening and told his story.

When he stood up, I was really skeptical – him with his cowboy boots and cowboy hat, Indian jewelry and silver… And I was from Washington where we all wore gray suits. But when he started talking – my goodness, my hair stood up. It was like hearing George Hagopian. He described all the details in a way that he had to have been there.

So we went to a little room, and I turned on my tape recorder and started to sketch what he was saying. It was crowded with people taking pictures, and as he was talking I needed more paper – because the picture grew bigger and bigger with his story. In the end I had about ten pieces all taped together. He was able to describe very detailed when he saw his testimony drawn on paper – just like Hagopian. It becomes visual, and he can then say, "No, put this rock there." This man who was supposed to be dying wanted to go on all night. I was getting tired.

The Conclusion

- What did you conclude out of the two eyewitnesses' stories and Navarra's wood?

- We did locate the different places where Navarra said he had seen wood on the mountain, and it came directly down from the Hagopian place with glaciers. We didn't know that is was broken at that time. Ed Davis told us that, and we think therefore pieces of wood were coming down from the Ark with the melting water.

- But still – the wood was too young. Couldn't it have been from a monastery in the mountain?

- Yes, it is possible, too. But the monastery we know of was way down in the Ahora Gorge. It wasn't up high. It couldn't come from a tree either. There are no trees above 11,000 feet. That's the timberline. This huge timber comes from 15,000-16,000 feet.

- But how could it be from the Ark when the carbon dating proved it was only 1700-1900 years old?

- That's another thing. We talked to Dr. Wilbur F. Libby who invented the carbon dating system. He said, "We have a problem with your wood samples. This wood is not dry like a piece of pottery in a New Mexico cave. This is wood that has been soaking in melt water at a high altitude bombarded by carbon of a more recent vintage."

This wood is contaminated of material from a more recent date. Also there are sheep and goats, and there are plants growing, but no trees. There are organic materials in this water, and these have contaminated it and made it much younger when carbon dating it.

- So the wood could still be from the Ark...

- I say, "What else is it?" It's a wooden vessel at 15,000-16,000 ft. It has three decks. It's open down the middle like a mall with a window in the roof with light and ventilation into the entire interior. Cages have been seen in the deck larger than any elephant we know. Smaller cages are on the second deck including rod iron bars that looked like a chicken-coop for birds. Some people say there was no iron at that time, but Turbal-Cain was an ironworker.[5] On the deck were still furniture and ceramic boxes and a stove to cook...

- You base all this on the claims of two people. If they lied to you, or if they imagined things or are confused in their heads, as old people sometimes are, what do you have left then?

- People don't believe someone walked on the moon. People ridiculed Columbus...

- But this is different...

- I knew these men, and if there were some lapses in their memories, it is forgivable. But usually when people get old, they forget about the time being and remember their childhood and what happened a long time ago.

- Are you still convinced that the Ark is on Mt. Ararat, or could it be on another mountain? (The Bible does talk about "the Mountains of Ararat" so it could be all over Armenia.)

- Yes, the Armenians call Mt. Ararat Massis — it means Mother Mountain. And there is only one mountain in Armenia that is high enough to be the mountain of the Ark..., says Elfred Lee.

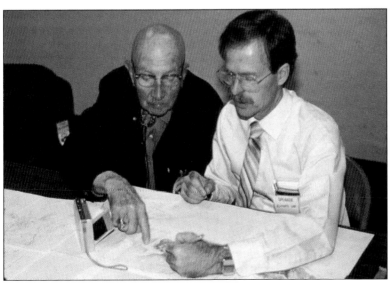

Ed Davis coaching Elfred Lee in drawing the Ark so that it matched his account. The picture is from the 1986 Ark-a-thon, an Ark-hunter convention, where Ed Davis turned up and impressed the audience with his story. The question is whether it was true or not...

Footnotes
[5] Genesis 4:22.

Ed Behling – Caught Boasting?

The American Ed Behling is the only living so-called eyewitness that claims to have seen the Ark not only from the air but on the mountain – Mt. Ararat.

In 1973 Behling was stationed in Diyabakir, Turkey, in the Air Force. One day after church back home in the States, Behling told how he had seen the Ark. He didn't know that an Ark hunter was there that day – a Bob Stuplich who had sedulously tried to find the Ark.

Behling was now brought forth in the news as a new eyewitness that confirmed the Ark's placement on Ararat.

In a radio interview in 1982 with *Prophecy in the News* in Oklahoma, he said that he and some Kurds conquered Mt. Ararat in 1973 and saw Noah's Ark there. But a number of his explanations don't fit in the puzzle. He estimated the distance to Mt. Ararat to be around 100 miles, while the real distance is 249 miles. The Ark hunter, Pat Frost, who has been up the mountain 9 times, believes that his description of the area is a copy of Lee's drawings from Hagopian's story. After the interview and the attention it created, Behling has withdrawn and refuses to answer any more detailed questions from other Ark hunters.

The most likely explanation is that this man's mouth was too big. One lie covered another and the snowball effect started and ended with Behling in a trap.

Chapter 23:

Ark Fever

After Navarra's incredible discovery of wood on Mt. Ararat, which isn't completely true, the real hunt began. Numerous expeditions, organizations, and private persons followed the so-called SEARCH expedition: A lot of money was invested, and a number of books were written and published retelling the tales without asking questions.

One might wonder why the Ararat Ark-hunters were not more critical of these stories or of the so-called eyewitnesses.

Maybe the big mistake was using this unscientific method before confirming the results: they *knew* that the Ark was on Mt. Ararat, and so they were all about finding it.

Dangerous Adventurism

It was probably more than religious convictions that caused all of these Ark-hunters to climb up Mt. Ararat. It was also adventurism, maybe childhood dreams. Most of these mountain adventurers were men. Among some it became an entire obsession. The Ark had to be up there. They were taken by Ark Fever and came back to their beloved time and time again. They put themselves in dan-

James Irwin was not only interested in the moonwalk. He attempted to find Noah's Ark on Mt. Ararat eight times. When he fell into a deep gorge in 1982 he nearly died. Nevertheless, Irwin came back again in 1985, '86, and '87…

ger, and some met a fatal end like the 28-year-old Paul Jernæs of Drammen, Norway. In September 1986, presumably killed in the mountains, Jernæs tried to reach the top and disappeared. He was never seen again, and his body has never been found.

James Irwin, who was the 8th astronaut to walk on the moon, fell from a cliff when he tried to find the Ark in 1982. According to the leader of the group, Bob Stublich, Irwin had four teeth knocked out, four gashes in his head, and his hands were torn and swollen to double their normal size.[1] Irwin still went back after a month in the USA to regain his strength. And again in 1985 and 86 and 87…

You have to admire these Ark-hunters' courage and stamina.

But you don't have to admire the non-systematic method many of them use in their search, nor their unwillingness to be discouraged by the geological and glaciological evidence that is inconsistent with their belief that the Ark can be found on Mt. Ararat. Geologically because Mt. Ararat is a volcano and glaciologically because ice moves at different speeds on the different layers and would therefore rip the Ark apart if it lay in the ice.

This doesn't rule out being able to find pieces of it, but it is unlikely that the Ark would still be whole as in Lee's paintings based on the accounts of Hagopian and Ed Davis.

Finally a Systematitian

One of the few Ark-hunters who has systematically researched the supposed Ark findings is an American, Dr. Charles Willis. He is a neurologist, has a degree in Religion, and has been interested in archaeology for many years. In 1973 an expedition in which his son John took place revealed with photographs that the rock at 12,000 feet thought to be the Ark, or at least a man-made object, was only a rock. Willis believes that this misunderstanding could have been the source of many false allegations including those of George Greene, Ed Davis, Ed Behling, and George Hagopian – the most well-known of the "eyewitnesses". And a large chunk of the Ararat Ark fever can be attributed to their work.

Willis also interviewed another self-professed eyewitness, Mr. Officer, and concluded that he was a pathological liar.

Willis studied the uppermost part of Ahora Gorge where many Ark-hunters continually return in belief that the Ark must be hidden here. Willis didn't find it here either. Afterwards he believed it may lie so deep in the ice that it wouldn't have been destroyed by the glacial movements. I 1983 he explored the eastern plateau. In 1986 he tried again where the whole group combed the eastern plateau with metal detectors. Their motivation was a new theory by Guy Leduc that the Ark was also built with iron and bronze. This too gave negative results.

But Willis was systematic. In 1988 he returned with an expedition probing the eastern plateau with radar, which revealed the ice to be 80 feet deep, but there was no trace of an Ark. They tried again further and further west on the top of Ararat where the ice was 95 feet deep. Again the radar returned with no signs of the Ark. Finally, they drilled holes to a depth of 40 feet which also told of ice alone.

The Ark Isn't Here

After all of these grueling expeditions, Willis and his team, which consisted of only committed Christians, concluded that the Ark was not to be found on Mount Ararat, and that the *assumed* find was of little or no value.[2]

Willis has no intentions of returning to Mt. Ararat. But he is interested in looking at Mt. Cudi, which lies much further south on the Iraqi border.

He hopes to find signs that Noah was there, but he doesn't believe that the Ark has survived all this time. Rather, he believes it has since been broken down and used for building material.

But the impeccable and systematic research performed by Willis hasn't caused other Ark-hunters to give up. Among the new Ark-hunters is the Italian, Angelo Palego, who has been on Mt. Ararat almost every year since 1990. He confidently claims that he has found Noah's Ark at a height of 14,000 feet and shows photographs in newspapers and on his website of

Footnotes

[1] Bob Stublich from *The Explorers of Ararat*, p. 100.

[2] Charles Willis in *The Explorers of Ararat*, p. 124.

the alleged find which he sets to be 39° 43' 0,08" N and 44° 16' 51,5" E. Not many of the other Ararat Ark-hunters support Palego's find. They believe that it is just another rock or a basalt cliff that has previously been mistaken for the Ark in aerial photographs.

The Long List

The following list of post-Navarra Ararat expeditions is made up of almost only Americans and is therefore not exhaustive. In addition to these expeditions, many others were planned and fell through because they were not given the necessary authorization or because of Kurdish terrorism. Most of the expeditions of the following list were carried out in full.

John Libi, USA – conquered Mt. Ararat 8 times from **1954-69**. The closest he came to a find was his discovery of some stone walls which could have been used as a stall for animals.

Secret expeditions by the **National Geographic Society**, the Smithsonian Institute, and David Duckworth in 1958, 1964, and 1968 – not officially confirmed but based on the evidence from multiple sources[3] most likely took place. The expeditions were held a secret because the prestigious institution did not want to put its reputation on the line claiming to search for Noah's Ark, which was considered a legend. The guard, Duckworth, believes to have seen a pieced together picture of a ship.

SEARCH Foundation - expedition 1968 and 1969. American financed with explorer Fernand Navarra as the main detective, Elfred Lee as the drawer, and others involved. The first expedition had to be cancelled when at the last moment Navarra sprained his foot. On the next trip in 1969 pieces of wood were "found" – wood that Navarra possibly laid one day when he separated himself from the group.[4] The wooden pieces were introduced at first as evidence of Noah's Ark, but later studies based on the carbon-14 method (studies which were held secret from SEARCH) showed that the wood was only 1300-1900 years old.

In **1972** Dr. **John Morris** together with John Bultema, Bill Ellison, Roger Losier, and John Seiter ascended Mt. Ararat and examined Ahora George, Cehennem Dere, and Parrot Glacier. Here John Morris was hit by lightning while he stood on Zap Rock and thanked God for his protection… (Talk about an electrifying experience!) Despite the paralysis and a snowstorm, they all made it down alive.

In **1973 John Willis,** Dr. Lawrence Hewitt, Eryl Cummings, Ray Anderson, Jerry Williams, Geoff McMahon, and Jack Darnell took on Cehennem Dere

*Dr. Charles Willis near the top of Mt. Ararat where he conducted expeditions in 1983, 1984, 1986, and 1988. On the last trip his team investigated the east plateau with radar and drilled holes in the ice. Dr. Willis's conclusion was that the Ark could not possibly be located on Mt. Ararat. Instead he has started looking on Mt. Cudy near the Iranian border.
(Photo: Charles Willis, www. ancientworldfoundation.org)*

[3] Rene Noorbergen's interview with a past employee, David Duckworth, letter from army chaplain Clair Shaffer to Dr. Willis about a group from The National Geographic Society that spent the night in Trabzon, Turkey, on their way back from Ararat, and shortly discussed in *The Explorers of Ararat* pp. 430-35.

[4] This is suggested by many including Bud Crawford, who was a part of the expedition in 1969.

(Hell's Canyon) and revealed that an object at 12,000 feet was only a rock.

In **1974** Bob Stublich and Dr. John Warwick Montgomery together with others climbed Mt. Ararat and saw a black spot in the ice on the upper part of the Parrot Glacier and the Abich I area.

In **1975** Bob Stublich climbed the Parrot Glacier on Mt. Ararat.

From **1976** until 1993 Ray Anderson was on Ararat five times.

In **1978** John McIntosh went up Mt. Ararat on his own, in 1982 with Jim Irwin, among others, in 1984 with Rick Hatch and Doris Bowers, in 1985 with Bill Crouse and others, in 1986 he was in Turkey to research Ed Davis's claims but had to give up any hope of climbing the mountain due to Kurdish terrorist activity. In 1987 he and Dick Bright also had to give up. In 1988 he went along with Al Jenny and Chuck Aaron's aerial photography trip. In 1989 other Ark-hunters asked him to stay home because of a book Dick Bright had recently published including a picture of John McIntosh baptizing a young man in the Euphrates River. They feared he would be arrested. He was in Turkey again in 1993 but in vain and in 1996, 1997, and 1998 where they again were not allowed to climb the mountain but instead looked at anchor stones and other things.

In **1982** the astronaut **James (Jim) Irwin**, who walked on the moon in 1971, climbed Ararat. At one point he left the group and fell. He survived but broke his leg and had his face all scratched up. All together he took part in six different expeditions to Mt. Ararat. The others were in 1983, 1984, 1985, 1986, and 1987. He died in 1991.

In **1983** Bob Stublich, Jim Kunes, and Bill Spear took on the mountain and photographed it from a small plane. The same year Dr. Charles Willis and a team climbed the eastern plateau. John Morris, Ahmet Arslan, Brian Bartlet, Ed Crawford, and Donald Barber were also on the mountain.

In **1984** Don Shockey took on Ararat, the first of 9 trips.
The same year Bill Crouse was also there. John Morris from the Institute for Creation Research was there with his group.
Marvin Steffens came with a group from International Expeditions, and
Jim Irwin with his High Flight Foundation group together with John Christianson, Dick Bright, and Ron Wyatt. On this trip Jim Irwin visited the boat-shaped formation on a close-by mountain together with Wyatt and was very taken by the site, but he continued looking on Mt. Ararat.

In **1985** Bill Crouse was in charge of the Probe-expedition on Mt. Ararat, where Elfred Lee, John McIntosh, Bob Garbe, Ken Alexander, Jim Willis, and others also took part.
The same year Jim Irwin, Bob Stublich, and Dick Bright reached the top from the south side but were called back by the authorities via radio.

The Institute for Creation Research sponsored a trip with **only Turkish** members to avoid problems getting authorized.

In **1986** Norwegian Paul Olav Jernæs disappeared and probably died on an illegal attempt to climb the mountain when it was closed.

The same year Jim Irwin and Bob Stublich were arrested for espionage but were quickly released. On the other hand Dr. Charles Willis and his Snow Tiger Team managed to find themselves on the mountain's eastern plateau for eight days. This huge team included Steve Connelly, Guy Leduc, Pat Frost, Bob Garbe, Carl Nestor, Richard Froiland, Deborah Redmer, James Willis, and Charles Willis himself.

Dick Bright, Ron Lane, and Ahmet Arslan climbed with their "Summit Expedition Team". Dr. Ole Honningdalsnes should have been on this expedition, but he disappeared.

In **1987** Bob Stublich and Jim Irwin again took pictures of the west side from a helicopter, and Dutchman Jon van den Boesch from Evangelische Omroep filmed for a series about the creation of the world. This same year John Morris represented ICR on the mountain with an expedition.

In **1988** Al Jenny, Chuck Aaron, and John McIntosh took more helicopter photos of the mountain.

And Dr. Charles Willis (as mentioned above) and Snow Tiger Team held an expedition with radar and ice drilling on the eastern plateau at about 16,500 feet. The team was large and comprised of Robert Baker, B.J. Corbin, Donald Davis Jr., Guy Leduc, Scott Little, Larry Mast, Ross Mehan, Willis Newton Jr. and Willis Newton III, Deborah Redmer, Robert, Margaret and Christopher Roningen, James Willis, and Charles Willis.

In **1989** Chuck Aaron, Bob Garbe, and B.J. Corbin climbed for an "Emmanuel Expedition" with underground radar testing on the western plateau. Other members of the team included David Montgomery, Kathy Montgomery, Paul Schiemer, Chuck Aron Jr., John Wanvig, and Debbie Redmer. In October of that same year John Morris, Bob van Kampen, Grant Richards, and Henry Morris III were there on an ICR-expedition.

In **1990** Robin Simmons, Don Shockey, Chuck Aaron, George Adams, Ahmet Arslan, Carl Baugh, B.J. Corbin, and others were in charge of "Ararat

The Snow Tiger Team in 1988 on Mt. Ararat's southern face at an elevation of 12,000 feet. The participants were Robert Baker, B.J. Corbin, Donald Davis Jr., Guy Leduc, Scott Little, Larry Mast, Ross Mehan, Willis Newton Jr. and Willis Newton III, Deborah Redmer, Robert, Margaret and Christopher Roningen, James Willis and finally Charles Willis who can be seen in the center behind the Turkish flag.

8 Team" filming and taking videos from a helicopter as well as "mountainside" research.

Also in 1990 Italian Angelo Palego climbed Mt. Ararat. He claims to have seen an outline of the Ark in three pieces under the ice near the places where Navarra claimed to have found sub-glacial shadows of the Ark – around Upper Parrot Glacier west of Abich I.

In **1993** Dick Bright and John McIntosh went to Turkey to land on the mountain by helicopter. They didn't get further than Kars where their authorization was terminated because of terrorism in the Ararat area. But the Italian explorer, Palego, was allowed.

In 1994, 95, 96, 97, 98, and 99 multiple Ark-hunters were in Turkey, but none of them were given permission to climb Mt. Ararat. Dave Larsen, USA, is on the list from 1999. In 1999 and 2000 a group of earlier Ark-hunters from USA BASE Institute (Bob Cornuke, David Faltot, Bob Stuplich, Larry Williams, and Dick Bright) climbed the Sabalan Mountain in Iran instead.

In **2000** the only things that took place were meetings at Ataturk University with Jim Hall, Rex Geissler, John Bradley, Peter Aletter, Michael Holt, and Yavuz Konca. But Palego climbed the mountain.

In **2001** there was an international "peace climb" on Mt. Ararat.

In **2002** the mountain swarmed with Ark-hunters due to the attention an (unsuccessful) satellite picture of Mt. Ararat created. According to local guides over 100 people were on the mountain this year, and there are now plans of opening a café and building more easily accessible paths. Tourism has taken over...

After the end of the tourist season Palego was up the mountain again in December...

In August **2004** Daniel P. McGivern, Hawai, planned to invest 900,000 dollars in investigating the "Ararat Anomaly" on the north-western corner of the western plateau with Ahmet Ali Arslan, professor at Seljuk University in Turkey as guide. The interest was due to the Washington Post Insight magazine having published secret CIA-photos. The paper paid for new satellite photos - in vain.

The wild goose chase continues year after year, but one question permeates: are we looking on the wrong mountain?

Chapter 24

Photographs – A Breeding Ground For Myths

One would think that photographs would be the best type of evidence to support all of this talk about the Ark being on Mt. Ararat. But in the last 50 years or so rumors of photographs and unclear satellite pictures have time and time again derailed the search for the Ark.

Pictures on a Retina

Three American soldiers from the Second World War believe that they have seen pictures of Noah's Ark in "Stars and Stripes" (the newspaper of the U.S. Armed Forces in Europe, the Mediterranean, and North Africa, 1942-present); **Vince Will** in 1943-45, **Lester Walton** 1945, and **Andy Anderson** in 1948. Ark-researcher Cliff Moody hasn't been able to find a single issue with pitures of the Ark in it (which could be attributed to the fact that "Stars and Stripes" is printed in multiple editions), but he has, on the other hand, found no less that 49 *articles* about the Ark from between September 1949 and August 1984 in "Stars and Stripes" alone!

The articles have obviously been so vivid and lifelike that they have printed pictures on the retinas of these soldiers.

Military Pictures

Many in the U.S. military have also heard second- or third-hand rumors about pictures of the Ark, which were supposedly taken from U2 spy planes, among others, and therefore top secret, of course.

But so far the American military has denied ever having had pictures of Noah's Ark even though pictures of Mt. Ararat have been taken.

One of the military photographers who believes he saw something that could have been Noah's Ark was **William Todd** from Yuma, Arizona. From 1951-55 the American military together with Turkish authorities took photos of Turkey in its entirety to use for new topographical maps in that the previous maps were inaccurate. William Todd was involved from 1953-55. During a shoot he saw something he believed to be abnormal jutting out of the ice around Ahora Gorge on Mt. Ararat about 14,500-16,000 feet. The plane was about 2,000 feet above an object everyone in the plane believed to be Noah's Ark. Even though Todd developed the negatives himself and delt 4-5 pictures to each of the crew members, they all disappeared! He

Is this the Ark or just a 620-ft. lava rock?
This picture is an enlargement of the so-called "Ararat Anomaly" from what was until recently a classified CIA photo from 1949 which can be seen at the bottom of the page.
This photograph has been popping up among Ark-hunters for many years for the simple reason that it was top secret.
New satellite photos seem to show that the anomaly has slid down the mountain.
But it is still not known whether this is anything more than a lava rock.

gave his own pictures (according to himself) to a baptist preacher who died. After his death the pictures were not to be found again. Todd has since then lost contact with his military buddies, and The Naval Photografic Science Center Archives in Washington D.C. who should have the negatives can't find them...[1]

George Greene, took pictures from a helicopter at almost the same time in1953 of a boat-like object on Ararat but couldn't raise the funds for an expediton. He was murdered in 1962, and his snapshots disappeared. About 30 people have affirmed that they too have seen his photos.[2]

But in the 1970's **Tom Crotser** from Holy Ground Mission established the object he photographed to be a large rock formation. Many other Ark-hunters who know this rock will also confirm that it is nothing more than just that, a rock.

Despite this confirmation, the photos were used in the film "In Search of Noah's Ark" – possibly retouched – with the asservation that planking could be seen. The rock is located at a height of 12,000 feet on the eastern edge of Ahora Gorgeand it is most likely the same rock Todd saw. Again this same formation was studied by **Bob Stuplich**, who in 1983 performed an extensive photographing of Mt. Ararat via helicopter.

Jet fighter **Gregor Schwinghammer,** USA, recounts that he saw some-thing that could have looked like an Ark from his F-100 when he flew over it in 1959. From the pictures he took, no one could figure out what it was. Someone concluded, "It must be Noah's Ark!" But this too was most likely another rock. Since then the pictures have been made public in a newspa-per without Schwinghammer's blessing.[3]

Pilot **Gus Pipkin**, California, also believes to have seen a ship on Ararat from his DC-4 in good weather when he was flying from Erzurum to Diyarbakir in 1963. But the route he describes doesn't seem realistic.

Captain **Walther D. Hunter** says he has seen snapshots taken from a U2 plane in 1969-70 containing an object resembling a ship. It had pointed ends, just like the photographs an employee at the Smithsonian Inst. be-lieves to have seen.[4] (Many of the so-called "eyewitnesses" tell of an al-most rectangular Ark.) What Hunter saw could possibly have been the pictures of the boat-shaped object the Turkish pilot Durupinar took in 1959. An object that was not on Ararat.

US Navy Lieutenant **Al Shappell** says that he saw a "boatlike structure" when he flew over Mt. Ararat in 1974 on a top-secret mission set to photo-graph the object thought to have possibly been a Soviet radarstation. He estimates the object to have been 300 feet long x 1-200 feet wide and 30-50 fod high, about 2/3 of the Ark's measurments according to the Bible. It was rectangular like a box and was close to the top of the mountain.

US Air Force General **Ralph Haven**, who was stationed in Ankara, Tur-key testified to Elfred Lee in 1985 that he had seen the object that Lee had told him about and shown pictures of. The general confirmed that the Air Force had pictures of the object and that he had even seen two slides of it at Fort Leavenworth, Kansas in a presentation for some people that were

Footnotes
[1] Bill Todd's information in state-ment to Rex Geissler, 27.3.1999 reported in The Eksplorers of Ararat.

[2] According to Violet M. Cumming: "Noah's Ark: Fable or Fact?" p. 144.

[3] Interviews with Schwinghammer in Ararat Report

[4] See chapter on Ark-hunters after Navarra

[5] The Eksplorers of Ararat p. 458-459

[6] "Field Notes" section of Research & Exploration, a Scholarly Publi-cation of the National Geographic Society, Autumn 1994.

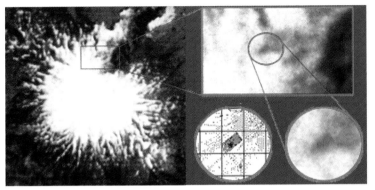

going to Turkey. But when he looked into it again, the slides were missing from the presentation.[5]

Special Photography from Space

Ed Crawford, a Canadian Presbyterian minister from Edmonton, claimed in 1987 to have seen the Ark - on a satellite picture. The picture he referred to was taken in 1973 by a land-based satellite and can be found on the internet at www.vonbora.com. It is probably the same formation that Bob Stuplich reported in 1974 as a "black spot". Land-based technology wasn't so advanced that it could give all of the information Crawford had.

Crawford had also climbed Mt. Ararat in 1983, 1987, and again in 1990, and on his last trip he made it to said object and marked it, according to his webpage. The find is located at lattitude 39° 42' 59,7" N and longitude 44° 17' 29,3" E.

Crawford also believes that he found proto-Sumerian inscriptions in the Ahora Gorge on Mt. Ararat in 1983.[6] The text, or proto-Sumerian signs, read after his interpretation, "God's sacrifical covenant of the sky-brought bow (rainbow), go forth, procreate, and be fruitful." In September of 2001 Crawford informed the Turkish authorities of his find and requested their cooperation in an excavation.

Scott van Dyke from the Mount Ararat Research Foundation in Texas got a Turkish firm to map-out 50 square miles of the border of Mt. Ararat at over 10,000 feet. They used a high resolution Zeiss camera with four different types of film, including infrared, and took 910 overlapping photographs in stereo pairs (displaced to show depth). The pictures were so sharp that both people and sheep could be seen. Afterwards a volcano expert, Matthew Kneisler from The Lunar & Planetary Institute in Houston, pointed out a number of objects that could be manmade, but he couldn't say anything concrete. But at least it has now been maintained that the Ark is nowhere to be found under the snow line. If it is on the mountain, it's up in the icy parts (unless it is buried deep under the lava.[7])

George Stephen III, who is a remote sensing specialist trained by the military, can evaluate pictures taken at great distances such as from satellites and airplanes. He believes that in 1989 he spotted two manmade

Footnotes

[7] Mt. Ararat is a volcanic mountain which has grown over a period of at least three eruptions. The last ones probably after the Flood.

objects near the top with an estimated distance of 1200 feet between them. He says that from time to time they are covered with 30-70 feet of ice. The area he is referring to is the same area that Ark-hunters Shockey, Simmons, Adams, and Arslan have looked at earlier.

George Stephen III won't state which picture he bases his results on which makes it difficult to take him seriously. The funny thing is that Stephen tells that he personally doens't believe in Noah's Ark. The same Stephen has previously worked on establishing the location of the Israelites' crossing of The Red Sea[8] based on similar distance photography. Currently, work is going on to photograph the area above the ice line with a hyperspectral camera (HSI) and a thermal IR-camera. The latter can measure temperature differences, and the hope is that a possible Ark will give off a different temperature than stone. Finally, a Synthetic Aperture Radar (SAR) that can "see" through the ice will also be used, says Tom Pickett.

David Montgomery, who was on B.J. Corbin's expedition to Ararat in 1989, claims that shortly before the expedition, he was given a message by a rich acquaintance with contacts high up. This contact knew about confidential reports of a satellite that supposedly got off course in the middle 70's thus finding an object on the top of the mountain. A national security meeting was called and a plane was sent out right away to take photos. There was fear of a Soviet missile installation. Apparently, the fear subsided and the conclusion was made that this instead was Noah's Ark. Because of fear of a "holy war" the discovery was stamped top-secret... Montgomery's acquaintance therefore thought that Montgomery could be in danger if he discovered the Ark.[9]

Another secret conspiracy put in the prolific Ark environment. It is very possible that the American military discovered a structure, and that they could see that it wasn't a Soviet missile. But even the government of the United States of America can't, based on a photograph, establish that this object is or is not the infamous Noah's Ark – just like all of the others!

New Satellites with Better Resolution

On October 18, 2001 earthwatch in London sent a new global observation satellite, the Quick Bird 2, into orbit from Vandenberg Space Center. This satellite can take pictures with a resolution down to one half meter (1.5 feet) which makes it the best commercial global observation satellite in the world.

Professor Porcher Taylor from Richmond University is a prominent member of the American think tank Center for Strategic and International Studies (CSIS) in Washington. He has since 1993 been gathering information about an abnormality on Mt. Ararat found on top secret military pictures and photos taken by the CIA. But until 2002 the CIA denied the exsistence of any such pictures as the CIA has a policy to destroy any photos after the information has been taken. However, the Defence Intelligence Agency (DIA) made six such pictures public in 1995. These pictures can still be seen on DIA's website. The claim that all pictures are destroyed is therefore not

Footnotes
[8] Mentioned in the book "The Gold of Exodus"

[9] Reported in The Explorers... p. 466

The large Turkish newspaper SABAH *reports a new attempt to find Noah's Ark by means of a satellite known as Quick Bird. The article is dated September 3, 2002.*

Nuh'un Gemisi'ni *hızlı kuş* **bulacak**

Amerikalılar, Ağrı'nın doruklarındaki Nuh'un Gemisi'ni bulmak için son teknolojiyle donatılan **QuickBird** (Hızlı Kuş) adlı uyduyu devreye soktu

BÜYÜK TUFAN'DAN BERİ AĞRI'NIN DORUKLARINDA BEKLİYOR

Nuh Peygamber'in Büyük Tufan öncesinde içine tüm canlılardan birer çift aldığı dev bir gemi yaptırdığı tüm semavi dinlerin kitaplarında yer alıyor. Bilim dünyası, geminin, tufanın ardından suların çekilmesiyle birlikte Ağrı Dağı'nın zirvesinde bir yerlerde karaya oturduğu konusunda da yaklaşık 60 yıldır hemfikir.

Uzaydan 61 cm'lik cismi bile çekiyor

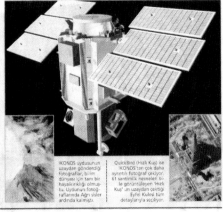

BİLİMADAMLARI Nuh'un Gemisi'nin yerini bulabilmek için seferber oldu. IKONOS uydusundan sonra şimdi de dünyanın en iyi ve en ayrıntılı fotoğraf çeken uydusu QuickBird (Hızlı Kuş), rotasını Ağrı'ya çevirdi ve fotoğraf çekmeye başladı. Bilimadamları, kısa süre sonra Büyük Tufan'da Ağrı Dağı'nın doruğuna oturduğundan emin oldukları geminin kesin yerini belirleyeceklerini söylüyorlar. Nuh'un Gemisi arayışları 1940'lı yıllarda başladı. 1949'da uydudan çekilen fotoğraflarda, Ağrı'nın kuzeybatı platosunda 3 bin 300 metre yükseklikte garip bir şekil tespit edildi.

FOTOĞRAFLAR ARŞİVLERE GİZLENDİ

1973 ve 76'da Keyhole adlı uydunun çektiği fotoğraflarda ise Ağrı anomalisi (bozukluğu) adı verilen garip şekil bilim dünyasının gündemine oturdu. Birçoğu, Amerika'nın gizli arşivlerinde tutulan bu fotoğraflarda görülen 183 metre uzunluğundaki şeklin Nuh'un Gemisi olduğu fikrinde birleşti. 1999'dan 2000 yazına kadar IKONOS adlı uydu Ağrı'nın çok sayıda fotoğrafını çekti. Bunların çok net olmaması üzerine Colorado eyaletinde bulunan DigitalGlobe şirketine ait QuickBird uydusu devreye sokuldu. Bu uydu, uzaydan 61 santimetreye kadar olan cisimlerin net fotoğraflarını çekebiliyor.

CIA DA GEMİNİN PEŞİNE DÜŞTÜ

PROJENİN başında Stratejik ve Uluslararası Araştırmalar Merkezi'nden Porcher Taylor var. Taylor, CIA'ya bağlı olarak da Ağrı'nın fotoğraflarının analiz uzmanı olarak çalışmış. Taylor, QuickBird fotoğrafları çekmeye başladığı zaman ellerinde Başkan George W. Bush'u Nuh'un Gemisi'nin tam yeri konusunda ikna edecek kesin deliller olacağını söylüyor. Taylor'ın ekibinde, efsane haline gelen Nuh'un Gemisi'nin peşinde birçok uzman kişi var.

DÜNYA FOTOĞRAFLARI BEKLİYOR

BUNLARIN başında Boston Üniversitesi'nden Faruk el Baz geliyor. Eski Mısır Devlet Başkanı Enver Sedat ve Ürdün'ün ölen Kralı Hüseyin'e danışmanlık da yapan Baz, Ay'a iniş programındaki çalışmalarıyla bilim dünyasının dikkatini çekmişti. Uygun fotoğrafı sabırsızlıkla beklediğini söyleyen Baz, "Araştırma yaptığımız nokta çok yüksekte. Burada bir buzul kütlesi olabilir. Hiç keşfedilmemiş bir bölge. İdeal hava koşulunda neler olduğunu göreceğiz. Sabırsızlıkla bekliyoruz" dedi. **DIŞ HABERLER**

| Sizinkiler |

IKONOS uydusunun uzaydan gönderdiği fotoğrafları, bilim dünyası için tam bir hayalkırıklığı olmuştu. Uydunun fotoğraflarında Ağrı sisler ardında kalmıştı.

QuickBird (Hızlı Kuş) ise IKONOS'tan çok daha ayrıntılı fotoğraf çekiyor. 61 santimetlik nesneleri bile görüntüleyen 'Hızlı Kuş' un uzaydan çektiği Eyfel Kulesi tüm detaylarıyla seçiliyor.

Bıçak Festivali'nde Üzeyir Garih'e saygı duruşu yapıldı

KAHRAMANMARAŞ'TA düzenlenen ve İnsan Haklarından Sorumlu Devlet Bakanı Ali Doğan'ın da katıldığı Bıçak Festivali'nde, bıçaklanarak öldürülen işadamı Üzeyir Garih için bir dakikalık saygı duruşu yapıldı. Dünya Barış Günü'nde düzenlenen festivalde Bakan Doğan, bıçak yarışmasında dereceye girenlere ödül verdi. **Sırrıberk ARSLAN (SHA)**

completely true.[10]

In 2001 Taylor got the Washington Post's magazine "Insight" to pay for a private satellite to take pictures of Mt. Ararat's northwest side. The pictures, taken from 15,000 feet, are of the side opposite Ahora George, where many mountain climbers up until this point have searched - despite the fact

Footnotes

[10] Insight, Washington Post, 4th April 2003.

that the Ark cannot possibly be in this crater that originates from a huge volcanic eruption. The pictures of the abnormality were given to experts. Four of these said it was a manmade formation, two believed it to be a rock, and one considered it undeterminable based on the pictures given.

The abnormality is thought to be more than 600 feet long, and one expert in historical nautical vessels believes he can identify the remains of the hull of a ship sticking out of the glacier. All previous examinations of this type have only shown lava blocks or rock projections.

In 2002 Porcher Taylor and the Washington Post magazine Insight succeeded in having top secret CIA pictures from 1949 handed out by using the law on openness in administration. Porcher Taylor found that the CIA had also in 1956 taken photos in high resolution from U2 planes and in 1973 by using remote-sensing from a KH-9 satellite and even more sophisticated photos in 1976, 1990 and 1992 from an advanced KH-11 satellite. But it is the 1949 photo that most clearly shows something 'abnormal'.

From October 1999 to the summer of 2000 a different satellite, Space Imaging's private Ikonos-2, took four pictures of this location without bringing the Ark to light.

But a team of analysts composing of seven scientists and picture experts couldn't come to an agreement about what was in these pictures. Some believed the object to have moved since 1949 which could mean that it isn't even a part of the mountain.

The pictures from Ikonos can only show objects that are one meter or more in size, but the team still believed the pictures to show an object broken in multiple places whose color makes it stand out against the surrounding volcanic rock. The surface of the object also looks smoother than the circumjacent sharp rock formations, they believe.

While waiting in the airport of Istanbul in September 2002 I happened to come across an article in a local paper, SABAH, about yet another American attempt to photograph Mt. Ararat from the satellite Quick Bird. At times it seems as if nobody knows that there are people living round the mountain who might pick out the Ark, climb the mountain and have a closer look at it. Apparently people have more confidence in unclear pictures taken from the space.

Each time large sums of money are put into these projects.

While I was finishing this book in 2004 another group (led by Daniel **McGivern)** had advertised that they planned to climb Mt. Ararat in August in order to examine the so-called "Ararat Anomaly". This was primarily due to the publishing of the so far classified CIA photos. But they didn't go in August 2004. Well, perhaps next summer...

Chapter 25

Conmen...

The problem the supporters of "The Ark is on Mt. Ararat" theory have always had is that they have not had tangible evidence. Therefore, all too much weight has been laid on the assertions of so-called "eyewitness sources" and rumors about photographs and secret military discoveries and paranoid notions that the CIA or communists are destroying all of the evidence, etc., etc.

This is a perfect environment for attracting the best liars. And unfortunately, some Ark-hunters and especially authors of books and film manuscripts about the Ark have in many cases believed them, thus revealing that a lot of Ark research has been built on an all too weak foundation.

Donald M. Liedmann – Fooled Them All for 9 Years

One of these liars was Donald M. Liedmann, who Violet Cummings wrote about in her book *Noah's Ark: Fable or Fact?*.[1]

Donald M. Liedmann simply approached James M. Lee, an employee at Search Foundation, who had a display about the Ark at the congress for Christian Businessmen in Chicago in 1969.

He told this complete stranger that he was Dr. Donald M. Liedmann, a neurologist from the University of Uppsala in Sweden with a Ph.D. from another university. Titles are always impressive, and this Dr. Donald M. Liedmann also told of photographs he had seen from the Russian expedition to Mt. Ararat which Ark-hunters believe to have taken place during the First World War.

According to Liedmann, he had been a squadron leader for the Royal Air Force and was shot down two times in 6 months and miraculously survived.

Actually, he kept up this deceit from 1969-1978...

Liedmann attended Trinity Church in Lubbock, Texas, for a short period in the 1970's under another name, Jakob Liedmann. Again he shared unbelievable stories that impressed. A pilot from the church took this Royal Air Force "veteran" up flying where he was uncovered as a fraud, not knowing the simplest aviation terms. The church took care of this poor liar, and after his public confession he was given counseling and pastoral care for three months after which he disappeared yet again.

The Ararat Report was now able to publish that this eyewitness had never even come close to Noah's Ark.

"George Jammal" – Cheated TV

It was even worse when in 1985 actor George Jammal claimed to have seen the Ark on Ararat. His deceit continued for eight years, and he was even filmed as an eyewitness on "*The Incredible Discovery of Noah's Ark*" which was aired on CBS on February 20, 1993. The program was produced by *Sun International Pictures* and was largely based on the film *"In Search of Noah's Ark",* which was produced by the same company in 1976. (More about this film later.)

In June of 1993 "The Skeptics' Society" was able to reveal that its counselor, Gerald Larue, together with Jammal stood behind this practical joke. They wanted to show Sun International Pictures' lack of credible research. The con was made public in March by "The Committee for the Scientific Examination of Religion", but it wasn't until *The Associated Press* and *Time Magazine* printed the story that it reached the entire globe. How embarrassing …

Easy to Cheat Ararat Support?

Jammal simply claimed that he had sought out the Ark in 1972, 80, and 84 and therewith tricked almost all of the recognized supporters of "the Ark on Ararat" theory. He claimed that he sought shelter in a cave on his last expedition, and this cave turned out to be the Ark itself!

In preparation he studied the books and maps of one of the most recognized Ark-hunters, Dr. John Morris,[2] in order to give a presentation that would live up to the pre-determined opinions of the Ark-hunters.

Jammal simply wrote Creationist Duanee Gish and was soon given interviews by people like Dr. John Morris and journalist Bill Crouse, who had revealed a number of other fakes. There were those that doubted, but they apparently did not check this guy and his claims out until it was too late, and that compromised their own credibility. I am sure that today they bitterly regret their past naivety.

For example, they could have simply asked to see Jammal's passport with a stamp from Turkey or hotel bills. They could have also easily found out that he was an actor if they only would have been more critical of a man confirming their own theory. But hindsight sees clearly, and there is no doubt that Ararat supporters have learned from this embarrassing story.

Pickled Railroad Planks…

Jammal produced the piece of wood he said he took out of the Ark.

But Jammal had never been inside the Ark; he had never seen the shadow of Mt. Ararat; he had never even been to Turkey. Jammal was just an actor from Long Beach, California, one of Gerald Larue's acquaintances, a member of the Skeptics' Society, and had previously been interviewed for a Sun International production. He felt he had been taken advantage of and wanted revenge.

The piece of wood Jammal claimed to have torn off of Noah's Ark was actually wood he found in the States. Jammal went out to a train graveyard and took a pinewood tie. He took the wood home and marinated it in teriyaki sauce, wine, and other fluids and then boiled it until the plank was black to his liking and sufficiently pickled. Afterwards he dried it with his hairdryer and then took it to Sellier, the producer, as evidence that he had been inside of Noah's Ark. But Sellier was not convinced. Therefore, he

Footnotes
[1] pp. 328-

required Jammal to find at least one recognized Ark specialist who could confirm his find in order for it to be a part of the program.[3]

Jammal got Dr. John Morris to conquer and therewith "prove" he had been inside of Noah's Ark as this was wood from that famous ship. He just couldn't believe someone could be so deceitful. In April of 1993, just after the program, he called Sun's program "a positive presentation".

But others suspected something. Shortly before the program was to be aired, Robin Simmons (who has made his own documentary, "The Riddle of Ararat") contacted CBS's attorneys to let them know there might be something fishy with the program, but CBS chose to air it anyway. TV researcher, David Balsinger, gave credence to Jammal – or just chose to send "a good story".

Afterwards *Time Magazine* wrote the following in their July 5, 1993 edition with irony: [4]

Phoney Archeology

"This piece of wood is so precious - and a gift from God." These moving words were spoken reverently by George Jammal as he displayed the relic that he said had come from Noah's Ark. His appearance was one of the highlights of The Incredible Discovery of Noah's Ark, a two-hour prime-time special that aired on CBS in February. What the network didn't know - and didn't bother to find out - was that Jammal was a hoaxer and that large segments of its program were based on blatant and ludicrous pseudo science. Jammal had obtained the wood, he unblinkingly told the network audience, during a 1984 search for Noah's Ark on snow-covered Mount Ararat in Turkey. With his companion "Vladimir", he had crawled through a hole in the ice into a wooden structure. "We knew then that we had found the Ark!" To prove he had been in the fabled vessel, Jammal hacked out a chunk of wood. "Then," he went on, "tragedy struck as Vladimir backed up taking photos of Jammal and the site. "He fell, and that made some noise, and there was an avalanche... and that is where he died." The film was lost, and Jammal was so distraught, he had been unable to tell his story - until now."

A Doubtful Ark Film

The Ark film that was the basis for much of the CBS program was aired on NBC on May 2 and December 24, 1977. This documentary is also one of the reasons so many believe the Ark to be found on Mt. Ararat.

Besides so-called "eyewitnesses", some Hollywood tricks were used to manipulate the viewers into believing the Ark is on Mt. Ararat – as mentioned previously in the interview with Elfred Lee.

At the end of the CBS program, a Dutchman states that he and Jim Irwin flew around Mt. Ararat and saw an object they knew was Noah's Ark... Then a photograph from a different situation was shown. That same photograph can be found on page 31 of *Noah's Ark and the Lost World*, written by John D. Morris in 1988. The caption under the picture clarifies that it was a blind picture taken above a ledge. The photograph could not in the slightest see what he was capturing.[5]

Here is the caption:

"A friend of mine took this photo by holding his camera out over the ledge of a cliff. It was too dangerous for him to reach the edge and look over, but he was able to take several pictures of the hidden canyon below. When the film was developed and the pictures examined, a strange object that looks like Noah's Ark could be seen, just as these enlargements show. But because he didn't actually see the object himself we don't know for certain what it really is. In fact, the more we study the picture, the less we believe it to be the Ark - but we certainly plan to go back and take a closer look! We call this picture the 'Mystery Photo'."

The program's narrator also tells us that Jim Irwin was sure that he had seen the Ark but kept it a secret until he was able to arrange an expedition on the mountain. Unfortunately, he died before that could happen. But the book with the picture was published in 1988 long before his death, so the 'secret' was not so well kept...

Stories from Ararat are full of these types of claims and evidence which has been lost, people who died before they could unveil the Ark, conspiracies, secret aerial photographs, and the list goes on.

But in the shadow of the impressive Ararat lies an overlooked mountain which is older than the volcano and can produce something concrete, namely, the boat-shaped silhouette which has the same measurements Noah's Ark had according to the Bible.

Naturally, this site can be debated, and as of yet there is no proof that these are the remains or the imprint of Noah's Ark. There are only indications. Hopefully, we will be able to get serious scientific research performed at this site.

In the last part of this book we will be looking more closely at the find with which we began.

Footnotes

[2] John Morris has climbed Mt. Ararat and is the leader of The Institute for Creation Research.

[3] Australian Ark-hunter in Discoveries: Questions Answered, p. 55.

[4] "Phoney Archaeology" in Time Magazine July 5, 1993, p. 51.

Foto: Henri Nissen 2002

PART 3:
The Neglected Mountain

"What would have happened
had this formation been found on Agri Dagh [Mt. Ararat].
I may be wrong, but I suspect that news of it
[the boat-shaped formation]
probably would have been heralded far and wide
as the discovery of the site where the Ark had rested.

What a difference a mountain makes."

Dr. William H. Shea[1]

ARCHAEOLOGY

FROM THE AIR the ship-shaped outline lies in the center of a landslide on the slope of a mountain that is only 25 miles from the Russian border. The landslides are of recent origin, may have packed thick mud and stones around the strange form. The photo was shot by a Turkish aerial survey plane from 10,000 feet.

NOAH'S ARK?

Boatlike form is seen near Ararat

The September 5, 1960 article printed in LIFE Magazine including an aerial photograph of the area surrounding the boat-shaped object sparked new interest in finding the Ark.

Chapter 26

Reshit Discovers the Ark

One day in 1948 a young Kurdish beau of 22 came running, yelling at the villagers in Nazar: "Noah's ship has been found!" This young man is a shepherd named Reshit. The village Nazar - which was renamed Uzengeli after this happening - lies about 13 miles south of Mt. Ararat according to the maps on the *opposite* side of the valley. In truth, it looks like they are much closer to each other, but it is difficult to judge distance from a large mountain.

An earthquake in the spring of 1948 shook the area causing a mighty mudslide that rushed from the top of the mountain called Al Judi (which is pronounced Al Cudi by some) and down its slope.

This green, grassy field where Reshit used to keep his sheep and goats has now become a river of earth, stone, and mud in an endless chaos flowing two miles down to the valley below. This wasn't the first time they had experienced such destruction.

From the middle of the mass of mud emerged an oval-shaped object, reminiscent of a colossal boat… The others in the village also went out to see. Reshit and the other local Kurds discussed what it could be. Reshit was convinced that it was Noah's boat.

This happened before western Ark-hunters seriously began to search for the Ark in these parts, so one might wonder why a Muslim shepherd such as Reshit immediately identified this oval object with the Ark. But still, the only boat to be found in the mountains would be the one from the story of Noah's Ark.

Reshit also went down to Dogubayazit and told about Nuhun Gemisi – Noah's boat – that arose where the sheep normally graze.

The Story Hits the Press

One day a well-off 69-year-old farmer, Shukra Asena, brings the story all the way to Ankara where he finds an Associated Press correspondent, Edwin B. Greenwald.

The Turkish papers brought forth the news on November 13, 1948; foreign papers followed suit by reproducing AP's story shortly afterwards.

Unfortunately, certain misunderstandings weaseled their way into the story under way. The story now told about a man named Reshit that had seen the remains of an object he claimed to be a boat high up on *Mt. Ararat* - for it was here the Western world assumed the Ark rested.

The story includes the expected addition of Mt. Ararat's description, of course with an unfathomable height and terrific glacial masses. The Ark had immersed due to an unusually warm summer with large run-off from the ice. AP also amends the story by Reshit seeing the Ark in a *fissure* from his field, which is about 2/3 of the way up the mountain. (Quite an awkward place to have a field!) Reshit, according to the AP version, "climbed down to it and with his dagger tried to break off a piece of the bow. It was so hard it would not break. It was blackened with age. Reshit insisted it was not a simple rock formation. 'I know a ship when I see one,' he said.[2]

But it wasn't on Mt. Ararat that Reshit had seen the curious object. One can almost imagine the old farmer trying to describe the site to the journalist. Maybe it was through a translator who also misunderstood that the Ark lay 2/3 of the way up *his* mountain, Al Judi. But the journalist only heard Mt. Ararat. "Simplification leads to understanding", we journalists argue as we cut away unnecessary information. But in this instance simplification made confusion.

Author Violet Cummings includes this mystical Reshit – whom no Americans had spoken with at this point – as one of her "eyewitnesses" in her book about the Ark[3] - on Mt. Ararat.

A Bible College Teacher Doubts

The dean of a Bible College in North Carolina, **A. J. Smith**, wanted to find this Reshit and speak to him one on one as well as have him show him the Ark. Smith went to Turkey in 1949 and offered a reward to anyone who could put him in contact with Reshit.

But no Reshit was to be found. Smith concluded that there was neither a Reshit nor anyone that had ever seen the Ark within a 100-mile radius, says Lloyd Bailey who has critically examined many of the Ark stories[4]. He doubts that the story is true and chastises author Tim LaHaye and Ark-hunter John Morris in his book for trying to excuse this dean's experience with the argument that, "maybe people wouldn't help him because they are Muslims, and he is a Christian."

Anyone who has worked with Muslims knows that this is nonsense[5]. The majority of Muslims are very helpful and hospitable, and if there is also talk of a reward, they will rarely hold back.

No, the problem was more likely that the dean only focused on Mt. Ararat. In Eastern Turkey very few speak English, besides the guides that have come only to earn money off of naïve tourists. Besides, there were probably not many people that just happened to know a young shepherd who randomly wandered through the mountains. It wasn't even him that brought the story to the media, but the farmer, Shukra Asena.

It wasn't until Reshit was an old man that now-deceased naval officer David Fasold found him and got the true story – some 40 years after the fact. The new revelation came out less than a year later, which should have put Ark-hunters onto the right trail, but preconceived notions kept the majority on their wild goose chases.

A Pilot Pictures It from the Heavens

In 1959 a Turkish pilot named Sevkut Kurtius was photographing the border area in Eastern Turkey in accordance with NATO's wish for a new and better map. This corner of Turkey lies adjacent to the former soviet

Footnotes

[1] Creation Research Society Quarterly, Vol. 13, Sept. 1976, "The Ark-Shaped Formation in the Tendurek Mountains of Eastern Turkey", by Dr. William Shea.

[2] Associated Press correspondent, Edwin B. Greenwald in an article from Istanbul, Nov. 13, 1948. See illustration on pg. 195

[3] Violet Cummings *Has Anybody Seen Noah's Ark?* 1982 Creation Life 0-890510865.

[4] Lloyd Bailey: *Noah*, 1989, University of South Carolina Press.

[5] I was surrounded by Muslims when I lived in Africa for three years. In Turkey, too, we met kindness, openness, and helpfulness from the Muslims' side, not counting a single attempt to use – and with that destroy – the finds.

Turk Reports 'Ship' Atop Mt. Ararat

By EDWIN B. GREENWALD

ISTANBUL, Nov. 13 (AP) —The petrified remains of an object which peasants insist resembles a ship has been found high up Mt. Ararat, biblical landing place of Noah's ark.

Apparently hidden for centuries it came to light last summer when unusually warm weather melted away an ancient mantle of snow and ice.

While various persons from time to time have reported seeing objects resembling a "house" or a "ship" on the mountain, Turks who have seen this new find profess it to be the only known object which could actually be taken as the remains of a ship.

Shukru Asena, a 69-year-old farmer who owns large acreage in that far-off eastern frontier district, told about the discovery in an unheralded visit to the Associated Press bureau here. This is his story:

Early in September a Kurdish farmer named Reshit was about two-thirds of the way up the 16,000 ft. peak when he came upon an object he had never seen before, although he had been up the mountain many times. He moved around it and then climbed higher to examine it from above.

There, Reshit said, was the prow of a ship protruding into a canyon down which tons of melting ice and snow had been rushing for more than two months. The prow was almost entirely revealed, but the rest of the object still was covered.

The contour of the earth, Reshit said, indicated the invisible part of the object was shaped like a ship. The prow, he added, was about the size of a house.

Reshit climbed down to it and with his dagger tried to break off a piece off the prow. It was so hard it would not break. It was blackened with age. Reshit insisted it was not a simple rock formation.

"I know a ship when I see one," he said. "This is a ship."

He spread the word among little villages at the base of the mountain and peasants began climbing up its northern slope to see the weird thing he had found. Each who came back said it was a ship.

There is no folklore there about the ark, Shukru Bey said, and persons who saw Reshit's find came away in great surprise. There are no cameras in the wild, isolated country where Turkey, Russia and Iran meet, hence no one came away with a picture. The snows have been falling again, perhaps have covered it again by now.

An expedition from America last September was reported hoping to see if it could find remains of the ark preserved in the ice atop Mt. Ararat, but no one in that eastern area has reported any foreign visitors.

(In Annapolis, Md., Frederick Avery, model ship maker for the naval academy museum who was to have been a member of the American expedition, said the trip had been "called off for the time being".

Avery said the "international situation and fighting in that area" had complicated plans and that the expedition could not get clearance and get ready in time. Mt. Ararat is frozen 10 months of the year. August and September are the only months of thaw.)

—Abaca Cartoo

TELLS OF FINDING ARK— Shukru Asena, bushy-mustached farmer from eastern Turkey, said that startled peasants had found the petrified remains of a ship high up Mt. Ararat, Biblical landing place of Noah's Ark. It was brought to light by extraordinarily heavy thaws that washed away the ship's ancient mant of ice and snow. Here, Shukru Asena points out the location of Ararat on a map.

---

republic of Armenia, thus, by heredity, the arch-enemy of the Soviet Union. While Sevkut Kurtius was flying over this area, he incidentally photographed a strange, boat-shaped object that didn't seem to belong in these mountains.

When Captain Ilhan Durupinar, who was both a captain in the Turkish Air Force as well as a cartographer, reviewed the pictures, he noticed this object and reported it to his superiors.

Could it be a Russian missile?

The photographs were sent to an expert in photogrammetry, Dr. Arthur Brandenburger from Ohio State University in Columbus, Ohio. Dr. Brandenburger has since then helped find Russian missiles on Cuba, which marked the beginning of the Cuban Missile Crisis putting the world on the verge of nuclear war.

Brandenburger immediately saw that this was a boat-shaped object and not a missile. But a boat-shaped object up in the mountains?

It couldn't be Noah's Ark, could it?

The article from the Associated Press's (AP) correspondent in Istanbul explained how a peasant named Reshit had found the Ark on Mt. Ararat. However… it was actually the boat-shaped object less than 15 miles south of Ararat Reshit had discovered.

The First Expedition

Journalist Rene Noorbergen, who has worked as a war correspondent and is now very interested in finding the Ark, tried to get an expedition in the works. Later Noorbergen wrote *The Ark Files* in 1974. He talked Brandenburger into going on the trip, and then his experiment came to a halt. The means to get this kind of expedition off the ground were not there, so Noorbergen got together with George Vandeman, an evangelist in the Adventist church who could get a hold of the necessary monies. In June of 1960 they traveled to Turkey along with Brandenburger and two researchers, Wilbur Bishop and Hal Thomsen. Noorbergen had also talked an archeologist into coming, Dr. Siegfried Horn, a respected name in the field of biblical archeology. In Turkey Captain Durupinar joined up with the group.

They were given military assistance and due to the lack of suitable roads were forced to travel on horseback. When they finally got there, the only thing they saw was mud. They used dynamite to see if there was anything interesting under the mud, but the only thing they found were some strange quadratic stones. They stayed at the site for only two days, after which they concluded that this was just a natural formation. But there were no geologists on the team that could have corrected their misunderstanding. The formation would not have been such if it were just a natural phenomenon. Even so many years after their surface level research, it is still difficult to get rid of this misunderstanding.

Pictures of the find were published in the Australian magazine, PIX in July and later in LIFE Magazine on September 5, 1960 with this text:

NOAH'S ARK?
Boatlike form is seen near Ararat.

While routinely examining aerial photos of his country, a Turkish army captain suddenly gaped at the picture shown above. There, on a mountain 20 miles south of Mt. Ararat, the biblical landfall of Noah's Ark, was a boat-shaped form about 500 feet long. The captain passed on the word. Soon an expedition including American scientists set out for the site.

At 7,000 feet, in the midst of crevasses and landslide debris, the explorers found a clear, grassy area shaped like a ship and rimmed with steep, packed-earth sides. Its dimensions are close to those given in Genesis: "The length of the ark shall be 300 cubits, the breadth of it 50 cubits, and the height of it 30 cubits," that is, 450x75x45 feet. A quick two-day survey revealed no sign that the object was man made. Yet a scientist in the group says nothing in nature could create such a symmetrical shape. A thorough excavation may be made another year to solve the mystery.

One member of the group, Arthur Brandenburger, still believed that this could be the Ark. But his doubt did not arise much support. The rising Ark-hunter community in the US was quick to conclude that this was not the Ark. The most prominent justification of this argument was probably that this object wasn't found on Mt. Ararat where they were convinced the Ark must be due to the mistranslation of "the mountains of Ararat" to "Ararat's mountain" or plainly, "Mt. Ararat".

As I have pointed out in the first part of this book, this is a misunderstanding that dates back to the 13th century – in the West.

According to the article, the distance to Mt. Ararat was 20 miles (which was later stated in Violet Cummings' book[6] as 50 miles! – far into Iran), when in truth it could be a maximum of 12 miles if measured from the peak of the mountain. And the 7,000 feet were actually only 6,350 feet.

The LIFE article was too quick to assume that the 300x50x30 cubits from the Bible were equivalent to 450x75x45 feet in that they used the normal conversion table from English cubit to the English foot. Since then we have realized that that cubit used in constructing the Ark was most likely not the same as that English cubit, but closer to the royal Egyptian cubit that Moses knew. These Egyptian cubits, which were also used when building the pyramids, were 20.6 inches or 52.82 cm. Therefore, the correct measurements would be 515x86x52 feet. The temples of the Jews were also constructed using the "old" cubit, which was longer than the new cubit by the length of the palm of your hand.

A Mesopotamian cubit was a little bigger than the Egyptian - 20.988 inches (about 53.3 cm).

A cubit is actually the length of one's underarm. As the length of a cubit became smaller the first two centuries after Noah, it could suggest that mankind was originally larger.

If Noah used his own underarm as a measurement, then he was about 7 feet tall. One theory suggests that people were larger before the Flood due to a hydrolayer in the atmosphere that protected them from cosmic radiation seeping in from the corners of the universe.

He Wasn't Talking About Mt. Ararat

So what is the real story about Reshit? Was he just a myth?

No. Reshit does exist and really had seen what he told about. He was just misquoted.

This was revealed when Ark-hunter David Fasold visited the village Kargaconmaz. The name means "The raven will not land" – which of course makes bells ring and sirens sound among those that are familiar with the different stories of the Ark. Birds play a large role in many of these accounts, and in Moses' it is written that "At the end of forty days Noah opened

Footnotes

[6] Violet Cumming: *Noah's Ark: Fable or Fact?.*

When the search team reached the boat-shaped object the only thing they saw was a lot of mud. The sides of the object were only about 3 feet high at the time. They set off some dynamite blasting a hole in the ground but only found a few square stones that resembled wood without the annual rings. They abandoned the find after only two days.

the window of the ark that he had made and sent out the raven; and *it went to and from* until the waters were dried up from the earth." (Genesis 8:6-7)

Kargaconmaz, like many of the other places close to the boat-shaped object, has a name that seems to have a connection with the Ark.

These names were given to their locations long before anyone started looking for the Ark here. Actually, the villages were repopulated about 100 years ago in tact with the Kurdish/Turkish and Armenian reckoning. The village names come from a distant time that no one can remember. But now, when the boat-shaped object has suddenly appeared out of the mud, the names take on meaning again and are even fascinating. We cannot know if the names come from days of Noah, but even if they do come from a later period, it suggests that someone at that time already associated the location around the boat-shaped object with Noah's Ark.

Reshit Pops Up

David Fasold found Reshit's scent in Kargaconmaz. He tells in his book[7] how on his second journey to the place of the Ark in 1985 he traveled east toward the Iranian border to the village of Kargaconmaz. The road leading to Kargaconmaz was washed out and impassable. One of his Turkish helpers, Dilavers, had to let his little car stay put.

The last part of the journey would have to be on foot. After stopping to rest three times, Fasold thought he would never be able to climb all the way to the top, but when they reached the next level they were surprised to find donkeys, goats, and a Kurdish campground. The first person to notice the foreigners was a woman who ran away screaming and hid herself behind a large stone. Another helper, Nuri, went over to her and explained who they were. He then yelled out to Mustafa, and Fasold overheard the name *Reshit* amongst a stream of words. The families that lived in this area were called Selman, Eraslan, Öser, and Sarihan.

"Reshit Sarihan," Fasold yelled as he remembered the name from the newspaper article.

Everyone looked at him, then Nuri smiled and said, "Evet, Sarihan" pointing at himself and then the woman behind the stone. They were related. Fasold then asked for Reshit Sarihan and Nuri answered, "In Dogubayazit." They told that Reshit often took care of sheep in the summer months and slept in a tent, but now he was in Dogubayazit where he had relatives.

If this was the same Reshit, a 38-year mystery could finally be cleared up. Fasold wanted to meet this Reshit immediately. Dilaver was to find Reshit, and they were to meet in the lobby of Hotel Ararat.

Ali Oglu Reshit Sarihan was now 60 years old. Fasold describes him as a calm and reserved person, a little bit bald and with a mustache. Everything he said came straight from his heart. He was polite and charming. Rumors spread quickly in Dogubayazit and guides from Mt. Ararat sat in on the conversation. They included Abdullab Turan, the son of Ahmet Turan, another well-known mountain guide, Halis Ceven, Yesil Gozlü, and

Footnotes

[7] David Fasold: *The Ark of Noah*, 1988, Wynwood Press ISBN 0-922066-10-8.

a helpful business man named Mustafa Yavus who had worked with Indian imports for many years. The elders from the village Uzengili were there too. Fasold tells that the taped interview lasted exactly 59 minutes and 50 seconds[8].

Yes, We Changed the Name…

Through a translator Reshit told that the "ship" came forth in the middle of the fifth month of 1948 on a field used for grazing sheep. Everyone in the village remembers it. There was an earthquake, and little by little the ship emerged. There was another earthquake in 1951 and some of it fell down. Fasold asked if the village was called Nasar until 1948.

Yes!

And did they change the village name to Uzengili then?

Yes!

Does Nasar (Nisir, Nesire) mean "to bring forth an offering?"

Yes, yes, an offering!

The reason Fasold is interested in this is that the epic poem of Gilgamesh names Nisir as the place the Ark landed. Fasold also names the slope of Masher (which means "the final judgment" or "risen from the dead" (Mashur Günü)) which fires a great deal of discussion amongst the Kurds. They are amazed that he knows the meaning of this name.

Reshit explains that the peasants knew that the happening with the "ship" wasn't normal, that it was "Nuh's ship", and that it was a *mu'cize* – a miracle.

Fasold asked if the earthquake had not destroyed the village. No, it didn't. But some people moved to other places far from the mountain.

Fasold also asked the leader of the village why they didn't see a connection between their mountain called Al Judi (Cudi), the place the Qur'an says Noah's Ark landed. He is told that it is only the top that is called al Judi because it is very high (Judi means tall, not mountain).

Reshit confesses that he can't read, so finding the connection in the Qur'an was not anything he could do. When the formation appeared in 1948, the villagers in Nazar had discussed if it could be Noah's Ark, but some of them reasoned that the Ark was on Mt. Ararat, so he kept quiet all of these years – until Fasold asked him now.

Reshit is still considered by some Ark-hunters as an eyewitness who saw the Ark - on Mt. Ararat. This story has still not been corrected[9] on NoahsArkSearch.com/eyewitness, for example, which otherwise tries to tell everything about the Ark. Unfortunately, it is colored with preconceived ideas about where the Ark is located.

Was He Cheated, Too…?

It should also be mentioned in the story about Reshit that Fasold's traveling companion, Ron Wyatt, who had rediscovered the boat-shaped object a few years previous, was not convinced that this was the real Reshit. In Wyatt's newsletter, he suggests that "an Ark-hunter" (Fasold) was fooled by

Footnotes
[8] David Fasold: *The Ark of Noah*, pp. 322-324.

[9] In 2004 when this is written, Reshit is still entered in the list of eye witnesses on the most official Mt. Ararat website: http://www.noahsarksearch.com/Eyewitnesses.htm - Here you read that Reshit saw the Ark in the "Mt. Ararat ice" and that it had the form of a "house" (the other possibilities are "box/barge" and "cigar"). However, it has not been filled out whether the Ark was damaged, whether it was lying on a ledge, wthether it had eaves etc.

a group of locals. Wyatt also stayed at Hotel Ararat (now Isfahan) in Dogubayazit together with the governor, Sevket Ekinci, and his Turkish contact, Mr. Mine Unler.

When he realized what had happened, he told Mine Unler and the governor. The latter went over to "Reshit" in the lobby and asked him straight out about the story. According to Wyatt, he admitted to the governor that he had been asked by a group of men if he wanted to earn some money by making a tourist happy. The only thing he had to do was say yes to said's leading questions.

But the Ark-hunter, who was surely Fasold, wouldn't believe that Reshit had fooled him, so he went home and told his story about Reshit. According to Ark-hunter Jonathan Gray, this Ark-hunter (whom he does not name) supposedly told that the earthquake – the phenomenon that caused the Ark to surface – happened exactly on the 15th of May (in the middle of the 5th month), which was the same day that Israel was established as a state.[10]

Unfortunately, communication between Wyatt and Fasold wasn't at its best at this point, and they both had strong, stubborn personalities. In his book, Fasold tells that he got mad at Wyatt just before all of this happened. The reason was that Wyatt wanted to measure the height of the Ark after biblical measurements, while Fasold had a different theory. In his theory, Fasold tried to get the 3 levels of the Bible to fit into the Sumerian telling with 6 levels. Fasold *doesn't* tell in his book that Wyatt and the governor doubted his story, only that Wyatt interrupted at one point because he had to go to Igdir in order to get a permit. He was not given any permit, so they had to give up looking any closer at the Ark.

They ate together that evening where Fasold shared his new discovery. After this trip, Wyatt and Fasold stopped cooperating together.

What happened?

My personal conclusion is that Fasold got a hold of the right Reshit, but the governor – who could not have known who Reshit was – gave Wyatt the impression that the man was just a swindler.

Wyatt believed him because he didn't know what had happened previously – and maybe he never heard it, because he and Fasold got on to unfriendly terms and broke their cooperation. Fasold over-interpreted the information about when the earthquake took place, because he was looking for a supernatural connection in everything he considered. He was very religiously interested. The Ark emerging on Israel's re-birthday fit into this pattern. He was also very interested in getting the formulaic expressions of the pyramids to fit with the measurements of the Ark and the ancient non-biblical myths to fit together with the Bible.

Wyatt was skeptical of all of these theories.

Footnotes

[10] Jonathan Gray in *Discoveries: Questions Answered*, p. 56, Adelaide, Australia, 1999.

Chapter 28

Ron Wyatt

For the 27-year-old Ron Wyatt, the picture in LIFE Magazine was decisive. Actually, he dedicated himself to the Ark and other controversial archeological discoveries which the Ark led him to until his death in 1999.

The information in this chapter is primarily based upon Wyatt's own information. Later we will come back to the criticism of Wyatt that exists, especially within Christian circles interested in Biblical archeology; criticism that is not without ground, but which has sowed greater doubt in the finds than is reasonably. But first of all, let's look at the enormous work that Ron Wyatt did, after all, contribute to the research of the boat-shaped object.

Friend and foe compared Ron Wyatt to Indiana Jones. (Watercolor from photo by Viveka Pontén.)

As previously mentioned, the first research team from 1960 dismissed the boat-shaped object as nothing more than a naturally occurring formation. But Ron didn't give up his belief quite so easily. He was determined to travel to Turkey himself and examine the site, but at that time it was impossible due to the extreme youth of his children. Instead, he had a single-mindedness to gather information about Noah's Ark, Turkey, the Mountains of Ararat, ship construction, and other things. The more he read and experimented, the more he was convinced that the Ark was not located on Mt. Ararat as most people believed.

Ships Don't Land on Mountains

He used this period of waiting to do things like construct a model of the Ark in order to see how it would react in water when it met various mountains. In this very concrete way he discovered the different hydrodynamic laws. Mt. Ararat is conical, and under a mighty flood its top would either have been under water or stuck up out of it.

A ship being drawn by the underwater currents to a pointed mountaintop sticking out of the water (like Mt. Ararat) would normally not sail into the mountain but be cast around it by the current. (Unless the ship was forcefully thrown into the mountain, but then it would be destroyed.)

Nor would it land on top of the mountain if the ship were floating above an underwater peak and the water sank. Again, the movement of the water would lead the ship away from the mountain. If the ship were to land on a mountain, it would have to sail into a natural port - such as a crescent-shaped mountain. Therefore, Wyatt was very anxious to see if such a mountain could be found near the boat-shaped object. (He would later discover that there actually was such a mountain, Yigityatagi, a good mile and a half above the object.)

From 1973-75 he and the children lived in Hawaii where he studied volcanoes in his free time. The largest volcano in the world, Mauna Loa, is

Wyatt constructed this mini-version of the Ark as a real boat - not as the square, box-shaped Ark the so-called eye witnesses from Mt. Ararat claimed to have seen.

located on Hawaii towering at almost 30,000 ft. tall (a large portion of it is underwater) and 75 miles wide.

Here he was also convinced that the Ark could not possibly have landed on a volcano; especially not if the volcano, Mt. Ararat, were erupting, which could be expected under such circumstances.

The Real Dimensions

Ron had noticed that the boat-shaped object didn't have the same dimensions as was normally expected of the Ark. It was more than 500 feet long, while many translations cited the Ark to be only 450.

But from his interest in Egyptian history, Ron knew the answer: the ancient Egyptians had a longer cubit of 20.6 inches, while an English cubit is only 18 inches long. The English cubit comes from what would later be Mesopotamia.

Moses, who wrote down the story of the Flood, didn't have other cubits to use than the Egyptian. And if these were used, the measurements fit much better. Actually, they proved to fit almost perfectly.

The pieces of the puzzle began to fall in place.

The measurement "cubit" originally comes from the length of an underarm. Noah could have possibly just used his own underarm as the measurement - otherwise he used a standard cubit equivalent to a normal underarm's length of that time period. If that is the case, Noah and the people of that time were 14% taller than they are now (assuming normal height now is 6 feet tall) making them 7 feet tall.

(However, we cannot be completely sure that the Egyptian cubit was equal to Noah's cubit because English and Egyptian cubits are not the only cubits that exist. While writing this book, I found an old cubit stick that belonged to my grand- and great grandparents. It is longer. Funny enough, the cubit used in the Nordic countries is actually longer than both the English and the Egyptian cubit measuring in at a full 24.71 inches, or 2.04 feet!_[1])

The Ark File

In 1975 Rene Noorbergen's book, *The Ark File* came out. Noorbergen had taken part in the first research group, and his information interested Ron so much that he contacted all of the other members of the team except for one in order to gather other particulars.

He found out that at least one of the other members, Dr. Arthur Brandenburger, still believed that the boat-shaped object really was the remains of a ship, even though the official conclusion was that it was just a natural formation.

Ron was determined to travel to Turkey. But none of the members from the team could help him find out exactly where the formation could be found, because they traveled via horseback led by the Turkish military. Not only did they not help Ron find the formation, but they didn't support him in looking closer into the object either.

Footnotes

[1] If it came from the underarms of the first Nordic people, they would measure in at about 246 cm, or 8 ft. tall. If this cubit were used then the Ark's 300 cubits would make 188 meters or about 617 ft. According to Thor Heyrdahl, the Nordic people came from the Black Sea area under the leadership of Odin, who was later made into a god. Was this cubit Odin's? Was he one of the first extra large people that also lived after the Flood according to the Bible – Genesis 6:4 – or is the explanation simply that the length of the hand was also included in the measurement?

To Turkey

But in 1977 Ron Wyatt traveled to Turkey to look with his own two eyes at the object he had seen in LIFE Magazine 17 years earlier. His two sons insisted on going, so it ended up being a party of three. Ron was not a rich man. He originally wanted to be a doctor but had to give up his studies and settle with becoming a nurse. But now he finally had enough money to go.

The first three days of their 14-day vacation went to traveling by plane, train, and bus deep into Eastern Turkey. Ron didn't know where he could find the Ark, but he had a child-like faith that God would lead him. So he and his sons prayed a little prayer that the taxi with which they were to travel the last leg of their journey from Erzurum to Dogubayazit would stop in the place where they were to start looking. Not long after, the taxi did just that. They gathered a heap of stones on the side of the road where they stopped, and the taxi drove off again. The taxi hadn't driven far when it stalled again – and again.

The Anchor Stones Were Found

The next day they found another taxi and found their way back to their three piles of stones. From here they began wandering around the area and soon ran across all eight of the enormous stones with holes in their tops. All of the stones, except one, were engraved with crosses. More of these stones were found later, 13 in all.

Discovering this large anchor stone (drag anchor) and several similar stones in the "Valley of the Eight" convinced Ron Wyatt that he was on the right track. This picture was taken at an elevation of about 5,000 feet; far, far away from oceans and seas. Here another Ark-hunter, Flemming Andersen, posing together with local Kurds. Note the engraved crosses. Wyatt connected these crossed with "the eight" that were in the Ark.

This clip from Wyatt's amateur film is the only known photo containing two stones; one of them is overturned. Unfortunately we cannot see the engravings because of the lighting. Here we have inserted engravings based on a sketch made by Mrs. Wyatt. The stones were later stolen and are yet to have appeared. But various people have seen them, including Dr. Bayraktutan. You could see the rainbow, the ship riding on the waves, eight people where two were larger than the others (Noah and Na'ama). Four of them were women, and their hair looked like a Z. All of the men had beards.

Drawing based on Mary Nell Wyatt's sketch.

The stones look like the anchor stones used all around the world, just in miniature form. No one had ever commented on these stones before, and the indigenous Kurds, who living in the mountains had no knowledge of ships, didn't know what the strange stones were.

Whether or not Ron Wyatt should be given credit for finding the boat-shaped object does not discredit the fact that he still deserves the title of discoverer when considering the anchor stones. They almost surely are connected with the Ark - some have been found on small peaks where anchors do not belong. One can imagine them being severed from the Ark as it sailed through this valley, which adjoins both Mt. Ararat and the mountains that are adjacent to the location of the boat-shaped object.

Discovered Graves

The second day Ron and the boys started off from the second pile of stones and found an old stone house where the floor lay at a depth of four feet. The roof was gone, and the building was fenced in by stone dikes. Outside of the house they found two headstones with etchings on them. One was standing upright, while the other was lying down.

A rainbow, a large wave, a boat, and eight people departing were - according to Wyatt - engraved on both of the stones. Four of the people had beards, while the other four had long hair. There was one man and one woman that were bigger than the others.

Naturally, Ron was sure that this was a reference to the Ark, and he assumed that these headstones possibly marked the graves of Noah and his wife. He based this conclusion on what he saw on the two stones. On the stone lying down, Mrs. Noah's eyes were closed. On the other, larger stone that was still standing, both of their eyes were closed.

Ron filmed the location on 8 mm film, but the engravings are unfortunately impossible to see on the film. On the other hand, Mrs. Wyatt has since reproduced the engravings in picture form. Since then the locals have removed all of the stones except for a boulder on the mountainside that Ron – probably a bit hastily - took to be Noah's Altar.

Mrs. Mary Nell Wyatt participated in a number of Ron's expeditions. Much of the information in this chapter is based on her newsletters.
Photo: Viveka Pontén.

The Boat-Shaped Object

On the third day the boys were exhausted, so Ron wandered into the hills alone. Again, he started at one of the stone piles he and the boys had built and let a taxi drive him as far as it could come up a dirt road.

From there he wandered up in the mountains until he found the boat-shaped object. But it was surrounded by mud, and right then Ron was not able to get anything done. Tuckered out, he lied down to rest his eyes.

The next day he and the children were stalked by locals apparently after their money. They fled, and the boys never got to see the object themselves. But there is no doubt that Ron saw it. Hassan, a local Kurd who guards the object testifies to that. As discussed previously, it was Hassan who found Ron sleeping just above the boat-shaped object.

No to Digs

Stateside again, Ron began to feel the pressures of seeing such fantastic sites and not being able to propagate them. He knew what he had to do: get archeologists and other professionals interested in his findings.

In 1978 Ron contacted an archeologist, Dr. Bill Shea from the Biblical Research Institute, who had published and article about the boat-shaped object in 1976. Shea applied to the Turkish government for permission to excavate the site but was given a negative response. Despite this obstacle, an earthquake in 1978 freed the formation from its surroundings.

Elin Berglund who worked together with Ron Wyatt on several travels tells that Ron - who was a very believing man - had actually urged some close friends to ask God for an earthquake so that "the Ark" would come

The letter from NORSAR confirming that the earthquake actually took place on the 25th of November 1978 at 8:57 in the morning.

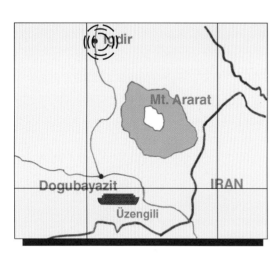

The circle marks the epicenter of the earthquake (39.90° longitude 44.07° latitude) close to the city of Igdir just 25 miles north of the boat-shaped object at Uzengili, which then became even more visible.

into view without anyone being injured. And whether you want to believe that God was behind it or not, there was actually an earthquake in November 1978. By this earthquake the sides of the "Ark" were set free at a height of approx. 7 metres.

It was as if the huge boat-shaped object had been lifted out of the earth because the earthquake caused the earth around the object to be shaken off its sides. For unaccountable reasons the boat-shaped object did not collapse as did the rest of the earth ....

Afterwards the object projected in the landscape in a very characteristic way so that nobody could fail to see it.

People around tell that on this particular morning the sky was silvered in such a special way that everyone had gone outside his house to watch this strange sight when the earthquake came. Therefore no one got injured.

But was there really an earthquake, the critical journalist asks? An interested Norwegian, Jon Kvam from Isfjorden, realized his scepticism and asked NORSAR, a Norwegian-American scientific center for geophysics and seismic measurements whether an earthquake had been measured in the Ararat area at this very time. In a letter dated 21.11.2000 senior research associate Tormod Kvarna answers affirmatively - I quote from the Norwegian letter (translated):

"With reference to telephone conversations concerning previous earthquakes near Mt. Ararat during the period November to December 1978 I send you information from the list published by the International Seismic Center (ISC). During this period only one earthquake has been reported within a radius of 150 km from the assumed co-ordinates of the mountain.

Date of the application is 25th November 1978 at 08.57.25 GMT.

Co-ordinates are 39,90 degr. northern latitude and 44,07 degr. eastern longitude. Assumed depth of the earthquake is approx. 10 km. The registration is based upon 41 global stations. A strength of 3.7 on Richter's scale has been given for this earthquake."

So whether you believe that God heard Ron's prayer or it was a natural coincidence, the earthquake did actually take place and on photos taken before and after it can be seen very clearly that the object has been set free.

As it appears from the map, the center of the earthquake was near Igdir, only about 24 miles from the boat-shaped object. The distance of it and its strength were just so that the object was shaken free without being damaged and without anyone being injured. The locals called the earthquake an unusual earthquake and a miracle that made Noah's boat rise from its grave. And the area was called *Mashur* - which actually means risen.....

515 Feet = 300 Egyption Cubits

In August of 1979, Ron returned with an Armenian preacher who spoke Turkish. They measured the Ark to be 512 feet. On top of that came a piece of the tail end that seemed to have broken off giving a total of 515 feet, which is equivalent to 300 Egyptian cubits.

Laboratory Tests

Ron brought samples of the curious, quadrangular "stone" found in the middle of the formation back with him and had them tested for mineral content at Galbraith Labs in Knoxville, Tennessee. A test sample from outside of the formation showed a carbon content of 1.88%, while the sample from inside of the formation reached all the way up to 4.95%. This content of the "stone", the carbon, was once living organic material from plants. Simply put: it is petrified wood. Or more correctly put: it is wood that has been turned to stone through a process where the cells of the wood were replaced, but the structure remained.

The test also showed a surprisingly high content of iron.

Jim Irwin Gets Interested

In 1983 Ron Wyatt contacted astronaut James Irwin, who had been on the moon with Apollo 15. Irwin was interested in finding the Ark on Mt. Ararat, and when he and Ron had had a meeting about Ron's findings, they decided to travel together to Turkey in August of 1984 so that Irwin could see the boat-shaped object.

While in Ankara, Jim introduced Ron to influential people[2] with contacts

Even though the outline of the boat-shaped object was easy to see from the air, before the 1978 earthquake it was difficult to differentiate between the surrounding dirt mounds close up. (See photo on pg. 199.) After the earthquake the sides were freed of multiple yards of mud causing it to stand out clearly as you can see in this picture taken by Dr. John Baumgardner's research team during the 1987 exploration.

in the Turkish government so that Ron could obtain permission to scan the area with two metal detectors. Jim Irwin and others from his group went out to see the object and witnessed its scanning.

To their surprise, the signals from the scanning showed the presence of metal at regular intervals in straight lines down the ship. There were also signals recognizing metal on the outer sides at 9-foot intervals.

On a video filmed by Wyatt, Jim Irwin said:

"Yeah, we got some real positive readings, didn't we, as we went up and down the long direction of the formation … The spacing (between positive readings) made it appear like, very much like it was, you know, a man-made object."

As for Irwin, he continued searching on Mt. Ararat - where up till this point everyone assumed was the location of the Ark - but he was very interested in the boat-shaped object and was of great help to Wyatt, who through him found contacts in the Turkish government. When British treasure hunter David Fasold was interested in looking for the Ark at the bottom of Mt. Ararat's lava flow, Jim Irwin referred him to Wyatt's research.

Jim Irwin's interest in Wyatt's work meant that other Ark hunters tried to steal the glory. Shortly after his visit, Marv Steffins called a press meeting in Ankara where he produced a stone and claimed to have found the Ark. This ended with his material being confiscated by the authorities and The New York Times printing libel about Ron Wyatt trying to export material illegally. He had been given permission, which was confirmed by the Turkish Consulate when he returned to New York.

Other Ark hunters - from Mt. Ararat - jealous of the interest created around the new find began to slander Ron Wyatt and his findings. For example, Ron Wyatt says that an envious rival got him arrested in Saudi Arabia by claiming him to be an Israeli spy. Ron was trying to cross the Red Sea, and before his journey he had only told Jim Irwin and the suspected Ark-hunter about this would-be trip.

At one time, a competitive Ark-hunter tried to have Ron's scanning equipment taken from him by the local authorities by publicly announcing in the

Footnotes

[2] Dr. Gulek, who had functioned as a minister for the government of Ataturk, as well as Orhan Baser and Mine Unler, became his government connections.

This old discolored photograph from Bill Fry's homepage anchorstone.com *confirms that Ron Wyatt, Orhan Baser, and others actually did find a stele near the Iranian border. It had been broken, but Ron reportedly took pictures of the engravings, and based on these photos and his explanation, Mrs. Wyatt drew a sketch. See page 212.*

hotel lobby that it was prohibited. (But Ron had been given permission.) Another Ark hunter, Elfred Lee, spread rumors that Ron tried to hide a stone in his baggage just before going through customs. Lee is probably "the artist" spoken of in Wyatt's newsletter as such:

"The artist was the second one (who tried to take the glory). The Turkish files show that he told their ministry that it was HE who actually showed Ron the site and that HE deserved to be recognized as the true 'discoverer'." [3]

This negative publicity from the Mt. Ararat Ark hunters is still the main reason that the site is questionable and that it has still not been possible to obtain enough sponsorship to conduct a mass-survey of the site and its surroundings.

The astronaut James Irwin (on right) was quite occupied with finding Noah's Ark. Here he is with Ron Wyatt in 1984 in Turkey.

Yet Another Imprint of the Ark

There was more than just the boat-shaped object:

Ron, together with Orhan Baser from Istanbul, now researched the area above the object - along the crest.

They found a formation here that was 20 x 40 feet surrounded by the same type of stone that Ron thought to be petrified wood and withheld other strange "stones".

Ron's theory was that maybe thousands of years ago this place was the original landing point before the Ark slid down through the valley to its present location. This happened due to the major mudslide of which clear evidence can be seen. The Ark was torn free and left the end part of the keel which Ron thought to withhold ballast. Again he had a stone to take home to the lab.

This boat-like formation that Ron believed to be the original location of the Ark was just below a crescent-shaped mountain and was surrounded by mountains on three sides - just like his experiments showed was necessary if the boat were to be caught in a port and land on a mountain.

A Stele Along Noah's Ark

Up here near the Iranian border the group found a so-called stele. A stele is an engraved stone. The stone was in pieces and was used as part of a border marking.

According to Wyatt, he took pictures of the pieces in order to later "reconstruct" the stone and decipher the markings. Whatever photographs taken were never released, but rather a drawing of the stone has been made public.

The stele was marked with multiple inscriptions. Ron estimated there to be three types of writing. One piece of the stele was especially legible; it contained a drawing of the entire crest and a peak in the background, a boat with eight faces in it, and two ravens - one over the ship and one over the mountain. What was amazing is that the shape of the boat was exactly the same as the form of the boat-shaped object when observed from above.

Footnotes
[3] www.wyattnewsletters.com\noahark\na11.htm

Turkey's most famous archeologist, Ekrem Akurgal, excavated the Hittite cities in Turkey.

And if Ron's drawing can be trusted, the discovery is really a guide: It is not difficult to find the characteristic crest on the drawing - it is, of course, Yigityatagi - the Wall of Heaven to the east. Both the boat-shaped object and what we call "the first imprint" of the Ark are to the right of the crest when viewing it from the north. But the peak to the right of the crest has disappeared ....

There are various theories of what has happened to this mountain. One theory is that it is a volcano in Iran, now exploded. Another possibility is that it is a small mountain, which has eroded in connection with an earthquake causing a lake to burst whereby earth and water rushed down through the valley carrying away the boat and burying it a good mile farther down.

Therefore, if the stele looked as described by Wyatt, it depicts the landscape as it looked before the mountain disappeared - and while the boat was still lying up on the mountainside below the crest.

The rest of the stele showed drawings of various animals. Quite a lot of stones have been found in the area with engravings from the time of the Hurrians - i.e. approx. 4,000 years ago. It is, indeed, a fascinating idea that this stone might have been engraved that long ago.

According to Wyatt, the stele was found just below the previously mentioned formation that was 12 x 40 feet.

On the "Ark" Ron found a fossil that looked like the remains of a metal fitting. When he came home, he again had his findings analyzed at Galbraith Lab. The possible metal fitting consisted of 8.08% iron, 11.55% ferric oxide (rust), 11.45% alumina (aluminum oxide), and 6.06% aluminum.

Ron sent a special stone he found in the smaller boat formation on the upper part of the mountain to Jim Irwin who then sent it on to Los Alamos National Laboratories in New Mexico.

The Turks Start Too

After Marv Steffins got his hot air going, the Turkish government decided to assign their own scientists to the task. Among these professionals was Dr. Salih Bayraktutan. In October of 1984 the Turks borrowed a metal detector from Ron Wyatt who went out to observe the location along with the Turkish experts. They agreed that there were positive responses to the presence of metal at even intervals.

According to Wyatt this unique crest, a mountain, a boat with eight faces, and two ravens, one above the boat and one above the mountain, could be seen on the stele. The drawing is from Mrs. Wyatt's drawing.

According to Wyatt's newsletter, they rediscovered various 4-ft. long metal rods under the soil. Wyatt never saw these himself, but was told that they were brought to the Mine and Mineral Museum in Ankara.

The world famous Turkish archeologist Ekrem Akurgal, who was in charge of the extensive excavations of the cities of the Hittites[4], confirmed Wyatt in March of 1985 when the two met in Ankara. He had followed his colleagues' scannings and had no doubt that this was a ship. He dedicated his book, *Ancient Ruins of Turkey* to Wyatt: "To Mr. Ron Wyatt, Congratulations for the successful discoveries". David Fasold videotaped a conversation between him and Wyatt where Akurgal said, "it is, at any rate, a ship".

Akurgal, who was a self-declared atheist, told the Turkish press that this *was* Noah's Ark. When asked why he thought that he answered: "because there is no other explanation".

Wyatt later met with various Turkish ministers of state who showed interest and approval of the discoveries and said they were willing to cooperate.

Metal in the Ark?

Ron had one more sample tested in the USA. This time it was what he thought could be ballast from the bottom of the ship. The analysis proved that the "stone" contained 84.14% manganese dioxide. But the sample didn't contain the minerals that were found in the previous samples, which confirmed Ron's suspicions that filling material was used as ballast. A chemist at Reynolds Aluminum inspected the sample as well, and he believed it to be waste from metal production.

Critics have mentioned that heaps of manganese have been found on the bottom of the ocean but are only about 2 inches in diameter, while these are 10 in. or more. The nuggets from the ocean floor have an average composition of 35% magnesium, where 50% is the highest that has ever been found. Ron's sample withheld over 84% magnesium. The sea nuggets are also made up of nickel and cobalt; this example was not. This is yet another sign that this formation is not natural.

A later test of three samples from the formation that Ron believed to be remains of metal proved to withhold 19.97%, 12.30%, and 11.55% of fer-

Footnotes

[4] The Hittites were only mentioned in the Bible, so many people thought they did not exist until they were rediscovered in the 19th century. They were a great empire c. 1500 B.C. They were the first to use iron and the first to use chariots in war with the kingdoms of Mesopotamia.

[5] Na'ama is also the name used for Noah's wife in the Book of Jasher 5:15 where she is the daughter of Enoch. This is not the same Na'ama mentioned here because her father, Tubal-cain, was one of Cain's descendents, while Enoch was one of Seth's. According to The Book of Jubilee Noah's wife was named Emzara and was the daughter of Rake'el. The Bible does not give a specific name for Noah's wife.

Compare the drawing with the picture on this page: On the left you can see the crest which looks even more like the drawing close up. On the right a mountain which has since disappeared was supposedly found at one time (added in).

ric oxide (rust) respectively. They also had 8.08%, 13.97%, and 8.60% iron. To compare, control samples from outside of the formation only held 0.77% ferric oxide and 0.54% iron. This confirmed that there was more iron in the formation than if it had been a natural phenomenon.

As opposed to other Ark-hunters, Ron believed Noah to have used metal in the construction of the ship. The Bible confirms this in Genesis 4:22 where we can see that pre-Noahic generations produced metal: "Zillah bore Tubal-cain, who made all kinds of bronze and iron tools. The sister of Tubal-cain was Naamah." [5]

*In March of 1985 treasure-hunter David Fasold accompanied Wyatt on a trip to Turkey.
Along with him he took a new type of scanner and, like Wyatt, was very excited about the find. But they were both lone wolves and ended up going each their separate ways.*

David Fasold

In March of 1985 Wyatt traveled to Turkey with British treasure hunter, David Fasold. During this visit he met Dr. Ekrem Akurgal and a Saudi Arabian prince, Samran Al Moteri.

Fasold had new equipment; a metal scanner that could distinguish between the different types of metal under the surface. He also knew of a new, so-called "sub-surface interface radar" which is a radar scanner that can measure and graphically reproduce objects hidden underground. If this were driven over the object multiple times, it could give a phantom picture of the boat-shaped object in 3D. Now this was promising.

The hard criticism of Christian Ark-hunters had thrown Wyatt for a loop, but Fasold was probably not Christian. He believed in the epic poem of Gilgamesh and other ancient myths. On the other hand, he was excited about Wyatt's find and was helpful in its being presented on the Discovery Channel, and he wrote a book about it as well. [6]

Footnotes
[6] David Fasold: 'The Ark of Noah, Knightsbridge Publishing Company, New York/1998 Wynwood Press *0-922066-10-8

When Wyatt, Fasold, and Prince Samran came to the area, they discovered that grave robbers had destroyed the "house" and the "headstones" that marked the resting place of Noah and his wife. Only portions of the stone with pictographs were left.

Enter Baumgardner

In June of 1985 Ron, David, and a geophysicist from the Los Alamos Laboratories, John Baumgardner, returned to Turkey.

Baumgardner and the others examined the formation with three different scannings. Every time the machine gave a positive reading, they laid a stone down and marked it with yellow tape. Baumgardner, who originally was skeptical, was more and more convinced that this could be Noah's Ark. But after some later readings he changed his mind which we will come back to.

Geophysicist John Baumgardner was very interested and traveled to Turkey eight times.

They went back to the boat-shaped object in August of '85 to take up their work again. David Fasold got Tom Fenner from GSSI - the factory that produced the radar equipment - to come out and manage the investigation with their new SIR-8 equipment. He also got ABC's "20/20"

to come and record the event. There was also a group sent out from Baumgardner's financial supporter to film it as well as two other scientists from Los Alamos.

Baumgardner also got CBN (The Christian Broadcasting Network) to bring the story onto The 700 Club.

Again, they scanned the area and set out tape. They measured the formation to be 515.77 feet long - the equivalent of 300 Egyptian cubits. Finally, it all seemed to be going well.

Then suddenly local Kurdish terrorists attacked in order to take advantage of the media coverage and bring attention to their freedom fighting. The military hit hard and killed many Kurds while others fled. Afterwards, the entire area was declared to be in a state of emergency.

Baumgardner and his team went home before Fasold could get there. Again, nothing went as planned.

In 1985 multiple extensive examinations were taken of the boat-shaped object with three different types of scanners. Tape was laid out to mark where positive results – and thus signs of an underground structure – were found.

Cheated Again

In October of the same year Ron Wyatt returned to the area with a home-made scanner, but he gave up. On this trip he had an author with him whom Mrs. Wyatt in the newsletter calls Mr. T.

Ron was convinced that this was the man that gave him over to the Saudis, but he still tried to cooperate with him because he believed Mr. T's book to be mutually rewarding. But after bringing the once Ararat Ark-hunter to the Village of the Eight, the fragile cooperation fell together ending in a scene where Ron refused to show the author where the Ark lay, because he found out that Mr. T had secretly taken a professional camera with him and filmed various scenes with the intention of selling them to BBC (the British Broadcasting Corporation) and others instead of their agreement that he was to research and take pictures for his book.

After the showdown in Turkey, this Mr. T supposedly tried to hurt Ron Wyatt with false statements. For example, he got a scanner company to require the return of a scanner Ron had brought with him to Turkey and had lost before he had to leave. Later Wyatt, by chance, found the scanner at the same hotel where Mr. T stayed.

That is, at least, what Mrs. Wyatt says in the newsletter. This unbelievable story has been more or less confirmed by a conversation archeologist Bill Shea had with Mr. T, which is also referred to in the newsletter.

There was a pit of darkness between the Ark-hunters - as if someone was pitting them against each other with slander and lies.

The Scanning Is Called Off

Ron was back in Ankara again in May of '86 to seek permission to scan, and in June he returned with Dave Fasold. They had fancy equipment, and Dave, who knew how to use it, was delighted with the results from the scannings.

Ron didn't miss this opportunity and called Baumgardner to convince him and Bill Shea to come to Turkey. After he was given permission to scan, they conceded. Baumgardner came with his wife, his financial supporter, and a camera crew. Bill Shea came shortly afterwards.

But again, things did not go as planned. This time it was due to a hot air balloon Baumgardner's film team brought to take aerial photographs. When running a test in the hotel parking lot it, along with all of their equipment, set ablaze calling off the entire mission. The cause is unknown, but the cooperation between Fasold and Wyatt, nonetheless, came to an end.

This is also quite possibly where Baumgardner lost his faith in Wyatt.

When Bill Shea arrived, the only thing Ron could offer him was a sightseeing tour of The Valley of the Eight and other historical sites. The Ark location was closed.

Since then Shea has involved himself in a find further up the mountain where there is evidence of a pre-historic city. He has also found a very old sherd (a so-called ostragon) in the vicinity of the boat-shaped object inscribed with the writing "Noah" on it. But we have already gone into that.

Scanner-Expert: Man-Made

After coming back to the States, Wyatt took the readings from the radar scannings that he and Dave Fasold had taken to GSSI, who had produced the radar. Neither Joe Rosetta nor Tom Fenner, who had performed the first Turkish radar scannings, doubted that this object was man-made. The manager later told Channel 9 news in Hudson, "This is not a natural object. The reflections are occurring too periodic(-ally) for it to be a natural type interface."

In an article in The Sunday Telegraph from August 3, 1986 Rosetta repeated that "You'd never see anything like this in natural geology … Some human made this structure, whatever it is."

Ron took a two-week course to learn how to operate the scanner, and in 1987 he took 5 trips to Turkey in order to scan the formation lengthwise and across. Dave Fasold now worked independently of Wyatt after their split and had teamed up with Salih Bayraktutan from the University of Ataturk.

With his scannings from 3, 5, and 10 feet's depth, Wyatt now believed that he was able to establish how the underground "ship" was built up. He believed he could see shapes of rooms and a door with a ramp leading to every level along with massive wooden beams sticking out of the back side.

He discovered that the keel had a large empty space in the middle that fit the imprint he found together with Orhan Baser in 1984 further up the mountain. David Fasold figured all of this out with his MFG device, but this instrument was often criticized for being an electric version of the twig that leads one to water. But in this case the same result was found with an approved scanner.

Turkish Recognition - And a Surprise

On June 20, 1987 the Turkish authorities officially recognized that this was Noah's Ark. There was an official groundbreaking ceremony where Governor Ekinci took the first shovel of dirt and - along with others - spoke of a future visitor's center. The military and the media covered the story, and Ron dug the second shovelful.

When everyone was about to go, the governor asked Ron to demonstrate the scanner for the journalists. During the demonstration, Ron explained that the radar had detected something under the surface that could be a piece of timber. The governor resolutely ordered one of the soldiers to dig it up. He found an 18-inch long piece of petrified wood. Everyone was amazed, most of all Ron, who had tried in vain over the past 10 years to get permission to excavate this site. The governor then ordered Wyatt to take the petrified wood with him to the US and have it tested. All of this was filmed by Turkish television and aired the next day.

Radar Scans

Radar scans performed with Geophysical Survey System SIR 3.
July 1986 through Nov. 1987.

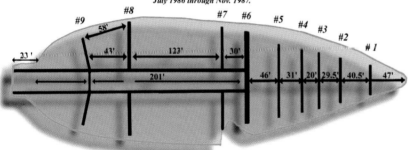

Based on the results from the scannings, Ron arranged the following possible divisions of rooms and walkways under the surface. (Illustration by Wyatt Archaeological Research)

A highpoint in Ron Wyatt's long hunt for the Ark; the Turkish authorities recognized his find with a press conference in February of 1987 where the governor of the Agri province, Sevket Ekinci, took part.

On Turkish maps, "Nuhun Gemisi" is plotted close to the village of Uzengili and official signs lead to the find.

The petrified wood was tested at Galbraith Labs on the 16th of September while Ron recorded the whole process. The results showed 0.7019 percent organic carbon - almost 100 times more than inorganic. Stone is not made up of organic carbon, but petrified wood is.

What Was In It?

Ron continued his scannings in July of the same year and thought it possible to draw a picture of what the Ark looked like based on the various scannings. The top two wooden decks could not be reconstructed. They were destroyed, and it was no longer possible to see if they had vertical or diagonal sides, for example. It was, however, possible to see that the uppermost deck was not quite as long as the deck below. This could be seen by the thickness of the sediment deposits.

The lowest deck was better preserved. It contained small rooms, and there was a double section that ran lengthwise where other rooms were located along the walls and these were not even separate.

That is how Ron recorded the scannings, but his interpretation can be discussed.

Hard Criticism

Even though Wyatt had now for 10 years tried to prove that the boat-shaped object was more than just a natural formation, a group of Ark-hunters from Mt. Ararat and their supporters stopped the findings from being taken seriously.

They continued to scornfully criticize Wyatt and his find - of which many nasty examples can be found on the Internet. Even when he and his traveling companions (Richard Rives, Marv Wilson, and Dr. Alan Roberts) were removed by Kurdish PKK terrorists (or freedom fighters, as they call themselves) in September of '91 and had to hike through the mountains for three weeks causing Ron to return home 20 lb lighter with a limp, one critic claimed that he had arranged the whole shenanigan...

And even after his death in 1999 the sling shooting continued. Despite this being extremely uncomfortable for the bereaved, this has considerably damaged the studies and research of the boat-shaped object.

In 1992 the Australian geologist Andrew Snelling, now working with the Institute for Creation Research in San Diego, California (run by the former Ararat Ark-hunter John Morris) made a scathing attack in the creationist magazine *Creation Ex Nihilo*. According to him, Wyatt's claims of Noah's Ark were all false.[7] The article was written with the usual stern dissociation and arrogance towards an amateur who could not come up with any Ph.D. titles. Ron's widow Mary Nell tried to oppose the accusations in a reply article which the magazine wouldn't publish, but which can be found on the Internet.[8] Snelling in return responded to this.[9]

Of course Ron was not without his faults. He was both stubborn and dictatorial. There is evidence that suggests that he suffered from a certain amount of persecution mania towards the end of the 80's, which made it difficult for others to work with him. But we cannot forget that it was Ron that revealed the secrets of the boat-shaped object at great personal cost. He didn't deserve the treatment he received.

Someone out there must have a black conscience.

As mentioned, Wyatt died in 1999 of cancer. Today, others have taken his work on the boat-shaped object. Independent of each other, people from Europe, the USA, Australia, and Turkey are working in each their manner to get to the bottom of the mystery behind Noah's Ark. Money, and in some instances experts, are in short supply. But little by little the mystery is being unveiled. Before long we will know if this is Noah's Ark - or not.

Ron Wyatt died in 1999.
Photo: Viveka Pontén

Footnotes

[7] Andrew Snelling's 1992 article *Could This Be Noah's Ark?* www.answersingenesis.org/docs/1154.asp

[8] Mrs. Wyatt's answer: Reply to "Ex-Nihilo Allegations" see: http://www.pllgrimpromo.com/WAR/discovered/html/chapter03.htm

[9] Snelling's response to the Mary Nell Wyatt can be seen at: http://www.answersingenesis.org/docs/526.asp

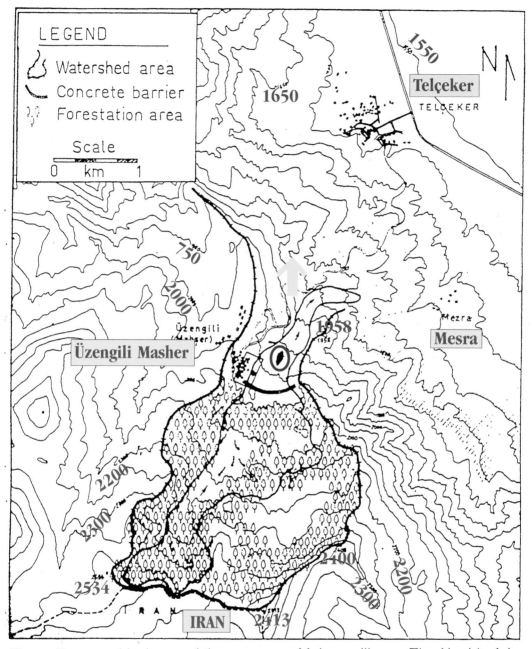

Fig. 1 Topographical map of the area near Mahşer village. The Noah's Ark site is approximately 0.5 km east of the village within an actively moving landslide environment. Features of a plan are shown for stabilizing the terrain including forestation, drainage, and construction of a retaining barrier.

Illustration from Dr. Bayraktutan and Dr. Baumgardner's report with numbers emphasized in color. The landscape abruptly slopes downwards in the north with the landslide flowing in the direction of the arrow. The numbers represent the altitude above sea-level.

Chapter 25

A Serious Critic

In my research I have run across many critics of Ron Wyatt and the boat-shaped object. Most just reiterate what others have already said without having researched the material themselves. But this is not true of John Baumgardner.

Dr. John Baumgardner, who has a Ph.D. in geophysics and works at the Los Alamos National Laboratory, New Mexico, visited the boat-shaped object eight times between 1985 and 1988. He participated in two large investigations together with Dr. Salih Bayraktutan in 1987 and 1988.

Dr. John Baumgardner answering questions – 15 years after he was in Turkey taking the scanning measurements.

In 1987 they used radar technology and scanned the boat-shaped object 72 times at 2 meters intervals. They took 1200 magnetometer readings in a detailed analysis. Besides this, they took multiple measurements with a seismograph. In 1988 they drilled and performed yet another seismographic scanning.

Baumgardner can be seen in different videos that have been shown on TV, and he is often quoted by both those that believe this is the Ark as well as those that don't.

At first, Baumgardner believed that this *could be* the Ark. But in a critical article about the boat shaped object by Dr. Andrew Snelling in Creation Magazine Vol. 14, Number 4, Baumgardner made his position very clear: This was not the Ark.

In a letter he wrote in 1996 that can be found on the Internet[1], he states:

"The footage of me in the video that has been shown several times on U.S. and British television during the last three years reflects my early enthusiasm about the possibility of a connection of the site with Noah's Ark, but it does not accurately represent my very firm conclusions reached after the extensive geophysical investigations we conducted at the site in 1987 and 1988. I realize this answer is brief, but I hope it is clear I am convinced the remains of the Ark must be somewhere else, that such remains are emphatically *not* associated with this boat-shaped formation. The central claims Wyatt and Fasold have been making about the site are bogus."

Why...?

It is evident that such a clear rejection has been like a waterfall on the critics' mill, which is why I contacted Dr. Baumgardner via e-mail in connection with this book in order to find out why he so abruptly jumped ship.

Was he afraid of losing face in the scientific community because he was working on a "religious" subject such as Noah's Ark? That is the most obvious assumption, so I asked him directly in an e-mail:

- *Were you afraid of your reputation as some rumors have it?*

"This is simply not true. Like Paul the Apostle I consider any loss of reputation I may suffer to be for the sake of Christ," Baumgardner an-

Footnotes
[1] www.tentmaker.org/WAR/BaumgardnerLetter.html (by Gary Amiraoult)

swered, being a believing Christian.

"Ron's assertion that I take the position I do because I am afraid I will lose my job is just not true. I am very bold in my creationist convictions here. For example, in February I presented a public lecture entitled "Exposing Evolution as Intellectual Fraud" in our community center. This has since been aired several times on our local cable television station."

"I am convinced that all of these data – including the seismic measurements we obtained in 1987 – are internally consistent and point to the very firm conclusion that the shape and stability of the site are due to a buried rocky ridge. Mud from one or several mudslides flowed around this crest-like obstacle, producing the very symmetrical almond-like shape," Baumgardner states.

The Mysterious V-Shape

As stated above Dr. Baumgardner scanned the object in 1987 together with Dr. Salih Bayraktutan. The two researchers' joint scanning was performed at intervals of two meters, effectively slicing through the site transversely, like a loaf of bread with a knife. This gives a good idea of what is

y = −20 m

y = −22 m

26

The results from the scannings showed a mysterious V-shape, which could be the keel of the ship.

hiding in the mysterious formation. Most interesting was a V-shape that appeared clearly in some of the resulting radar images – for example in -18y, -20y and -22y.

What could be the cause of this V-shape? It is tempting to imagine that this could be the keel of the Ark.

But Baumgardner had another explanation:

"In 1988 we drilled four holes in order to collect samples to determine the composition of the subsurface material. This drilling revealed a large, mostly subsurface, ridge of rock below the centre line of the site. As a matter of fact, this rock body is actually exposed at the surface for approximately one third of the full length of the object – from just above the middle to near the lower end

"In the drill cores it was rather easy to distinguish the material associated with the mudslide from the underlying rocky ground because of the presence or absence of pea-sized gravel. This gravel was ample in the mud, but totally absent in the underlying rock body.

"The V-shape we found in 1987 matches the location of the ridge we identified in connection with our drilling in 1988. The V-shape in the radar reflection profiles actually represents a horizontal layer several meters below the ground surface. As we crossed the site dragging the radar antenna over the ground surface, we first climbed several meters vertically to the top of the crest and then descended an equal vertical distance on the other side. The V-shape in the radar profile was the result of the greater vertical distance to the horizontal reflecting layer of rock when we were at the top of the crest compared with when we were in the depressions on either side of the crest. In other words, the V-shape was due to the large variations in the surface topography as we crossed the site with the antenna.

"The drilling cores gave us actual samples of the material below the surface and enabled us to interpret the radar measurements with a high degree of certainty."[2]

No Mystery

In other words: Baumgardner concludes that the "mysterious" V-shape is just the reflection of the radar pulses from the flat interface between two layers of rock having strongly different electrical properties.

The radar apparatus had to be pulled up over the eminence where Baumgardner believes the V to have occurred.

The V appears in the radar data because the radar antenna had to be dragged over a pronounced ridge down the middle of the boat-shaped object. The ridge had the shape of an inverted V, and the radar pulses took longer to make the round trip to the reflecting interface when at the top of the ridge than when at the bottom on either side.

Gray's List of Evidence

After this I confronted Baumgardner with a list of "evidence" that the Australian archeological author, Jonathan Gray, has collected about the boat-shaped object in his book.[3]

Jonathan Gray has undergone a huge task in collecting information about Ron Wyatt's find (which also includes the place where the Ark of the Covenant is supposedly hidden, another Mt. Sinai than we normally refer to, a different location for the Israelites' crossing of the Red Sea, and other thing.)

Wyatt didn't always publish his evidence, and critics have accused him of lying or having a very lively imagination. Gray, who was originally skeptical of Wyatt's extraordinary find, concluded - after his research – that all of Wyatt's claims were true. Gray has established a specific method of examining the findings based his and others visits at the boat-shaped object over 30 times.

Let's look at Gray's list of evidence, or indications, that the boat-shaped object is the remains of Noah's Ark:

1. **Ship's anchor stones** in the vicinity
2. **Metal** nowhere in the ground around the boat shape, but only inside the formation.
3. **Inside, an organized pattern** of iron at regular intervals
4. **Radar evidence** of man-made structure (walls, cavities, tank shapes, passage ways, side doorway, ramp, etc.)
5. **Regular vertical structure** around the sides - crossed by

Footnotes

[2] Dr. John Baumgardner in an e-mail to the author from October 2001 to april 2004 - which he allowed us to publish. Baumgardner has also read this chapter and accepted the quotes after some corrections.

[3] These are from his compendium "Discoveries - Questions Answered" that deals with all Wyatt's discoveries.

horizontal formation to form a "lattice work"

6. **Petrified, laminated wood**
7. **Fossilized rivets** containing a sophisticated alloy
8. **4-foot-long metal rods**
9. **Iron angle bracket**
10. **Slag** (waste product) from some type of metal production, coming out of the boat-shape from a location which suggests it could have been ballast
11. **The formation is the correct size** (both length and breadth) to be Noah's Ark
12. **It is in the correct location** (the biblical "mountains" - plural – of Ararat).

Quite an impressive list! And if even some of these indications actually prove to be true, then we will be closer to finding Noah's Ark than we have ever been. For the first time, we have concrete evidence – something we never had on Mt. Ararat.

But Baumgardner doubts and denies most of these claims:

1) "Ship's anchor stones in the vicinity"

"First of all, that these gravestones marking Armenian graves areactually anchor stones from Noah's Ark is not at all clear. They seem to be made from the local basaltic rock that forms most of nearby Mt. Ararat. Moreover, the nearest gravestones like this to the Durupinar site are about 10 km away.

"They are unquestionably Armenian sepulchral monuments; the question is whether they were genuine anchor stones prior to their present use. Given the fact they all appear to be made from the local basaltic rock so abundantly available, I believe the case is strong they were not," says Baumgardner.

2) "Metal nowhere in the ground around the boat-shape, but only inside the formation."

-"This is a false statement as far as I know. There is *no* metal associated with this formation," comments Baumgardner.

- But you are quoted in a newspaper and in David Fasold's book for saying that there were metal occurrences in straight lines.

Baumgardner: "On my first visit to the site in 1985 I was seduced by David Fasold's claims based upon his interpretation of the results of what he called his 'molecular frequency generator' technique.

It was merely Fasold's interpretation that there was actually metal beneath our feet.

It was only later I realized that Fasold's technique was a type of dowsing and had no scientific basis undergirding it whatever."

3) "Inside (the formation), an organized pattern of iron at regular intervals".

Baumgardner: "This claim is based on Fasold's and Wyatt's use of a dowsing technique which I am convinced is a form of divination, activity condemned unequivocally in the Law given to Moses by God Himself. There was and is no tangible evidence for subsurface iron. This was simply their interpretation of the results they were seeing from their dowsing technique. In terms of the normal laws of physics, there is no explanation whatsoever for how such a method might work."

My comments to 2 and 3:

1) According to Gray the claim of metal is based on not only the MFG but also on pulse induction and ferromagnetic metaldetectors. Ron found the metal lines in 1984 using conventional White's metal detectors, and John and Ron used conventional metal detectors to verify the readings of the MFG, according to Gray (and this can be seen on both David Fasold's video 1985, and 1986 Field Surveys, and the video "Discovered – Noah's Ark"). Photographs show red and yellow tape that was laid to mark the results confessing findings of straight lines of metal. The results showed iron in 5,400 different locations, according to Gray.

The lines are interrupted around the area where a large stone was found pertruding from the "ship", which suggests that the stone destroyed a pattern because the object grounded on the stone.

4) "Radar evidence of man-made structure (walls, cavities, tank shapes, passage ways, side doorway, ramp, etc.)"

Baumgardner: "These claims, in my opinion, represent the use of a lot of imagination relative to the actual facts. The black boulders in the site are pieces of the volcanic basement rock, and they do not form any regular pattern. These rocks are the heavily weathered remnants of a pre-Flood or Flood-aged slice of volcanicly formed ocean floor."

5) "Regular vertical structure around the sides - crossed by horizontal formation to form a "lattice work"

Baumgardner: "There has been differential weathering of the almost vertical fault scarps on both side of the site. The softer zones have eroded more than adjacent zones that are somewhat more resistant. But if one examines the material comprising these vertical walls carefully as I and others have done, there is no evidence of any large scale internal structure or variation in composition. The material comprising these vertical walls is the identical mudflow material full of pea-sized gravel one finds in the terrain surrounding the site itself. And there simply is no 'lattice work' horizontal structure inside the site itself."

6) "Petrified, laminated wood

Baumgardner: "I am persuaded this claim is adeliberate fabrication on

27th June, 1991

I hereby certify that on June 17, 1991 I was on the Akyayla site where there is a large boat formation which could be Noah's ark and I can verify that Mr Ron E. Wyatt found a large metal rivet that appears to have been struck when hot, in or upon the boat formation.

[signatures]

I was walking with Ron Wyatt when he picked up the object described above, just outside the 'hull' of the boat formation. Foster James

A large rivet was found in June of 1991. Above 26 witnesses confirmed the find with their names and signatures.

the part of Ron Wyatt. I examined the piece of rock he claimed was petrified laminated wood around 1990, and I found it to be nothing more than a slab of igneous basaltic rock. Its internal fine-grained crystalline structure was evident from a place on one end that had been chipped. I offered to have samples from this slab analyzed at Los Alamos National Laboratory, but Ron refused. This offer is still good, by the way."

My comments:

Ron's "petrified wood" – a piece of "deck timber" was found on June 20, 1987 while the governor was present as mentioned above. This was filmed and shown on television. The rock or wood was analyzed at Galbraith Laboratory in Knoxville, TN. The results showed that the sample contained about 100 times more organic carbon than non-organic. If this was a stone, it would not have withheld organic carbon, but wood would. The "deck timber" was also examined by removing a thin layer and looking at it under a microscope. This took place at Teledyne-Allvac Labs in 1992, where it was also filmed. Under the microscope, it was confirmed that there was woodstructures, the video explains.

It also showed that there were three layers glued together – that is, laminated wood – and there were also signs of bark. The wood from the top two layers was a type of cypress.

As mentioned, Noah was told to build the Ark out of "gopher wood". There is no type of wood known as gopher, but the Armenian word (which is the root of the Hebrew) for gopher means laminated. Gluing multiple layers of wood together was a technique that was also used in ancient Egypt for things such as coffins.

7) " Fossilized rivets containing a sophisticated alloy."

Baumgardner: "During the eight visits I made to the site between 1985 and 1988, I and all the individuals on our research teams were constantly on the alert for any type of human artifact that might exist at the site. This included, for example, pottery shaerds that ought to mark any ancient site visited by large numbers of pilgrims as ancient historians such as Josephus indicated had been true for centuries in the case of the site of Noah's Ark. We found nothing consistent with what these ancient historians described

Footnotes
[4] wyattmuseum.com/noahs-ark-10.htm + /na24.htm

and certainly nothing of the way of rivets that Wyatt has claimed.

I realize this is a serious charge, but I personally suspect Wyatt deliberately planted these supposed artifacts." , says John Baumgardner, who earlier was quoted in a newspaper in Livermore, California, that these metal rods had been found.

- Was this based on Ron's claim? And did you later find out that this was not true?"

- That is correct.

Radar expert Tom Fenner in the foreground on his way to the boat-shaped object, seen here from the back side where it is lowest laying.

My comments:

Just to understand what the claims are based on:

A round nail was found in June of 1991 where 26 witnesses confirmed the find with their names and signatures.[4] (See opposite site).

In 1984 a number of these nails were found on the side of the ark with the help of metal scanning. They were photographed by Ron Wyatt, who didn't have permission to remove them. It looked like they were in groups of seven.

We ourselves saw one nail on the eastern side of the object in May of 2001 and again in September of 2002, which we have already discussed.

A laboratory test at Teledyne-Allvac on the 11th of February 1992 of the nail Ron Wyatt brought home showed a special alloying of titanium, aluminum, iron, and other metals in the remains of the nail. Just one centimeter from this point there were no alloys, however, there was a 1,350 percent higher organic carbon content, which, when translated, means that the round ring was some type of metal while the material around it had once been wood. Organic carbon is not found in stone or basalt, but it is found in petrified wooden remains.[5]

8) "4-foot-long metal rods."

Baumgardner: "Ron made this claim to me in late 1985. It is my opinion that it is without any basis in fact. I interviewed the Turkish authorities that Ron claimed had found these rods, and they emphatically asserted that nothing of this sort was recovered from their excavations at the site in September of 1985.

My comments:

In 1985 the Turks examined the find and tell Ron Wyatt (according to him) that they have found 4-ft. long iron rods. Ron never actually sees

Footnotes

[5] "The 4 analyses they ran showed that location 1 yielded a 1.88% and 1.97% carbon content while location 2 yielded a .14% and .13% amount. The scientists involved in the analysis made the following notation in their report: *"It is interesting to note that location 1 (presumably fossilized timber members) was found to contain much higher carbon (1.9%) than location 2 (presumably fossilized metal."*

(http://www.wyattmuseum.com/ noahs-ark-12.htm)

[6] Discoveries. Section B: Has Noah's Ark been found? Pg 71-.

[7] MUL.APIN, Tablet Nr. 86378, British Museum

these rods but believes what the Turks tell him. About a month later he tells this to a young scientist named Baumgardner, who also naively believes that it is true. *He* then tells it to a newspaper, states it in his newsletter and at a seminar he holds for the employees at the Lawrence Livermore National Laboratory.

BUT when he queries the Turks about these rods, no one can produce them. The closest we come is Ron finding out that the rods were brought to the *Mine and Mineral Museum* in Ankara. I have also tried to ask Salih Bayraktutan about these rods, but to no avail.

9) "Iron angle bracket."

Baumgardner: "I have half of this object in my desk drawer here in my office. My own earnest conclusion is that it is a natural piece of the seafloor basement rock at the site. Please note that its composition is iron oxide and not metallic iron."

My comments:

Gray's claim is based on Fasold's video in which Dr. Baumgardner in May of 1985 is examining the boat-shaped object with a metal detector. Suddenly he shouts, "Undecomposed iron!" The metal detector shows a perfectly rectangular area.

But Baumgardner comments now: "I never said, much less shouted, such a thing. It was immediately evident to me that the material was rock, probably iron oxide, and obviously not metallic iron."

Gray continues: "Fasold ran in close with the video recorder. There in the wall, surrounded by mud, was a perfectly rectangular beam end and from it projected what appeared to be iron flakes, which had given the signals.

Earlier he had held in his hand a piece of wrought iron. It was a stretched and hammered angle bracket, (No, that was Fasold's interpretation!) with the grain clearly visible. The angle bracket was tested by the Los Alamos National Laboratory. It showed 91.84% FE203," Gray writes.[6]

But Baumgardner comments now: "This emphatically was not wrought iron! It was a chunk of iron oxide. To call it a "stretched and hammered angle bracket" was Fasold's interpretation —a product of Fasold's own very fertile imagination."

- But can "a natural piece of the basement rock" contain almost 92% iron without being iron? Asks the ignorant journalist...

"Note this is *iron oxide*, and not metallic iron. Iron oxide occurs commonly in the natural world," says Baumgardner.

10) "Slag (waste product) from some type of metal production, coming out of the boat-shape from a location which suggests it could have been ballast."

Baumgardner: "I personally had the sample analyzed here at Los Alamos.

The team that examined the boat-shaped object. From left: Producer James Burroughs, a Turkish helper from Masher, Jeffrey Wayman, a Turkish chauffeur, co-producer Dan Devaney, yet another Turkish chauffeur, Semsi Yazici, Necmettin Tamas, Salih Bayraktutan, and John Baumgardner. Tom Fenner is in front of everyone. Not pictured are Mahlon Wilson and Thomas Anderson who also took part.

Its composition, although unusual for continental rocks, is not that un-usual for volcanic rocks formed on the seafloor and subsequently altered by vigorous hydrothermal processes, which is the case for the basement rocks at the site."

- Does this mean that these metals (31,44 pct. manganese, 41,95 pct. titanium, 11,33 pct. silicon and 7,19 pct. aluminum) could just inci-dentally be found in volcanic rock?

"Note these numbers represent the elemental compositions in terms of oxides. I suggest that this particular sample is not volcanic but hydrother-mal in its origin, formed on the seafloor near a hydrothermal vent. In other words; it is a manganese nodule. Remember, the bedrock beneath the site was originally a slice of seafloor.

My comments:
The manganese nodules that are found at the bottom of the ocean are normally about 2 inches in diameter, whereas the slag ballast that Gray is talking about here are nodules of up to 10 inches.

The smaller manganese nodules at the ocean bottom normally contain 35% manganese and 50% at the most. Some of the slag material contains more than 84%. The nodules on the ocean bottom also withhold nickel and cobalt. The ballast material doesn't, according to Gray.

Baumgardner states that the only sample he has seen and tested was 3 cm. and claimed by Wyatt to come from the Durupinar site.

He wrote a report to Ron Wyatt that according to Gray stated that the sample was "tailing of aluminum aloud production". And Ron concluded that this was a proof for a very early form of aluminum production in ancient times.

"This was a gross misinterpretation of the analysis reports I sent to Ron. He inferred the existence of modest levels of aluminum in rocks implied these rocks represented 'tailings of aluminum production', when in reality aluminum is a common component of most crustal rocks," says Baumgardner.

11) The formation is the correct size (both length and breadth) to be Noah's Ark

Baumgardner has repeatedly affirmed the formation to have approximately the correct length. (The same length as Noah's Ark.)

My comments:
Actually, it is only the length that fits the 300 (Egyptian) cubits – the equivalent of 157 meters. (Measured to be 515.7 feet by Baumgardner and Wilson in 1985, and 515 feet by Fasold in the same year.)

And this only if the back portion, which seems to have broken off, is incorporated. The width is apparently too big at 138 ft. (42 meters), whereas it should be 86 ft. (26 meters) in order to equal the 50 cubits mentioned in the Bible.

The most *simple* explanation – if this is the Ark - is that the sides have fallen together under the weight of the mud.

The more complicated explanation from Fasold and Gray is, that the 50 cubits refer to the average width, which is exactly 50 cubits at the boat-shaped object, and the Ark is built based on a natural logarithmic curve of .6180 which can be found everywhere in nature - such as in the shell of a muscle. The difference between the largest radius and the average is .6180. The depth of the Ark is 30 cubits (15 meters), which, in inches, equal this reoccurring number: 618.0 in.

Jonathan Gray has a very complicated calculation which causes non-mathematicians' brains to hurt, but the interesting thing is that if you use this model, then the area of the Ark was exactly one acre (4,047 sq. m.), which equals the "ash IKU" that is mentioned in the Sumerian tablets[7], according to Gray.

12) "It is in the correct location (the biblical "mountains" - plural – of Ararat)."

Baumgardner repeatedly affirmed his conviction that the ark came to rest in "the mountains of Ararat". In our correspondence he mentions that he doesn't think that the Ark is on Mt. Ararat itself because *that* mountain seems to be an extremely young, post-Flood volcano. This is one of the reasons that he became interested in the boat-shaped object in the first place.

Who Is Telling the Truth?
The Whole Truth, and Nothing but the Truth…

Baumgardner's conclusions are dramatically different than what Wyatt claimed and what Gray explains in his book. – And, as we shall see in a later chapter, his colleague in geology, Dr. Bayraktutan, is in almost complete disagreement.

Is somebody just lying or could there be another explanation?

I personally have the impression that there is more to Baumgardner's firm denial of the boat-shaped object than just the scientific reasons. I think the foremost reason is Wyatt's personality. His "jumping to conclusions" and intuitive reasoning some people see as simply lying.

Baumgardner doesn't hide that he thinks Ron Wyatt was a liar:

"The reason I dissociated myself from Ron in 1986 was my conclusion that he could not be trusted, that he was given to lying as part of a deeper psychological problem," Baumgardner says.

Disappointment – and Fear of Seduction

Personally Baumgardner could feel burnt by Wyatt and with good reason. Once in 1985 and once in 1986 he went to Turkey with a film crew at the request of Wyatt without bringing anything useful home again. That was embarrassing.. (My comment: I had nothing to do with the film crews' appearing on the scene in 1985.) (But still it must have been embarrassing, so let's leave that.)

But what were possibly most decisive were Baumgardner's publications of the 4-ft. long iron rods that have since disappeared. (See pt. 8.)

"I believe the rods never existed but that Ron invented the entire story. All the Turkish authorities deny their existence, including Dr. Bayraktutan, who participated in the investigations in the fall of 1985 and who was present at the time Ron says the rods were dug from the ground," says Baumgardner.

Anyone with just a bit of professional and vocational honor in life can imagine just how disappointed a young Baumgardner might have felt with this fatherly Ron. He had put his professional credibility on the line, and there were no iron rods! What Baumgardner forgets is that it is not necessarily Ron that has lied. Possibly no one lied. But like so many other things in Turkey, these rods have disappeared. They may be rediscovered one day. We are still looking.

Maybe we should also look at the *theological* world in order to understand why Baumgardner (and some Christian-Creationists) take such distance from Wyatt.

In 1985 Baumgardner was "seduced" (as he puts it) by scanning from an instrument that some consider being occult. At this point in time many American Christians were almost in panic of being seduced by new religiosity that was appearing all over the place. Books were warning of New Age being sheathed in every possible way. . Baumgardner came to the conclusion that it was a form of dowsing.. "It was my reverence for God and His communication with humankind through the Bible that I distanced myself from involvement with it. Moreover, I became keenly aware there was no scientific basis whatever for the method, he remembers.

Molecular Frequency Generator

In 1985 David Fasold, who could possibly be seen as New Age , brought a so-called molecular frequency generator (MFG) to the Ark-site. This is an instrument that appears to involve electrical induction – an instrument, critics have compared to the infamous twig with two branches that point down when they "fell" water. This actually happens, but no law of physics can explain it. So critics claim that one is border-lining the occult and refer to Deuteronomy 18:10, where there is a warning against all types of witchcraft. But it seems like a major misinterpretation to call this instrument witchcraft! The twig and two branches is not called witchcraft in the Bible, and the MFG has nothing to do with the twig besides that they both have two rods to hold on to.

The MFG is claimed to be sending an electrical radio frequency towards the ground, and when the signal hits metal, it shows a disruption in the electromagnetic field, which can be read. The person who holds the MFG in his hands functions as a type of antenna, just like the ability to strengthen or interrupt a tuner by putting your hand on the antenna.

Even though it can be difficult to understand what is happening, there is nothing mysterious or occult in it. But Baumgardner disagrees on that point.

And one can imagine the impact such an allegation of occultism against Wyatt and his supporters has had in the largely religious circles that so far have had the strongest interest in finding the Ark.

It doesn't make it any easier to identify the truth from among all the rumors and confusion, claims and counter-claims…

Continuing the Hunt

In September 2002 I spoke with Dr. Bayraktutan about the problem. He didn't understand his old friend Baumgardner's point of view. but he added with a reference to Wyatt:

"We don't have to exaggerate or conclude something that isn't sure yet. Facts speak for themselves:

We have a boat-shaped object at an elevation of 2,000 meters that did not occur naturally. We haven't found anything that refutes the possibility of this being Noah's Ark. We can see signs of specific structures in our scannings that are not naturally occurring. The way in which the object is thought to have traveled down the mountain in a mudslide is very interesting. We have now found signs of an early civilization up on this mountain, etc, etc, etc.

All of this requires our continuing the investigations."

Chapter 27

Back to the Ark

The Danish/Norwegian group assured themselves Dr. Salib Bayraktutan (on right) as their geological guide. The Coptic geologist, Saïd Kirollos (on left), was also a part of the group.

Again in September 2002 I traveled with a group of Norwegian and Danish Ark-enthusiasts to the Ararat Mountains.

Elin Berglund and I, both of whom had been on the first journey, led the trip.

Elin is especially good at the mythological and historical side of it, like for example how the first tribe arose in the area, why the Assyrian Empire named itself after a god, Assur – funny, that was Noah's grandson's name – or that the Aramaens' name suggests a root in Asur's brother, Aram. Most of us know that the Semites come from Noah's son Shem, but fewer know that Egypt was once called Mizrm or Mizraim, after Ham's son who was the first king of Egypt. A quote from the Book of the Dead, which originates from that same period, tells us that in Egypt's earliest history, they believed in only one almighty God, just as Noah did.[1]

But with Ham's grandson, Nimrod, the son of Cush, polytheism – worshiping multiple gods – had already started. Among these the mother god, after Noah's wife, and many other people-gods were included.

Elin also thinks she can trace the ancient Nordic gods back to the Black Sea area. Most nations' gods are in reality their ancestors, and thousands of years ago it was very normal for peoples and lands to be named after their progenitors.

The Nordic god, Odin, was actually just a forefather or chief of the Odin-clan from which the Nordic people and the Anglo-Saxons and probably the Franks and the Westphalians originate. The world-famous Norwegian scientist, Thor Heyrdahl, believed that the origin of these peoples is to be found in the area of Caucasus, i.e. not far from where the Ark landed. This theory is built especially on the sagas written by the Icelandic historian Snorre Sturlason from around 1200 A.C. where also the earth is described as "Kringla Heimsins", i.e. "the round ball we live on", as described in the thesis of the contemporary Irish monk Johannes Sacrobosco "Sphaera Mundi" about the roundness of the earth. As you will see, they were well informed, these writers!

Heyrdahl was made a fool of by religious historians who meant that Odin was a mythical god and not a human being. But Heyrdahl followed Snorre's descriptions and found that Odin's "heavenly" castle Asgaard was actually the Russian town of Asov where the river Don flows into the Lake of Asov. Odin was chief of the Aesir. Before they were chased north by the Roman troops c. 1200 B.C. their castle stood here. So As-ov, As-gaard (in Danish) or As-gorod (in Russian) was actually the farm, the castle of the Aesir. "As" means fire and the Aesir were called so because they worshipped the fire as did the Zarathustra followers further south in Iran.

Footnotes

[1] God is one and alone, and none other existeth with Him – the one who hath made all things – a divine spirit, a hidden spirit – God is from the beginning, and He hath been from the beginning. He hath existed from old, and was when nothing else had being. He existed when nothing else existed, and what existeth He created. God is life and through Him only man liveth. He giveth life to man, He breatheth the breath of life into his nostrils. He fashioned men and formed the gods (angels). (The Egyptian Book of the Dead, E.A. Wallis, Dover Publications Inc.:New York, 1967.)

The name of the neighbouring country Azer-baidjan means the Country of the Fire - or the Country of the Aesir?

The Odin-people originally came from Azerbaidjan - not far away from the Ark. In 1991, when the Iron Curtain between the East and the West was unraveled, the author Bjørn Wegge discovered that about 10,000 members of a group known as the Udin People were still found in the Caucasus Mountains in Azerbaidjan[2]. They apparently stayed behind when Odin journeyed to Asov and later on to the North.

(Incidentally, these Udin People later became some of the first Christians and have partially kept their own religious form, in sharp contrast to the surrounding society, which converted to Islam around 1300.)

Heyrdahl also refers to the Anglo-Saxon Chronicle and the Canterbury Chronicle where Odin is mentioned in the English dynasty. Odin is a good example that the "gods" of the past were simply kings or ancestors.[3]

Where is Salih?

In advance Elin Berglund and I had agreed with Dr. Salih Bayraktutan, professor of geology at Erzurum University, that he was to come out and lead our troops, but the bus that was supposed to pick us up at the airport in the ancient Armenian city of Kars and then drive us to Dogubayazit never showed up.

Elin, who was in charge of the logistics of the trip, was shocked that this could happen and found an airport telephone from which she tried to call everyone she could think of but with no luck. This area of Turkey isn't quite the same as our modern cities of Oslo and Copenhagen, and from my time in Africa I knew that this type of unforeseen impediment was to be expected.

So we were forced to improvise.

I stood on the stairs in front of the airport and held an extended lecture for the group, which was forced to listen while Elin tried to contact Salih. Hours later in a even more populated terminal, we are a couple of men who decide to go into town and rent another bus at a much higher rate, or course, because it had to get there and back the same day. But in the end we made it to Dogubayazit and before dark to boot.

We drove to the border of what is now Armenia, but political reasons had unfortunately closed the border. It could otherwise have been interesting to find some Armenians whose families came from the area to hear what they had to say.

The Coptic Geologist

Despite our missing geology professor, we were lucky enough to have another geologist in our group: Saïd Kirollos, an experienced Danish geologist with Egyptian origins – or as he prefers it, with Coptic origins (one of Mizraim's descendants). He studied at Alexandria University in Alexandria, Egypt, and has since then taken courses at the University of Aarhus in Aarhus, Denmark. He has worked in Denmark and Norway

Footnotes

[2] Udin is the correct spelling of the name Odin.

[3] Thor Heyerdahl og Per Lillieström: Jakten på Odin. På sporet av vår fortid. J.M. Stenersens Forlag A-S, 2001

most of his life with such things as subsoil studies and has most recently worked as a consultant in environmental research.

Kirollos was an interesting person to know. He had heard about the Ark through the radio. DR1 ("Danmarks Radio 1") had aired an interview I gave, and afterwards he contacted the interviewer, Anders Laugesen. "Where can I find this man," he asked and shortly after contacted me. His penmanship resembled hieroglyphics, and it turned out he knew much more than just geology. But his vocation and knowledge of geology was what interested me most.

Saïd Kirollos passes on his knowledge of geology during the bus ride from Kars to Dogubayazit.

What did it matter that *mythological* and even *historical* sources suggested the existence of the Ark? It would always be a point of discussion. Some would be convinced by the place-names at which we will later look. But these can surely be explained away with the misconceptions of later periods.

No, we need to get a hold of a geologist. We have to have samples of petrified wood and other mentionable objects from the boat-shaped object that might otherwise just look like dirt to the untrained eye tested. We have to have samples of the earth and test them to see what has happened over the last 5-10,000 years and if there are any signs that there has been a flood. We have to have the lava on the near lying Mt. Ararat examined to establish whether or not the Ark could possibly still be there.

Maybe it was his background in the ancient Coptic culture that kept him open to researching something as geologically unthinkable as the Ark.

Anti-Authoritarian, Yes Please!

When I started looking for Noah's Ark, I never considered that the search could seriously question such things as the theory of evolution. That was not my purpose for interest in the Ark, but it wouldn't have stopped me from researching the possibilities. Where are we at when a *theory* turns to such dogma that alternative theories may not even be considered? That is deeply unscientific. But still, it is apparently a very accepted opinion in some circles. Too few dare to question these out-dated theories, even though many can sense they can't hold water.

Saïd Kirollos didn't come with that type of stumbling block. In everything he considered, he was open to all the possibilities. He had the right type of anti-authoritarian attitude. This was the same attitude I had to learn when studying to be a journalist: don't be afraid to run your head into a wall. Maybe the wall won't hold!

Kirollos' constant refrain when he heard something new was, "This is *very* interesting. No, no, that cannot be ruled out…"

His contacting me was a great encouragement. Now I had the opportunity to ask a man who knew his geology. Journalists can't know everything about everything.

Footnotes
[4] This theory tells us that all things have developed at the same tempo or pace that we can now see. That is, almost immeasurable, which leads to millions and billions of years of development.

Our plan was to have Kirollos perform presearch that would act as a foundation for later, more in-depth scientific research that we were hoping top geologists would get interested in.

The Impressive Mountain

When the bus arrived to the city Igdir, we could see the mighty Ararat mounting the horizon. Impatiently we began to photograph the mountain with its snow-clad top, even though the chauffeur encouraged us again and again to wait. "We'll come right past it. We'll be very close," he explained – at least that's what I could make out. None of us understood much Turkish, and he and his colleague couldn't speak anything else. We wanted to stop and look at some of the old cities on the way, but they didn't understand a word of what we said, or maybe they didn't want to understand.

As we came closer to Mt. Ararat I couldn't deny the feeling of disappointment that "our Ark" wasn't on this impressive mountain. If it were at the foot of this mountain, it would be much easier to find sponsors. But we were looking somewhere 12 miles away on an unsubstantial mountain that no one had ever heard of, even though it is believed that Gilgamesh and other pilgrims had been there… Bill Shea was right, "What a difference a mountain can make."

The bus huffed and puffed up the road winding its way around Mt. Ararat's southern effacement. We were soon on the other side, and except for the mighty mountain, the landscape was quite flat. The sun radiating down on us created an inner peace which made it difficult to imagine that not too long ago bloody battles had taken place here between the Kurds and the Turks, not to mention the violent revolt with the Armenians that occurred in the same place just around the turn of the century.

Dogubayazit was now in front of us, marking the last city before Iran. This time we found a hotel in the city to use as our base, and the next day we drove out to the Ark site.

Petrified Wood from the Port Side?

Erosion had taken its mark in the 1½ years since last we had been here. The shed water from the winter had taken a great deal of the mud with it down toward the valley again. The Ark – as we now called it – was where

In Igdir we could finally make out the impressive Mt. Ararat from the bus. But we were still 15 miles away…

It was so peaceful standing here in the sun. It was difficult to imagine the bloodbaths that took place between the Kurds and the Turks here recently, not to mention the violent showdown the Armenians were involved in almost a hundred years ago.

it had always been, but now it had cracks and porous sides suggesting that the entire formation could well be destroyed within a short amount of time. It was thought-provoking that this boat-shaped object that so many critics had called a "natural formation" maintained its form so well when everything around it sailed down the mountain.

The first day we noticed that something had changed; just east of the Ark a portion of the ground was raised. It looks like part of the Ark's port side had fallen off – probably a long time ago. Afterwards the Ark and the piece that has fallen off were covered with mud.

The Ark was again made visible due to the earthquake in 1948 and again even more visible after the 1978 quake. Due to the snow and rain, the mud around the formation is cleared away more and more each year and carried down the slope. The entire area slants down for about 3 miles toward the flat valley between this mountain and Mt. Ararat. Down in the valley the road from Dogubayazit runs to the Iranian border.

On the eastern "port side" there are now some places that are up to 9 meters (30 feet) from the surrounding area and up to the "rail". If it continued like this, it wouldn't be long before we made it down to the keel!

Due to the large amounts of watershed in the winter from 2001-2002 a large part of the hill has disappeared, and under the mud a gathering of "stones" can now be seen. Offhand they look like a bunch of loose rubble, but on closer examination they look like petrified wood. We could make out lines and signs of bark.

Geological Discussions

Geologist Saïd Kirollos is walking around with his special hammer, banging, while he tells about the great amount of minerals and fossils in the area. He is gathering samples to take home for further research.

Odd Standall from Strømmen, Norway, works for Statoil, Norwegian state-

Elin Berglund shows the intense erosion on the eastern side; or in maritime terminology: off the starboard side.

owned oil and natural gas company that also exports to the United States. He also has a great knowledge of geological relationships. Both are skeptical and careful, but both also agree that the earth samples from the sides of the Ark are of a completely different nature than the mud around it that moves while the Ark stays put.

We have been told that this is due to the limestone that is protruding in the middle of the formation, but later Dr. Bayraktutan dismisses this misunderstanding. The stone is mobile along with the Ark. He believes the explanation to be that the formation is being stopped by a narrowing of the landscape which creates a bottleneck effect for the mudflow.

Bill Fry

Again, we were so lucky to meet an Ark-specialist, Bill Fry, who was also in the area the first time we were here. Bill was a friend of Ron Wyatt, who rediscovered the boat-shaped object. Bill says that before his death in 1990, Ron asked him to take care of his project because he was afraid of the way it might continue.

Ron's widow, Mary Nell Wyatt, and the new curator of Wyatt's Museum in Tennessee, Richard Reeves, believe *they* have sole rights to Ron's controversial life's work.

Bill started on the Ark project in 1997 and has used all of his time the last few years to help find the solution to the Ark mystery and the other spectacular discoveries Wyatt was involved in. Bill has made an agreement with the authorities and will establish a museum in the building close to the Ark which is now the visitor's center, which has otherwise stood empty since this site's official recognition.

The Turkish authorities have not recognized this site as Noah's Ark. We are not talking about an archeological verification but rather a type of memorial to be protected – a kind of national park. The authorities have unfortunately not had the means to dig deeper, so Bill Fry has stepped in as the sponsor.

Over the entrance to the visitor's center a sign had already been posted naming the official sponsor to be Bill's website, www.anchorstone.com, with which different activities are connected. Bill told that he was now working on a project together with a local travel agency, because the authorities, understandably, wanted a Turk to be in charge. But as noted, Turks are not the only ones in the area...

The Kurds

When traveling about Dogubayazit and the surrounding area it doesn't take long to notice the tension between the Turks and the Kurds (the two groups making up the majority of the local population) resting under a fine surface.

The first night I went out of the hotel and immediately met a Kurdish guide. He is the grandson of a Kurdish revolutionist from Iran who

Bill Fry discussing with a group in The Valley of the Eight.

claimed an independent Kurdish state in vain. He and other Kurds believe that they have the sole rights to visitors and don't look well upon the Turks taking over. One time Elin experienced a Turkish driver having his life threatened if he dared to take a group of foreigners. He did it anyway and it still living. Not everything should be taken so literally. But casting murder threats shows how quickly the kettle can boil.

It hasn't been very long since the Kurdish Independent Movement was blamed for unrest in the area and multiple murders. Ron Wyatt was even carried off to the Iranian mountains for two weeks.

(In 2002 we found out that the man that used to carry out the local mafia's dirty work was now behind bars for a murder he *had* committed.)

The Petrified Nail

On the Ark formation we again found the petrified nail in the port side, and Bill confirmed that it was such a nail that Ron Wyatt found in June of 1991 in the opposite side of the ship in the presence of a visiting American travel group. They all signed that they had seen it.

"But where is the 4-foot long metal rod Ron Wyatt found and many witnesses had confirmed that they saw," I asked Bill.

"I have also tried to find it. The trail ends with the Turkish authorities who won't confirm its existence but won't deny that it is possible the authorities have it in their possession. There are many other found objects that later disappeared and in some cases probably some type of theft by the local people or others," says Bill Fry.

Honor is Everything

Here is something people in the West have a hard time accepting. Seen from a Western perspective, the authorities don't have anything to loose by releasing information that an archeological artifact has been stolen

But it is completely different in countries with an Eastern mentality. Here, honor means everything!

If an archeological artifact were to disappear, the government would often just close the entire case because it is embarrassing.

Instead of open politics, which through the ideals of Christianity have become a part of the Western system, in the East it is often preferred to keep quite to maintain honor. Rather than, as in the West, bringing it into the light, it is better to forget the uncomfortable.

We Are Guests

When researching Noah's Ark, we are Turkey's guests. We have to respect the rules that apply here.

Therefore, we can't find the sarcophagus that was supposedly discovered and dug up in what many believe to be Noah's vineyard either. This "vineyard" was found in "The Valley of the Eight", close to the Kurdish village Arzep where two very old tombstones were found engraved with pictograms about the Ark. The sarcophagus disappeared. It was taken during the night, and the Turkish authorities know nothing about it.

The whole story is told in the chapter entitled "Noah and Naamah's Graves".

Chapter 30

Bayraktutan Comes

Dr. Salih Bayraktutan

After days of waiting, Salih Bayraktutan finally showed up. And it turned out he was worth the wait. The little absent-minded professor went through the scientific data on the boat-shaped object. We were all deeply impressed by the serious, scientific methods he used – despite the disappointments, lack of equipment, and other obstacles that otherwise could have hindered him.

Actually, he has worked with geological research of the boat-shaped object and the surrounding area since 1983, but it has been stopped three times because foreign partners have pulled out before the research was done.

"The project has never been finished. We have begun three times, but each time we've found some evidence and then the partners have pulled out for different reasons. I'm still waiting for a more stabile partner so we can finish," recounted Salih the evening we had a seminar with him in the lobby of Hotel Ararat in Dogubayazit.

"Which partners have there been?" I asked

"First of all there were the large, serious studies together with Dr. Baumgardner who unfortunately pulled out quickly. Next I did some research together with Wyatt and Fasold, but they couldn't get support and were forced to pull out due to the civil war (with the Kurds) and other problems. Then there was also a German-American group that was maybe more occupied with proving that it *wasn't* the Ark. They also disappeared suddenly. There was also an Australian man here that used it in a court case where he lied in court about what I said in order to have books about Creation forbidden in Australian schools."

"Don't trust the foreigners" this little Kurdish girl from Üzengili seems to be thinking.

What do you think of Dr. John Baumgardner?

"I regard him very highly. He has a great family and is a good scientist. I have visited him in his house," Salih shares with joy in his voice.

"But I don't understand his reaction," he states. "While he was here we agreed on the conclusions of our research, but two years later I heard that he has changed his mind. I do not understand why.

"Through the last 4-5 years I have worked together with men like Professor Robert Michelson, Bill Fry, and Dave Deal. Yeah, Mr. Deal is good at 'remote sensing' of photographs. Actually he found an area further up the mountainside full of graves, and in one of the graves we found bones, fossil soil, paleosoil, ceramics, and other things that dated back circa 3,600 years. And we expect that there are still deeper graves lying in the ground.

"But after 15 years' work, I have reached the conclusion that this find is so meaningful that it shouldn't be given to random people like me and a

few others to study it. We need geologists, geoformologists, climatologists, paleoclimatologists, architects, archeologists, geophysicists, mathematicians, computer specialists, scientists that can decipher satellite pictures, remote sensing specialists, and others.

"All of these professionals should be gathered and study the entire area."

When trying to find scientists is it problematic that the Ark is spoken of in the various holy books?

"Yes, in one way because there is an unwillingness to deal with things that reach outside of positivistic science. That is why it is important to find sponsors that can see that this is a meaningful cultural-historic find, which is worth looking further into - no matter what we find."

Unnatural

What do you think about the claim that the formation formed around the large stone sticking up through it?

"If the stone had lain in the upper end of the formation, it could be possible. Either during a mudslide or a flow of lava it met an obstacle in the landscape. We see many examples of this type of formation in river beds. But this formation cannot be made in that way, because the stone is in the middle of the formation.

"When there are rivers of lava, sometimes the rivers split in two and then come back together again later. This creates a formation that could look like the boat-shaped formation. Such formations can be found on Little Mt. Ararat, for example. But in both of these examples an obstacle in the front causes it to happen, so a shadow is formed after the obstacle.

"Therefore, based on normal hydro-dynamic laws, it is impossible for the great stone in the middle of the formation to have caused the formation. Whether the stone was there or not, we would still have this object with its special shape. It has its own 'framework' with its hydro-dynamic and symmetric shape, the ship-like length-width relationship, etc."

A Hidden Internal Structure

"There is a hidden internal structure that we have yet to concretely prove. But the evidence we already have is, in my opinion, enough to conclude that there is a regular internal structure. The materials that made up this structure have most likely dissolved, but there is a type of fingerprint left after many years of the replacement of materials."

How do we know these internal structures exist?

"These structures give readings in the form of radar signals on GPR measurements (Ground Penetrating Radar).

"It is my opinion that this is a highly unusual object, especially in an earthquake area. Normally this type of object in a geomorphologic region would be destroyed and mixed with its surroundings, not maintain its own structure. This is completely unheard of.

"But we are not finished with the research. Our goal is to find the materials that are giving these readings and carefully collect samples in order to analyze them chemically, isotopically, and for age. But at the moment we have no possibility of accomplishing this."

Drilling Proved Nothing

"We drilled three holes along the middle of the object one year after taking the GPR-scannings in 1988. But we couldn't hit the lines that sent out the signals. When we started to drill we ran into obstacles that forces us to drill on the side, and then we were disoriented.

"We originally laid plastic strips of various colors to mark where the line had been observed on the scanning, but the strips were unfortunately taken by the locals. We videotaped where the strips lay, so if we work hard enough, we may be able to reconstruct where the lines go...

"Otherwise we'll have to perform a new scanning.

"Another reason we couldn't hit these abnormal lines was that our drilling equipment was out-of-date; it used water to cool the drill down as well as to get through the soil. But in this case the water mixed with the clay we thought the signals came from, so all of the fine factions disappeared when we got the samples up. We only had a few samples with gravel and clay.

"We used the wrong technique. In the future we will have to use dry drilling with air pressure instead. There is also foam. We have decided to use better equipment in future drillings, and we also need to find the radar lines that were previously measured."

Dr. Baumgardner, with whom you took these drillings, says that the drilling showed rocky ground under the object which gave these results. Therefore, he concludes that this is not the Ark.

"No, no. These drillings really didn't show us anything because we couldn't hit the lines that had given feedback, and we couldn't use the samples that we obtained. Baumgardner cannot conclude if the Ark exists or not based on that."

The Mysterious V-Shape

In the scannings we can see a V-shape in the bottom of the object. Where does this V come from?

"Actually, many places show a W – a double U. In these W's there are about 2½ meters between the lines. This W shows the underground topography, and due to the radar technique used, elevated ground is shown as a V. But Tom Fenner, who took the radar samples, has set-off the results from this topography. You have to set-off these results so that you get an idea of what results the object would give if it were on level ground. When the V is removed in this fashion, there is still another V left over (– or more correctly, a U). The curve isn't as pointed as before. It is more rounded – not 40 degrees, but maybe 10-15.

"We hadn't expected to find a pointed V either, because if this is the Ark, it would be more like a ferry, i.e. the keel would be more rounded (than a sailboat, for example).

"This V-shape reoccurs in about 80 percent of the object, but there where the large rock has crept in this inner-structure is ruined. (That means the structure existed before the rock. HN)

"We have found abnormal lines on the scannings that are completely vertical and horizontal. As far as I remember, there are no less than 9 vertical lines along the object. Some have thought these just to be fissures, so they left the project," laughs Dr. Bayraktutan in amazement. "...Because these are not fissures by any means. We have measured along the sides and there are no cracks. We have even found weak abnormalities in the middle.

"We know that differentiation in the material gives these results, but we don't yet know what material it is, whether chemical differences or just a difference in the stiffness of the different materials."

Three Layers and Internal Structures

Do your scannings show multiple layers?

"Yes. There is one close to the surface and two others near the bottom."

But some people claim that the bottom of the boat is still up in the upper area?

"No. We have examined the first object three times. It is located about 100 meters up the slope below the rock. It is parallel with the rock. But we have found no signs of the bottom up there. On the other hand, we haven't taken any radar scannings up there, so we can't say for sure what is in the ground.

"We have located this first impression from the aerial photo, and afterwards we found it in the area. It has the same geometrical shape and size, but the orientation is different. But recently a road has been built over the impression, so it is partially destroyed. Besides that, the military has driven around the area with bulldozers and other large machines," says Salih.

On the aerial photograph you can follow the route the "boat" took from the upper site to its present location.

If the boat could cope with a trip down the mudslide, its inner structure must have been strong. But it doesn't look that way today. What could be the explanation for this?

"The object must have a strong structure holding it together, that is obvious. We can see on the radar that there is something in there."

If we imagine that there is a framework holding the "Ark" together, why, then, is it not visible on the exterior?

"In some places there are some plank-like stones sticking out. But erosion would cause such things to disintegrate after they have been freed from the mud."

Is it possible that the ship slid down the mountain around 2,000 years ago when the structure was still strong enough but has now more or less disappeared?

"Yes. That is possible. We still haven't dated the landslide. But with the modern techniques we have, it is possible to date the soil – if we have the means."

Three Landslide Periods

"We have established that there have been three different landslides. The first landslide started on the Iranian side of the border from south to north. At that time there was a lake in the Dogubayazit area.

"The banks of the lake were located where the mudslide turns 90 degrees east. A fault created by an earthquake stopped the flow from going that direction. The first landslide occurred while there was a lake here, and Mt. Ararat was only half of its present-day size.

"During this first slide, earth slid into the lake that was there, because we can see it is like a delta."

Do you mean that the whole valley was flooded?

"Yes. At that time there was a lake here." (Or Noah's Flood?)

"But later there was another landslide. Actually, there were multiple landslides but at the same time. When you go up by the white ridge of rocks next to the Iranian border, you can see that the rock has been raised by an earthquake that happened in connection with the landslide.

"With this second event there was no longer a lake in the area but rather a kind of farm land.

"The third landslide happened as late as 1949, and it is still active. The earth is still moving. This landslide was initiated by a series of earthquakes that came close to each other. It wasn't until this last landslide that the boat-shaped object became visible.

"The people in Uzengili village remember quite well how the fields were even and easy to cultivate normally.

But with the earthquake the entire area became uneven.

"I have a picture that was taken 10 years later where the sides of the "Ark" are only about 3 feet high. The contour is untouched and the ends are not yet destroyed.

"But since then, the earth around the Ark continued down into the valley while the Ark ended up in the open. It may have been lifted about 10 percent, but 90 percent of that is due to the erosion of the surrounding soil.

"Since 1984 I have followed and measured the movements of the object by using geodetic methods and an expensive GPS-system. I set marks on the object and the surroundings, but these have unfortunately also been removed by the local population," the hard-pressed professor accounts.

Dismissed Too Quickly

"If you stand on a high point and look out over the surrounding area, you can see that the landslides are moving down toward a smaller area, a bottleneck, that is about 300 meters wide and 1.2 km long.

"The Ark looks like it has stopped just at the beginning of this bottleneck. It isn't by chance that it is located where it is, because according to the laws of physics, it would stop right there!"

Do we know when the first two landslides happened?
"No, we have no dates, but I have taken samples over the last ten years that are ready to be dated when the opportunity arises.

"When I first saw this object in 1983, my first reaction was that this was just a landslide area where the object was formed naturally and by chance.

"Other geologists from Ankara and Istanbul said the same thing. They said that this type of object appears in areas where there has been an earthquake or a landslide.

"But two things got me thinking and caused me to look at the area more closely:

1.   First of all, I thought about the large rock. If it were placed towards the front of the object, I would have gone home right away. But it wasn't.

2.   Secondly, I saw the object from a helicopter and could see that it lay at the beginning of the bottleneck. It looked just like when you fly over the Atlantic and see the gargantuan boats floating down there. According to aerodynamic and physical laws it made sense that the "Ark" lay precisely where it did in the middle of a mudslide.

"Then I understood that the formation had not emerged around the great stone which we are quick to conclude. It is independent of the stone. It is its own entity."

Chapter 31

The Report

One evening Salih Bayraktutan showed me the report that he and Baumgardner, among others, wrote in July of 1987. He showed me the simple radar measurements, whose graphs were copied in the report, as well as the seismic measurements.

There is no doubt that something is down there, but what it may be is difficult to conclude as long as satisfying drilling hasn't been completed.

In 1987 radar, magnetometer, and seismic measurements were taken. All three showed signs of an unidentifiable material in even layers about 15-25 feet below the surface.

Radar Measurements

From the 19th -23rd of July, radar measurements were taken.

In some of the 71 graphic printouts that resulted from these measurements the material showed up as a V about 20-25 feet below the surface. If one were to imagine this object as the remnant or imprint of a great ship, then the V would resemble the keel of the Ark.

This V was found by means of a small radar vehicle driving across the boat-shaped object 71 times at 2-meter (6.5-foot) intervals. Because the surface of the object curves outward in the middle, this V needs to be flattened out.

Artist David Deal (or Big Deal, as he calls himself) wasn't present at the time of the measurements, but he has created a graphic reconstruction in which he sets off the arc. He has set the arc off by so much that it is almost flat. I think that Dave is overcorrecting the V, though, because the surface bulge is not that big. But the V is flatter. Tom Fenner, who was the radar specialist on the team and conducted the layer studies, also adjusted the

Tom Fenner with ground-penetrating radar (GPR) in addition to control apparatuses, magnetic tape recorders, graphic measuring devices and batteries.

An example of the V that appears in many of the results.

This printout is from scanning Y -20, 20 meters (65 ft.) below the middle. See the blue marking on the co-ordinate figure below. The V shows up clearly on all of the scanning results from the yellow area.

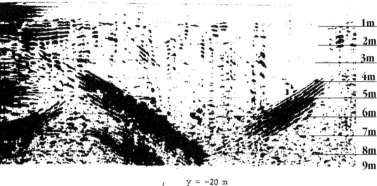

y = −20 m

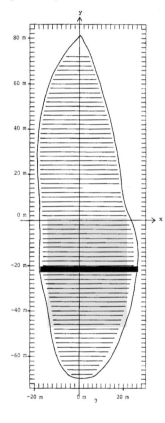

measurements, tells Dr. Bayraktutan.

The radar measurements also show other layers and stripes that Fasold and Wyatt understood as rooms and hallways. This cannot be proven, but these irregular stripes are found in the results – what are they?

Magnetometer Measurements

After the radar measurements, the team performed 1,177 magnetometer tests. These can be seen in fig. 8 and show a smaller swing reflecting limestone. This is probably because there is less metal in limestone than in the surrounding area.

Because these results are only found in a restricted area, it suggests that the limestone is only a part of the subsoil and does not lie under the entire formation – and for that matter is not the cause of the formation.

To the right we can see David Deal's somewhat overexaggerated graphic correction in which the V is almost made flat. Tom Fenner had actually already corrected it quite a bit due to the uneven surface of the formation. Deal believes that the scanning results also show signs of several collapsed decks.

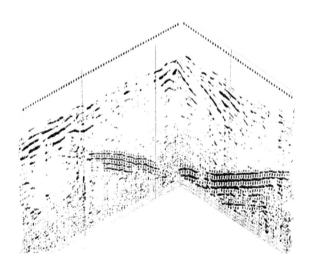

Seismic Measurements

Finally, the group performed seismic measurements. These measurements added new knowledge to those previously taken. The seismic measurements showed two straight lines with high amplitude along the middle of the "boat" and one long line just to the right of the middle – on the port side.

(The lines can be seen between the following points
x = 0, Y = 68 and x = 0, y = -4 (see fig. 9)
x = 0, y = 0 and x = 0, y = -76 (see fig. 10)
x = 0, y = 68 and x = -10, y = -4 (see fig. 11)

The layers in figures 9 and 11 were the deepest and gave a result of between 2400-3300 m/s, which is quite a high velocity. On the other hand, the layer in figure 10 gave a result of only 1500 m/s. This result presumably comes from the limestone that is protruding from that part of the formation.

Because of the great difference between the two measurements, the writer of the report assumes that the results in the deeper layer are <u>not</u> from limestone but rather something else.

This coincides with the radar measurements in which each layer was separated into 4-8 meter (15-25 ft.) deep portions. It is probably the same deep layer that gives these results in the seismic measurements.

Provided that the layers have the same thickness, the writer of the report calculates that the layers are relatively thick: 5.9 meters (19.4 ft.)for the fig. 9 layer (which is most likely limestone) and 2.3 meters (7.5 ft.) for the fig. 10 layer, as well as no less than 7.9 meters (25.9 ft.) for the layer in fig. 11.

But what these layers consist of can only be established through drillings, concludes the author of the report in November of 1987.

The following year some drillings were taken, and Baumgardner concluded that these illustrated the fact that the previous results were caused by the peculiar nature of the subsoil. After these drillings he discontinued his involvement with the Ark. But Salih Bayraktutan completely disagrees. The drillings showed nothing that could be used to form such a conclusion, because the drillings were unsuccessful, he says. (A type of drill was used that integrated water in the cooling process, and the water destroyed the material.)

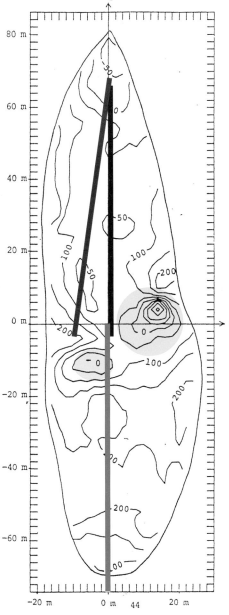

Figure 8 above: the results of the 1,177 magnetometer measurements. The contours of the magnetic fields revealed a slight fluctuation around the limestone, marked here in yellow. The colored lines show layers that were discovered by the seismic measurements

Then why didn't he perform new drillings?

Simply because he didn't have the necessary equipment. After all of the mess with Wyatt and Fasold (who are both now deceased) and Baumgardner, who suddenly changed his mind and began writing against the find, the Western sponsors are understandably quite confused.

This type of drilling, with the proper equipment – air and foam, not water-cooling – is what we need to get the ball rolling.

Conclusion: It Could Be Noah's Ark

The report comes to a conclusion on page 49:

> We conclude that the data from our geophysical investigations in no way conflict with the proposition that the unusual boat-shaped site near Mahser village contains the remains of Noah's Ark. Indeed, the existence of remains of a large man-made structure in the site is an attractive way to account for the highly anomalous feature of the extensive, almost planar, reflector observed in the radar data. However, without actual samples of the subsurface materials we feel that definitive interpretations of our data are not possible. On the other hand, we believe samples obtainable through core drilling a small number of holes in the site can provide the information required which, together with the geophysical data we already have, can allow very solid conclusions to be reached. We therefore urge the Turkish authorities to support efforts to conduct core drilling as early in 1988 as weather conditions allow.

Afterwards, a thank you to all the Turkish authorities that have helped with the research followed: We want to express our thanks to Prof. Dr. Hursit Ertugrul, Rector of Ataturk University, for sponsoring this joint research project. We also thank Mr. Rüsdü Naiboglu (Emeritus General), Director for Security Affairs, and Mrs. Reyyan Odemis, Director of the Department of Foreign Affairs, Turkish Prime Ministry, as well as the Governor of Agri for their sincere efforts and assistance in making this project a success.

The report is dated November 10, 1987, Erzurum.

We can conclude that more than 15 years have passed since this report was made and that the drilling that was performed the following year did NOT give an acceptable solution. This means that more drilling is necessary.

Chapter 32

Mysterious Place Names

We're going out to the "Ark" again.

The view from the Ark formation – looking out over the valley flowing from the mountain over to Big and Little Ararat – is absolutely sumptuous.

For some, being here is solemn, even ceremonious in the "holy place" thinking about what the Ark symbolizes. For others it's all about collecting information and material that will either confirm or deny this being the Ark of Noah.

If this should be the case, then we are among the most privileged allowed to walk here before the site begins to overflow with or be closed to tourists. Talk of a fence around the formation to protect it has already been thrown back and forth by many, including the locals who hope to get in on any possible profits.

The Mountain Referred to in the Qur'an

We also wandered through a section of the mudslide that supposedly brought the Ark to its present resting place. The locals call it Al Judi, and there is about a mile to the top of it. Ark-eologist David Fasold was key in finding the ancient name of this area, and he described it in his books.[1] The Arabic name Al Judi means "the high" and is also the name the Qur'an uses for the landing place of the Ark:[2]

Then the word went forth:
"O earth! swallow up thy water, and
O sky! Withhold (thy rain)!"
And the water abated,
and the matter was ended.
The Ark rested on Mount Judi,
and the word went forth:
"Away with those who do wrong!"

٤٤-وَقِيلَ يَٰٓأَرْضُ ابْلَعِى
مَآءَكِ وَيَٰسَمَآءُ
أَقْلِعِى وَغِيضَ الْمَآءُ وَقُضِىَ الْأَمْرُ
وَاسْتَوَتْ عَلَى الْجُودِىِّ
وَقِيلَ بُعْدًا لِّلْقَوْمِ الظَّٰلِمِينَ ٠

Salih Bayraktutan, who grew up with Islam, tells that the Arabic text is not talking about a peak, but rather an eminence, or rise in the ground: "the high".

In the English translation of the Qur'an, the nuance is often lost where "Mount Judi" is written (as in the most famous translation, Abdullah Yusuf Ali's translation with commentary.[3])

The First Mountain

The pronunciation of *Al Judi* is very close to *Al Cudi*, meaning the *Kurdish* mountain in Arabic. The Turkish name for this place is *Cudi Dagi* – the Kurdish mountain. Because *kurd* can also mean "first", the original mean-

Footnotes

[1] David Fasold. *The Discovery of Noah's Ark*. Sidgwick & Jackson Ltd. 1990, pp. 93-102, 324. David Fasold. *The Ark of Noah*. Knightsbridge Publishing Company, New York / 1988 Wynwood Press * 0-922066-10-8.

[2] Hud Surah 11:44 – all of Surah 11 is about Noah. The last sentence in verse 44 refers to a story about Noah's son, who will not separate himself from evil people but is still saved in the Ark. He should be destroyed because of his unrighteousness, but because of Noah's prayer, he is allowed to live, though promised to be punished later.

[3] The Holy Qur'an, published by Tahrike Tarsile Qur'an, Inc., New York.

ing could well have been "the first mountain". This, of course, is interesting in relation to the landing of the Ark. The mountain does not necessarily get its name from the Kurds. The Kurds may have gotten their name from the mountain.

The name *Al Judi* probably originates from a later period. Islam, and with it the Arabic name, did not come to the area until the 8th century when the Arabian army made it all the way to Constantinople (Istanbul). But the area wasn't put under Islam until the 14th century with the defeat of the Turks.

At this time the Kurds had lived in the mountains for centuries along with the Armenians.

To avoid confusion, I must again say that another and more famous Al Judi Mountain can be found about 200 km (125 miles) south of this location on the Iraqi-Syrian border. It is called *Jabal Judi*. There a local tradition says it is the resting place of the Ark. This is mainly based on the fact that a monastery existed on the top of the mountain at one point, and this monastery was possibly built in the form of a ship. After the Muslim takeover, it was re-constructed into a mosque.

But the Al Judi or Al Cudi we are looking at lies just across from the boat-shaped object.

The Heroes' Anchorage

Because this location is guarded very carefully today, we cannot go all the way up to the crest marking the border to Iran. On the map this crest is situated between two peaks known as "Yigityatai" which, when translated, mean "the bed of heroes" or cradle. The locals have also called it "the Wall of Heaven".

This is the same mountain with its characteristic crest between two peaks that was carved into the stele Ron Wyatt found here in 1983. On the stele a boat was engraved with eight faces below a hill.

When we read Gilgamesh's description of the place where he visited Ut-napishtim (Noah), he mentions one mountain[4] with two bosoms – two peaks.[5]

Wyatt thought that it was this crescent-shaped mountain that made a natural port for the Ark, as discussed previously.

Judgment Day and the Resurrection

The northern most part of the slope is called "Masher", which means "Judgment Day" according to Fasold. This is a clear reference to the judgment day the Flood exemplified, not just according to the Bible and the Qur'an, but according to most ancient sources.

The location to where the Ark has slid down, if we accept that theory, is called "Mashur", which means "the Resurrection". It is notable that these places had these names long before the earthquake in 1948,[6] when the boat-shaped object appeared.

Why were these places named such? Is it thinkable that their origins can

Footnotes

[4] In the Sumerian version KUR in the sentence *"a-na KUR ni-ir i-te-mid GIŠ eleppu"* does not mean mountain, but hill or country or area. This fits well with the area above the boat-shaped object but not with a peak like that of Mt. Ararat.

[5] To the Sumerians, Mashu was a sacred mountain. Its name means "twin" in Akkadian, and thus was it portrayed on Babylonian cylinder seals —a twin-peaked mountain, described by poets as both the seat of the gods, and the underworld (60). References or allusions to Mt.Mashu are found in three episodes of the Gilgamesh cycle which date between the third and second millennia B.C.

[6] According to Fasold in "The Ark-Update", May-June 1991 and in his book pg. 100.

The Mountains of Ararat

The Urartu Mountains = fits the entire region

> *2 miles to >*
> *the village of*
> **Karga-con-maz**
> *= The crow-land-will not*

Al Cudi = the first or the Kurdish mountain
Al Judi = the high, the Ark-mountain of the Qu'ran
Mashu = the twin-mountain in Gilgamesh

Yigityatagi = the Bed of the Heroes
„Wall of Heaven"

Ziyaret Dag = pilgrimage Mt.
Ritual burial place

1ˢᵗ boat-shaped imprint

Stream of mud

**Masher =
The Judgement Day**

**Mashur =
Resurrection**

300 Royal Egyptian cubits = 515 feet = 158 meter

Sides up to 30 feet high
(9 meters)

> *Only 500 yards to >*
> *the village Uzengili*
> *before 1948: Nazar*
> *(promise, to hide)*
> *- or Nisir as*
> *in Gilgamesh*

Photo: Henri Nissen September 2002. NB: This picture has been lengthened to compensate for the long distance. See the aerial photograph for the correct proportions.

be traced all the way back to the Ark? It is peculiar that these insignificant mounds and fields where the shepherds guard their sheep were given names at all, especially these names…

The expectancy of the Judgment Day, a day where justice will finally be seen, plays a big role in both the Bible and the holy book of the Muslims, the Qur'an. But why did they call these specific places these important names?

Whether the names were formed in Christian or Muslim time – that is within the last 2,000 years – these names would have referred to either the above mentioned Judgment Day and Resurrection or to the Judgment Day and Resurrection of Noah's day. Why these names for these areas, unless they were already associated with the Ark.

Also, if the names date back to the pre-Christian era, then those who gave the names must have had a reason to refer to the Judgment Day in this specific location. What other explanation could there be, except for the Ark…? These names keep running through my head.

Noah in the New Testament

One of the female members on our journey had a crisis a number of years back that led to a spiritual openness. Therefore, she was more interested in the spiritual realm than geological facts that the rest of us might think more important. People that are very spiritual often sense more here than just rock and mud. They sense a dimension that cannot be seen or touched.

She took a New Testament with her and sat up on the limestone in the middle of the formation reading aloud the texts about Noah and the Ark. The New Testament, too, withholds multiple references to the story of Noah from the Old Testament. For example, the apostle Peter writes a great deal about the coming judgment day in his second letter, and he warns the reader that God "did not spare the ancient world, even though he saved Noah, a herald of righteousness, with seven others, when he brought a flood on a world of the ungodly".[7]

Jesus also prophesies somewhere else about a time when he will return to earth as Messiah. According to Jesus this will be a time where everything is "business as usual" just as it was when Noah sent out the warning:

> "For as the days of Noah were, so will be the coming of the Son of Man. For as in those days before the flood they were eating and drinking, marrying and giving in marriage, until the day Noah entered the ark, and they knew nothing until the flood came and swept them all away, so too will be the coming of the Son of Man. Then two will be in the field; one will be taken and one will be left. Two women will be grinding meal together; one will be taken and one will be left."[8]

Just like Noah, Jesus (Isa) is also in the Muslims' holy book, the Qur'an. He is a great prophet called Messiah because he will come again to judge the world.

Footnotes

[7] 2 Peter 2:5.

[8] Matthew 24:37-41.

[9] Hebrews 11:6-7.

We don't know if the place names originate from Christians or Muslims, or even a distant past when the location of the Ark was possibly known.

For the believer, the account of Noah and the Flood is not only a terrible catastrophe and a warning, but also an inspiring example that faith conquers all. In the book of Hebrews Noah is used as an example of a man who was saved by his faith:

> "And without faith it is impossible to please God, for whoever would approach him must believe that he exists and that he rewards those who seek him. By faith Noah, warned by God about events as yet unseen, respected the warning and built an ark to save his household; by this he condemned the world and became an heir to the righteousness that is in accordance with faith."[9]

The Aras River rises from the Anatolian Highlands, runs east, and constitutes the border between Turkey and Armenia. It then flows behind Mt. Ararat, creates the border between the Azerbaijani enclave Naxcivan and Iran, and finally runs out into the Caspian Sea.

Aras is the modern name for the Greek Araxes, which can be translated as "where the boat anchored"... Which boat?

Araxes – Where They Anchored

Peace and beauty. The wind cools us so that the long sunrays intensified by the altitude are hardly felt at all, and in the evening we are as red as lobsters.

Together with the Norwegian Kåre Vik I am standing at the top of the "bow" looking out at the valley below as it spreads towards the west.

This valley continues northeast into the valley through which the Araxes flows. The Araxes most likely flowed here as well when the water level was higher. The Arxes or Araks is the ancient name for the 606-mile-long Aras River that constitutes the border between Turkey and the present-day state of Armenia as well as a part of the border to Iran before it ends in the Kura River in Sabirabad, Azerbaijan.

The Aras is the most important river for Armenia as the majority of the population and industry is found along its banks.

Unfortunately, the border to Armenia is closed because of political and historical disagreements, similar to the trade boycott on the Iranian-Turkish border due to religious power in Iran, and the surrounding countryside suffers under both.

The interesting thing for us is that Araxes (Arazes) is Greek and means something like "where the boat anchored". Arazo means "to moor", "to anchor", or "to come to anchor". Araxo is the verb, while Arazes is the past tense form. I wonder where the Araxes got its name...?

How Did the Animals Get Down?

Kåre Vik is recording with his fancy digital DVD-video camera for a program that I will be editing when we get home.

While others are taken by how Noah got the animals *into* the Ark, Kåre is

Kåre Vik in a film clip where he wonders how the animals came down the steep Mt. Ararat on the other side of the valley alive…

more curious how he got them out again! Or better yet, how did he get them down the mountainside?

He is surveying the steep Mt. Ararat that looks as though it is just on the other side of the valley, while in reality its peaks lie almost 15 miles away.

This warm summer where the snow has receded more than normal is expecting over 100 mountain climbers to dare the dangerous slopes of Ararat – especially Americans. The conical top of this volcano is covered in ice and its slopes are highly dangerous. One risks slipping or even finding rock, ice and stones flying towards one's head. To imagine that animals could make this trip down is absolutely absurd. It just couldn't happen.

The whole idea of the Ark lying up there on Mt. Ararat is unrealistic. Everything is against it. At a distance – in the US and Europe – it may be thinkable, but when one is standing here looking at the steep slopes, one is forced to conclude that it is not possible, concludes Kåre.

But here where we were standing, in the peaceful, soft mountains, it is not as difficult to imagine the Ark quietly coming to a rest in the almost U-shaped port the mountains form here, nor to imagine the animals spreading out through the landscape with the rainbow vested overhead.

"I can easily picture how the animals swarmed out and could have moved safely down the rolling hills into the rich valley below with little difficulty," says Kåre, who thinks this place to be one of the most peaceful and marvelous locations he has ever seen – and this coming from a Norwegian.

The Idyll Is Broken…

But this idyllic picture is harshly destroyed when Bent Callesen from Ringsted in Denmark comes running back to the Ark after a lone walk through the countryside. He met some Kurdish kids keeping sheep. At first they were just talking, and then the boys asked if he didn't want to go around the mountain to see their animals. When he got to the other side where no one could see him, they wanted money. When he said no and turned away, they ran after him and grabbed his shirt. He had to run away as they threw stones after him!

That kind of thing makes us mad, so a few of us chased the boys to scare them. Afterwards I spoke with the old Kurdish *Keeper of the Ark*, Hassan, who comes from the same village, Uzengili. He showed me, with two whips of the hand, what he thought they deserved.

Uzengili – Originally Nazar

The village of Uzengili hasn't always been called such. This comes from an interview with David Fasold from the 24th of June, 1986 which was published, among other places, in the May-June 1991 issue of "The Ark-Update". In this interview Fasold is speaking with Ali Oglu Reshit Sarihan, who discovered the Ark – or the boat-shaped object – in 1948 as a 22-year-old. Fasold states that on the 1945 map of Dogubayazit/Erivan, the village was called Nazar. But in connection with the earthquake, the inhabitants of the village changed its name to Uzengili, which translated means "to spur with the stirrup".

Nazar isn't a Turkish word, but possibly borrowed from Arabic where the root NSR can mean "to conceal a secret thing". It could also come from the Assyrian word *nazãru*, which means "to protect". The inhabitants of the village took Nazar as if it were the Turkish word *nezir*, which means "vowing", or "devoting vow", or "a thing vowed", just as that which is surrendered when a prophet warns about the wrath of God, or otherwise *nezire*, which can mean a thing done, given or sacrificed in fulfillment of a vow.

This is quite important, because the name Nisir is named five times in Gilgamesh[10] as the landing place for Utnapishtim's ship!

Father and son, Bent and Jakob Callesen, exploring the area. Here we are on the western side of Mt. Ararat. Bent was attacked by a couple of youngsters who wanted his money. As he walked away they threw stones after him…

In the Forbidden Zone

After this, three of the younger people from the team came back from a forbidden trip. Vivien Broughton and Thomas Samsing together with Bent's son, Jakob Callesen, had gone all the way up into the military zone. They made it up to the new military road that rips through the landscape where the Ark once lay – according to the working theory and the aerial photography that can be found in this book.

Unfortunately the military had built a road directly through the "landing place"…

In order not to provoke the military, the three youths didn't dare to go so far so they could see the burial place or the stele to the right of the mountain's crest which marks the border. An ancient Hurrian petrograph can supposedly be found on a stele – that is, a carved drawing on a stone, and the drawing is thought to date back to the Hurrian period, as far as we can come, to the age of Noah.

Unfortunately, only one picture of this stele exists, and it is impossible to see what is on the stele. We are forced to trust what Ron Wyatt has described and his wife's drawing of the same until we are given permission to photograph the stele ourselves. We are working on that, the legal way.

A Place of Pilgrimage

There is also a ritual burial site just below Yigityatagi, the special brow or saddle between the two peaks. This site is called Ziyaret Da, which means "volunteer pilgrimage".

As we will discuss in a later chapter about Naxuan, an artist and historian named David Allen Deal found in an aerial photograph signs suggesting the existence of multiple graves and buildings underground. Ruins make marks that can be seen in aerial photographs.

Footnotes
[10] Tablet XI, col. III, lines 140-44.
or
Tablet XI, col. 134-138
134. To the country of Nizir, went the ship;
135. the mountain of Nizir stopped the ship, and to pass over it, it was not able.
136. The first day and the second day, the mountain of Nizir the same.
137. The third day and the fourth day, the mountain of Nizir the same.
138. The fifth and sixth, the mountain of Nizir the same.
(from The Chaldean Account of the Deluge by George Smith)

When the SEPDAC-expedition was here in 1998 they were affirmed that graves and ancient ruins can be found here underground. Professor Robert Michelson from Georgia State University is working hard to put together and find funding for a scientific expedition team to explore the area.

So much suggests that a building existed here at one time – maybe the fabled Naxuan, the first city after the Great Flood. This place was possibly a necropolis, a burial city where ancient peoples traveled because it was the holiest place for everyone. Maybe they came to give alms at the place their forefathers started and leave behind the bones of the deceased. Those that believed in a resurrection surely hoped that theirs would happen in this unique place.

More Symbolic Names

If all of these meaningful and symbolic names haven't yet convinced our readers that we are in the vicinity of Noah's famed Ark, then there is another place, further east, called Kargakonmaz.

Karga means crow, *kon* means to land, and *maz* means will not. The crow will not land. Noah sent a raven out – translated as crow in many versions – and it wouldn't land...

> "Then it came about at the end of forty days, that Noah opened the window of the ark which he had made; and he sent out a raven, and it flew here and there until the water was dried up from the earth. Then he sent out a dove from him, to see if the water was abated from the face of the land" (Genesis 8:6-8, NAS).

There is also an ancient castle up here called Daronynk. It stands on a place which means "where the years were turned". A strange maritime phrase to use up here in the mountains... unless a boat had once been here.

And as mentioned, the valley to the southwest is called "The Region of the Eight", and in that valley lies the village Arzap which is full of headstones with eight crosses. A clear allusion to the eight from the Ark.

The place name Arzap can come from the Turkish *Arz zapt* which means "to capture the earth" or maybe even further back from the Semitic "eretz tsap", which can be translated as "to cling to the earth".

The first anchor stones were found in Arzap. Could the name be a reference to the anchor scraping the tops of the hills, thus giving an idea of "land ho!" or rather "land below!" ..."to cling to the earth"?

Let's go to Arzap.

Chapter 33

The Graves of Noah and Naamah

Thursday September the 5th, 2002 – We drove out to "The Valley of the Eight" where evidence suggests that Noah and his wife Naamah may have lived. According to the book of Jasher, which we will look at in the next chapter, Noah's wife's name was Naamah, the daughter of Enoch, who – according to Genesis 5:18-20 – was the father of Methuselah.[1]

We drove from Dogubayazit, the most eastern city in Turkey just a few miles from the Iranian border, west of Mt. Ararat, to a small village called Arzep[2] about 20 miles from the Ark formation.

Like in 2001 we have come to have a closer look at the big stones that are found here. They look like anchors found in other places of the world - but these are much bigger. How have these huge anchors of stone ended up here in the mountains where sailing isn't possible at all? The anchors are one of the clearest indications that Noah's Ark has something to do with this region.

The stones have been engraved with crosses, but these are most certainly of a later date - probably from the time of the crusaders or from the Armenians. The reason why we assume that the crosses have been added later on is simply that Ron managed to find some partly buried anchors which had not (yet) been engraved with crosses.

Above: A stone with a cross and a very old Hurrian or Hittite symbol.

Below: A close-up of the upper portion of the stone with an inscription written with letters that were at the time yet to be deciphered. We later found out that it was either West Armenian or Old Armenian…

But there are also other engravings on the stones. On one of the stones e.g. we find a so-called "zigurrat", a temple tower and, of course, that makes you think of the Tower of Babel mentioned shortly after the Flood. We also find an old symbol similar to the symbols of the Hurrians. And finally this engraved a very old writing which has not yet been deciphered as far as we know.

To Tea at Feizal's

Before we get the chance to look at the stones, we receive an invitation by Feizal, the "leader" of the village. His grandfather is the official head of the village.

A lot has changed over the past few years. In the beginning, the villagers were hostile towards foreigners; they even threw stones after them. Maybe this is due to the Armenian and Christian origins of this village whose ancestors were persecuted over a hundred years ago. The Armenians were not completely innocent in that they sought help from Russia, but that is another, and very complicated, story. War and strife have left a dark shadow of hate and hostility against "the others" – or maybe it's the feeling of guilt?

Whatever the case, being on guard against foreigners is a part of Eastern

The stone with the Tower of Babel or at least an engraved zigurrat. Close-up below:

Footnotes

[1] According to the Book of Jasher 5:16-18 Noah's wife Naamah was little sister to Methuselah whose name means „when he dies, it will come". And the same year he died, the Flood came. Interestingly enough, it does not say that Noah's father-in-law, Enoch, died, but rather, "Thus all the days of Enoch were three hundred sixty-five years. Enoch walked with God; then he was no more, because God took him." Genesis 5:23-24.

[2] This village has previously been mistakenly called Kazan. But Kazan is a few miles up in the mountains and does not have any headstones (not anymore, at least). This is the village we visited in the valley, Arzep, which has the many headstones connected to the name "The Region of the Eight".

culture. The others are the enemy until proven otherwise. But once a friend, the hospitality of the East is at one's feet. This is shown by, among other things, eating together.

Last year when we came there was no stone throwing, and as the day progressed, the atmosphere became more and more friendly. This year we are even invited into Feizal's house, which is equipped with a satellite dish on the roof and woven carpets on the floors.

We put our shoes outside and sit on pillows on the floor as Feizal and his wife and children welcome us with tea served in glasses. Pictures from earlier visits are brought forth and given to those that are in them.

A group of children pop their heads in the open door in order to see the strangers. After tea and talk we go to the stones together.

The Tower of Babel and the Writing on the Stone

The stones are still there, we are glad to see. We study them and take pictures - pour water on them to see the shades more clearly. And Feizal and other people from the village are very helpful.

We find the stone with the "tower of babel". But I doubt that this engraving is rather old. As a matter of fact I think that it has been added after the crosses as it can clearly be seen that *The Tower of Babel* has been made in a more primitive way than the crosses. This could, of course, be due to its having been engraved at a very early time. But I can't imgine that the crusaders, or whoever engraved the beautiful crosses, would do it without paying respect to an old symbol like that. *The Tower of Babel* is probably added much later by hands not that artistic.

On another stone are engraved some characters which nobody has been able to decipher so far and which we therefore assume to be very old, Elin tells. And they do, indeed, look a bit primitive. And below them again some crosses and a beautifully engraved tree or flower.

In May 2004 I managed to partly clear up the mystery of the unknown writing. I sent the picture to Michael Westh, a theologian who has been living in Armenia and is something of an expert in that field. He was able to tell that it was Armenian:

- The first line goes: "Put up cross". Then follows a line that makes no sense: "jare khav sjusi". Third line begins with: "aj. Ira (or Illa)".

It is written in West Armenian, the dialect where the orthography up to this day is closest to Old Armenian.

In the line "Put up cross" (3rd person singularis, aorist) the "writer" has used the second 'v' and not the first 'v' in the Armenian alphabet which usually characterizes 3rd pers.sing.aor. In other words, he used the 'v' which a modern Armenian would use in East Armenian or which an non-academic would use.

The Armenian alphabet came into existence shortly after Byzantium and Persia divided the Armenian kingdom in 387 A.C. which meant that it stopped existing, Westh tells.

In Armenia like in Iran/Babylon the writing used to be cuneiform, Syrian or Greek, and it was to preserve Armenian identity, language and culture that the alphabet was created only few years later.

However, Michael Westh doesn't think that the writing on the stone is more than 250 years old and compared to Armenian standard it is more like graffiti. But the exact meaning of the text we still don't know.

Feizal shows off one of the largest anchor stones in Arzep.

- You find a similar poor style in the bad years from the middle of seventeen hundreds in Armenia, i.e. toward the end of the Iranian period, Westh says, who thinks that the cross and the ornamentation, on the other hand, are very old. You find the ornamentation *under* the big cross in the middle used in the same way in Armenia as part of a cross where the cross may appear as a tree of life. But here you find an extra "bar" under the cross which might indicate that the cross and the bar with the ball have been made at different times.

Hot Springs

After having seen the stones in the village, we begin, together with Feizal, on a long trek through the surrounding area to find the other stones.

The Region of the Eight is filled with natural hot springs and natural soda water. A Turkish family is having their family washing day at one of the springs that forces water up through the ground forming a little pond. Of course, it is the women that do the hard work while the men and boys swim in the pond. They invite me in, and after having walked so much in the blistering sun, I'm ready. So I pull up my pants and wade in the cool soda water together with them.

Hot springs pop up all around the volcanic area like this one, a dammed pool in the vicinity of Arzep.

We're running around with cameras, so we are naturally asked to take pictures of these lovely people and we promise to send them copies. When they find out that we are here because of Nuhun Gemisi – Noah's Ark – they point to Mt. Ararat. No, our Nuhun Gemisi isn't there, we explain.

Noah and Naamah's Graves Plundered?

The Valley of the Eight has its namesake in the eight that survived the Flood. Maybe that number had already increased by the time they left the Ark, and non-biblical accounts tell of others. Whatever the case, the numbers grew quickly because after just a few centuries we can read about the existence of thousands of people, even nations.

We assume that the survivors gathered quickly and grew to a number too large to live in this valley, so the sons and their descendants spread out.

They followed the rivers - for example, the Euphrates - down from the mountains and into the open plains.[3] They called the plains Shinar. Even today Shinar is the name of a large plain in southern Turkey that can be found by following the Euphrates down through the mountains and then turning east. But most Bible experts think that Shinar refers to an area further south in Iraq.

That is where they set roots, and that is where they built the Tower of Babel. And there, in Mesopotamia between the two great rivers - the Euphrates and the Tigris - the first known civilizations developed.

The Stone House

But Noah and Naamah probably stayed up here in the Valley of the Eight in the Ararat Mountains. In 1977 Ron Wyatt's two sons, Danny and Ronny, actually found two very interesting gravestones. Both markers had eight crosses engraved on top of an older engraving (a so-called petroglyph, a drawing in stone) that suggested the death of Noah on the one and the his wife on the other. The stones were found in front of a very old stone house in a flat, open field just below some small mountains.

The site was videotaped, and Mrs. Mary Nell Wyatt later drew a sketch of the engravings (See the chapter about Ron Wyatt). In it we can see a rainbow over eight people. Half of them have long hair (women), and half have long beards (men). Six of the people are smaller than the other two, who most likely represent Noah and Naamah. On the drawing Naamah is looking down with closed eyes, which could show that she died first, while both have closed eyes and bowed heads on the second stone. This might suggest that Noah, too, had died.

There is also a boat on top of a wave, which is quite a sight up here in the mountains where there are neither lakes nor seas. There can be no doubt that this engraving is a reference to the story of the Ark.

Besides all of this, the story of the Flood was found described on one of the walls of the house. This is documented on a video recording in the possession of the Wyatt's who have, for the time being, not made the tape available in its entirety. On a video sold by the Wyatt Archaeological Museum the two gravestones can be seen but the engravings cannot due to the lighting which causes the headstones to show up black. These stones and the wall were probably engraved long after Noah and Naamah, but we don't know because the stones were removed by local thieves shortly after, and the house was destroyed by the villagers who used the stones from the building in constructing their own houses. But the video proves that this is not just a good story. The stones and the house were there, and to this day remains of the house are there too. If one looks closely, the plundered graves can be found as well.

Personally, I doubt that this stone house dates back to the days of Noah. But, of course, that cannot be ruled out completely. The local Armenian people have had the opportunity to protect this place for thousands of years; a place that has naturally been holy for the Christian Armenians and

Footnotes

[3] „And as they migrated from the east, they came upon a plain in the land of Shinar and settled there." Genesis 11:2

[4] The Ark Conspiracy was released in 1993 for Australian Seminar Services, P.O. Box 3370, Greenfield Street, Adelaide 5000, South Australia, Australia.

maybe, too, for the believing Muslims. Even after the Ottoman Muslim rule (c. 1000 A.D.) this house and these graves were not touched. That would make sense if it were a holy place. The Muslim Turks have also respected the prophet Noah they know from the Qur'an.

But it is a well-known fact that there was a fierce clash between Turks/Kurds and Armenians at the time of World War 1 and after that period much is destroyed.

Today where the graves were claimed to have lain, we find only a big hole in the ground where the house stood. There are also two new holes on the right side of the house where Mary Nell Wyatt's drawings show the gravestones were. Gold fever has hit the locals and not without merit! A large treasure of gold and jewelry has supposedly been removed from Naamah's grave along with everything else that may have been there.

Examining an anchor stone high up on a hilltop. How did that get here…? This stone also has crosses engraved on it but is partially destroyed on the other end where the hole can be found.

A strong local rumor that I had confirmed on multiple occasions says that a large sarcophagus, 18 feet in length, was dug up from under Naamah's headstone. The sarcophagus disappeared; it was taken during the night.

This happened the same year that Wyatt and his sons had to flee from the local Kurds who tried to capture them at their hotel, according to the video. When one has visited this part of the world, one realizes that it is not as absurd or even abnormal as it may sound.

As a modern Turk says a little slightingly, "It is a part of their mentality. They are used to acting that way in the mountains where they come from. It has become a bad habit..."

The Kurds surely do not completely agree with this Turkish explanation.

Who Were the Grave Robbers?

Jonathan Gray, Australian Ark-hunter, claims in his book, *The Ark Conspiracy*[4], that Ron Wyatt conceded to another Ark-hunter viewing the site. He assumed that this colleague could be trusted, but this unnamed hunter returned the favor by supposedly going in cahoots with the village chief, Mehmet, and opened the grave, placing all of the goods on a truck in the middle of the night. Gray may have this story, or parts of it, from Wyatt.

While we were there I found a different explanation, though. Rumors now say that a prominent official stood behind the looting, and the villagers don't claim responsibility for the robbing. Feizal explained to Bill Fry that he and his wife heard a truck in the middle of the night and saw it drive off with its lights turned off, and the next day the grave was empty. That's what they say. Is it thinkable that the governing officials removed the precious sarcophagus in order to protect it? Ron should have mentioned that the sarcophagus has possibly been brought to the museum in Ankara. Both

Feizal helping us to find "Naamah's grave"...

...and Elin immediately sees how much room is in the grave by crawling down into the dark hole, lit up on this photograph to show the size.

We're finding a number of stones from the Hurrian or Urartu Period. Here is one with a sword.

Bill Fry and Jonathan Gray have asked in vain about the stone coffin there, but no one knows anything about it. In Ikonium where there is a museum with sarcophagi, there is no knowledge of such an 18-foot-long example from the Region of the Eight.

Gray claims in his book – with Mrs. Wyatt as a partial source – that the large amounts of gold and jewels were sold on the black market in Istanbul for over 100 million dollars.

This is probably exaggerated. If we were talking about 100 million in Turkish currency, it would make more sense. Besides, who other than the thieves themselves would know how much the jewels were sold for? But about there being gold in the grave, the locals agree.

Not a Coffin, but a Tomb

More interesting than gold and jewels is of course whether or not a skeleton was in the grave – this could be the actual Mr. or Mrs. Noah.

This question is more difficult to answer. But many agree that there was such a sarcophagus. Gray writes that it was over 20 feet long.

"Yeah, but even 18 feet," I protested. "That would be 6 yards long! There's no way..."

Many things suggest that Noah and the people before the Flood were larger; Gray thinks they were up to ten feet tall, but a 20 ft. long coffin...? How could they even find a stone long enough to chisel a sarcophagus of that magnitude...?

A few days later, when talking with Dr. Bayraktutan, I got my answer. Bayraktutan, who has been involved in research in this area for over 20 years, is by nature skeptical of all of these stories. Neither does he support the account of an oversized skull that we will look at later.

"But," he says, "on the other side of the border, in Iran, there is a place where the Muslim pilgrims go; it is called 'Noah's wife's grave'. There is a grave here too that is 5-6 meters long. It is also a type of sarcophagus, but the body – if there is one – is not lying in a stone coffin. The walls of the grave are made of stone. It is very normal in Eastern Anatolia to find old graves that are 5-6 meters long. The body doesn't fill the entire grave. It is just the grave chamber that is so large. As far as I know, that is also the way it was out here in the Region of the Eight. The stones made a grave chamber that was 18 feet long. They have since been removed, just as the local peoples take everything else they can use," sneers Salih.

"They have no understanding of the archeological worth. What they see is stone – and gold."

Noah's Altar?

We have heard from Bill Fry that Noah and his wife's graves were not to the right of the missing house as the sketches suggest. This was supposedly also one of Wyatt's tricks to hold the gold-hunters away. In the beginning, Wyatt naively revealed all of his discoveries to anyone and everyone, but later he learned to be more careful. He supposedly sent dishonest people on wild goose chases many times.

We walked around looking for the place that Wyatt and others suspected of being Noah's altar. It is supposed to be found a short distance up in the small mountains towards the west. We were just a handful of people, and we had Feizal from the village with us when we got to the supposed Altar. We were not very convinced. There may have been a groove carved in the large rock for the blood to run out, but it does not look like an altar. With "sign language" we ask Feizal if this is Noah's altar. "No," he answers and points further up the mountain. We follow him and together find some large stones with crevices chisled in them so the blood from offered animals could run out. It would also be more likely to build an altar here, further up the mountain.

We took pictures and video taped it as proof.

Encouraged by Feizal's guidance, we also ask about the grave of Noah's wife. He points in the opposite direction of the house, and again we follow him over rocky terrain. After a longer hike, he shows us a large hole with flat walls. This is clearly a grave chamber. It is not 18 feet long, though, and definitely not any longer. Feizal claims that three people lay in this grave. We've got to get this cleared up. We find a local guide and translator, Zafer Önay, and ask him to explain what Feizal has shown us. When he starts translating, it suddenly turns into a very complicated story. We ask again and Zafer tells us a different story...

Vivien Finds a Finger

We make it up to an area where there is an entire cemetery of ancient Urartu graves from the first kingdom in this area – Urartu; a word that is later changed to Ararat in the Bible. Urartu was a great kingdom that ended c. 700 B.C. but whose beginnings is unknown. Maybe it went back to the days of Noah. The only other nation that may have been in this area before them is the Hurrian. The name means the ancient or the noble. No one really knows if they were an independent people or if this was a term for the first, probably *larger* people that lived up here after the Flood.

The rock some believe to be Noah's altar.
Bellow: The possible "altar", the groove to channel blood we found further up the mountainside.

Larger people...?

1. In connection with the Flood, the Bible tells that *before* it (the Flood) "but also since" there have been giants.

2. Both the Bible and the Sumerian tablets tell of ten kings that lived before the Flood and who lived much longer than those that came after it. The Sumerian is the oldest known kingdom in Mesopotamia – and the world. Their age of the kings is much longer than that of the Bible, which is under 1,000 years, while the Sumerians' is tens of thousands of years long. This could be because of a mistranslation where weeks became years in the ancient scriptures.

3. Ron Wyatt found a human bone here, specifically the top joint of a thumb, which was almost twice as big as ours are today; almost four inches. And there is a picture of this bone.

But as the skeptics we are, we want to see proof ourselves.

Suddenly, something happens. Vivian Broughton, a young Norwegian nurse, hops down from one of the tombs the grave robbers have recently emptied in their search for treasure. And here she finds some human bones. Together, we move some of the stones lying on the bottom, and more bones come forth. Some of the bones seem to come from a child. But one bone surprises us. Again, it is a finger joint, and Vivien says it is longer than a normal finger joint. We photograph and film it, gather the bones in a plastic bag, and go on.

I find a grave that not only contains the remains of a ram's head with its curly horns, which suggests that this is an Urartian grave, but also contains a curved sword! It is not just buried. No, the sword is prominent because part of the stone around it has been removed.

Again, we have to settle with photography and film, and then leave this fantastic memory of prehistory to grave robbers and treasure hunters. It's very frustrating, but at the same time it's impossible to protect an entire valley 24 hours a day.

After a long day of trekking dusty trails with the harsh rays of the sun beating down on us, we return to the hotel in Dogubayazit. I find the Book of Jasher, which has been mentioned previously, and read the story about Noah and Naamah hoping to discover something new.

Ron Wyatt (right) with the thumb bone too long to be from any living human being…

Chapter 34

The Book of Jasher

The Book of Jasher is named twice in the Old Testament.[1] *Sephir Ha Yasher* means "the book of the upright". Around 1500 the book disappeared, but in the Middle Ages a scroll with the same name showed up once again. It was printed in Hebrew in 1625 in Venice (possibly 1613) and was later translated and published in sections in Krakow, Prague, Frankfurt, Constantinople (Istanbul), Amsterdam, and Calcutta.[2] It was finally published in English in 1839 in the USA.

That translation was given by a well-known American-Jewish politician, Mordecai M. Noah.[3] Moses Samuel, a professor in Hebrew from Liverpool, England, started the translation, but when a fake book of Jasher came out, he gave up his work and sold the translation for £150 to M. M. Noah. The 19th of November 1828 he wrote in a letter to the editor in *The London Courier* that he had been given the Hebrew text by a Jew from North Africa. This English version has been reprinted many times and is also accessible via the internet.[4]

An Amazing Work

A number of false copies of the Book of Jasher have shown up, but they have all been easy to detect. The Book of Jasher we will be looking at is different from these others.

It's about the same people the Bible discusses – from Adam, all the way to Joshua – and for the most part it agrees with the Bible. It also includes some interesting details about people, places, and dates. The dates given here actually clear up 60 missing years around the time of Abraham's birth, a mistake brought in by the Irish archbishop James Ussher (1580-1656) when he tried to create a chronology of the Bible. (Though there are parts that are thought to be added from other time periods and could even be taken from Greek mythology, unless Greek mythology is built up from a common past.)

The book is so inclusive and detailed that it would be almost impossible to recreate. And according to translators it is written is a very clean and ancient Hebrew in such a beautiful style that it should be read as a great literary work, even though it cannot be proven that this is the same Book of Jasher that existed 3,000-3,500 years ago

Where does it Come from?

Josephus, the famous Jewish historian who cooperated with the Romans in Jesus' time, also knew about the Book of Jasher. He says that "by this book are to be understood certain records kept in some safe place on

Footnotes

[1] In Joshua 10:13 and 2 Samuel 1:17.

[2] The book is translated into Ladino, Latin, Spanish, and English. A number of these translations can be found in the British Library's catalog (1893-1960 catalog, Vol. II). A Jewish German edition and a Hebrew edition for youth printed in Warsaw in 1923 exist as well as a Greek translation called "Lo Libris de los divitiis".

[3] **Mordecai Manuel Noah** (1785-1851) journalist, playwright, diplomat, attorney, and politician in New York. In 1825 he planned on gathering all of the world's persecuted Jews to create a state in the western part of New York State – together with the Indians. He became the consul in Tunis in 1813. Owner and editor of the New York newspaper, *The National Advocate*, which supported state independence and slavery. From 1820-28 he was elected New York City sheriff and in 1829 director of the Port Authority. In 1826 he founded *The New York Enquirer*, which merged with *The New York Morning Courier* in 1828. In 1833 he started *The Evening Star*, which went down in 1842. Continued as a journalist and politician until his death in 1851. At this point he was the most well-known Jew in America.

purpose, giving an account of what happened among the Hebrews from year to year, and called Jasher or the upright, on account of the fidelity of the annals." It can also be translated as "the correct record".

According to the Hebraic version the scrolls were found during the destruction of Jerusalem in the year 70 under Emperor Titus. While sacking and plundering a house, an officer named Sidrus found a false wall behind which a room full of Jewish books was found. In the middle of it all sat an old man hoping to escape the plundering of the Romans. The officer took the old man and all of the books along with him from city to city until they ended up in Seville, Spain, where he built a spacious house for himself, the old man, and the books.

When Seville was attacked by "the kings of Edom" (the Muslims?), 12 identical copies of the book were taken to Napuli (Naples) and later printed.

Possibly from the Library in Alexandria

Even if this story isn't true, the manuscript could be real. It could come from the Great Library that King Ptolemy II of Egypt built in Alexandria c. 280 B.C. He gathered all of the world's works of wisdom and holy books, but in 391 A.D. the library was destroyed and the manuscripts spread throughout North Africa.

We know that many Jews sought refuge in Morocco and Spain. They also brought a large number of their holy scrolls. Many of these were placed in their school in Cordoba in southern Spain in the 11th century.

Doubtful Paragraph

A French professor, Jacqueline-Lise Genot-Bismuth, who has researched the Book of Jasher as a reproduction of the Hebrew Venice-version from 1625 at the *Université de le Sorbonne Nouvelle* in 1986[5] believes the work to be written in the Middle Ages by a learned Jew. She bases this theory on the fact that European words are seen in the text, words that should come from a newer period.

Others believe that these European pieces could be newer additions, a kind of updating, but that the work itself is much older. Besides this, Genot-Bismuth proves the likelihood of the book being brought to the Venetian publisher from Morocco by *Jacob Son of Atya,* whom she believes to be the same person as *Jacob the Scribe*, a famous man from the Portuguese connection with Morocco in the 16th century.

When the Rabbi Council of Venice took it upon themselves to publish the Book of Jasher, it was done with great difficulty. They had to decipher the ancient Hebrew text from a tattered scroll where at times it was almost illegible. We are told so by the translator, Joseph Haqatan from Venice, in the printed Hebrew version of 1625.

What Can We Use it for?

We do not know if the Book of Jasher is the same as the book mentioned in the Bible 3,500 years ago, but even if it came later, it withholds the

Footnotes

[4] See http://www.ccel.org/a/anonymous/jasher.

[5] *Seminaire sur le Sefer Hayashar de le Centre des Recherches sur la Culture Rabbinique.* Ginzberg, *The Legends of the Jews* (Philadelphia: Jewish Publication Society of America, 1912) includes Jasher 3:2-38 (vol. 1, pp. 127-30) and the end note (vol. 5, pp. 157-8) assumes that The Book of Jasher is a collection of older sources. Jasher is considered an authentic source in *The Jewish Encyclopedia* (NY: Funk and Wagnall, 1905), XII:588-9 and *The Universal Jewish Encyclopedia* (NY: Universal Jewish Encyclopedia Co., 1942), 6:41.

[6] Hugh Nibley writes the following concerning Jasher 3:5-10, "Passages such as this which closely follow both the Hebrew and the Slavonic Enoch show that the book of Jasher used very ancient sources and was far more than a medieval romance." Collected Works of Hugh Nibley, Vol. 2, p. 301, fn. 380.

[7] Deane Schaub, Logos Resource Pages, logosresourcepages.org/jasher.htm

information the Jews – either orally or in writing – passed down since the ancient times.[6]   For example, that Noah's wife was the daughter of Enoch and was named Naamah, that the people were given 120 years to turn from their ways, or that it took five years to build the Ark.

Unfortunately, we cannot be sure of this information, just as we cannot be 100% sure of other sources. Therefore, we must accept reading the Book of Jasher as an interesting book that may well contain reliable information. That is why we have taken it into account here.

For the believing Christian it is important that the book has not been canonized by the church as inspired, and as one critic of the authenticity of The Book of Jasher remarks, "I can only conclude that while Jasher is an interesting book to read, the reader must be very discerning as to the truth of all or any of the writings in Jasher."[7]

The Book of Jasher

We shall now read chapters 4-6, which deal specifically with Noah and the Ark. Footnotes refer to the equivalent biblical text. My own notes are marked with the initials, HN:

CHAPTER 4

1 And all the days that Enoch lived upon earth, were three hundred and sixty-five years.

2 And when Enoch had ascended into heaven, all the kings of the earth rose and took Methuselah his son and anointed him, and they caused him to reign over them in the place of his father.

3 And Methuselah acted uprightly in the sight of God, as his father Enoch had taught him, and he likewise during the whole of his life taught the sons of men wisdom, knowledge and the fear of God, and he did not turn from the good way either to the right or to the left.

4 But in the latter days of Methuselah, the sons of men turned from the Lord, they corrupted the earth, they robbed and plundered each other, and they rebelled against God and they transgressed, and they corrupted their ways, and would not hearken to the voice of Methuselah, but rebelled against him.

5 And the Lord was exceedingly wroth against them, and the Lord continued to destroy the seed in those days, so that there was neither sowing nor reaping in the earth.

6 For when they sowed the ground in order that they might obtain food for their support, behold, thorns and thistles were produced which they did not sow.

7 And still the sons of men did not turn from their evil ways, and their hands were still extended to do evil in the sight of God, and they provoked the Lord with their evil ways, and the Lord was very wroth, and repented that he had made man.[8]

8 And he thought to destroy and annihilate them and he did so.

9 In those days when Lamech the son of Methuselah was one hundred and sixty years old, Seth the son of Adam died.

Footnotes
[8] Jasher 4:7-8 :: Genesis 6:6-7.
[9] Jasher 4:10 :: Genesis 5:8.
[10] Jasher 4:13-14 :: Genesis 5:29.
[11] Jasher 4:18b-19.21 :: Genesis 6:5-8.
[12] Jasher 5:1-4 : Genesis 5:11-20.
[13] Jasher 5:13 :: Genesis 6:9-10.
[14] Jasher 5:17-18 :: Genesis 5:32, 6:10.
[15] Jasher 5:20 :: Genesis 5:31.
[16] Jasher 5:25-33 :: Genesis 6:13-22.
[17] Jasher 5:36 :: Genesis 5:27.
[18] Jasher 6:1-31 :: Genesis 7:1-24.
[19] Jasher 6:32-42 :: Genesis 8,1-22:9,1.

10 And all the days that Seth lived, were nine hundred and twelve years, and he died. [9]

11 And Lamech was one hundred and eighty years old when he took Ashmua, the daughter of Elishaa the son of Enoch his uncle, and she conceived.

12 And at that time the sons of men sowed the ground, and a little food was produced, yet the sons of men did not turn from their evil ways, and they trespassed and rebelled against God.

13 And the wife of Lamech conceived and bare him a son at that time, at the revolution of the year.

14 And Methuselah called his name **Noah**, saying, "The earth was in his days at rest and free from corruption", and Lamech his father called his name Menachem, saying, "This one shall comfort us in our works and miserable toil in the earth, which God had cursed."[10]

15 And the child grew up and was weaned, and he went in the ways of his father Methuselah, perfect and upright with God.

16 And all the sons of men departed from the ways of the Lord in those days as they multiplied upon the face of the earth with sons and daughters, and they taught one another their evil practices and they continued sinning against the Lord.

17 And every man made unto himself a god, and they robbed and plundered every man his neighbor as well as his relative, and they corrupted the earth, and the earth was filled with violence.

18 And their judges and rulers went to the daughters of men and took their wives by force from their husbands according to their choice, and the sons of men in those days took from the cattle of the earth, the beasts of the field and the fowls of the air, and taught the mixture of animals of one species with the other, in order therewith to provoke the Lord; and God saw the whole earth and it was corrupt, for all flesh had corrupted its ways upon earth, all men and all animals.[11]

19 And the Lord said, "I will blot out man that I created from the face of the earth, yea from man to the birds of the air, together with cattle and beasts that are in the field for I repent that I made them."

20 And all men who walked in the ways of the Lord, died in those days, before the Lord brought the evil upon man which he had declared, for this was from the Lord, that they should not see the evil which the Lord spoke of concerning the sons of men.

21 And Noah found grace in the sight of the Lord, and the Lord chose him and his children to raise up seed from them upon the face of the whole earth.

CHAPTER 5

1 And it was in the eighty-fourth year of the life of **Noah**, that Enoch the son of Seth died, he was nine hundred and five years old at his death.

2 And in the one hundred and seventy ninth year of the life of Noah, Cainan the son of Enosh died, and all the days of Cainan were nine hundred and ten years, and he died. [12]

3 And in the two hundred and thirty fourth year of the life of Noah, Mahlallel the son of Cainan died, and the days of Mahlallel were eight hundred and ninety-five years, and he died.

4 And Jared the son of Mahlallel died in those days, in the three hundred and thirty-sixth year of the life of Noah; and all the days of Jared were nine hundred

HN:

• Chapter 4 is more or less the same as the biblical explanation, but the evil of man is defined more precisely here. In the Bible, Genesis 6:5 states, "Then the Lord saw that the wickedness of man was great on the earth, and that every intent of the thoughts of his heart was only evil continually" and in 6:13, "…for the earth is filled with violence because of them…".

·In verse 20 it is mentioned that the righteous died out before the flood came. This is reiterated in chapter 5, verse 5.

and sixty-two years, and he died.

5 And all who followed the Lord died in those days, before they saw the evil which God declared to do upon earth.

6 And after the lapse of many years, in the four hundred and eightieth year of the life of Noah, when all those men, who followed the Lord had died away from amongst the sons of men, and only Methuselah was then left, God said unto Noah and Methuselah, saying,

7 "Speak ye, and proclaim to the sons of men, saying, 'Thus saith the Lord, return from your evil ways and forsake your works, and the Lord will repent of the evil that he declared to do to you, so that it shall not come to pass.'

8 "For thus saith the Lord, 'Behold I give you a period of one hundred and twenty years; if you will turn to me and forsake your evil ways, then will I also turn away from the evil which I told you, and it shall not exist,' saith the Lord".

9 And Noah and Methuselah spoke all the words of the Lord to the sons of men, day after day, constantly speaking to them.

10 But the sons of men would not hearken to them, nor incline their ears to their words, and they were stiffnecked.

11 And the Lord granted them a period of one hundred and twenty years, saying, "If they will return, then will God repent of the evil, so as not to destroy the earth."

12 Noah the son of Lamech refrained from taking a wife in those days, to beget children, for he said, "Surely now God will destroy the earth, wherefore then shall I beget children?"

13 And Noah was a just man, he was perfect in his generation, and the Lord chose him to raise up seed from his seed upon the face of the earth.[13]

14 And the Lord said unto Noah, "Take unto thee a wife, and beget children, for I have seen thee righteous before me in this generation.

15 "And thou shalt raise up seed, and thy children with thee, in the midst of the earth"; and Noah went and took a wife, and he chose Naamah the daughter of Enoch, and she was five hundred and eighty years old.

16 And Noah was four hundred and ninety-eight years old, when he took **Naamah** for a wife.

17 And Naamah conceived and bare a son, and he called his name Japheth, saying, "God has enlarged me in the earth"; and she conceived again and bare a son, and he called his name Shem, saying, "God has made me a remnant, to raise up seed in the midst of the earth."[14]

18 And Noah was five hundred and two years old when Naamah bare Shem, and the boys grew up and went in the ways of the Lord, in all that Methuselah and Noah their father taught them.

19 And Lamech the father of Noah, died in those days; yet verily he did not go with all his heart in the ways of his father, and he died in the hundred and ninety-fifth year of the life of Noah.

20 And all the days of Lamech were seven hundred and seventy years, and he died.[15]

21 And all the sons of men who knew the Lord, died in that year before the Lord brought evil upon them; for the Lord willed them to die, so as not to behold the evil that God would bring upon their brothers and relatives, as he had so declared to do.

22 In that time, the Lord said to Noah and Methuselah, "Stand forth and proclaim to the sons of men all the words that I spoke to you in those days,

- In verses 8-11 mankind is given a 120-year warning. In the Bible (Genesis 6:3) 120 years is also mentioned, but this is normally translated as a limit on the age of man being 120 years.
- In verses 15-18 Noah marries Naamah, who is 91 years older and the daughter of Enoch. We are also told that Japheth was born first and then Shem (the father of the Jews and the Arabs) and Ham. In Genesis 6:10 they are named as Shem, Ham and Japheth. We are not told who is the oldest.
- In verses 22-24 we are told that Noah and Methuselah tried to warn the „sons of men", but when that did not work, God decided to fulfill his threat. In the Bible we do not hear about this.
- In verse 28 Noah is to „finish above" "a cubit". That is, add one more cubit "above". In Genesis 6:16 the text is a bit shaky. Some Bibles translate is like in Jasher, while others understand it to mean a row of windows.
- In verse 32 Noah chooses wives for the boys, while the Bible just says they took their wives with them on the Ark. In verse 35 we are told that they were siblings and Methuselah's daughters.
- In verse 34 we are told that the Ark took 5 years to build.

peradventure they may turn from their evil ways, and I will then repent of the evil and will not bring it."

23 And Noah and Methuselah stood forth, and said in the ears of the sons of men, all that God had spoken concerning them.

24 But the sons of men would not hearken, neither would they incline their ears to all their declarations.

25 And it was after this that the Lord said to Noah, "The end of all flesh is come before me, on account of their evil deeds, and behold I will destroy the earth.[16]

26 "And do thou take unto thee gopher wood, and go to a certain place and make a large ark, and place it in that spot.

27 "And thus shalt thou make it; three hundred cubits its length, fifty cubits broad and thirty cubits high.

28 "And thou shalt make unto thee a door, open at its side, and to a cubit thou shalt finish above, and cover it within and without with pitch.

29 "And behold I will bring the flood of waters upon the earth, and all flesh be destroyed, from under the heavens all that is upon earth shall perish.

30 "And thou and thy household shall go and gather two couple of all living things, male and female, and shall bring them to the ark, to raise up seed from them upon earth.

31 "And gather unto thee all food that is eaten by all the animals, that there may be food for thee and for them.

32 "And thou shalt choose for thy sons three maidens, from the daughters of men, and they shall be wives to thy sons."

33 And Noah rose up, and he made the ark, in the place where God had commanded him, and Noah did as God had ordered him.

34 In his five hundred and ninety-fifth year Noah commenced to make the ark, and he made the ark in five years, as the Lord had commanded.

35 Then Noah took the three daughters of Eliakim, son of Methuselah, for wives for his sons, as the Lord had commanded Noah.

36 And it was at that time Methuselah the son of Enoch died, nine hundred and sixty years old was he, at his death.[17]

CHAPTER 6

1 At that time, after the death of Methuselah, the Lord said to Noah, "Go thou with thy household into the ark; behold I will gather to thee all the animals of the earth, the beasts of the field and the fowls of the air, and they shall all come and surround the ark.[18]

2 "And thou shalt go and seat thyself by the doors of the ark, and all the beasts, the animals, and the fowls, shall assemble and place themselves before thee, and such of them as shall come and crouch before thee, shalt thou take and deliver into the hands of thy sons, who shall bring them to the ark, and all that will stand before thee thou shalt leave."

3 And the Lord brought this about on the next day, and animals, beasts and fowls came in great multitudes and surrounded the ark.

4 And Noah went and seated himself by the door of the ark, and of all flesh that crouched before him, he brought into the ark, and all that stood before him he left upon earth.

5 And a lioness came, with her two whelps, male and female, and the three crouched before Noah, and the two whelps rose up against the lioness and

smote her, and made her flee from her place, and she went away, and they returned to their places, and crouched upon the earth before Noah.

6 And the lioness ran away, and stood in the place of the lions.

7 And Noah saw this, and wondered greatly, and he rose and took the two whelps, and brought them into the ark.

8 And Noah brought into the ark from all living creatures that were upon earth, so that there was none left but which Noah brought into the ark.

9 Two and two came to Noah into the ark, but from the clean animals, and clean fowls, he brought seven couples, as God had commanded him.

10 And all the animals, and beasts, and fowls, were still there, and they surrounded the ark at every place, and the rain had not descended till seven days after.

11 And on that day, the Lord caused the whole earth to shake, and the sun darkened, and the foundations of the world raged, and the whole earth was moved violently, and the lightning flashed, and the thunder roared, and all the fountains in the earth were broken up, such as was not known to the inhabitants before; and God did this mighty act, in order to terrify the sons of men, that there might be no more evil upon earth.

12 And still the sons of men would not return from their evil ways, and they increased the anger of the Lord at that time, and did not even direct their hearts to all this.

13 And at the end of seven days, in the six hundredth year of the life of Noah, the waters of the flood were upon the earth.

14 And all the fountains of the deep were broken up, and the windows of heaven were opened, and the rain was upon the earth forty days and forty nights.

15 And Noah and his household, and all the living creatures that were with him, came into the ark on account of the waters of the flood, and the Lord shut him in.

16 And all the sons of men that were left upon the earth, became exhausted through evil on account of the rain, for the waters were coming more violently upon the earth, and the animals and beasts were still surrounding the ark.

17 And the sons of men assembled together, about seven hundred thousand men and women, and they came unto Noah to the ark.

18 And they called to Noah, saying, "Open for us that we may come to thee in the ark—and wherefore shall we die?"

19 And Noah, with a loud voice, answered them from the ark, saying, "Have you not all rebelled against the Lord, and said that he does not exist? and therefore the Lord brought upon you this evil, to destroy and cut you off from the face of the earth.

20 "Is not this the thing that I spoke to you of one hundred and twenty years back, and you would not hearken to the voice of the Lord, and now do you desire to live upon earth?"

21 And they said to Noah, "We are ready to return to the Lord; only open for us that we may live and not die."

22 And Noah answered them, saying, "Behold now that you see the trouble of your souls, you wish to return to the Lord; why did you not return during these hundred and twenty years, which the Lord granted you as the determined period?

23 "But now you come and tell me this on account of the troubles of your souls, now also the Lord will not listen to you, neither will he give ear to you on

- Here we are given a vivid description of how the animals got into the Ark (verses 1-10). The Bible only mentions that "...they went into the ark to Noah, by twos of all flesh in which was the breath of life." Genesis 7:15.
- In verse 11 the way the Flood came is revealed: "...the Lord caused the whole earth to shake, and the sun darkened, and the foundations of the world raged, and the whole earth was moved violently, and the lightning flashed, and the thunder roared, and all the fountains in the earth were broken up, such as was not known to the inhabitants before...". This leads one the think of the theory that the Flood was caused by a mighty meteor or that another planet came too close to the earth causing violent upheaval.
- Both the Bible and Jasher speak of "the fountains of the deep" that were broken up (a volcanic eruption?) so that water (came spraying?) up.
- In verses 16-25 we are shown a picture of people that want into the Ark – even by force.
- Verses 28-31 reveals that the Ark did not just float around but was thrown violently, and all were afraid.
- Verse 35: The resting place is the same: the *mountains* of Ararat.
- Verse 36: tells they were tired of being closed up in the Ark.

this day, so that you will not now succeed in your wishes."

24 And the sons of men approached in order to break into the ark, to come in on account of the rain, for they could not bear the rain upon them.

25 And the Lord sent all the beasts and animals that stood round the ark. And the beasts overpowered them and drove them from that place, and every man went his way and they again scattered themselves upon the face of the earth.

26 And the rain was still descending upon the earth, and it descended forty days and forty nights, and the waters prevailed greatly upon the earth; and all flesh that was upon the earth or in the waters died, whether men, animals, beasts, creeping things or birds of the air, and there only remained Noah and those that were with him in the ark.

27 And the waters prevailed and they greatly increased upon the earth, and they lifted up the ark and it was raised from the earth.

28 And the ark floated upon the face of the waters, and it was tossed upon the waters so that all the living creatures within were turned about like pottage in a cauldron.

29 And great anxiety seized all the living creatures that were in the ark, and the ark was like to be broken.

30 And all the living creatures that were in the ark were terrified, and the lions roared, and the oxen lowed, and the wolves howled, and every living creature in the ark spoke and lamented in its own language, so that their voices reached to a great distance, and Noah and his sons cried and wept in their troubles; they were greatly afraid that they had reached the gates of death.

31 And Noah prayed unto the Lord, and cried unto him on account of this, and he said, "O Lord help us, for we have no strength to bear this evil that has encompassed us, for the waves of the waters have surrounded us, mischievous torrents have terrified us, the snares of death have come before us; answer us, O Lord, answer us, light up thy countenance toward us and be gracious to us, redeem us and deliver us."

32 And the Lord hearkened to the voice of Noah, and the Lord remembered him.[19]

33 And a wind passed over the earth, and the waters were still and the ark rested.

34 And the fountains of the deep and the windows of heaven were stopped, and the rain from heaven was restrained.

35 And the waters decreased in those days, and the ark rested upon the mountains of Ararat.

36 And Noah then opened the windows of the ark, and Noah still called out to the Lord at that time and he said, "O Lord, who didst form the earth and the heavens and all that are therein, bring forth our souls from this confinement, and from the prison wherein thou hast placed us, for I am much wearied with sighing."

37 And the Lord hearkened to the voice of Noah, and said to him, "When though shalt have completed a full year thou shalt then go forth."

38 And at the revolution of the year, when a full year was completed to Noah's dwelling in the ark, the waters were dried from off the earth, and Noah put off the covering of the ark.

39 At that time, on the twenty-seventh day of the second month, the earth was dry, but Noah and his sons, and those that were with him, did not go out from the ark until the Lord told them.

40 And the day came that the Lord told them to go out, and they all went out from the ark.

41 And they went and returned every one to his way and to his place, and Noah and his sons dwelt in the land that God had told them, and they served the Lord all their days, and the Lord blessed Noah and his sons on their going out from the ark.

42 And he said to them, "Be fruitful and fill all the earth; become strong and increase abundantly in the earth and multiply therein."

The World is Split into Three

After all of this, in chapter 7, the names of the children of Japheth, Ham, and Shem are given. The interesting thing is that the names of the children and grandchildren become the names of the new peoples and their regions. Based on this information, Wayne Simpson[20] has created a list in which he identifies the nations that emerged. It is too inclusive to get into now, but it is very interesting. The most important thing is that the sons of Japheth spread towards the West and got Europe, Shem's took the later Arabic lands and the East, and Ham's descendents got Egypt and Africa.

But there are a bit of modifications:

There are indications that Indo-Europeans settled in the Indus Valley - some of Japheth's decendents went along to build the first great civilization in the East.

Ham's grandson took a portion of Shem's area (i.e. later Israel, which was called the land of *Canaan*, one of Ham's sons). And Ham's grandson Nimrod was the first ruler of Mesopotamia the blooming grounds of the world's first great civilization. The Semites and Indo-Europeans later fought ravishingly for the same.

The third great civilization, Egypt, which flourished on the Nile around the same time as the other two was most likely founded by Ham's descendents but later taken by the Greeks, who were among Japheth's seed, the kings of Egypt. Going on...

Adam and Eve's Clothes in the Ark?

In chapter 7 we see the story about Nimrod, the first ruler in the new world. He was the son of Cush, the son of Ham. He became a tyrant that later built the Tower of Babel. We can read about this in Jasher 7, from verse 24:

24 And the garments of skin which God made for Adam and his wife, when they went out of the garden, were given to Cush.

25 For after the death of Adam and his wife, the garments were given to Enoch, the son of Jared, and when Enoch was taken up to God, he gave them to Methuselah, his son.

26 And at the death of Methuselah, Noah took them and brought them to the ark, and they were with him until he went out of the ark.

27 And in their going out, Ham stole those garments from Noah his father, and he took them and hid them from his brothers.

- In verse 38, Jasher tells us that Noah and the others were in the Ark an entire year. The Bible names two specific dates: the 17th day in the second month where the fountains of the great deep burst open and the floodgates of the sky were opened (Genesis 7:11). On the 27th day in the second month (the following year), the earth was dry (Genesis 8:14). One year and ten days.

Footnotes

[20] Found as an appendix to Wayne Simpson's version of The Book of Jasher: *The Authentic Annals of the Early Hebrews*. Morris Publishing, 1995.

28 And when Ham begat his first born Cush, he gave him the garments in secret, and they were with Cush many days.

29 And Cush also concealed them from his sons and brothers, and when Cush had begotten Nimrod, he gave him those garments through his love for him, and Nimrod grew up, and when he was twenty years old he put on those garments.

30 And Nimrod became strong when he put on the garments, and God gave him might and strength, and he was a mighty hunter in the earth, yea, he was a mighty hunter in the field, and he hunted the animals and he built altars, and he offered upon them the animals before the Lord.

31 And Nimrod strengthened himself, and he rose up from amongst his brethren, and he fought the battles of his brethren against all their enemies round about.

32 And the Lord delivered all the enemies of his brethren in his hands, and God prospered him from time to time in his battles, and he reigned upon earth.

33 Therefore it became current in those days, when a man ushered forth those that he had trained up for battle, he would say to them, "Like God did to Nimrod, who was a mighty hunter in the earth, and who succeeded in the battles that prevailed against his brethren, that he delivered them from the hands of their enemies, so may God strengthen us and deliver us this day."

34 And when Nimrod was forty years old, at that time there was a war between his brethren and the children of Japheth, so that they were in the power of their enemies.

Sumer Is Founded

We also hear that Nimrod goes to war with Japheth's descendents and increases his power. He builds his first city, Shinar - probably the same word as Sumer, the name of the oldest known civilization in Mesopotamia:

43. And they found a large valley opposite to the east,[21] and they built him a large and extensive city, and Nimrod called the name of the city that he built Shinar, for the Lord had vehemently shaken his enemies and destroyed them.

44. And Nimrod dwelt in Shinar, and he reigned securely, and he fought with his enemies and he subdued them, and he prospered in all his battles, and his kingdom became very great.

Abraham and Noah

But Nimrod falls to evil and haughtiness, and later in the Book of Jasher we hear that Abraham, the son of Nimrod's general, Terah, has to flee and seeks refuge with Noah where he stays for 39 years learning all the wisdom Noah and Shem can give him. In this period he stops worshiping the sun, moon, and stars (the astrology of the Chaldeans) and begins to worship the Creator himself – God. Later he stops his father from worshiping the trees, and after a long bout with Nimrod, Terah and Abraham leave Ur. They end up in Haran – as it is told in the Bible.

Footnotes
[21] Here it says, "opposite to the east. The Bible formulates this phrase as, "journeyed east (Genesis 11:2).

Chapter 35

SEPDAC - A New Experiment

With the surveys already taken of the boat-shaped object, most people would have already assumed that they had found what they were looking for. This is not the case with Noah's Ark.

We have to first surpass the obstacle that the Ark, according to prevalent theories and conventional thought, never even existed and that the Flood it sailed upon did not take place either.

Therefore, it is neither easy to get professionals from recognized institutions involved, nor to get the necessary funds. If the "evidence" that is found fits into the theory of the Ark, it will have to be even more convincing than that which is normally required.

Professor Robert Michelson and artist David Deal with their Turkish bodyguards when they in 2000 were given permission to probe the military zone where they found ancient graves, traces of houses, and other things.

It's about time that recognized professionals in the field are put together with recognized institutions, so that the results we already have can be verified or rejected - whatever the case may be.

As Professor Robert C. Michelson has explained, "The time for lone-wolf, half-baked 'cowboy archaeology' has come to an end." This is probably a reference to two deceased pioneers in the field: the late Ron Wyatt and the late David Fasold.

This may not be completely fair though, for if it weren't for these two competent, recognized scientists, the boat-shaped object may never have been examined. The first "experts" established that the site was of no interest. Sometimes we need those lone wolves who are willing to continue searching for scraps even when stones are thrown after them.

People such as Wyatt and Fasold offered themselves for this matter, and there was something symbolic about the private memorial service held by a group of Ark-explorers in October 1998 in Turkey, where the ash from David Fasold's urn was sprinkled over the ark formation. It was also symbolic that people from both camps gathered together; both the Ararat group and the Durupinar group. They were invited by Dr. Salih Bayraktutan, and among them were Michelson.

Michelson and SEPDAC

Robert C. Michelson is the principal research engineer at The Georgia Tech Research Institute at The Georgia Institute of Technology in Atlanta, Georgia. In October 1995 he visited the area together with Dr. Bayraktutan, and three years later in 1998 they arranged a workshop at Atatürk University in order to gather scientific resources for a more serious exploration. Again in September of 1999 and October of 2000, Michelson was in Eastern Turkey in the military zone close to the Iranian border.

The workshop in 1998 was called "The First International Workshop on the Noahic Flood and the First Settlement in the Agri Mount Region". It took place from October 5-9, 1998. The participants, who came from Turkey, the United States, Azerbaijan, and Uzbekistan, were also on expeditions to the Durupinar find, to the adjacent presumed ruins of the ancient cities of Nazuan and Seron, to "Kazan", that is Arcep along with its anchor stones, and to the southern side of Agri Dagi (Mt. Ararat).

The participants have established a research project called SEPDAC (Scientific Enterprise in Pursuit and Discovery of Ancient Cultures) in which Michelson is the main driving force.

Others have had this same idea but have given up because of the many complications and difficulties. Maybe Michelson has more perseverance.

One of Michelson's forefathers was the Norwegian prime minister, Christian Michelsen, who helped Norway gain independence from Sweden in 1905. At this time, he became the first prime minister of an independent Norway. While the Swedish king stood threatening with sables, Michelsen held an election in which 368,208 ballots were thrown in support of his idea for independence and only 184 against! Undoubtedly, he had the support of the people. Today there is a Christian Michelsen Institute in Bergen, Norway, which acts as both a scientific and humanitarian organization.

With the work of SEPDAC, today's American Robert C. Michelson is setting the stage for research to be performed under a common entity instead of many solitary researchers working in each their specific area. SEPDAC hopes to get the support of local authorities to research different things such as the remains of ancient campsites that lie within the security zone on the Iranian side of the border – a place where civilians are not allowed without military escort. There are also plans to attempt involving the Iranians in the research from the other side.

Michelson shows an ancient grave found in the military zone above the boat-shaped object.

Rib Bone Fragments

Without Preconceived Notions

SEPDAC is a privately owned institution in the U.S. and has been given status as a non-profit organization.

- We are operating in several modes at the moment," says Michelson.

- First, we are assembling the right team of experts to conduct meaningful and credible research in the area. Second, we are seeking targeted donations to support this research.

Michelson was the driving force behind SEPDAC's 1998 seminar in Turkey where he is seen here foremost to the left together with Matt Kneisler and B. J. Corbin. In the back row Michael Holt, Dave Deal, and Bill Shea stand together with Dr. Salih Bayraktutran. The other people are Turkish soldiers who were present to protect the team.

- Of critical importance is the objectivity of SEPDAC research. We do not, and cannot go in with preconceived notions about these sites. Of course we are investigating valid theories as to the origins of the Durupinar "formation" (is it natural/man-made/an imprint/the Ark/etc.?) as well as the history of what Dave Deal is calling "Naxuan".

When asked if it *is* Naxuan, Michelson replied:

- We have our individual beliefs and hopes, but until we do the research at the site, we cannot be dogmatic to state uncategorically that it *is* Naxuan. The SEPDAC mission is to get to the truth. If the answer is not what we'd personally hoped, at least we can focus on other areas, having hopefully solved the question at hand.

The SEPDAC team will be comprised of experts from all beliefs (Islam, Jewish, Christian, Atheist…), but all must be objective. The reason for this is not only necessity, but to defuse allegations that data is somehow tainted or biased if we come up with conclusions that might counter the fundamental assumptions of academics or certain religious leaders.

Unscientific Jaunts

Michelson is not impressed by the mostly "unscientific jaunts" on Mt. Ararat over the past 50 years.

- In my opinion, most of the Ararat work is based solely on rumor.

There is very little substance. We have come across more significant tangible evidence at Durupinar and the area in the military zone above Durupinar than all of the mountain men have in the last 50 years of fuzzy photos of squared-off rock outcroppings that can never be found again (assuming that the film or camera with the definitive pictures of the Ark made it back without being lost in a crevasse or whatever the excuse of the day happens to be). This kind of thing is what has spurred me and others on to do some credible scientific work that may resolve the issue.

Wyatt and Fasold were pioneers in that they broke away from the rumor-mill and started considering the evidence at hand and what the Bible and ancient extra-biblical texts actually said. Neither was qualified to do the

[1] The boat-shaped object (also known as Durupinar), seen on the top picture to the right, has often been criticized for being nothing but some natural formation in the landscape.

On the website of the Mt. Ararat supporters, NoahsArkSearch.com, you can e.g. see a picture of "similar formations" - painted in by Rex Geissler in red. And the text reads: "Just a few of the many phantom ark formations in the lava and mud slips near Mt. Ararat".

But in this illustration professor Robert Michelson points out that there is no comparison at all between the boat-shaped object and these random shadows most of which will be gone two hours after having taken the picture ...

He then shows in fun on the bottom picture that you can also find several rectangular arks - like claimed by Hagopian that it looked - by using the same superficial analysis.

(A great part of the Ark-search on the Mt. Ararat mountain itself consists in discussions of rectangular rocks which the mountaineers claim to have seen or shadows that can be seen on photos - latest on satellite photos.)

Michelson:
„Another fallacious argument proffered by those who are not grounded in the understanding of fluid dynamics and flow effects, is the incorrect belief that flow diverted around an obstruction will separate and rejoin down stream, thereby forming a boat-shaped „shadow" immediately downstream from the obstruction. All one needs to do is observe the wake formed by a rock in the flow of a stream to see that the classic

This aerial photograph shows the unique boat shape of the Durupinar site. Contrary to the claims of several detractors, there are no other formations of this shape in the vicinity. Often oblique pictures of unidentified lava structures are said to be boat shaped, but inspection from above, as in this photograph, would show that these are circular or oval features. As can be seen in the following figures, a circle when viewed from the side will appear oval or boat-shaped.

Durupinar Site June 1987

Another fallacious argument proffered by those who are not grounded in the understanding of fluid dynamics and flow effects, is the incorrect belief that flow diverted around an obstruction will separate and rejoin down stream, thereby forming a boat-shaped "shadow" immediately downstream from the obstruction. All one needs to do is observe the wake formed by a rock in the flow of a stream to see that the classic Kelvin wake spreads at a 38.8° angle, never to return to a point. Compounding the error of those making these claims is the fact that had they visited the Durupinar site and studied its morphology, they would observe that there is no obstruction at either end of the boat shaped formation that would account for a separation of the flow in the first place.

In the photograph below entitled, "Other Canoe/Boat Shapes Around Little Ararat Across Valley: Photo Courtesy of Charles Willis", Rex Geissler of ArcImaging portrays at his NoahsArkSearch.com web site "Just a Few of the Many Ark Formations..." found in the lava near Küçük Ağrı.

From NoahsArkSearch.com
http://216.117.163.114/

JUST A FEW
THE MANY
ARK FORMATIONS
IN THE LAVA AND MUD
FLOWS NEAR ARARAT

Durupinar Site 1960's

Is there realistically any comparison between the rock shadows in the snow on the picture to the left and the distinct physical shape of the Durupinar site shown in the down-looking view above? Even drawing boat-shaped figures around these shadows doesn't make them convincing.

Most of the "Phantom Arks" above disappeared two hours after this picture was taken as the Sun illuminated the scene differently, but the Durupinar site 17 km away remained unaffected. ☺

Just for fun, lets consider the same photograph and see how many rectangular "Hagopian Arks" can be found using the same faulty analysis:

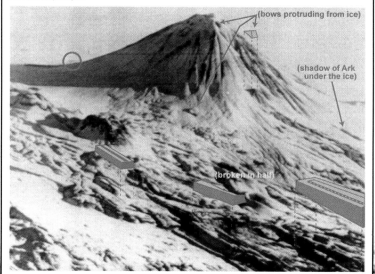

(bows protruding from ice)

(shadow of Ark under the ice)

(broken in half)

science, but they did open the way for SEPDAC's work.

What is Needed?

SEPDAC defined a long list of areas that should be researched. The list is given as a footnote for interested professionals that may want to be a part of the project.[1]

First of all, there is a need for soil analysis, which can help establish how old the find is, when there have been periods of drought or flood, when there has been volcanic activity, etc.

There is also a need for an analysis of what may lie underground. Radar-scanning of different types which can show (again) if there are any signs of abnormal structures in the boat-formed object which may be man-made such as rooms, halls, a keel, etc. will help with this.

That is the geological and physical research.

There is also a need for language people that can research the interesting names that have been found; for anthropologists specializing in pre-bronze age; for metal experts (metallurgists) that can research the different marks and symbols engraved in the metal that has already been found or will be found. There is a need for historians that can translate the ancient texts about the Flood; for archeologists who are given permission to dig (which has been forbidden up to this point; for cartographers, data-experts, lists of the different documents, and of course people who can do the practical organizational work.

If SEPDAC were to succeed in building such a team, then we would be that much closer to finding an answer to this mystery.

Michelson also has plans of flying an unmanned, computer-steered airplane, which he has helped develop at Georgia Tech Research Institute, over the area to take pictures. With the use of infra-red and two other types of photography, Michelson thinks that he can reveal new secrets that are yet to be discovered. It will be a very expensive project, and the first thing that needs to be done is to raise the funds.

Very Old Graves and Foundations

At the workshop in 1998, Dr. Bayraktutan revealed his discovery of a grave that held ancient soil and human remains of which both were able to be dated. Bayraktutan found the grave in a Turkish patrol road cut along the Iranian border, in the area that is now called "Naxuan" by the researchers. Naxuan was perhaps the name of the first city Noah built after the Flood. (More about that later.)

- Samples of bone and pottery were taken back to Atatürk University for analysis. In addition, on the first day at 'Naxuan' I found a gravesite which appeared to be an ancient cairn burial, explains Michelson.

Kelvin wake spreads at a 38.8° angle, never to return to a point. Compounding the error of those making these claims is the fact that had they visited the Durupinar site and studied its morphology, they would observe that there is no obstruction at either end of the boat shaped formation that would account for a separation of the flow in the first place."

Michelson with a micro UAV-airplane developed by a team at the Georgia Tech Research Institute which can be used for infra-red aerial photography.

***Below** Michelson discussing the technical applications of remote-controlled airplanes with the actor and instructor Alan Alda at the International Aerial Robotics Competition in 1995.*

Footnotes

[2] Ground surveys would include:
· volcanism/geothermal
· tectonism (paleoseismicity)/dating
· sedimentation analyses
· geochronology
· remote sensing

Geophyisics surveys include:
· Ground Penetration Radar (GPR)
· gravitometry
· ground resistance
· acoustic seismology
· satellite photo analyses

Anthropological interests include:
Linguistic Translators (from Istanbul Museum, the University of Pennsylvania and elsewhere),
Anthropologist (perhaps someone from Ankara who is versed in "neolithic through early bronze age")
Metallurgist (to analyze any metal artifacts located at any of the sites)
Historian (to understand and correlate the early writings describing any particular site of interest. Some of our present members are already versed in this area)
Other skills/services that will be required include:
Excavational archeologists
Cartographers
Data Acquisition experts
Documentation specialists
Logistics managers (various)
Security (military)
Archeological preservation experts

- This was later uncovered to reveal the sunken lid or base, if robbed, of the cairn which was lined with cut limestone blocks.

The lid was approximately one meter by 2 meters. Other graves were found and documented photographically without disturbing them.

GPS fixes were taken at various prominent locations visible in the 1959 aerial reconnaissance photographs, as well as several of the gravesites[2]. In addition, a number of rectangular building foundations were identified and documented photographically."

Signs of Life

In 1999 Michelson, Bayraktutan, and David Deal were again in the area. This time they were further up the mountain in the area referred to as Naxuan – Noah's first city. In order to get into this tightly guarded area of the border, it was necessary to have a military escort.

During their visit they found multiple foundations and man-made structures just under "the Wall of Heaven" – the characteristic crest with two summits.

- One outstanding find was a one-meter diameter ossuarial burial urn containing bones and a protected incursion of soil, tells Michelson.

- These bones (samples of what appear to be ribs have been collected) along with a quantity of the paleo-soil and ceramic urn fragments can be cross-dated by at least four independent methods. Carbon dating of the bone, analysis of pollen in the paleo-soil, and dating of the soil itself and the pottery will provide an accurate dating of this burial. This data will help to establish the age of the cultural activity just below the escarpment thought to be the Wall of Heaven.

It was near such an escarpment that the Ark is said to have landed, and the first post-flood city established according to Babylonian accounts. "The sun rises over the Wall of Heaven", and indeed, the sun does rise over this escarpment, Michelson concludes.

[2] GPS is the abbreviation of Global Positioning System, i.e. the technological possibility to determine any place on earth based on measurements of range and angles to satellites.

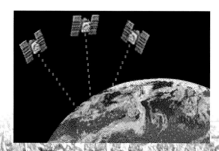

Chapter 36

Deal's Discoveries

David Allen Deal with the Ark formation in the background. Photo: Jerry Kitchens

Attending the first SEPDAC-seminar was artist David Allen Deal, who also researches the past and has written two books about the connection between the Mayan and Hebrew languages and histories[1] as well as a third book about the origin of the world and the ancient past. He was a good friend of David Fasold, and when Fasold died, Deal took over quite a bit of his material. Among that material is the very interesting aerial photograph taken by the Turkish military in 1959 when mapping out the border areas.

It was from this picture that the boat-shaped object was detected. Air Captain Ilhan Durupinar took the picture from 20-25,000 feet and sent it to his instructor in photogrammetry, Dr. Arthur Brandenburger in Ohio, which - as mentioned before - led to an American expedition.

Afterwards the picture was published in the Australian magazine PIX in 1960 and in LIFE magazine in September of the same year. Due to the superficial expedition that was conducted, the case died after that.

But Brandenburger gave a copy of Durupinar's picture to an archeologist at Ohio State University, a Dr. Siegfried Horn, who later gave it to Arkhunter David Fasold. Deal got the 8x10 in. detailed negative from Horn in 1994.

This picture, along with other photos, drawings, and explanations from Deal, are reproduced here with permission. Parts of these and other pictures can be found in the 1999 revised edition of David Deal's book "The Day Behemoth & Leviathan Died". [2]

Under the Microscope

Deal immediately enlarged the picture and started studying the details more closely. His most important discovery took place in 1995 when he found evidence of an ancient civilization that he believes to be Naxuan - Noah's first city.

In 1998 Deal was able to visit the sight together with Professor Michelson, Bayraktutan, and others under the SEPDAC seminar. Here he confirmed that there was such evidence in the deserted area close to the Iranian border. This discovery is so important, we will return to it in its own chapter.

But the photograph also showed two other phenomena which tell us about the Ark (or should we still be satisfied with the boat-shaped object?):

Footnotes

[1] *Discovery of Ancient America*, 1984, Kherem La Yah Press, Irvine, California. *The Nexus Spoken Language*, Isac Press, Institute for the Study of American Cultures, Columbus, Georgia, 1993.

[2] The book was released in 1988. The title refers to two monsters spoken of in the Bible which Deal believes to belong to a period before the Creation written of in Genesis. He believes the Hebrew text to be mistranslated and thinks this was a re-Creation out of the chaos that existed.

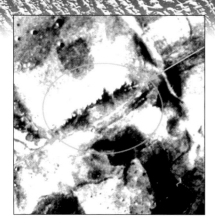

An enlargement of the so-called „first imprint" from the aerial photograph.

1. A new imprint of a boat-shaped object almost identical to that which we have already studied.

2. A clear s-shaped flow of mud leading from the new object to the old!

In the 1959 photograph we almost have a marked journey from the first imprint to the latter.

Wyatt's Imprint - or Another?

In 1984 Ron Wyatt printed in his newsletter that – together with Orhan Baser from Istanbul – he had surveyed the area above the object along the slope and found another imprint.

The measurements he gave were much smaller: 120 x 40 feet. This raises the question, are they the same imprint?

Dave Deal doesn't think so. He argues that the measurements are completely different and that the discovery is his alone. Because of this he had a map with his discovery of the boat-shaped imprint as well as what he believes to be the ancient city of Naxuan registered and copyrighted by the Library of Congress in 1997.

Ron Wyatt's publishing smaller measurements could be due to his inability to see the entire object in 1984, though it was visible in its entirety in the 1959 aerial photograph. The area Ron describes was encircled by stones that he believed to be petrified wood, and a test he later ordered could suggest the same.

The new boat-like imprint that we are assuming to be the original resting place of the Ark is about 1½ miles from the other imprint. It is located further up Al Judi at about 7,400 ft while the other is around 6,200.

Only few have been allowed in this strictly guarded military area on the Iranian border, but those that have had the chance confirm that such an imprint exists about 100 yards below the characteristic crest (Yigityatagi).

"It looks like the other object. It has the exact same shape, but it is narrower" tells Dr. Salih Bayraktutan.

"I had already named the 'first impression place' in 1985 and (mentioned) that the object had moved from that site to its present site. Actually, Wyatt, Fasold, and I had an argument about where the exact location was. Now Deal has pointed it out."

The location was open and obvious until the military built a road over the impression recently - long after the aerial photograph was taken.

In the photograph we can faintly make out the impression in its full length (which is equivalent to the lower object). It is found near the start of the mudflow, which can be seen twisting down through the landscape. The flow starts in the middle of the picture and then turns to the left, then to the right where it again takes a left turn ending in a narrowing where the boat-shaped object seems to be stuck in the bottleneck created here.

How do they connect - two boat-shaped objects?

Let's just reconsider the theory in the new light this information sheds:

NAXUAN

NAXUAN

NAXUAN

NAXUAN

NAXUAN

ARK LANDING SITE
2,244 METERS ABOVE
SEA LEVEL

CENTER OF MESHA NAXUAN
NOAH'S CITY CALLED

"PLACE OF FIRST DESCENT"

ARK'S FINAL REST
AT NASAR-UZENGILI
VILLAGE 2,046 METERS
ABOVE SEA LEVEL

NASAR-UZENGILI

SERON

The Theory in a Nutshell

♦ The Ark is stranded on Al Judy as the Qur'an states, or Nisir as Gilgamesh claims. Whatever the case, it is in the Ararat Mountains as Moses more broadly tells us in the Bible.

♦ According to tradition (but not named in the Bible), a city – Naxuan or Nachidsheuan, possibly Noakh-Tsywn (there are different spellings) – is founded.

♦ A catastrophe strikes in the area at some point. It could be the close-lying volcano, Agri Dagh (Mt. Ararat), blowing 1/6 of itself in the air; possibly when a volcano 25 miles into Iran explodes. If we believe Wyatt's account of an engraving of a drawing on a stele from this forbidden area, then a mountain has disappeared since the engraving, probably in the Hurrian Era (c. 2,000-1,000 B.C.). This could be the volcano in Iran that was barely visible in the background or a smaller local mountain to the right of our peak.

♦ Due to an earthquake or something else, an inland lake was "popped" and huge amounts of water came flowing for miles down the mountainside and through the valley. The water and mud (from the lost mountain?) flowed down and took the Ark with them.

♦ The Ark leaves an initial imprint up top. Some people believe that it is a section of the keel.

♦ The Ark apparently is still intact enough to glide down the mud river in one piece. This could suggest that it happened many thousands of years ago. Otherwise it would have already rotted.

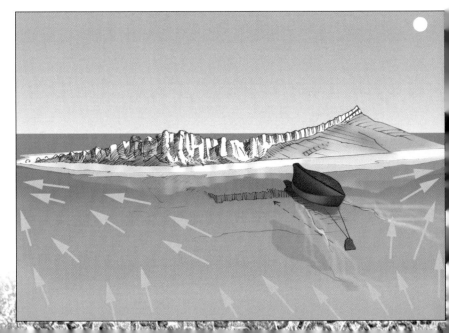

This is how David Deal imagines the Ark, with anchor stones hanging from behind, sailing into a U-shaped, natural port at Al Judy - or Nizir as called by the Babylonians

♦ The Ark stops about 1½ miles further down Al Judi in a place the Turks, strangely enough, call Masher = Judgment Day or Mashur = resurrection. There could be two locations. (Deal believes the name to come from the Hebrew Masheh, saved from the water, which sounds like *Mosheh* – Moses, taken up from the water.)

♦ The Ark is taken by the mud to its present day resting place and covered in mud, covered for maybe thousands of years.

♦ Back in the days of Josephus and other sources there is only "a little piece of the Ark" which lay in the place of the Ark's "first descent" - a place local Armenians probably knew about since the area was invaded by Turks from the northeast around the year 1,000.

♦ Due to erosion and later earthquakes, the Ark comes forth again in 1948. According to Fasold this occurred on the date of Israel's independence. It does happen, however, in the same month.

♦ The military later catches a glimpse of the object from the air, and in 1978 another earthquake causes the object to become even more visible and to stand out from its surroundings. This process continues with the annual rains and erosion, but if no protection is offered, it will eventually be destroyed.

♦ Now no more than an imprint of the Ark exists along with a few iron nails and signs of other metals (like the Viking ship, Sutton Hoo, that left an imprint though it had rotted away). The strange rocks we found could possibly be planks of wood that have petrified through the thousands of years that have passed.

Aerial Photographs
Require Revision

Deal also questions the given length of the Ark by his old friend Fasold. Wyatt and Baumgardner (along with others) have measured the object to be 515 feet which fits the biblical 300 cubits perfectly - that is, if you use the ancient Egyptian royal cubit.

But who says that Noah used Egyptian cubits, challenges Deal. He surely used his own cubit (elbow) as a measuring device. Deal believes the full length of the ship to be 538 feet. And that is not taken out of thin air. At the end of the boat-shaped object there is some earth that seems to have been broken off of the Ark.

The Path of the Ark:
A mudslide tears the boat away from its original location. The boat possibly turns in the way down.

When Fasold and Wyatt scanned the Ark with a Molecular Frequency Generator they noticed that this extra piece also contained parallel lines. But these lines were only one foot apart. The piece with the small parallel lines is 34 feet long. 11 of these feet run into the supposed ending of the object. Therefore, they took these 11 feet into consideration in the equation which now gave 515 feet.

They assumed that the 23 feet that now lay away from the object had originally ended the ship horizontally.

But Fasold realized that this could be questioned when the Ark is one day excavated, so he clearly stated how he calculated the length (p. 12 in his book *The Ark of Noah*).

Six months before Fasold died Deal wrote with him about this same problem. Deal noticed on the blow-up of the photo that not only the lower part of the boat-shaped object had an extra separated piece, but the upper part did too! It also had this special narrowing bottleneck in the stern and was 538 feet if measured on this extremely detailed photograph.

"That is why I do not doubt that the Ark was originally at least 538 feet, probably more, because the impression shows the section of the boat lying in the mud, but there could also have been a section hanging over. I believe that is the explanation why the upper impression is smaller. The boat didn't lie so deep here where the earth is harder.

"So I believe that the boat's length was 550 feet," says Deal.

A Longer Cubit?

But what about the 300 cubits. Do they still fit?

Yes. As mentioned, Dave Deal doesn't believe that Noah necessarily used the Egyptian royal cubit (20.6 in). Noah used his own cubit, about 22 in. (55.88 cm). Deal found this length in two different ways. First of all he divided 550 feet by 300 cubits, and then he compared the distance between the bulkheads of the ship.

It turned out that if he divided the distance with three different cubit measurements, the 22-in.-cubit fit best. Besides the Egyptian and his own 22-in.-cubit, he also tried a supposed 21.52-in.-cubit (538 feet divided by 300 cubits). The 20.6" Egyptian cubit only fit in 30% of the cases, while the 21.52" cubit (which fit a ship length of 538 feet) fit in 40% of the cases. The 22" cubit fit 60%, and if he assumed an erosion factor of 6.5 cubits on each end, then he ended at 80%.

So Deal is convinced that the Ark was longer than the 158 meters we almost bought. He believes it to be 167.64 meters, that is 550 feet.

And nothing suggests that a cubit could not be longer than the Mesopotamian or Egyptian. The old Danish cubit that the first invaders from the south and east most

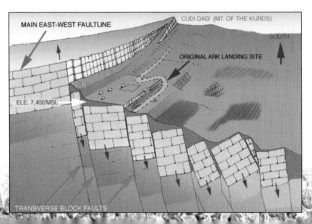

Illustration by David Deal. Here we see how the earthquake changed the landscape under „the first imprint", which he and others believe to be the original landing place of the

MAIN EAST-WEST FAULTLINE

CUDI DAGI (MT. OF THE KURDS)

SOUTH

ORIGINAL ARK LANDING SITE

ELE. 7,400'MSL

TRANSVERSE BLOCK FAULTS

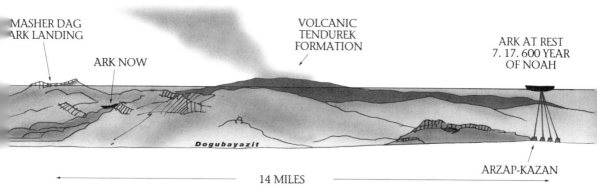

MASHER DAG
ARK LANDING

ARK NOW

VOLCANIC
TENDUREK
FORMATION

ARK AT REST
7. 17. 600 YEAR
OF NOAH

Dogubayazit

ARZAP-KAZAN

← 14 MILES →

*„In the seventh month, the 17th day the Ark came to rest in th mountains of Uratu" but it is not until the 10th month „the tops of the mountains were seen". David Deal assumes that during this 2½-month interval the Ark set anchor over what we know as **Arzap** (which means to seize the earth), the city where the anchor stones can be found today. It is likely that Noah decided to sail the 14 miles to the peak of **Masher Dag** (Mt. Curdu – the first mountain), a large limestone rock that protruded out of the water to the southeast forming a natural harbor. He would not have gone to the smoking volcano **Tendurek** in the south (Iran). If **Agri Dag** (Mt. Ararat) even existed at that time it would have been situation in the northeast, probably another steaming volcano. Here we are looking at David Deal's illustration in an almost southern direction. In the middle you can see where Dogubayazit now lies.*

likely brought with them thousands of years ago is no less than 24.7 English inches or 24 American. That is the equivalent of two very large Danish feet...

There is no doubt that ancient Nordic legend tells of giants. Maybe they were only Noah's first descendants, but that, again, is a whole other story.

Was the Ark also Wider...?

Deal believes, like most other modern Ark-hunters, that Noah's Ark was shaped like a boat. This doesn't agree with the Mt. Ararat-hunters' idea that it was a quadratic, rectangular Ark. The latter built their idea on Middle Age and Elfred Lee's paintings, the somewhat doubtful "eye witness" accounts, and a lack of ship building knowledge. These cut and dry suspicions are being broken down along with the discovery of the boat-shaped object.

In the meantime, the boat-shaped object is wider than the Ark should have been according to Moses. At its widest, the object is about 138 feet, and Moses described it as only 50 cubits = 85.8 feet or 26 meters.

Wyatt and Fasold's explanation was that the sides of the Ark must have fallen out under the weight of the mud. Since the upper impression on Al Judi is narrower, this also sounds like a plausible hypothesis.

But again Deal has his own:

"I think that the ship has always been as wide as we see in the lower impression. That it doesn't look like that in the upper impression is probably due to the ship not being stuck so deep in the hard earth up on the mountain. Not even in water would such a ship stick so deeply that the entire width would touch the surface of the water," says Deal, who doesn't see a problem in different measurements for the width. He believes that it was normal practice to give the average width of a ship as its width instead of its outermost points.

As we can see in Deal's drawings, we end up with a wide ship that - except for its size - could remind one of the hull of modern sailboats.

Australian archeologist-author, Jonathan Gray, who otherwise agrees with Wyatt on almost everything, does not agree with Wyatt's hypothesis of the sides falling out. He also believes that the present width of the object is its original. His argument is that the sides of the "Ark" don't seem to have heeled over because the (presumed) support beams which are sticking out of each side and thought to run throughout the ship are still level. They don't bend down as they would if the sides had given way. [3]

"Doesn't Fit the Biblical Measurements"

For the time being our ship expert from earlier in this book, Hans Otto Kristensen, accepts the idea that a ship's width could be measured based on its average:

Footnotes

[3] Jonathan Gray: *The Ark Conspiracy*, pg. 63.

[4] The Swedish-Estonian ferry, "Estonia" sunk on the 28th of September, 1994 becoming the worst European ship catastrophe since World War 2. Almost 900 people lost their lives due to a combination of bad weather and safety problems with the ship's bow.

"In ship building we work with two measurements of width: how wide the ship is at the waterline, i.e. the distance from one side of the ship where it meets the surface of the water to the point of penetration on the opposite side, also at the waterline. This width is called the waterline width.

Another is the total width, which can often be greater than the waterline width. There are no other definitions for width," concludes Hans Otto Kristensen.

He doesn't agree that Deal's drawing is equivalent to the biblical account which requires the roof to be raised by one cubit - that is 1/50 of the width of the ship. Kristensen believes that the roof in Deal's drawing has been raised by at least 6 cubits. And Deal's boat only has two stories, whereas the Ark should have three according to the Bible.

Hans Otto Kristensen

-Wouldn't a broad ship like Deal's be more sea worthy than a narrow one?

"The broader a ship is, the more stable (and with that safer) it will be, but it will also roll from side to side more quickly. From a motion point-of-view it would be uncomfortable and insecure", answers Kristensen.

An example illustrates this: Modern ferries that have been built after the reconciliation of the *Estonia*[4] are built as wide as possible in order to attain stability, but a compromise is still necessary so that passengers and cars are not thrown from side to side. With animal transport, the animals risk breaking bones if the ships are too wide. Therefore the dimensions of the Ark are perfect for animal transportation.

Chapter 37

Naxuan Found?

When Turkish captain Ilhan Durupinar took his aerial photographs of the Ararat Mountains the snow had melted and the crops were harvested. The light was great; the sun was low. This is why the landscape stood clear enough in the negatives that he could send them to Dr. Arthur Brandenburger. Many details could be observed with a trained eye.

In the subsequent photographs published in PIX and LIFE in lower resolution, the section picturing the boat-shaped object was the point of interest.

But a few people were able to look at the whole picture and began to look at the surroundings. For Dr. Salih Bayraktutan, the picture was decisive in his continuing work on the project:

"When I saw the picture I could immediately see that this was something very special. The boat-shaped object didn't only resemble a ship, but the manner in which it lay in the mudflow looked exactly like when you are in a plane looking down on the enormous ships in the Atlantic. And I thought, 'this is just like a ship'.

"I could follow the mudflow and see it narrow into a bottleneck below the object. I am convinced that the object had to have moved with the flow, and it didn't stop because of the limestone that is now penetrating the middle, but because the flow ended in a bottleneck. Moreover, it is still slightly moving."

Rectangular Houses by the Hundreds

David Allen Deal got the negative from Dave Fasold and began studying the area above the object. He believed he could point out evidence of about 20 houses and in June of '97 had a portion of the negative enlarged from 1x1.75 in. to 16x18.

"I could immediately see tons of rectangular houses. Not visible ruins, but a color variation in the surface of the earth, which is due to underground ruins," tells Deal and continues explaining:

When an earthen house is not well kept it will be destroyed by rain and snow within 100 years. Nothing is left besides a shadow where the foundations are buried. But in barren areas like this an imprint remains much longer. Even if the ruins disappear from the surface, they will be able to be seen from above because areas where the crops don't grow as well due to the hard earth are left behind. Even in agricultural countries like England, shadows in the earth left from ancient Roman castles can be seen after two

*Robert Michelson and Salih Bayraktutan find signs of ancient buildings and graves only 100 yards from „the Port of Heaven".
Photo: Deal*

Extract from the aerial photo that convinced Bayraktutan that this was a ship. The boat-shaped object is shown in yellow. Notice that the mudslide narrows into a bottleneck.

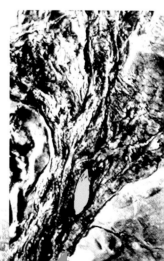

Footnotes

[1] Quoted from Jewish Antiquities, Vol. IV, p. 43, Loeb edition, Classic Library.

[2] The sons of Shem (were) Elam and Asshur and Arpachshad and Lud and Aram. The sons of Aram (were) Uz and Hul and Gether and Mash. Arpachshad became the father of Shelah; and Shelah became the father of Eber. Two sons were born to Eber; the name of the one (was) Peleg, for in his days the earth was divided; and his brother's name (was) Joktan. Joktan became the father of Almodad and Sheleph and Hazarmaveth and Jerah and Hadoram and Uzal and Diklah and Obal and Abimael and Sheba and Ophir and Havilah an Jobab; all these were the sons of Joktan. Now their settlement extended from **Mesha** as you go toward Sephar, the hill country of the east. These are the sons of Shem, according to their families, according to their languages, by their lands, according to their nations. (Genesis 10:22-31.)

[3] Epic of Gilgamesh, Tablet IX , 47.

thousand years of plowing and harvest.

"When I studied the photograph more closely I was able to see multiple straight vertical lines imprinted on the ground over a large area – maybe thousands. What appeared were the blueprints of an ancient city that hadn't been visible since before Josephus' time," believes Deal, who considers this the remains of Naxuan - Noah's city.

Is This Naxuan?

Naxuan isn't mentioned in the Bible but it shows up in various ancient sources. The Jewish historian Josephus (c. 75 A.D.) possibly names Naxuan. He quotes the Chaldean historian Berosus (c. 270 B.C.) who refers to a place of pilgrimage:

"The Armenians call it the place of the decent ("apo bah tay reon" in Greek) because it was there the Ark safely landed, and relics appears to this day." [1]

William Whiston, who translated Josephus into English in 1737, suggested in a footnote that the Greek name for the landing place was a section of the name of the Armenian city, Nachicevan (Naxuan), supposedly the first city after the Flood. Linguists, though, disagree how correctly this is translated. If it is correct, then Josephus (or Berosus) actually writes, "the Armenians call the place Nachidsheuan".

The city that Winston thought of was the present city Nachivan (also spelt Nachidcevan and Naxcivan etc.) which is situated at least 150 miles away in an Azerbaijani enclave by the same name, wedged between Armenia and Iran.

According to Deal, Nachidsheuan or Naxuan(a) comes from either Noach + tsywn, which mean Noah's and Zion, that is, great city, or Noach + tswaneh, which means Noah's (sheep)fold.

But the important thing here is that Josephus speaks of the existence of a city or place where the Ark once landed and that in Berosus's time relics appeared. The place or city he refers to could just as well be the recently found city located on Al Judi above the boat-shaped object.

As seen in the chapter on Josephus, the Ark had probably already disappeared when he lived (75 A.D.). He doesn't write that the actual Ark can be found, but only mentions relics from it, or "a little piece of the Ark" (as Eusebius later writes in the 3rd century).

Most likely the first dwellings were build near the Ark. Maybe even from material from the Ark. Illustration: Deal

But what is this "little piece of the Ark"? Could it be the first imprint?

Are Naxuan and Mesha the Same?

"Naxuan" is also mentioned by the Armenian historian Moses of Chronen. The Chaldean (Babylonian) writer Berosus also names "Naxuan" as Noah's city. Claudius Ptolomy includes "Naxuana" on his map of the world in his book of geography vol. VII, chapter 12.

Further south – where the Kurdish village Uzengili now lies - there are signs of underground houses, says Deal, and he believes this to be the city Seron that Josephus also mentions.

In Winston's translation of Josephus' works he writes in a footnote on page 29 that Seron was the second city and that Naxuan was "the place of the first decent".

As mentioned, the name Naxuan is not directly mentioned in the Bible, but in Gilgamesh, Mesha is Noah's city, and this name *is* found in the Bible in Genesis 10:22-31.[2]

So Deal's theory is that Mesha and Naxuan are one and the same. Noah himself called the city that grew around the Ark Mesha, because it means "lifted out of the water". It was later known as Naxuan:

I don't believe that Noah was so vain to name the city after himself, but rather Noah was later honored and the city was named after him, known as "Noach–tsywn" – Naxuan – Noah's great city.

Gilgamesh told about a mountain with twin peaks where the Ark landed and where wise Noah (called Utnapishtim in the poem) dwelled after the Flood. Gilgamesh called the place "Mashu" (the Mountain of Mashu).[3]

He also mentioned "the gate to Heaven" that guarded the rising sun. The steep slopes between the two pinnacles are called the Wall of Heaven by the locals today.

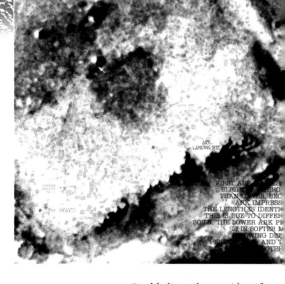

Deal believes he can identify all of these „shadows" of ruins on the aerial photograph. Here shown in yellow. The so-called „first imprint" of the Ark is shown in red.

Dr. Salih Bayraktutan shows the remains of a housing the military zone. Note the road in the background the military has established.
Photo: Robert Michelson

Semitic Names

Deal believes that the original name - Mesha/Mashu - remains among the local peoples. The Kurds, who live in the area, call the mountainside below the Wall of Heaven two different names that resemble Mesha: Masher, which can mean the day of judgment, and Mashu-r, which can mean resurrection. But what language did Noah speak?

Tradition tells us that Noah's son Shem continued living in the same area as Noah. If this is true, then it is possible that Noah spoke a form of Old Semitic. So maybe the Semitic language can give us better explanations of the place names than Armenian or Turkish.

Biblical Mesha, from which the sons of Joctan (who were Semitic) spread, could have been in this area. It was "in the mountains of the East" seen from Egypt or Mesopotamia. Mesha has the same Hebrew signs as in Moses (MSH), and the meaning is the same "to be taken up from water".

There is a connection between these names and the Flood, the deliverance, and maybe the resurrection. Deal believes that this place has been used as burial grounds; a Necropolis.

Necropolis – a Place of Pilgrimage

If this is the place where Noah's Ark landed then it was the point of origin for all nations, and they had to have seen it as a holy place. It probably continued like this for thousands of years, even if the different peoples developed their own religions. Religions with eight forefather gods can be found as far away as the Americas in Native American religions. Stories about the Ark and the Flood are found all around the globe in various forms.

Deal thinks that this place was a cultural burial site. He believes that people from distant lands journeyed here in order to be buried as close as possible to this holy place.

Support of this theory can be found in a place up here called Ziyaret Dog, which should mean "volunteer pilgrimage".

Many historians write about pilgrims traveling to this area, and some even scraped pitch off of planks to use as talismans for protection. We do not know how long this continued after the Ark disappeared, but the accounts suggest that it took place for a number of centuries around Jesus' lifetime. With the crusaders' journey to the Holy Land through Turkey around 1200, it is not unlikely that some of the more serious crusaders decided to venture into this area in order to find themselves and God. According to tradition, this was the resting place of the Ark.

In the uppermost area close to the peak at least one cult grave has been found, confirms Salih Bayraktutan. A Christian burial dated to 1245 names "the boat... God's son".[4]

Unfortunately, the area is not normally accessible due to the extreme closeness to the Iranian border.

In September of 2002 we were not allowed to go there, but Dr. Salih Bayraktutan has surveyed the area multiple times, and he confirms that

Footnotes

[4] Fasold, *The Ark of Noah*, 2nd to last page in the photograph section after page 140.

[5] Pieces of this and other photographs were also published in the 1999 revised edition of David Deal's book *The Day Behemoth & Leviathan Died*.

graves and signs of ancient buildings exist there.

"I don't think that a very large city existed there as David Deal believes he has found evidence of, but there has been some type of a city, " he admits.

If Professor Michelson and co. can get the necessary support for the SEPDAC project, then archeologists will start excavating this site. While I write this, it hasn't happened yet, but there are probably many archeological treasures buried here.

David Deal's photographs and drawings along with his elaboration are printed here with permission. [5]

A Potsherd

One of the participants from the SEPDAC seminar in October 1998 was Dr. William Shea.

Because of a bad leg he was unable to follow the other participants into the upper military area and instead wandered down around the boat-shaped object.

While Shea was wandering around the object, he found a potsherd about 20 meters west of the formation's starboard side. The potsherd was about 3.7 x 3.7 in., but only 1.8 in. at the bottom. The sherd rounded off a bit and looked like it came from the middle part of a medium-sized pot. It was 1.2 in thick.

When he came back to the hotel in Erzurum in the evening of October 8th, he cleaned the potsherd and looked closer at it with a magnifying glass he had brought along.

"At that time it looked as if the markings on the sherd had something to do with the story of Noah and the Ark. Further study has borne out that connection," tells Shea.

Shea quickly concluded that on the outer side of the sherd (the convex side) one or more fish were engraved and a number of figures were painted in black, possibly with the help of ink made out of coal.

In the upper left-hand corner he found a drawing in black ink of two birds flying to the left. Under them he found a man releasing the two birds. Of course, the thought of Noah releasing a raven and a dove looking for dry land comes to mind.

The outer side of Shea's potsherd in two different lights. Photo: Bill Shea

On the inner side (the concave) it looked like a man with a crown and a beard was carved. He apparently had a hammer in his hand and hammered a nail into something that is no longer visible because it was beyond the edge of the sherd.

Possibly the Oldest Writing in Existence

In the meantime Bill Shea is taking a huge step in deciphering the ostracon. He believes that the small figures throughout the sherd are actually letters.

Shea already knew an ancient writing, Proto-Sinaitic,[6] which he had studied inscriptions of in a turquoise mine in Korhar, Sinai, in 1996. Based on this knowledge he believes he can make the three figures out to be three words

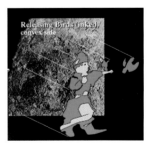

Dr. William Shea found a potsherd near the boat-shaped object which he is still investigating.

- brace yourself - raven (oreb), dove (yonah), and Noah...!

If this is ancient Proto-Sinaitic, then the sherd is at least from 1500 B.C. A new find in Egypt proves that the writing was used around 1800 B.C.

Painted and Engraved

After Bill Shea worked on revealing the drawings and texts on this ostracon for over two years, I contacted him and he had so much information about signs and figures that his outline filled 18 pages on top of 12 pages of illustrations and photographs!

Bill Shea now believed he had found drawings and names of not only the eight who were in the Ark but also two other families.

Shea has reached this conclusion by studying the ostracon under microscope. Looking at it with the naked eye, however, it is difficult to see much and I am afraid that Shea may be overinterpreting the sherd and reading more into it that it can bear. But why did the artist make them so small?

I am also forced to consider why the names and letters have been written from right to left and from left to right as well as up-down and vice versa. There are examples of writing in basically all directions, but so far no sherds have been found with more than one type.

But until then we will keep to the fact: a sherd has been found near the Ark formation that may show drawings and maybe letters that have a connection to the Ark.

The Proto-Sinaitic Inscriptions and Their Decipherment, Harvard Theological Studies, vol. XXII (Cambridge: Harvard University, 1966).

Phon. Value	Schematic Forms	Early North-west Semitic	Early South Semitic	Early Letter Names	Meaning of Names
ʾ		(14th) (13th)	(Jamme)	ʾalp-	ox-head
b		(17th) (13th)		bêt-	house
g		(15th) (12th)		gaml-	throw-stick
d		(10th)	(Jamme)	digg-	fish
ḏ	?		(Jamme)	?	?
h		(10th)		hô(?)	man calling
w		(10th)	(? used for y)	wô(waw)	mace
z		(16th) (10th)		zê(n-)	?
ḥ		(12th) (10th)		ḥê(t-)	fence (?)
ḫ	?		(Jamme)	ba( )	hank of yarn
ṭ		(16th) (10th)		tê(t-)	spindle?
y		(13th) (10th)	(orig. w)	yad-	arm
k		(17th) (13th)		kapp-	palm
l		(14th) (13th)	(Jamme)	lamd-	ox-goad
m		(15th) (13th)	(9th) (8th)	mêm-	water
n		(14th) (12th)		nohš-	snake
s		(10th)		(samk-?)	?
ʿ		(12th) (10th)		ʿên-	eye
ġ		(15th)	(Jamme)	ġa( )	?
p		(10th)		piʾt-(?)	corner?
ṣ/ẓ		(10th)		ṣa(d-)	plant
ḍ	?	?		?	?
q		(14th) (10th)	(Jamme)	qu(p-)	?
r		(16th-14th)		ra'š-	head of man
š/t		(13th) w(10th)		tann-	composite bow
ś		?	(Jamme)	?	?
t		(13th)	(Jamme)	tô(taw)	owner's mark

Chapter 38

One Last Check

I've been working on this Ark book for a number of years now, and often I've been at the point of desperation, overwhelmed with the endless number of matters that *should* be combed through. My publisher has reset the printing date multiple times because I have found new, exciting areas to explore.

The rescue party reaches the earthquake-stricken villages; 18 have already been lost.
(Photo: Zafer Onay, 2004)

In the beginning of 2004 I had to accept the fact that writing this book could continue for the rest of my life, partly because we are unable to make any conclusions about whether or not this is Noah's Ark, and partly because the subject is so exciting I could continue writing into eternity. For example, we could have looked more closely at:

1.   What do the exiled Armenians have to tell about the names and locations in eastern Turkey?

2.   What information can be found about Nachidcevan – Noah's city – situated 100 kilometers east in Azerbaijan's enclave?

3.   What else is hidden in Iran besides "the grave of Noah's wife"?

But the publisher is starting putting on the pressure, and therefore I decided to put a temporary stop to it by making a two weeks' trip to the Ark area around Dogubayazit in Turkey in June 2004. Together with me were two other Ark enthusiasts: Norwegian John E. Madsen and Danish Flemming Andersen. I think I had a futile hope that some new revelation would appear – and it almost did.

Another earthquake – 18 Dead

The week after we returned home, on the 2nd of July, another earthquake hit the Dogubayazit area. Possibly new evidence is lying around again, as after the quakes in 48 and 78.

Though no life was lost in Kazan-Arzep, many houses were destroyed.
(Photo: Zafer Onay, 2004)

I'm sorry to say that 18 people were killed and 27 injured, most of these taking place in the mountain village of Yigincal, just a few miles from "The Village of the Eight". The epicenter was about 15 miles northwest of Dogubayazit – in the mountains surrounding The Valley of the Eight.

I immediately contacted Zafer Onay, a local guide I know. He relayed that the big wall that cut through the village had

Feizal, who had received us with great hospitality only a week ago, lies in the open air. An earthquake struck „The Village of the Eight" and destroyed his house. (Photo: Zafer Onay)

The wall next to the largest of the anchor stones was shaken by the quake. (Photo: Zafer Onay)

fallen and many houses were damaged, but luckily none of our friends in the village were hurt.

One of the photos he sent included our friend Feizal lying on a mattress in the open air. When we had visited him shortly before, he was bedridden due to a broken leg from a trip he had taken to Iran. There was a cart behind him full of clothing, upon which his little son sat. So I wrote Zafer to hear a bit more.

Zafer replied and told us that there had been multiple earthquakes and though no one had been hurt, Arzep was destroyed and the government planned on moving the inhabitants to another location. Hopefully this means the relics of the past will be taken better care of from now on.

Unlike Arzep, the "Ark" – another 12 or so miles away - didn't seem to have noticed the 5.1 quake, a measurement considered moderate on the Richter scale. Turkey is like California in that earthquakes are quite normal. Just a few years ago an earthquake claimed the lives of 15,000 people…!

A Mix-Match of Names

As you can see, we managed to visit Arzep just before it was destroyed. Even though Feizal was stuck in his bed, we were invited to tea where pictures of Bill Fry, Elin Berglund, and other foreign contacts were brought forth. I was even in one of the pictures. One would never know I had been here before when I tried to find it again! When I asked for directions to Arzep, I was pointed in one direction. But when I asked for Kazan I was sent in another. Arzep wasn't even on the map we had, and where I remembered Kazan/Arzep to be, the map showed Sagliksuyu… We followed the map the other way to Kazan and finally made it to Arzep.

"How does this all fit together?" I asked Feizal.

"Kazan is the Armenian name. That is what the village was called long ago," Feizal answered. "Arzep is the Kurdish name it is now known by and Sagliksuyu is the Turkish. But they are all names for the same village."

Later the Turkish teacher, Dudy, told us that Sagliksuyu means "healing water", so we assumed that the Turks had named it after the springs of rich mineral water that bubbled up all over the valley. We even tasted the water for ourselves.

Despite Feizal's narrative, we knew that there was another village known as Kazan

located somewhere else in the vicinity.

Zafer later explained, "Only you foreigners use the name Kazan for Arzep. Arzep is the original Armenian name that the Kurds use too. Kazan is an entirely different village about 10 kilometers away."

Arzep was the village's real name.

I remembered the many stone monuments from the Hurrian or Urartu period we found, but as we traversed the area this time, they were nowhere to be found. The local boys followed us around, and when they found out what we were looking for, they brought us to a house in Arzep-Kazan.

In a closed courtyard in Kazan-Arzep we found this ram, which probably dates back to the Hurrians or Urartu, ca. 3-4,000 years ago.

Inside the private courtyard stood an animal made of stone. What I understood was that the locals took all of the stones from the surrounding area and brought them back to the city to protect them. It was evening and therefore difficult to see whether it was a bull or a ram, but we were given permission to take pictures with flash so we could later see what it was.

The stones were painted, which the locals surely thought was beautiful, but that might not be the best way to take care of ancient relics...

Take Your Own Ark Journey!

If you are thinking visiting the Ark to see it with your own eyes, be encouraged that it is no longer as difficult to get to as it once was. There are regular flights to the larger cities like Erzerum, Kars, and Van in eastern Turkey, and from there busses can get you to your point of destination. Some busses are small and overcrowded, but the bus from Erzerum to Dogubayazit is large and comfortable and usually leaves on time.

The other stone ram had an engraved curved sword, which the locals accentuated with green paint.

A number of hotels can now be found in Dogubayazit, Turkey's easternmost border town located in the cartographic hack into Iran. The best hotel is probably *Grand Derya* with a near-by restaurant that dishes up food in which there is a bit of hope not to get a stomach infection. There are other hotels as well, like *Hotel Ararat* and *Hotel Nuh* (Noah) or the camping grounds high up the mountain close to *Isac Pasa* if that better suits your fancy. The prices are very reasonable, though Dogubayazit is a bit more expensive than other eastern cities due to its popularity among tourists – many of which come from Turkey, Iran, and other neighboring countries.

There is periodic political uproar because of the large numbers of Kurds wanting a sovereign state, but with the new Kurdish freedom in Iraq there may be hope that the problem can be solved by non-violent means.

Just before we were to leave, the Kurdish rebel group, PKK, announced a cease fire against the Turkish government, so we were expecting something to happen. It did, but not until after we had left. A car bomb exploded in downtown Van just as the governor's car drove by. Five innocent bystanders were killed and 22 were wounded. The governor escaped unharmed. While in Turkey there were terror bombings in both Ankara and Istanbul from other groups because of a meeting of top NATO officials, and in Iraq the most terrible kidnappings and torture took place.

Unfortunately that is the world we live in. If we only traveled under favorable conditions we wouldn't be able to get very far. The same thing goes for natural catastrophes.

As with earlier trips, it was our experience that the Turks were generally more than hospitable, especially in the western half where there is a focus on being European and "modern" – so much, in fact, that visitors almost feel as if they were in Paris or another of Europe's western metropolises. In 2004's Istanbul most of the women were (bleached) blondes with up-to-date hairstyles and western taste in clothing.

Not so in eastern Turkey.

Hospitable – but What are They Saying?

There is much more reservation towards foreigners, and their own culture is sacred; not just thrown away at the drop of a hat, thankfully. The biggest problem, however, is that so few speak a foreign language.

This time we decided not to have an English-speaking guide who could trick us into paying too much for things. We wanted to make it on our own. Besides, that is much more fun.

On the other hand, you often wander around not understanding a word that is spoken.

For example, if you hike up around the boat-shaped object, you're sure to meet irritating and naughty boys constantly asking for "payro-payro" (it must mean money), trying to sell you worthless junk they've found, or wanting to function as guides. They are quite a nuisance, and they don't just disappear after having their advances rejected. Instead they just insist more noisily and maybe even bring out their slingshots. At this point the authorities have to step in and speak with the parents.

Part of the Kurdish and Turkish cultures is inviting strangers in for tea, as we were one day when visiting the Castle of Isac Pasha high in the mountains beyond Dogubayazit.

The Silk Road behind the Mountains - and Past the Ark?

The existing fortress is only 400 years old, but the remnants from a much older cave castle are located on the steep mountainside east of the fortress. Since I am somewhat afraid of heights, I left the mountain climbing to John, who as a Norwegian is used to getting around in the mountains. Instead, I was brought into a tent for tea with a Kurdish family consisting of three or four generations. They motioned to me by raising a glass of tea, and they were wonderfully hospitable. Though we didn't have a common language, we communicated with signs and some help from Kurdish and Turkish dictionaries.

I showed them our primitive map and asked them about the area beyond the mountains. Until then we thought the Silk Road continued into the valley, but a local expert told us that it went through this pass. I asked the Kurds where the road led to and deciphered that we could follow it past Isac Pasha all the way into Iran. The official border was no longer located there. It now lay in the valley by the main road, and it was necessary to take a 30 kilometer detour to get there. But in days gone by, the road unfolded in the mountains here, leading past the castle.

At first glance it only seemed to be a small trail, but further south it turned into a passable road. We put the car into first and followed the Silk Road toward the east and then later north. We traversed steep and narrow mountain roads on a nerve-racking journey, which after 25 kilometers led us all the way to Uzengili and the boat-shaped object. This was the back way. We were three men, so the vehicle wreaked of testosterone, but still fear was present – and with good cause – that portions of the road might suddenly slip out from under us, as was prone to happen with the not so infrequent landslides. The road was not always quite there, we experienced, and there were a few instances when we had to get out of the car and decide if we dared take

Among the magnificent attractions the boys from The Valley of the Eight brought us to was „Noah's footprint". There is a „footprint" in the rocks adjacent to this which some believe to be Noah's altar, however it might have gotten there…

The hotel's Turkish Anatolia car seething again as we travel up the steep mountain roads…

the chance. Evening was approaching, and it would be difficult to turn around. But staying the night out here would not be too wise either, not as much because of the wolves as the people.

We also had to keep an eye on the dark sky above. If it began to rain, the steep trail could turn lethal. As we drove past the Kurdish villages throughout the afternoon, dark-skinned men and women mummified with their scarves stared at us with disbelief as their dogs ran into or in front of the car to stop us, as if we were one of the sheep they were trained to herd.

The last leg of our journey unfolded in darkness, so we were relieved when we finally made it down the mountain onto the main road in the valley. Now we knew for sure that the Silk Road went behind the mountains all the way to Iran and took travelers past the location of the Ark. Before the military laid the twisting, five-kilometer long road from the valley up to the boat-shaped object, this was the only way to get to the village of Uzengili.

Is Reshit Still Living in Kargakonmaz?

As previously mentioned, the boat-shaped object was discovered by a Kurdish shepherd named Reshit in 1948. I remembered that David Fasold later found him in Kargakonmaz, and his full name was *Ali Oglu Reshit Sarihan*.

I asked the old Kurdish Ark-keeper, Hassan Öser, about Kargakonmaz and Reshit. He explained how to find Kargakonmaz, but told us that Reshit had passed away.

"Reshit is dead, but Hassan is here," he said with a certain matter-of-factness.

Driving in the steep mountains seems to be an acquired taste, so we took the main road a bit further out toward the Iranian border and then turned off on a side road and crawled up the hairpin bends.

On the way up the mountain we came to a small village. We neared Yigityatagi from the other side.

The saddle-shaped mountain of Yigityatagi can be seen on the main road leading to the Iranian border.

Kargakonmaz means "restless crow", which we had a school teacher named Dudy confirm. Dudy knew nothing about our theories. I imagined Kargakonmaz lay in the mountains so the crow could fly overhead restlessly, but I was wrong.

After we made our way as far up the narrow road as possible in our rental car, we ended up in front of a small patch of houses with a military post not far behind us. The motor overheated multiple times on the way up. A Kurdish farmer named Achmed immediately went to the creek and washed himself before sending the children after tea and a blanket so we could sit in the ditch.

"Is this Kargakonmaz," I asked.

"No. Kargakonmaz is down there," Achmed replied and pointed down the mountainside.

"Then what is this village?"

"Yigityatagi," he answered as he motioned with his arms referring to the mountains all around him. The entire area is Yigityatagi.

We were dangerously close to the forbidden mountain top. The military hindered us in coming any further, but I had another plan...

Video clip: On the way up to Yigityatagi.
Mt. Ararat in all of its beauty lies on the opposite side of the valley.

Up to Yigityatagi

Yigityatagi is the characteristic saddle-shaped crest located about 2 kilometers above the boat-shaped

Video clip from the Yigityatagi climb with a view of Uzengili.

En route we pass a lake with colossal frogs. Mt. Ararat is behind us.

object. It is up here Wyatt claims to have seen a stele upon which the crest and the Ark were etched. This is also where Michelson and Salih found an ancient grave and where David Deal believed that he could see dimly an entire city in the soil imprints he saw in an aerial photograph.

Unfortunately, Yigityatagi is not accessible because of the Iranian border. This is also why you cannot go more than a mere jaunt above the boat-shaped object. But were we men or mice? We had to attempt climbing Yigityatagi to see what was up there. I noticed that military vehicles regularly drove through Ûzengili, so there had to be a road cutting through the town leading up to the military grounds behind the peak. If we just followed that road a bit, maybe we could come in from the eastern side.

We trekked on, the one hairpin bend after the other, until we reached a peak. Suddenly, we saw Turkish soldiers less than 200 yards away. We quickly shifted into reverse and turned around, rolling back down the slope as a couple of soldiers drew in. At that point we were more than happy that the name of the hotel was plastered on the side of the car so the soldiers didn't doubt that we were just stupid tourists who had just gotten ourselves lost.

But we had caught the Ark-fever and simply had to get closer to the "untouchable" mountain. Therefore, we stopped the car after a short stretch – when we thought we were outside of the military zone – and hiked in. We were significantly closer to Yigityatagi than ever before, but there was still half a mile to the top of the mountain, and there was a guard to pass that might not think highly of our endeavor. We changed our minds and decided to drive all the way down to Uzengili where we found a smaller road. We quickly ran into a creek and had to abandon the car.

The Kurdish boys saw us and were immediately at our heels demanding loose change. John was very kind and bought his freedom with candy while Flemming and I chose to implement the harsher methods we had learned from Hassan.

We are just below Yigityatagi's crest; the earth has eroded.

When we started up the steep hills they let us be, though we didn't get off the hook without a few shots from their stinging slingshots. From here we trekked more than a mile up a steep incline trying to get into the uppermost area while at the same time trying not to draw too much attention to ourselves. There was a guard in the eastern corner of Yigityatagi, and we were unsure whether he would allow us to hike there or not. As we wandered through the untouched landscape with its rare flora and loud-croaking frogs Flemming and John sagged behind while I picked up the pace, lit by my burning Ark-fever. I headed for the highest area as far west as possible in order to avoid detection. Huffing and puffing, I finally made it up to the pathway, which is barely distinguishable from the Ark as it lies just below Yigityatagi's impressive white crest. A bit more hiking led me all the way to the top where I was able to touch the crest. I was the happiest man in Urartu.

The military road cuts through. Lush grass hides the „first imprint".

Not Much to See

This year had given more precipitation than ever, Salih informed us. I then realized that we should have put off our trip until the fall because lush grass covered the area so that the boat-shaped imprint, Michelson's grave, and Deal's ruins were all hidden. There was, however, a quadrangular stone, probably from a house, to be seen, but the area seemed a bit too small to encompass Deal's original Naxuan. The area also produced evidence that the soil found just before the crest had sunk and slid over a long period of time, so it is probable that a larger plateau was once located here with a village, but there was surely no large city.

My two companions caught up to me, and as we made our way east, we were detected by guards who started shouting, which made us realize that we needed to turn around. Afterwards Uncle Hassan scolded us for going too far up the mountain, but since Kurdish shepherds are allowed to be there, it is difficult to understand why we shouldn't be allowed to look for traces of the Ark. But now we at least had a more realistic idea of what was to be found around the mysterious mountain crest. As for me, that was the highlight of the 2004 trip.

We couldn't buy a local map anywhere in Dogubayazit. But on the wall in a restaurant there was a simplified map, which we copied. After trying out the roads - if they were there - I draw this simple map. The boat shaped object is close to Uzengili – on some old maps called Nazar, the former name. Close to Uzengili are the mountain Yigityatagi and the village Kargakonmaz. On the other side of Dogubayazit we find The Valley of the Eight with Kazan / Arzap / Sagliksuyu. South of this village is another Kazan. The village Yigincal that was hit by an earthquake is just a little north of Arzap.

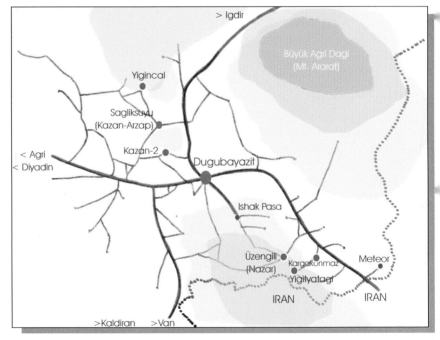

Chapter 39

Has the Ark Been Found?

Has Noah's Ark finally been found?

When I started writing this book a number of years ago I had hoped to come to a conclusion, but unfortunately there is no conclusion to be made.

I thought – and I still think – that the remains of Noah's Ark lie under the earthen hill we know as "the boat-shaped object".

Dr. John Baumgardner seems to have convincingly shown that the Ark is not there. Or more correctly put, in his opinion there is no scientific *evidence* that the Durupinar find is more than a coincidental and natural formation among the landscape. Also others have in the same way tried to explain away the Durupinar find, most of them because they are convinced that it is somewhere else, some again because they don't believe it exists.

But Dr. Salih Bayraktutan just as convincingly argues that the object is *not* natural. And as time goes on, new evidence is constantly popping up in the near vicinity suggesting that the area is hiding something very special. Just think about the place names.

Viveka Ponten took this picture of Wyatt at the Sea of Galilee on one of his last journeys.

Ron Wyatt's Credibility

We have to give it to Baumgardner, Lee, and other critics that Ron Wyatt can at times appear less than credible. He jumps to conclusions too quickly and does not always base them on facts but rather on a certain kind of intuition – or was it conceit? Some of his "evidence" can easily be dismissed, either because he was unable to present it or because he had it examined in such a way that doubt could be sown in with the results.

In his June 1, 2000 newsletter, Bill Fry writes about an old wall in the village Kazan which Ron claimed to have blue-green tiles finished with a painting of the Ark and animals on it. When Bill saw the wall in June of 2000 there were no paintings. Later, in May of 2001, he returned and the wall was completely destroyed by the villagers! (See Barbara Pratt's pictures to the right of this document.) Bill contacted the authorities and questioned the village heads. They claimed that they took the wall down to be free from visitors. (If that is how the locals think, then maybe we have an explanation as to why so many things have disappeared or have been destroyed.) Later Bill asked one of the village leaders' wives what had happened. She said that at one point precious stones were found in the wall (probably Christian, Byzantine). He asked if there was anything else special about the wall. Yes, a few years ago there were some tiles on it, almost blue-green.

"It's this type of experience that convinces me that Ron was telling the truth," remarks Bill Fry.

June 2000

May 2001

photo courtesy
of Barbara Patt

The distance from the capital of Armenia, Yerevan, to Ararat is only about 30 miles. From the border to the mountain there is less than 15.
The border between these two countries is marked by the Araxes River which runs through this lush valley situated between the two countries.

Ron Wyatt actually did make a lot of exciting discoveries, whatever the reason was. A lot of the criticism directed towards him *was* unfair and exaggerated and was often caused by either jealousy on the part of other Ark-hunters or attempts to defend their own prestige and/or doubtful "eye-witnesses".

Interestingly enough, critics have been harder on Wyatt than Fasold despite Fasold's speculation and circumstantial theories. We could also question Dr. Shea's exposition of the potsherd.

But the boat-shaped object does not stand or fall based on Wyatt's, Fasold's, or Shea's credibility. No matter what mistakes or shortcomings there have been, they have no influence on whether the object is or is not Noah's Ark.

It *Could* Be Noah's Ark

Bayraktutan – and Baumgardner – conclude in their report that, "the data from our geophysical studies in no way conflicts with the assumption that the unusual boat-shaped object near Maher village contains the remains of Noah's Ark.

"The existence of remains from a large man-made structure in this location is surely an obvious explanation for the highly unusual markings on the stretched-out, almost flat reflector, which can be observed in the radar data."

In other words: it *could* be Noah's Ark.

Later Dr. Baumgardner concluded that this was not the case, while Dr. Bayraktutan is even more convinced that it is.

As we saw in the chapter about Baumgardner, there is good reason to question whether his complete rejection is based on scientific measurements alone. Personal disappointment and anger connected with Wyatt and Fasold and personal religious reflection – such as the fear of being religiously persecuted – have without a doubt played a role. Would Baumgardner have repudiated the find so strongly if gravel found in drillings had proven to be the cause of the boat-shaped object? Wouldn't a normal scientific reaction simply be to conclude that the boat-shaped object was most likely a natural formation? But instead Baumgardner completely dissociated himself from Wyatt's unscientific methods and Fasold's flirtation with the occult and thus conjured the boat-shaped object away – again. When we talk about the object being formed by a river of mud creating a tail after an obstacle, we have to remember that the formation *suddenly* appeared out of the ground after an earthquake, according to local villagers. The theory that the object is formed around an obstacle requires that the mud flowed past the obstacle for a period of time, and the people wanted to accentuate that point. But their – unscientific, but none the less credible – explanation is that the shepherd, Reshit, noticed the strange new formation after an earthquake in the spring of 1949, not in a strange

Journalist Tage Bechmann bought this painting in 1998 in the marketplace in Yerevan and sent it to the author of this book to remind him of the knowledge of the Ark hidden among the exiled Armenians on the other side of the border. The Monastery of St. Gregory lies only about 20 miles from Mt. Ararat. A poor artist painted this work on a piece of brown cardboard.

location he had never seen before, but rather on the fields where he was used to watching his sheep. This did not occur over a longer period of time. He was amazed and thought it must be a colossal boat, Noah's Boat – Nuhun Gemisi.

Remember, the formation was *buried* up till the earthquake. Therefore, the theory that the object was formed by mud surrounding an obstacle is completely unrealistic.

With all respect for Dr. Baumgardner's competence and his ground-breaking scientific work in relation to the geological development of the earth, we will allow ourselves to take his decision about the boat-shaped object with a grain of salt.

This cannot be thrown away so easily.

Need for Scientific Research

Here it is, plain and simple: despite decades of private research in the area, there has yet to be taken any definitive scientific research that cannot be doubted. Therefore, new studies have to be made.

Wyatt, Fasold, Baumgardner, and Bayraktutan's research give exciting indications that the boat-shaped object is anything but natural. It is possible that Wyatt and Fasold will have their hasty conclusions confirmed, but it is necessary to conduct new studies to come to any type of conclusion. Robert Michelson's SEPDAC-project is the best bet to date, but the project needs money.

It's hard to believe that there isn't more interest and support for such and interesting cultural and historical project; the basis for the three largest monotheistic religions in the world, not to mention the large and small religions and people groups that have clear memory of the Flood and Ark in their oldest scriptures and oral traditions.

Flood research is also highly relevant for the entire scientific community inclusive of research and teaching, which in many ways are based on the assumption that there have been no major catastrophes like the Flood.

Imagine what would happen if we found a flaw in the foundation upon which many theories are built. What a discovery that would be.

Anyone and everyone should be interested in researching that.

But as Dr. Bayraktutan tells us, there is a certain lack of support from the scientific community for research outside of the so-called positivistic boundaries of science. At the same time this research seriously questions ruling theories about the development of the world.

Hopefully this book will relight the fire in the hearts of those interested in scientific projects that possibly could clear up whether the boat-shaped object is the remnant or just the imprint of Noah's Ark.

Many of us simply cannot rest until this question is answered...

What About Mt. Ararat?

As this book suggests, there is little or no reason to continue the search on beautiful Mt. Ararat. The impressive crest possesses an amazing attractive force, but it has been tested and prodded in almost every nook and cranny possible over the last 50 years.

We have looked at the historical sources, which do not point to this specific mountain, and found that it is rather a Western European misunderstanding that has led many to assume the Ark can be found here. We have clearly shown that the loads of Ark stories flourishing around Mt. Ararat are highly unreliable and that they have been received with much too great ease among naïve Ark enthusiasts.

Mt. Ararat's geological composition also argues against it being the most likely candidate for the location of the Ark, if the volcanic mountain even existed at that time. Whether it existed or not, we do know that it didn't look in Noah's day like it does today.

The intense research on this mountain with radar measurements deep into the ice and satellite photos that have already been taken only confirm that Mt. Ararat, though impressive, does not hold a ship from Noah's time.

It is somewhat embarrassing that so much time and effort continues to be invested in this superficial Ark hunt when support is lacking for research of the much more tangible boat-shaped object.

A Very Different Past

Whether or not we can prove here and now that the remains of Noah's Ark have been found in Turkey on the Iranian border, I hope that this book has created a new and exciting understanding of our common history – as opposed to the one we are constantly indoctrinated with via the concentrated and outdated theories of evolution and the eternally dawdling change of the universe over a period of billions of years.

We can find the Flood and Noah in most of the ancient cultures of the world, though other names and other geographic circumstances are used.

We have seen that in the past mankind was not a conglomeration of primitive apes but rather constructed highly developed societies whose intelligence amazes us even today.

We cannot let ourselves be locked into the idea of our forefathers being unintelligible cart-wheeling primates, when in fact there is considerable evidence that in certain areas they were even superior to us.

Can We Trust the Bible?

Doesn't all of the amazing information and proof hidden in this book make the biblical account of Noah's Ark not seem so unrealistic an adventure as it often is presented to be?

Of course the number of animals and other specifics can be debated, but the occurrence of a Flood – a mighty deluge – is only obvious when we look at the evidence. Whether it was world-wide or just local so that it "only" covered one part of the world is a point of discussion learned theologians have discussed over and over again. For some, it is easier to believe in a local flooding.

This doesn't contest the validity of our established understanding of the world, but who is to say our understanding is right?

There are actually – as mentioned in the Velikovsky chapter – many sites that suggest it spanned the entire globe. We don't know whether it was caused by planets coming too close or meteors crashing down and ripping up the crust of the earth causing lava to spew out raising the level of the oceans – as Baumgardner's research suggests – or if there was a whole other explanation.

The Bible simply tells us that God was behind it and the deep was opened and the rain fell down.

And of course it tells us there was an Ark – a mighty boat whose muddy waters we hope future research of the boat-shaped object will clear up. There is already so much evidence indicating the presence of a ship. If a gigantic ship were to be found at an elevation of 6500 feet in the mountains of Ararat and the ancient kingdom of the Urartu, then I personally would have no doubt as to how the ship got there and which ship it was.

You don't have to be a believer to be convinced, but you might be convinced and become a believer…

The Bible Has Often Led to Amazing Discoveries

My approach to the Bible is that it is *reliable*. Surprisingly reliable, it may be safely said when comparing it to other sources.

As Nelson Gluck, an expert in archeology noted:

"No archeological discovery has ever controverted a Biblical reference. Scores of archeological findings have been made which confirm in clear outline or in exact detail historical statements in the Bible. And, by the same token, proper evaluation of Biblical descriptions has often led to amazing discoveries."[1]

On the other hand, it has on several occasions turned out that hasty criti-

Footnotes
[1] Dr. Nelson Gluck excavated some archeological sites in Jordan and 500 in the desert of Negev. He located Solomon's copper mines, the place near the Red Sea where Solomon met the Queen of Sheba, and much more by comparing the facts found in the Bible with archeological knowledge. In 1963 he was pictured on the cover of Time Magazine.

```
0141    18U84        0147   3929       3205     310     14960
מְתוּשֶׁלַח  אַחֲרֵי  הוֹלִידוֹ  אֶת־לֶמֶךְ  שְׁתַּיִם  וּשְׁמֹנִים  שָׁנָה
years    eighty-   two    Lamech  fathered he   after   Methuselah

3117      1961     1323      1121      3205  8141   3967      7651
27  יִשְׁבַע  מֵאוֹת  שָׁנָה  וַיּוֹלֶד  בָּנִים  וּבָנוֹת:  וַיִּהְיוּ  כָּל־יְמֵי
the all   And     and      sons    he and ;years  hundred   and
of days  were    .daughters  fathered                          seven

              4191  8141  3967  8672    8141       8346    8672    4968
מְתוּשֶׁלַח  תֵּשַׁע  וְשִׁשִּׁים  שָׁנָה  וּתְשַׁע  מֵאוֹת  שָׁנָה  וַיָּמֹת:
he and ;years hundred nine and  years    sixty-   nine   Methuselah
died

1121   3205  8141   3967     8141      8084      8147    3929   2421
28  וַיְחִי־לֶמֶךְ  שְׁתַּיִם  וּשְׁמֹנִים  שָׁנָה  וּמְאַת  שָׁנָה  וַיּוֹלֶד  בֵּן:
.son a he and ;years one and   years    eighty-    two    Lamech And
fathered        hundred    2088                                  lived

6093      4639     5162      559    5146  8034        7121
29  וַיִּקְרָא  אֶת־שְׁמוֹ  נֹחַ  לֵאמֹר  זֶה  יְנַחֲמֵנוּ  מִמַּעֲשֵׂנוּ  וּמֵעִצְּבוֹן
the and   from     shall   This  ,saying ,Noah  name his  he And
of toil  work our  us comfort one                        called

310    3929    2421     3068   779       834        127  4480  3027
30  יָדֵינוּ  מִן־הָאֲדָמָה  אֲשֶׁר  אֵרְרָהּ  יְהוָה  וַיְחִי־לֶמֶךְ  אַחֲרֵי
after   Lamech And .Jehovah  has     which   the  from   our
          lived            cursed           ground        hands

3967     2568   8141    8673   2568  5146        3205
הוֹלִידוֹ  אֶת־נֹחַ  חָמֵשׁ  וְתִשְׁעִים  שָׁנָה  וַחֲמֵשׁ  מֵאוֹת
hundred  five and   years   ninety-   five   ,Noah        he
                                                        fathered

7651   3929    3605    1961    1323   1121    3205  8141
31  שֶׁבַע  וַיּוֹלֶד  בָּנִים  וּבָנוֹת:  וַיְהִי  כָּל־יְמֵי־לֶמֶךְ  שֶׁבַע
seven  Lamech the  all    And      and     sons    he and ;years
        of days   were  .daughters             fathered

1961              4191  8141   3967  7651  8141      7657
32  וַיִּהְיּ         ס    וַיָּמֹת:  שָׁנָה  מֵאוֹת  שֶׁבַע  שָׁנָה  שִׁבְעִים
And                    he and ;years hundred  and    years   seventy-
was                    .died                                 5146

2526   8055      5146   3205  8141   3967  2568  1121
נֹחַ  בֶּן־חֲמֵשׁ  מֵאוֹת  שָׁנָה  וַיּוֹלֶד  נֹחַ  אֶת־שֵׁם  אֶת־חָם
,Ham   ,Shem   Noah  And  .years  hundred  five  a  Noah
                     fathered                      of man
                                                    3315
וְאֶת־יָפֶת:
.Japheth and
```

An example of the genealogical lists in Genesis chapter 5 from the Hebrew Masoretic version. Here is added a word-to-word translation into English. The text is to be read from the right to the left. (From The Interlinear Bible, Hendrickson 1986.)

cism of the statements in the Bible cannot hold. Many books have been written about this with examples showing that the Bible was, after all, telling the truth. Experience shows that there is, actually, good reason to trust its historical details. And personally I believe that we are dealing with *Divine inspiration*. But this is the kind of opinions that you cannot argue for as it belongs to the spiritual, metaphysical field. It implies that you admit the spiritual dimension and as is well known, science is rather ignorant in this field. I am not claiming that I am wiser, it only depends on experience whether you have this dimension or not.

The authors of the Bible never claim that the word just fell down from Heaven or that it was dictated by God, with the exception of sections specifically noted as supernaturally revealed.[2]

The Bible plainly and clearly tells us that it was written by everyday normal people – and there is no attempt to hide the authors' sins – but multiple times we are reminded that it was written with God's *inspiration*.

At Least 1,000 Years Further Back

But in spite of respect for the Divine inspiration of the Bible – which I also recognize – we have to understand its numerical declarations as they truly are. As we saw in the chapter entitled "Confused Chronology", most translations of the Bible include mistakes with the years of the patriarchs. We also have to add in the omission factor where periods under foreign rule, or the "years of evil", have been left out.

Without changing the truth of the text, the Flood lies at least 1,000 years further back in history than otherwise recognized by most Bible experts. Apparently, there are still finds that are dated to too early a period, and there is also the question about whether Adam and Eve were created at the same time as the earth or if their creation took place thousands of years later. (The story of Creation speaks of days which might not be literal since "for God one day is as a thousand years".) As previously mentioned, some theologians also believe the Bible's account of Creation to be a re-Creation of the earth after chaos from an earlier civilization.

All of this is speculation, but for me it is important that we don't make a rock solid *assumption* of what the distant past was like and then give no room for adjustments or change.

Other People's Stories

We have looked at the historical ancient accounts from *other* cultures, and as mentioned, I think we have all too often treated these sources with little or no respect taking them simply for myths or fables. Now we see that they may contain nuggets of truth about the history of the world hidden behind mystical and fairy-tale-like language. We often have to peel off the additional layers to get to the original story.

In his book *Eternity in Their Hearts*[3] anthropologist Don Richardson goes through a long list of examples of research showing that ancient peoples and "untouched" tribes had their own versions of God long before Chris-

[2] Such as the prophets in the Old Testament and the Book of Revelation in the New.

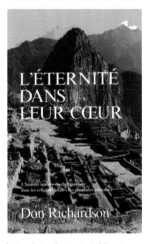

[3] Regal Books, G/L Publications: Ventura, California (pg. 198).

tian influence stepped in. And the native versions of God were in fact very similar to the whites'. These groups were often originally monotheistic – that is they believed in one Almighty God – before they started worshipping many small gods and spirits. Anthropology teaches that an understanding of the Divine has developed from a primitive belief in many gods to advanced monotheism. But actually, it's the opposite. Apparently, there was a time when they all believed in one God. Abraham's descendants – the Jews and the Arabs – held onto this belief, which flowed over into Christianity and Islam, while most other peoples started worshipping multiple gods, such as the stars (Kaldis), spirits (as seen in Africa), or ancestral and royal worship where humans became gods.

We need to get away from the idea that everything developed from lower stages to higher ones. The opposite has also been the case.

As with the origin of the gods, there are many examples of biblical ingredients of creation, sin, a flood, an ark, and the dispersion of mankind that can be found in the original accounts of various peoples. This suggests that, whether Aboriginal or Greenlandic, German, African, or Indian, we have a common ancestry. Our history can be backtracked to "the eight" from the Ark and even further.

This is a (unfortunately all too often ignored or forgotten) piece of cultural history that has the ability to give us a whole new world of information about the past.

What Was Moses' Source?

Personally, I think that Moses, who gathered information about the ancient past and put it down in writing in the first book of the Bible, Genesis, also had some of his information from these sources. He didn't get it from the Bible, but we *know* that:

1.   He had the oral tradition from his own Hebrew people.
2.   He possibly had written Hebrew material: the Book of Jasher, tablets, papyrus scrolls.
3.   He had access to the writings in the royal library about the beginning of history, both Egyptian and others (such as Babylonian) as he was an Egyptian prince.
4.   He spent 40 years with another desert people in the land of Midian, a people who were the descendents of Abraham and his third wife, Ketura.

The Midianites also had to have their oral history, and Moses' father-in-law, Jethro, priest for these (heathen) people, would naturally have told Moses what he knew.

Moses could have possibly had supernatural revelations in the form of dreams and visions as well. Of course, materialistic science doesn't understand this kind of thing, but there is no reason to restrict ourselves due to the limitations of science. But the Bible never mentions Moses having revelations of ancient history, though it does mention him having other revelations. So let's keep to the idea that he built his account on handed-down stories and oral tradition.

Based on these sources, he wrote in specific detail the best kept and most coherent history of the origin of the world.

The Message of the Past

On top of all of this, it is a biblical principal that the message is more important than the means. So let's look away from the details for a moment and consider the message.

The message of the Bible, when looking at ancient history, is that mankind is not an amazing coincidence generated from an unbelievable amount of correctly timed mutations, but that mankind is an exalted creation formed by a positively intelligent being (God) who has given us favor and a purpose.

We normally think of ourselves as evolving from lower life forms (low to high), but the Bible says the opposite. The first people were more perfect than we are. We have not evolved from vine swinging ancestors into higher life forms, rather we have degenerated – as we have also destroyed much of the wonderful, paradise-like world in which our forefathers lived. These forefathers were extremely developed when the mighty Flood hit.

The question is: have we reached the same level(s) since the Flood?

Surely, we have invented things that did not exist before the Flood, such as cars and televisions, atom bombs and computers. But our human intelligence has not necessarily improved – not to mention out spiritual state.

If people really did live for hundreds of years at that time due to the climate, then they also had the opportunity (and time) to gather more knowledge and experience than we can in the short span of our lives.

With this understanding of the ancient past, the Flood was a dramatic change caused by God trying to limit the spread of evil in the world. As we all know, it didn't go as planned...

There Is an End...

"Development" is not eternal from a biblical perspective. There is a beginning and an end. And Jesus Christ told us that the end is going to look just like the days of Noah:

> For the coming of the Son of Man will be just like the days of Noah. For as in those days before the flood they were eating and drinking, marrying and giving in marriage, until the day that Noah entered the ark, and they did not understand until the flood came and took them all away; so will the coming of the Son of Man be.
>
> Then there will be two men in the field; one will be taken and one will be left. Two women (will be) grinding at the mill; one will be taken and one will be left.
> *Matthew 24:37-41*

Most people won't learn from the past, nor will they notice the signs of the times. They will continue with business as usual just as the people of Noah's day did, until one day when Noah went into the Ark and it started to rain.

But Noah is an example of a person that lived a righteous life, even though the world around him was full of unrighteousness. He was a man that was spiritually open and could hear God's warning. A man that trusted God and acted on *faith* – and therefore made it through the catastrophe and experienced the rainbow vested across the blue sky of the new world.

I would have loved to spend an evening with that Noah and his beloved Naamah as they sat by the bonfire set on the mountainside in the Valley of the Eight telling their great-grandchildren how life was before the Flood.

What a story!

Thanks to Mikel Rice   (See Genesis 6-8)   10-06-2004

GEE DAD ... I HOPE THAT PEOPLE IN THE
FUTURE WON'T BE LOOKING FOR THIS ARK

Thanks

Photographs, illustrations, information, etc.: The author would like to thank the following people for their kind permission to use pictures and other material:

The artist **Elfred Lee** for his historical pictures from the Ark search and for paintings made on account of the eyewitness testimonies.

Dr. John Baumgardner and **Dr. Salih Bayraktutan** for photos and illustrations from their cooperative explorations of the boat-shaped object.

Dr. William Shea for information and photographs of the Durupinar potsherd. **Dr. Robert Michelson** for information and material from his personal research. The artist **David A. Deal** for permission to use his photographs, illustrations, and research. Ark-researcher **Bill Fry** for permission to use photos from his website www.anchorstone.com and historical photographs he was given by Ron Wyatt. Mrs. **Elin Berglund** for her helpful cooperation on trips and material from Ron Wyatt. Dr. **Lennart Möller** for his photos from southern Turkey used in his book "Exodus". Miss **Viveka Ponten** for information and photos of Ron and Mary Nell Wyatt.

Translation: My best thanks to our patient and enduring American translator, **Tracy Jay Skondin**, who had the difficult task to translate simultaneously as the chapters were written - and rewritten - for more years. He even named his firstborn Noah. Thanks also to co-translator **Dorthe Orbesen** for a great help with all the corrections and editing.

My very special thanks to my wife Birthe for backing me up in writing this book - even though it took me thousands of hours. You even used your holidays and allowed me to use mine in the Mountains of Ararat.
And thanks to Henrik, Maj-Britt and John
for your never failing interest.

The author

Henri Nissen trained at the Danish School of Journalism in Århus and has written thousands of articles, produced radio and television, and has written seven books, of which four have been translated into other languages. He has traveled extensively in Asia and Africa and worked in Cameroon for three years. At present he is the editor-in-chief of a newspaper and a communication consultant to The Lutheran World Federation in French-speaking Africa. Noah's Ark is his personal hobby, and he has visited the area around Mt. Ararat and the boat-shaped object several times.